Advances in Enterprise Technology Risk Assessment

Manish Gupta
University at Buffalo, SUNY, USA

Raghvendra Singh
University at Buffalo, SUNY, USA

John Walp
University at Buffalo, SUNY, USA

Raj Sharman
University at Buffalo, SUNY, USA

IGI Global
Publishing Tomorrow's Research Today

Vice President of Editorial	Melissa Wagner
Managing Editor of Acquisitions	Mikaela Felty
Managing Editor of Book Development	Jocelynn Hessler
Production Manager	Mike Brehm
Cover Design	Phillip Shickler

Published in the United States of America by
IGI Global Scientific Publishing
701 East Chocolate Avenue
Hershey, PA, 17033, USA
Tel: 717-533-8845
Fax: 717-533-8661
E-mail: cust@igi-global.com
Website: https://www.igi-global.com

Library of Congress Cataloging-in-Publication Data

Names: Gupta, Manish, 1978- editor. | Singh, Raghvendra, 1992- editor. | Walp, John, 1967- editor. | Sharman, Raj, editor.
Title: Advances in enterprise technology risk assessment / edited by Manish Gupta, Raghvendra Singh, John Walp, Raj Sharman.
Description: Hershey, PA : Engineering Science Reference, [2025] | Includes bibliographical references and index. | Summary: "The objective of this book is to serve as a definitive resource that bridges the gap between traditional audit practices and the demands of modern technology-driven business environments. It offers research-rich content that encompasses a wide spectrum of practical solutions, frameworks, and technological insights related to technology auditing. The impact of the book is multifaceted: it extends the knowledge base of practitioners by providing a holistic view of how technology is influencing auditing and risk management, and it serves as an academic cornerstone for research in this dynamic field"-- Provided by publisher.
Identifiers: LCCN 2024042542 (print) | LCCN 2024042543 (ebook) | ISBN 9798369342114 (h/c) | ISBN 9798369350881 (s/c) | ISBN 9798369342121 (ebook)
Subjects: LCSH: Technology--Risk assessment. | Technology assessment.
Classification: LCC T174.5 .A29 2025 (print) | LCC T174.5 (ebook) | DDC 363.1--dc23/eng/20241211
LC record available at https://lccn.loc.gov/2024042542
LC ebook record available at https://lccn.loc.gov/2024042543

British Cataloguing in Publication Data
A Cataloguing in Publication record for this book is available from the British Library.

Table of Contents

Detailed Table of Contents

This research chapter examines strategies to optimize the technology audit lifecycle, focusing on the growing reliance on IT and evolving regulatory demands. It reviews traditional IT audit phases—planning, fieldwork, monitoring, and follow-up—starting with the planning phase, which sets the audit's direction through analysis of standards, economic conditions, and prior findings. Fieldwork involves assessing controls, conducting interviews, and evaluating risks. Monitoring tracks the implementation of recommendations and management responses. Proposed optimization strategies include integrating data analytics in planning, adopting control self-assessment (CSA), utilizing generalized audit software, and enhancing reporting and follow-up. The chapter also explores the impact of artificial intelligence (AI) on auditing, emphasizing the need for effective project management and stakeholder engagement. Additionally, it covers continuous auditing techniques and automation to improve audit effectiveness and efficiency.

This study addresses the critical field of information security risk mitigation introduced by humans. Recognizing and fixing risk factors resulting from human behavior is essential at a time when complex cyber threats plague digital environments. This research is significant because it acknowledges that human vulnerability plays a major role in information security breaches. Despite technological advances, insufficient training, malicious intent, and human error remain major obstacles. Organizations that ignore these factors risk devastating data breaches, financial ruin, and serious harm to their reputation. By addressing human-related vulnerabilities, companies can better protect their digital assets and ensure a more secure working environment. The research illustrates the importance of comprehensive training programs, strict security policies, and a culture of awareness to mitigate risks associated with human factors. Effective risk mitigation requires a multifaceted strategy that combines technology with human-centered strategies to safeguard against evolving cyber threats.

The Critical Security Controls (CIS) and National Institute of Standards and Technology Cybersecurity Framework are both important for increasing organizational cybersecurity, with each catering to certain demands and implementation approaches. The CIS Controls, which were initially announced in 2008, are organized into Implementation Groups and provide a prioritized approach suitable for companies with varying levels of cybersecurity maturity. Also, the NIST Cybersecurity Framework was established in 2014 and employs a risk-based framework focusing on six essential function. This framework includes technology like risk assessment tools, continuous monitoring systems, and incident response platforms. While the CIS Controls give specific, practical actions for immediate adoption, the NIST Framework focuses on overall risk management and compliance with larger regulatory requirements, providing a holistic, customized approach for improving cybersecurity resilience.

This study digs into the critical intersection between the Sarbanes-Oxley Act (SOX) and corporate audits of information technology (IT). SOX, which was initially intended to improve financial transparency, has had a significant impact on IT controls, data security, and reporting accuracy. The study delves into SOX regulations, particularly Section 404, as they apply to IT, necessitating strong internal controls, data integrity, and secure record-keeping processes. This chapter highlights the strategic application of SOX for comprehensive IT audits using real-world case studies and practical insights. It emphasizes the interdependence of financial and IT controls, highlighting how SOX serves as a foundation for maintaining the integrity of electronic data and safeguarding enterprises' economic well-being.

As organizations increasingly rely on third-party entities, managing third-party risks has become crucial for overall risk governance. This chapter explores third-party risk management (TPRM), highlighting past events, challenges, opportunities in due diligence, and evolving strategies for safeguarding organizational interests in a complex, interconnected business landscape. The study reviews the current state of TPRM, recent security breaches, and challenges in managing third-party risks. It identifies common pitfalls and gaps in existing frameworks, focusing on due diligence processes, risk assessment, and mitigation techniques. Insights into various third-party risks, including cybersecurity vulnerabilities, data privacy concerns, and regulatory compliance, are provided through an extensive literature review and case analyses. Additionally, the chapter examines the role of technology, agreements, and key indicators in enhancing TPRM practices, aiming to streamline risk assessments and response mechanisms.

With increasing reliance on internet technologies, auditing plays a critical assurance role. This chapter explores the evolution of the internet into the emerging landscape of Web 3.0, built on decentralized and semantic technologies like blockchain that transform today's web architecture. It analyzes the vision, potential applications, and inherent governance, risk, and business impact considerations involved in this blockchain-powered reinvention of the web. It further discusses key risk domains in Web 3.0 that warrant audit scrutiny, including decentralization, blockchain, cryptocurrencies, and semantic inaccuracies. This chapter provides technology leaders, auditors, and regulatory stakeholders with an overview of Web 3.0 while highlighting the pivotal governance, risk management, and assurance challenges involved in this transition. It prepares readers to evaluate the analyses and recommendations centered on securing this next-generation, decentralized web future.

PCI DSS is a contractual obligation rather than a mandatory regulation to be taken up with diligence and care in organizations. But PCI DSS is a globally recognized standard that applies to organizations involved in processing, storing, or transmitting payment card information. This chapter provides an overview of PCI DSS, emphasizing its key components, objectives, and significance in the world of electronic payment security. PCI DSS sets rigorous security requirements for organizations that oversee payment card data. Compliance with PCI DSS helps organizations reduce the risk of data breaches, fraud, and financial losses while also safeguarding consumer trust and ensuring the integrity of payment card transactions. Endpoint security is a critical facet of modern cybersecurity. Endpoint security is vital for ensuring the confidentiality, integrity, and availability of sensitive data, as well as maintaining the overall security posture of organizations. This chapter will focus on the key requirements of endpoint controls within PCI DSS compliance and their effectiveness.

Businesses frequently manage the complicated challenge of transitioning from on-premises systems to the cloud in the evolving world of technology. An integrated risk framework is critical for analyzing and auditing this transformation, ensuring a smooth transfer while limiting potential risks. This methodology provides proactive risk management by predicting issues such as compliance gaps, and service outages. In addition, this framework includes a thorough selection procedure for the best cloud service providers (CSPs). Organizations may find the best partner for their specific needs by examining criteria like security standards, compliance adherence, scalability, and data governance. This complete strategy not only reduces possible interruptions during migration but also fortifies the company against unanticipated obstacles, promoting a safe and efficient cloud environment, and educated decision making. As the technology landscape is changing exponentially, it is important to integrate risk framework as a strategic compass in intricacy of migration to reinforce digital infrastructure.

Preface

In today's rapidly evolving technological landscape, the traditional practices of auditing have been profoundly disrupted by emerging innovations and the increasing complexity of modern business environments. This book, Advances in Enterprise Technology Risk Assessment, is born out of the recognition that the field of technology auditing is at a pivotal crossroads. Bridging the gap between long-established auditing practices and the new demands of technology-driven organizations, this work serves as both a practical guide and an academic foundation for anyone navigating the intricate intersection of auditing, technology, and risk management.

Our goal with this publication is to provide a definitive resource that offers research-based insights alongside actionable strategies. Throughout the chapters, we delve into a broad spectrum of topics ranging from the integration of emergent technologies like artificial intelligence (AI), machine learning (ML), blockchain, and Agile methodologies, to the evolving frameworks that have reshaped IT audit in response to global events such as the COVID-19 pandemic. The content is meticulously crafted to ensure that practitioners, students, and academicians alike can derive tangible value, whether it be through enhancing their audit methodologies or extending their understanding of how modern technology influences risk and compliance.

The unique value of this book lies in its pragmatic approach. We do not merely discuss theoretical frameworks; instead, we demonstrate how these ideas can be applied in real-world contexts. From auditing complex environments like DevOps and Platform-as-a-Service (PaaS) applications to addressing the critical security needs of Point-of-Sale (POS) systems, each chapter offers a comprehensive roadmap for navigating today's technological audit challenges. This book also sheds light on the role of technology auditing in supporting organizational resilience during periods of unprecedented change.

By focusing on both the current state and future trajectory of technology auditing, Advances in Enterprise Technology Risk Assessment positions itself as an essential tool for organizations looking to enhance their audit practices and for auditors who wish to stay ahead in an era of continuous innovation. We explore how the integration of emerging technologies into audit processes not only transforms traditional approaches but also opens up new avenues for ensuring comprehensive risk management and operational efficiency.

We hope that readers will find this book to be a valuable companion in their journey towards modernizing audit practices and integrating cutting-edge technologies into their work. It is our aspiration that this book will serve as both a resource for professionals seeking practical solutions and a cornerstone for ongoing academic research in the dynamic and ever-evolving field of technology auditing.

We extend our gratitude to the contributing authors who have shared their expertise and insights, making this endeavor possible. It is our hope that the knowledge imparted within these pages will inspire a new generation of auditors and contribute to the ongoing discourse on the intersection of technology and assurance.

ORGANIZATION OF THE BOOK

Chapter 1. Optimizing Technology Audit Lifecycle

This chapter explores strategies to optimize the technology audit lifecycle amid increasing reliance on IT and evolving regulatory demands. It reviews traditional IT audit phases, such as planning, fieldwork, monitoring, and follow-up. The planning phase sets the audit's direction by analyzing standards, economic conditions, and prior findings. Fieldwork involves assessing controls, conducting interviews, and evaluating risks. Monitoring tracks the implementation of recommendations and management responses. Proposed optimization strategies include integrating data analytics in planning, adopting control self-assessment (CSA), utilizing generalized audit software, and enhancing reporting and follow-up. The impact of Artificial Intelligence (AI) on auditing, continuous auditing techniques, and automation are also examined, focusing on audit effectiveness and efficiency.

Chapter 2. Mitigating the Human Risks to Cybersecurity Posture

This chapter addresses the importance of mitigating human-related risks to cybersecurity posture. Despite technological advancements, human vulnerability remains a major factor in security breaches. The chapter emphasizes how organizations that overlook training, malicious intent, and human error are at risk of serious breaches, financial loss, and reputational damage. It highlights the need for comprehensive training programs, stringent security policies, and fostering a culture of awareness to reduce risks. Effective risk mitigation involves a combination of human-centered strategies and technological measures to enhance protection against cyber threats.

Chapter 3. Bridging the Gap: A Comparative Study of CIS and NIST Cybersecurity Frameworks

This chapter provides a comparative analysis of two prominent cybersecurity frameworks: the Critical Security Controls (CIS) and the National Institute of Standards and Technology (NIST) Cybersecurity Framework. CIS Controls, organized into Implementation Groups, offer a prioritized approach suitable for organizations with varying cybersecurity maturity levels. The NIST Framework, focusing on risk management, presents a more comprehensive, risk-based approach. While CIS provides specific, practical actions for immediate implementation, NIST offers a broader focus on overall risk management and regulatory compliance. This chapter guides organizations in selecting a framework that best fits their cybersecurity needs.

Chapter 4. Safeguarding Financial Integrity: Utilizing Sarbanes-Oxley for IT Audits in Modern Corporations

This chapter explores the relationship between the Sarbanes-Oxley Act (SOX) and IT audits in corporate settings. Originally designed to enhance financial transparency, SOX significantly impacts IT controls, data security, and reporting accuracy. Section 404 mandates robust internal controls, data integrity, and secure record-keeping processes. Using real-world case studies, this chapter emphasizes the strategic application of SOX for comprehensive IT audits, highlighting the interdependence of financial and IT controls. The discussion showcases how SOX contributes to maintaining electronic data integrity and protecting a company's economic well-being.

Chapter 5. Identifying Opportunities in the Enhancement of an Organization's Third-Party Risk Posture

This chapter examines Third-Party Risk Management (TPRM) in the context of an interconnected business landscape. It identifies common challenges and gaps in managing third-party risks, including cybersecurity vulnerabilities, data privacy concerns, and regulatory compliance. The study reviews past events and evolving strategies for mitigating these risks through improved due diligence, risk assessment, and mitigation techniques. By leveraging technology, agreements, and key risk indicators, the chapter offers insights into enhancing TPRM practices to protect organizational interests and streamline risk assessments.

Chapter 6. Ensuring Sustenance of Innovation

This chapter discusses the evolving role of internal audits in improving healthcare systems and adopting new technologies. The research focuses on how risk management and internal audits ensure the controlled and sustained implementation of innovative medical practices. It emphasizes the importance of data analytics, modern information systems, and relationships with third-party providers, all while addressing evolving management needs and regulatory compliance. As healthcare institutions continue to leverage new technologies, this chapter explores how audits contribute to enhancing the quality of care and operational efficiency.

Chapter 7. IS Auditing in Modernizing Legacy Systems Using Salesforce

This chapter explores the challenges of modernizing legacy systems and migrating them to cloud platforms like Salesforce. The paper delves into modernization strategies, highlighting how financial institutions face issues such as system inflexibility, high maintenance costs, and limited analytical capabilities. Salesforce's cloud based architecture offers a solution, improving data governance, regulatory compliance, and decision-making processes. The chapter emphasizes the importance of modernization to overcome the limitations of legacy systems and Salesforce's potential in driving digital transformation in competitive industries.

Chapter 8. Auditing Risks of Web 3.0

This chapter explores the emerging landscape of Web 3.0, built on decentralized and semantic technologies like blockchain. The chapter provides an analysis of the vision, applications, and governance challenges of Web 3.0, focusing on risks such as decentralization, blockchain vulnerabilities, cryptocurrencies, and semantic inaccuracies. It highlights the need for audit scrutiny in this evolving internet paradigm and provides recommendations for addressing key risk domains. The chapter aims to prepare auditors and regulatory stakeholders for the governance and risk management challenges involved in securing Web 3.0.

Chapter 9. Endpoint Controls Through a Lens of PCI DSS

This chapter focuses on Payment Card Industry Data Security Standard (PCI DSS) compliance and the critical role of endpoint security in ensuring the confidentiality, integrity, and availability of sensitive data. PCI DSS is a globally recognized standard for organizations handling payment card information. The chapter discusses the key components of PCI DSS, its significance in electronic payment security, and the importance of endpoint controls in safeguarding against data breaches and fraud. Compliance with PCI DSS is positioned as vital for maintaining consumer trust and ensuring transaction integrity.

Chapter 10. Risk Management Framework for Cloud Migration and Selection of Suitable Cloud Service Providers

This chapter outlines a risk management framework for cloud migration, emphasizing the selection of suitable Cloud Service Providers (CSPs). It addresses the complexities of transitioning from on-premises systems to the cloud, proposing proactive risk management strategies to mitigate compliance gaps, service outages, and other potential risks. The framework offers a thorough process for selecting CSPs based on criteria like security standards, scalability, and data governance. By incorporating this framework, organizations can ensure smooth migration and fortify their digital infrastructure against unforeseen challenges.

Moksh Gupta
University at Buffalo, SUNY, USA

Abinash Jena
University at Buffalo, SUNY, USA

Monal Gupta
University at Buffalo, SUNY, USA

Raj Sharman
University at Buffalo, SUNY, USA

Chapter 1
Optimizing Technology Audit Lifecycle

Moksh Gupta
University at Buffalo, SUNY, USA

Abinash Jena
https://orcid.org/0009-0001-5103-2956
University at Buffalo, SUNY, USA

Monal Gupta
University at Buffalo, SUNY, USA

Raj Sharman
https://orcid.org/0000-0001-5838-7330
University at Buffalo, SUNY, USA

ABSTRACT

This research chapter examines strategies to optimize the technology audit lifecycle, focusing on the growing reliance on IT and evolving regulatory demands. It reviews traditional IT audit phases—planning, fieldwork, monitoring, and follow-up—starting with the planning phase, which sets the audit's direction through analysis of standards, economic conditions, and prior findings. Fieldwork involves assessing controls, conducting interviews, and evaluating risks. Monitoring tracks the implementation of recommendations and management responses. Proposed optimization strategies include integrating data analytics in planning, adopting control self-assessment (CSA), utilizing generalized audit software, and enhancing reporting and follow-up. The chapter also explores the impact of artificial intelligence (AI) on auditing, emphasizing the need for effective project management and stakeholder engagement. Additionally, it covers continuous auditing techniques and

DOI: 10.4018/979-8-3693-4211-4.ch001

automation to improve audit effectiveness and efficiency.

1. INTRODUCTION

With a greater requisite and necessity on Information Technology for business functions and fresh and additional rules affecting the assertion of Information Technology for these events, the key role of information technology (IT) auditing has amplified more than ever. Diverse explanations of IT audit quality might result from the various purposes and goals of numerous participants and stakeholders within a corporation that IT audits assist. The field has evidence that the information audit (IA) is not widely used or fully acknowledged, despite its centrality to the efficient management of information within organizations. Three issues with present practice are highlighted and discussed in this paper: the absence of a standard methodological approach, unclear connectivity to relevant ICT development processes, and limited guidance on scope management. A two-dimensional matrix is suggested as a means of managing scope, and the function and scope of the IA are reexamined in response to these difficulties. Additionally, important connections between information strategy and information system architecture (ISA) are established and mapped (Buchanan and Gibb, 2007). Ideas like effectiveness or impact, audit completeness in accordance with numerous standards, time taken for the audit process, and cost efficiency may be considered in these definitions. As a primary objective, assuring management that a system or automated process is accomplishing its goals is key (Stoel, Havelka, & Merhout, 2012). Technology audits are performed up by internal or external consultants in close cooperation with company management, second line of defense and business owners.

It follows a basic structure:

- Scoping the audit to decide the objective
- Gathering of material information for investigation
- Compiling all the evidence in a report
- Recommendation for findings
- Meetings with stakeholders before presenting the report to the management
- Monitor

Then efficiently windup the audit which will allow for systematic and technical progress that could be in terms of resolving the finding, adding necessary controls, or acquiring new and vital technologies. It is carried out by highly experienced audit consultants when carefully acknowledged and accepted by the management of the business.

Although, we must understand that the technology audit itself with the current process cannot resolve the essential problems, i.e. produce prompt responses or benefits, correct faults, and reduce coordination issues. Since, this process takes time and the result to reflect in the system is not immediate.

The general goal of technology audit is to evaluate the capability of firms, companies, and organizations to find material errors and communicate that to the management before it affects the organization adversely. There are three main stages that the audit procedure is often conceived of, consisting of three main stages: planning, fieldwork, and the evaluation of audit evidence (Cushing & Loebbecke (1986), Wallage (1991). Within the auditing profession, it is widely acknowledged that judgments made on evidential planning are crucial to an engagement's efficacy and efficiency. (Mock & Wright, 1992). Technology audit helps to integrate emerging and essential technologies by assisting technology stakeholders and partners and explain what needs to be done to successfully incorporate the new technologies into the company for add value to business (Kuttybaeva, Raikhanova, Zhaparova, Kozhabatchina, & Akmolda, 2022).

While technology audits are essential for incorporating new technologies and enhancing a company's value, it's also critical to take into account any risks that could jeopardize an audit engagement. Several risks that might compromise an audit engagement are listed below (8;17). The auditee's integrity and professionalism are being questioned; the auditee is involved in illegal activities, fraud, and/or unusual financial reporting; there is a lack of commitment to improve governance and internal controls; the auditee wants to limit the scope of the auditor's work; and there are significant threats that could erode the auditor's independence.

Based on previous research results on the advancement of episodic memory (e.g., Kolodner, 1983; Anzai, 1987; Einhorn, 1974), we may deduce that novices will apply fewer heuristics than experts and, as a result, necessitate additional information and intermediate cognitive processes in order to solve a given problem.

Materiality is not a single idea that can be applied globally to all types of enterprises. Furthermore, it is a relative concept (Leslie, 1985) from the following two perspectives: the first of the two factors will rely on the size of the company and the second will depend on the auditor's assessment of the issue areas unique to the client.

There is widespread recognition within the auditing profession that evidential planning decisions are critical to the effectiveness and efficiency of an engagement (Mock & Wright, 1992).

Materiality is thus not one concept which is uniformly applicable all over the world for all kinds of businesses. More than that, it is a relative concept (Leslie, 1985) from two points of view: first, it can be expected to be dependent on the size of the business and second, it can be expected to be dependent on the auditor's perception of client-specific problem areas.

CURRENT STAGES OF AN AUDIT:

Planning

As per AS210, the planning phase of an audit process makes sure that the auditor's aim to perform the audit effectively and successfully is achieved. The audit engagement and its outcome are the audit team's responsibility. The audit should be judiciously planned by the auditor and the responsibilities of the auditor for properly establishing the audit is drawn. Determining the overall audit approach for the engagement and crafting an audit plan, which emphases on planned risk assessment methods and responses to critical risks, are two parts of planning the audit. So, planning is a continuing, iterative activity that might begin soon after the close of the last audit and continues until the existing audit is complete.

The scope and complexity of the firm's business, prior audit reports, and any deviations in the audit's environment will impact the scope of groundwork activities that are necessary. The issues should be considered and measured by the auditor when creating the audit strategy and plan to determine their impact on the company's risks and internal control, as well as in what way the issues could impact the auditor's processes. Below are few such factors that decides the scope and objective:

I. Issues like applicable standards, economic circumstances, legal and regulatory frameworks, and technology changes and progression which have an impact on the firm.
II. Issues relating to the business of the company, methods of operation, domain, or industry it deals with or any third-party service providers.
III. Issues related to control weaknesses or lack in controls previously stated to senior management or audit committee.
IV. Issues pertaining to the type and size of information and data which is available on the efficiency of the firm's internal controls. (PCAOB, 2010)

The direction of the audit is established at this first phase by deciding the scope of the audit. It is outlined and defined by auditors, by judiciously laying out the particular topics or tasks that will be examined and considered for an audit in a stipulated time duration. This decision is dependent on couple of factors such as audit's goals, risk assessment, past audit results, etc. This process includes validating IT general controls, IT application controls, checking the accuracy of financial statements as part of FAIT, assessing internal control design and control effectiveness, confirming compliance with regulations, etc. The scope of the audit is also modified by the auditors. by considering its goal in order to collect the most pertinent and appropriate data. For example, an internal audit that is focused on the effectiveness of the procurement process will be more restricted in scope when compared to a financial audit of a publicly listed corporation. (IAASB, 2004) Setting up the scope of an audit during the planning phase is the most important aspects of an audit as it makes sure that important business processes is included while performing the audit. The auditors while deciding the scope of a technology audit consider several factors to determine the scope and objectives in an effective manner. Different aspects such as the risk maturity of the audited firm, the size of the organization, sector or industry an organization belong to, and most importantly previous audit results plays a big role in setting the objectives and scope. Similarly, key elements like existing and changing laws and regulations, rules, and standards that control the firm's business activities and financial reporting are carefully examined by them. This involves any technology that has been implemented to achieve business results which also falls under the scope of the audit. After the scope has been set, the auditors hold meetings with senior management to identify places where risk is present, fully understand the procedures, and discuss any concerns management may have about their business processes. So, these comprehensive procedures help auditors to construct a precise scope and goals that serve as the foundation of a successful audit (AICPA, 2021).

Fieldwork

The evaluation and assessment phase of the audit process is known as fieldwork. This part encompasses investigating the adequacy and sufficiency of internal controls for the associated risks and compliance, testing and validating control environment, transactions, and resources, and performing various processes necessary to achieve the audit's goal and objectives. The audit team hold interviews with employees, staff as well as examine business units' documents and processes. There are efforts that are taken to reduce disruptions and collaborate with auditee to make sure that the audit process runs well and smoothly. The span of an audit fieldwork phase varies according to the scope, audits with a limited scope takes only a week or two, but broad scope audits take many months. Also, access to staffs, employees as per their bandwidth and access to records, as well as how timely audit needs are answered and responded, all have a bearing on the duration of an audit. During the process of audit, clients are kept up-to date and informed of the audit progress by routine status updates and meetings. The audit team put all their effort to reveal audit results and findings, possible complications, and any recommendations as they result from the audit. (Austin, 2024) The auditors collect data and carry out processes to evaluate and assess the risks of substantial issues and lack in control measures in the technology implementation after the scope and goals have been established. Auditors implement a risk-based strategy, focusing their attentiveness on areas and business processes where mistakes or control deficiencies are more likely to appear. The reason for this assessment's importance is that auditors are unable to review every transaction. Auditors request for existing documents and examine a array of papers in order to get information. These consist of contracts, network configuration, past breach records, vulnerabilities assessments reports, financial statements, and regulatory and compliance details, etc. Moreover, auditors also carry out analytical tasks including contrasting data with industry standards or spotting anomalous and odd patterns in the data itself. This could include an unanticipated rise in inventory turnover, increase in failed login attempts, rise in external devices try to connect to the network, etc. Auditors leverage interviews in accessing the security posture of an organization. Auditors interview important employees from throughout the company by asking them set of questions to understand the control mechanism that exist and whether the employees are performing there assigned duty in alignment with the security policies placed in the organization. The purpose of these interviews is to learn more about the company's procedures, safety measures, and risk control methods. Employees from a variety of areas, including human resources, information technology, accounting, and operations, may be interviewed by them. Auditors can find any control gaps or places where more audit processes could be required by using these interviews. This help them to understand the control measures implemented in different technologies which have been employed by the business. It also involves auditors checking the awareness of employees about the implemented controls and their role in protecting the information assets of the firm.

Lastly, auditors evaluate how well the company's internal controls are working. Policies and processes known as internal controls are put in place to protect assets, guarantee the completeness and integrity of financial records, and encourage adherence to legal requirements. Examining how internal controls are applied in real-world scenarios, running test transactions to verify that the controls work as intended, and repeating controls are some methods for testing internal controls. (PCAOB, 2007) This goes for technology controls from Cloud implementation to network security controls, the auditors evaluate each technology and the risk associated with it. By understanding the different implemented controls, auditors ensure that all the information assets are in compliance with the industry standards and regulations. So, when it comes to IT Audits, the auditors categorically focus on five key aspects: (Alvello, 2023)

1. System & Applications
2. Information processing facilities
3. Systems development
4. Management of IT & Enterprise architecture
5. Telecommunications

Monitoring and Follow-Up

The final phase of an audit process depends on monitoring and examining the response of the senior management to the audit recommendations given by auditor. Then they conduct follow-up audit on implemented control measures as per the recommendations given and a subsequent process involve evaluating paperwork or performing more control testing in future audits, depending on the risk level and results generated from initial audits.

Optimization Steps

Utilize Data Analytics During Planning

Previously, data analytics is being considered through the fieldwork stage of audit. But it could be meaningful to use data analytics at an early phase of audit. During audit planning phase if an audit engagement permits access to firm's data for the subject under the scope, it would be very effective going forward in the audit process. It would be viable to find and categorize which countries, business units, business processes, and other areas cover irregularities that could signify greater risk or compliance issues by analyzing the data. (Kress & Hildebrand, 2017) The scope of the audit may be further defined by refining the data analytics results, incorporating, and expanding the scope and extent in higher risk areas, and reducing the scope in regions where analytics illustrate the risk may be lesser, after a business unit has been decided. So, incorporating data analytics at the initial stage of audit planning can save a lot of time and resource need as the auditor further goes into the fieldwork phase. (Cooke, 2018)

Adopting the Control Self-Assessment

Control Self-Assessment (CSA) is a managerial practice in which employees of business units assess their own controls. This method not only provides assurance regarding the reliability of internal controls to stakeholders, clients, and related parties but also significantly aids auditors. By involving operational line managers and staff in assessing their unit's controls, CSA helps in identifying and correcting control failures in a timely manner, leading to more accurate and reliable information for decision-making and financial reporting (Li, Peters, Richardson, and Watson 2012; Feng, Li, and McVay 2009). This practice is particularly valuable for auditors as it can save a substantial amount of time, especially in companies where material evidence is predominantly collected through meetings and interviews (Cooke, 2018).

The effectiveness of CSA depends on several factors, including the intentional identification and employment of internal subject matter experts, appropriate oversight, and strong levels of organizational trust. Furthermore, CSA requires clear assignment of control accountability (Salka 2014; KPMG 1999). CSA involves asking the auditee to answer a series of questions about control measures, standards, and benchmarks, providing auditors with valuable insights into the effectiveness of the controls in place (ISACA, 2016).

Recent studies underscore the importance of CSA in managing internal control costs. Prior research suggests that CSA can be an effective means of controlling costs associated with internal control compliance (Masli, Peters, Richardson, and Sanchez 2010). Thus, CSA not only enhances the internal control environment but also contributes to reducing overall compliance costs. By leveraging CSA, organizations can benefit from a more accurate and reliable control monitoring process, ensuring that control deficiencies are identified and addressed promptly, ultimately leading to improved decision quality and financial reporting.

Documentation: Get Primary Access to the Evidence

Generally, in a fieldwork stage of an audit, an IT auditor collects and attains data and evidence to assess against the specified control criteria. Conventionally, it is done through interviewing employees and performing walk-throughs with business process owners, where the IT auditor will ask for a print screen, copy of an existing report, control implementation documents, and additional evidence to corroborate that the controls measure criteria have been met. But to optimize and audit process and IT auditor can be given primary, read-only access to this evidence, which will reduce the required time the auditor needs to spend with the business owners, controls owners, auditee, eventually saving the company money. (Cooke, 2018)

Further, the IT auditor need not be limited to sampling. Some examples follow:

- **Change management**—If a change management application is in place and the IT auditors have direct access to it, they do not necessarily need to walk through the changes with the auditee. They can sample or test all changes directly on the application or by extracting the data from the application for further analysis.
- **Vulnerability management**—If the IT auditors have direct, read-only access to the vulnerability scanner, they can tell if the associated assets are being scanned by the tool. Further, by reviewing the results of previous scans they

can gain assurance on whether an ongoing process is in place and vulnerabilities are continuously being mitigated.

- **Audit and logging**—If the IT auditors have direct, read-only access to the enterprise's security information and event management (SIEM) tool, they can tell whether the related application assets are captured in the tool and the auditing is at a level that matches the required criteria.

This concept could also be applied to other processes where automated software is in use or evidence is captured and maintained by second-line functions. This could include the leavers and movers process, disaster recovery testing, backup restore testing, and database scanners. (Chartered Institute of Internal Auditors, 2020)

Repurpose Generalized Audit Software

As per ISACA, generalized audit software (GAS) is a multipurpose audit software that can be used for general processes, such as record selection, matching, re-calculation, and reporting. From an IT audit perspective, the use of GAS tools is usually limited to supporting operational or general audits by assisting in extracting and analyzing data from the database for applications. To help auditors in enhancing and audit process, these tools can equally be used for data extraction from servers, application logs, and meta data from databases. Which can help support expedite audit processes. (Cooke, 2018) After the data has been extracted, it can be examined and compared against accepted compliant data sets and other different sources of data, such as the application login access, past threat assessment results, company payroll. This practice can be repeated for a continuous audit and monitoring.

Effective Reporting/Follow-Up: Track and Measure Progress

IT audit reports can be complex documents containing layers of interrelated findings that affect multiple areas of the business and often require further explanation. This may be overcome by meeting the audience face-to-face and providing further detail. However, due to the size, complexity, and geographical dispersity of some enterprises, this is not always possible.

ISACA's Information Technology Assurance Framework (ITAF) recommends that a report on the status of agreed-upon corrective actions arising from audit engagement reports, including agreed-upon recommendations not implemented, should be presented to the appropriate level of management and to those charged with governance (e.g., the audit committee). This can be achieved by bringing the recommendations together in an assurance-finding register.

In addition, if these findings are allocated attributes (e.g., significance, status, owner, country, department, region), the data can be analyzed, summarized, and presented in a meaningful manner—becoming information. This information can then be used to clearly show compliance to standards and regulations and even act as lead indicators for new initiatives. (Cooke, 2018)

AI USES IN BUSINESS OPERATIONS

The auditing industry has been utilizing leading-edge digital technology and procedures in recent years. The agile methodology which was used for software development process is now implemented as agile auditing techniques. Companies apply technological capabilities like big data to create methods for continual auditing, natural language processing-based AI programs, such as Siri, Google Home, Alexa, etc.

1. Development of audit program using Chatgpt - Creating and audit program is a key aspect of an audit engagement. A basic audit program can be created by utilizing the current AI technologies by using prompt engineering which can help auditors save a considerable amount of time, and auditors will only need to make minimal amendments or adjustments to the audit program as per the specific goals and scope of the audit.
2. AI may help auditors to relieve tedious and repetitive work by reducing a lot of manual processes, which can save them a great deal of time and money. Additionally, it will support auditors in focusing more on areas that are of high risk or needs critical thinking and creativity.
3. Not only AI technologies help just experienced auditors, but also junior auditors make use of them to improve and advance their skill sets for both existing and upcoming methods and technology, as well as to save time and gain information more quickly. Moreover, auditors can use AI solutions to improve their technology auditing proficiency by understanding innovative technologies like blockchain, driverless cars, linked gadgets, etc. AI can also help the audit function fulfill skills shortages up to a certain extent. (Jaleel, 2023)

The rise in Artificial intelligence (AI) is changing how businesses are run and managed, and auditors are making sure to improve their own procedures in accordance with this change. They are doing so by leveraging artificial intelligence for complex algorithms and machine learning to predict different activity and manage business functions, which can include assessing inventory lists, improving internal auditing tasks like monitoring, etc. As these business changes might produce operational risks which are not necessarily audit issues, using AI based tools to drive business decisions does not necessarily bring new audit risks. But auditors should understand and validate the entity's business process flows, that includes the creation of reports or data analytics, which could get affected by the implementation of AI. Auditors should also consider whether the management is using AI to make decisions or AI is making decisions on behalf of the senior management. Auditors must comprehend where there is reliance on AI and whether there are other controls over the activities when AI is used in monitoring, for example, by identifying specific reconciling activities within a population or by using predictive analytics to focus management's attention on particular items. If internal audit uses AI to focus more on supervision, auditors need to know why this happened, how future risks could be handled, and whether current risks are receiving enough attention. Comprehending these modifications may lead to adjustments in the audit methodology. (Lindsay, Doutt, & Ide, 2019)

EFFECTIVE PROJECT MANAGEMENT OF AUDITS

Since every audit is a project, and projects need management to be successful, internal audit supervisors never receive project management training. Rather, we elevate competent auditors to managerial roles with minimal, if any, formal project management education.

Every aspect of the audit may function more efficiently when project management is done appropriately, and effort is dedicated to preparation beforehand. In addition to managing the team and the project, audit managers are usually required to oversee the team's completed audit work, communicate with stakeholders, and frequently finish some of the audit themselves. Enhancing our project management skills may help teams and supervisors concentrate on the important work without being sidetracked by unmanageable deadlines or projects that get out of hand. Devoted project management necessitates setting precise, quantifiable goals; monitoring the team's performance on allotted assignments; proactive, recorded stakeholder involvement; risk management; and utilization of appropriate tools and technology. (Grabis, 2022)

Project management and the internal audit function's value proposition are closely associated. Project management is defined by the Project Management Institute (PMI) as "the application of knowledge, skills, and techniques to execute projects effectively and efficiently." Audit engagements can be completed timely and, in a cost, effective manner by implementing efficient project management practices. If a project is managed well, it helps in adequate delivery of an audit engagement which is beneficial to the company.

Although project management is an essential component of any audit, internal auditors also need to take project motivation into account. A purpose is a clearly defined, well-understood goal or ideal that drives motivation. Although the overarching goal of the internal audit function is conveyed through a charter, the objective of each engagement is established and refined throughout the planning and beginning stages. Too frequently, audit management planned and begins work in isolation, omitting audit professionals and even internal audit stakeholders. Consequently, these parties may remain unaware of the goal of the engagement until the execution phase and are not made aware of the efforts made during the engagement. These stakeholders might not be as committed to the audit engagement, which might be bad for the project's chances of success. Initiating and preparing the internal audit engagement with all pertinent stakeholders involved is crucial.

As the audit process moves forward, audit management has to make sure the audit team stays focused on the engagement's goal, which was established at the beginning and planning stages. This is pertinent to long-term initiatives when audit staff entered the engagement later and were not exposed to the goals of the engagement as stated in the planning and commencing stages. Throughout the whole company, delivering excellent internal audit engagements depends on effective project management and motivation. (Bayhi, 2014)

CONTINUOUS AUDITING

Understanding continuous auditing and how to use the technique successfully is one of the major difficulties facing internal audit, control experts, enterprise risk management teams, and business managers worldwide.

Continuous Auditing has been around for a while, but there has always been a lively debate over what exactly it means and how best to use the targeted testing approach inside an already-existing audit department. The ability to distinguish between continuous monitoring and continuous auditing is another difficulty for internal audit units. One thing is constant: a monitoring strategy won't offer any control validation, even though there doesn't seem to be a significant difference between the two. There's always a chance that audit departments would skip over important stages of the continuous auditing methodology's development and implementation in an attempt to adopt a more efficient testing technique.

As global markets become increasingly complex, the demand for timely and accurate audit procedures grows, driven by the interrelated risks and evolving technology landscape (Beasley et al., 2005; Santoro et al., 2018). The rise of new technologies necessitates innovative knowledge management systems to keep pace with these changes (Santoro et al., 2018). In this context, establishing a robust system of internal audits is crucial for enhancing procedures, preventing cyber-attacks, and recruiting skilled risk-prevention professionals (Ebaid, 2011; Drogalas et al., 2016; Abdullatif and Kawuq, 2015).

One particularly relevant approach is continuous auditing, which is especially beneficial for smaller and developing countries that may lack advanced digital auditing platforms. For example, following its fiscal deficit announcement in 2007, Greece embarked on a significant digital transformation effort (Kontiadis, 2008). The literature from that period emphasized how information technology impacts internal audit procedures and highlighted the need for increased investment in technology (Spathis, 2007; Woodroof and Searcy, 2001).

Continuous auditing involves the integration of traditional audit methods with new technologies. Studies such as those by Alles et al. (2006) and Vasarhelyi and Halper (2018) showcase how continuous auditing systems, like Siemens' internal IT audit practices and AT&T Bell Laboratories' Continuous Process Auditing System (CPAS), enhance audit processes by providing real-time metrics and analytics. CPAS, for instance, monitors operational analytics, compares them with benchmarks, and flags issues for auditor review. Meanwhile, research by Rikhardsson and Dull (2016) highlights the implementation of continuous auditing technology in small businesses, indicating its growing relevance.

The successful implementation of continuous auditing requires significant initial investment in time, preparation, and resources (Mainardi, 2011). Despite the effort required, the long-term benefits are substantial once the system is operational. Continuous auditing represents an evolutionary step in audit practices, combining traditional methods with technological advancements to improve accuracy and efficiency (Woodroof and Searcy, 2001; Chan et al., 2018).

For instance, deploying technology for remote auditing has enabled the reorganization of internal audit procedures, allowing staff to work virtually and enhancing overall audit effectiveness (Teeter et al., 2010). Moreover, continuous assurance is increasingly recognized as a vital tool for enterprise risk management, facilitating early detection of fraudulent activities and improving financial oversight (Onulaka, 2015; Chan et al., 2018).

By embracing continuous auditing and leveraging technological innovations, organizations can better manage risks, streamline audit processes, and achieve more reliable financial oversight.

The way financial information is conveyed and commerce is done has changed dramatically as a result of the digital economy. Online and real-time business and financial report publication is being used by an ever-increasing number of enterprises. Continuous auditing will probably be required in order to give ongoing confidence over the accuracy and reliability of the data provided in real-time financial reporting. Due to need, the audit process changed from being a traditional manual audit to one that was computer-based, and it is currently required to create ongoing electronic audits. The fast advancement of information technology and the need for prompt information dissemination to corporate stakeholders necessitate that auditors devise novel approaches for consistently tracking, obtaining, and evaluating audit evidence.

AUTOMATING THE AUDIT

Organizations that have traditionally relied on human audit processes might gain by approaching the next audit piecemeal. Under such a strategy, a pilot study would essentially be carried out to determine the possible advantages of audit automation. Since resistance to change is a common occurrence, it will probably be easier to progress gradually and cautiously. In the long run, this might greatly increase the likelihood of finally reaching the future audit and lead to increased support for the growth of automated audit procedures and programs.

An effective and cost-efficient way to begin automating audit processes is by utilizing basic Computer-Assisted Audit Techniques (CAATS). These tools simplify tasks such as data extraction, sorting, and analysis. CAATS provide comprehensive audit logs for documentation, have no file size limitations, require no extensive training, and allow for the generation of tailored reports applicable to both current and future data sets (Chan, Chiu, Vasarhelyi, & Miklos, 2018).

The initial deployment of these technologies is best suited to replace manual auditing efforts, where the greatest benefits are often realized. For example, CAATS can automate functions like selecting statistical samples, generating confirmations, balancing ledgers, and detecting unusual transactions, significantly reducing the need for human resources and making transaction verification more cost-effective (Chan, Chiu, Vasarhelyi, & Miklos, 2018).

Furthermore, integrating automated systems into the audit process enables real-time or near real-time data analysis against predefined benchmarks (Brown, Wong, & Baldwin, 2007; Chan, Chiu, & Vasarhelyi, 2018; Kuhn & Sutton, 2010). This approach not only enhances efficiency but also reduces the cost of verifying a larger volume of transactions (Brown et al., 2007). However, it's important to consider that automation might lead to behavioral changes among managers. The awareness of being monitored through automated systems can alter their decision-making processes, a phenomenon often referred to as the "Big Brother" effect (Brown et al., 2007; Kogan et al., 2018). By leveraging these automated tools, organizations can significantly improve the accuracy and efficiency of their audits, facilitating better control monitoring and cost management.

The Administrative Officer's openness to use contemporary auditing technology internal auditors cause to reconsider the practices and techniques they were employing on a daily basis. The internal auditors sought to replace their manual procedure with an ongoing automated one in order to increase productivity and make the process more flexible and all-encompassing. This type of leadership is seen as being crucial to the implementation of continuous audit success.

CONTINUOUS AUDIT IMPLEMENTATION PROCESS PHASES

Phases Criteria

1. Planning 1.1 Establishing priority areas based on risk management
2. Process Evaluation 2.1 Evaluating routines and procedures used by the department
   2.2 Identifying controls already implemented
   2.3 Conference on whether the department has sufficient systemic data
3. Scope Definition 3.1 Limitations and risks
   3.2 Frequency of the audits
   3.3 Opportunities
   3.4 Crosschecking definitions
4. Pilot Test 4.1 Script writing
   4.2 Testing application
5. Alignment with the Business Area 5.1 Treatment of exceptions
   5.2 Follow-up process
6. Project Maintenance and Execution 6.1 Adjusting the script
   6.2 Project execution
7. Continuous Follow-Up 7.1 Definition of indicators for continuous monitoring in conjunction with the business area (Anne Hardy & Laslett, 2015)

The internal auditors discovered that comprehensive databases and sufficient reports were necessary for a proper execution of continuous audit as their plans for it developed. Internal auditors wouldn't be able to apply some forms of automation and parameterize test procedures without these tools. Among other things, the availability of computer-readable data formats determines one's capacity to parameterize a test. (Appelbaum & Nehmer, 2017)

EFFECTIVE STAKEHOLDER ENGAGEMENT

Stakeholder collaboration is a vital, two-way process that benefits both internal auditors and stakeholders. Internal auditors can underscore the importance of their role in good governance and highlight the value of providing independent, unbiased assurance through regular face-to-face meetings. These interactions offer stakeholders an opportunity to discuss the effectiveness of internal audits, express their concerns, and identify risks or issues they wish to be addressed in the audit strategy. However, organizing these meetings can be challenging and easily postponed, especially when stakeholders are juggling multiple assurance providers. Proactive planning is essential to maintain regular communication and address stakeholder needs effectively (Chartered Institute of Internal Auditors, 2023).

Despite shared interests and expectations among stakeholders (Knechel et al., 2013a), conflicts of interest are inevitable, with some emphasizing professional aspects and others focusing on commercial interests (Sweeney and McGarry, 2011; Cooper and Robson, 2006; Suddaby et al., 2007; McNair, 1991). Auditors develop their professional perspective through education, training, and regulation, which emphasizes adherence to auditing standards (Li et al., 2017; Che et al., 2018; DeFond and Lennox, 2011). Although previous studies have explored auditors' ideal views on audit quality (Brivot et al., 2018; Gonthier-Besacier et al., 2016; Warming-Rasmussen and Jensen, 1998; Carcello et al., 1992; Schroeder et al., 1986), there is limited understanding of how these general views align with self-assessments of actual audit engagements.

Balancing stakeholder expectations with professional standards and managing potential conflicts of interest is crucial for effective internal auditing. Regular and well-planned interactions between auditors and stakeholders can help mitigate these challenges and ensure that audit strategies remain aligned with the needs and concerns of all parties involved.

In order to guarantee the audit's accountability and openness, stakeholder participation is essential. It is becoming more widely acknowledged that in order for work to have an impact and, eventually, to generate value and benefits, an ecosystem of interrelated actors, circumstances, and processes must support and collaborate.

Working in an emergency scenario may make stakeholder participation even more crucial. For instance, companies must take into account how stakeholders' priorities are changing, how rising risks may affect stakeholders' behavior, and the possibility that audit work may obstruct stakeholders' ability to provide emergency response. Furthermore, when the company is able to be there, stakeholders' continuous presence on the ground during an emergency means they may play a crucial role in audit selection, risk assessment, and evidence collecting.

Key steps in stakeholder analysis, and the outputs from each, may be summarized as follows:

1. Identify Stakeholders - Register/list of stakeholders
2. Map Stakeholders - Stakeholder MAP, e.g. power/interest grid
3. Stakeholder Consultation - Record of stakeholder views and inputs
4. Analysis and Decision Making - Summary analysis table and identified actions (Initiative, 2020)

Additionally, there could be both internal and external stakeholders, therefore the audience will determine how important certain messages are emphasized. Some key requirements that can be added into a stakeholder engagement plan as part of the larger audit strategy incorporate creating an orientation scheduled program for senior management, internal stakeholders, external stakeholders, and new members of the audit committee. Also, the plan can have schedule separate meetings for management for related updates and appropriate information, such as any changes in laws and regulations, information technology risk management practices, and professional internal audit exercises that could have potential effects on the organization and internal audit delivery. Also, they can build an intranet or website with necessary and relevant content to help stakeholders with required information and also it is updated with the latest information. (Chartered Institute of Internal Auditors, 2023)

CONTROL SELECTION

It is very necessary to establish compliance, information technology security audits for evaluating the efficacy of IT controls, which plays a key role. So, most companies are placing a high premium on adhering to the increasing privacy laws and regulations, and standards. The issue of whether to conduct a security audit become decisive factors of an organization's control process in light of the numerous expenses, including controls costs. (Herath & Herath, 2014) Therefore, deciding the right set of controls can help in optimizing the audit lifecycle. Understanding the entity's information system, including the IT environment pertinent to the flow of data and information processing through the system, is necessary for an auditor in order to prepare the reports. It is crucial to comprehend how your client's information system relates to the major business operations because using IT applications or other elements of the IT environment increases the risks associated with using IT. The nature and degree of IT reliance in the information system may also be better understood in light of the entity's business strategy and how they have integrated and utilized IT. As part of the control activities, you must also identify the IT applications and other elements of the entity's IT infrastructure that are vulnerable to risks associated with using IT for the specified controls. The information processing controls that directly address information integrity are the focus of these identified controls. Next, you may determine the associated risks associated with using IT and the entity's GITCs that deal with those risks. Your proposed methods to ascertain whether the control has been implemented for each of these identified GITCs will be informed by your assessment of how well the control is designed to support the functioning of other controls. (Lee, 2022)

Control baselines, which are pre-defined sets of controls put together to meet the protection needs of a group, organization, or community of interest, are used in the baseline control selection technique. Information, information systems, and people's privacy are all protected beginning with security and privacy control baselines. The proposed NIST Special Publication 800-53B defines the baselines for federal security and privacy controls. The information and information systems that have been classified as low-impact, moderate-impact, or high-impact—that is, the potential negative effects on the organization's missions or business operations or a loss of assets if there is a breach or compromise to the system—are protected by the sets of security controls and control enhancements found in the three security control baselines.

The selection of security control baselines from draft Special Publication 800-53B can be guided and informed by the system security categorization, risk assessment, and security requirements derived from stakeholder protection needs, laws, executive orders, regulations, policies, directives, and standards.

Because the organization does not begin with a pre-defined set of controls, the organization-generated control selection technique is different from the baseline selection approach. Instead, the organization chooses controls via a procedure of its own. This could be required in cases where the system is extremely specialized (like weaponry systems or medical devices), has a narrow scope or purpose (like smart meters), has to be protected from a particular set of threats, or the nature of the data processing presents particular privacy problems. Instead of starting with a pre-defined set of controls from a control baseline and adding or removing controls through the tailoring process, it could be more efficient and economical for an organization to choose the controls for the system in certain circumstances. Similar to the baseline control selection approach, the organization-generated selection approach's requirements for specific controls can be determined by stakeholder protection needs, laws, executive orders, regulations, policies, directives, and standards, as well as by system security categorization, risk assessment, and requirements derived from these sources. (Ross, Pillitteri, & Lefkovitz, 2020) The relationship between the effectiveness of internal controls and how audit programs are planned can help optimize an audit process. A generally accepted auditing standard requires that a study be made of internal control as a basis for assessing the extent of audit tests. But there is a need for a theoretical framework to guide auditors in exercising judgement about how much to modify their audit programs in response to their evaluation of internal controls. There should be a conceptual framework for a "minimum" audit program, which would be the set of auditing procedures necessary if there were no internal controls because the extent to which an auditor can reduce the scope of his or her substantive auditing procedures should depend on his or her assessment of the effectiveness of the client's internal controls. (Mautz & Mini, 1966)

CONCLUSION

To conclude, this research book chapter probes into the complexities of optimizing the technology audit lifecycle, recognizing the ever-expanding dependence on Information Technology in modern-day business functions. The research explored various optimization methods to enhance the effectiveness and efficiency of IT audits. Initially, it emphasized on the current audit lifecycle, including planning, fieldwork, monitoring, and follow-up stages. It then explored into optimization strategies such as incorporating data analytics in the planning phase, utilizing control self-assessment (CSA) processes, granting auditors primary access to evidence, repurposing generalized audit software (GAS), and implementing effective reporting and follow-up procedures. Moreover, the paper acknowledged the increasing influence of Artificial Intelligence (AI) in the audit landscape. It discussed the potential of AI to streamline tedious tasks, facilitate continuous auditing, and improve understanding of emerging technologies like blockchain. Auditors can leverage AI to adapt their methodologies and stay ahead of the curve.

The concluding section highlighted the significance of effective project management practices and stakeholder engagement in achieving positive audit outcomes. Finally, the paper explored the concept of continuous auditing and automation as promising avenues for optimizing the audit process.

By adopting these optimization strategies and embracing emerging technologies, IT audits can evolve into a more proactive and insightful function, adding significant value to organizations.

REFERENCES

Abdullatif, M., & Kawuq, S. (2015). The role of internal auditing in risk management: Evidence from banks in Jordan . *Journal of Economic and Administrative Sciences*, 31(1), 30–50. DOI: 10.1108/JEAS-08-2013-0025

AICPA. (2021). *aicpa.org*. Retrieved from Planning an Audit: https://us.aicpa.org/content/dam/aicpa/research/standards/auditattest/downloadabledocuments/au-c-00300.pdf

Alles, M. G., Brennan, G., Vasarhelyi, M. A., & Kogan, A. (2006). *Continuous monitoring of business process controls: A pilot implementation of a continuous auditing system at Siemens*. Published in the International Journal of Accounting Information Systems.

Alvello, M. (2023, October 19). *What Is an IT Audit? A Definitive Guide to Safeguard Your Data*. Retrieved from G2: https://track.g2.com/resources/it-audit#:~:text=Fieldwork%3A%20Once%20the%20plan%20is,evidence%20that%20supports%20their%20findings

Anne Hardy, C., & Laslett, G. (2015). Continuous Auditing and Monitoring in Practice: Lessons from Metcash's Business Assurance Group. *Journal of Information Systems.*

Appelbaum, D., & Nehmer, R. A. (2017). Using Drones in Internal and External Audits: An Exploratory Framework. *Journal of Emerging Technologies in Accounting*, 14(1), 99–113. DOI: 10.2308/jeta-51704

Arens, A. A., Elder, R. J., & Beasley, M. S. Hogan, & Chris E. (2017). Auditing and assurance services: An integrated approach (16th ed.). New Jersey: Pearson Prentince Hall.

Austin, T. U. (2024). *The University at Texas at Austin: Office of Internal Audits*. Retrieved from Audit Process: https://audit.utexas.edu/audit-process#:~:text=The%20evaluation%20phase%20of%20the,the%20objectives%20of%20the%20audit

Bayhi, J. (2014). The purposeful audit: effective project management is fundamental to delivering valuable internal audit engagements across the organization. *Internal Auditor(Vol. 71, Issue 1).*

Beasley, M. S., Clune, R., Hermanson, D. R. (2005). Enterprise Risk Management: An Empirical Analysis of Factors Associated With the Extent of Implementation.

Brivot, M., Roussy, M., & Mayer, M. (2018). Conventions of audit quality: The perspective of public and private company audit partners. *Auditing*, 37(2), 51–71. DOI: 10.2308/ajpt-51772

Brown, C. E., Wong, J. A., & Baldwin, A. A. (2007). A review and analysis of the existing research streams in continuous auditing. *Journal of Emerging Technologies in Accounting*, 4(1), 1–28. DOI: 10.2308/jeta.2007.4.1.1

Buchanan, S., & Gibb, F. (2007, June). The information audit: Role and scope. *International Journal of Information Management*, 27(3), 159–172. DOI: 10.1016/j.ijinfomgt.2007.01.002

Carcello, J. V., Hermanson, R. H., & McGrath, N. T. (1992). Audit quality attributes: The perceptions of audit partners, preparers, and financial statement users. *Auditing*, 11(1), 1–15.

Chan, D., & Chiu, V. (2018). *Continuous Auditing*. Emerald Publishing Limited.

Chan, D. Y., Chiu, V., & Vasarhelyi, M. A. (Eds.). (2018), Continuous Auditing: Theory and Application, Emerald Group Publishing, Howard House, Bingley, UK.

Chartered Institute of Internal Auditors. (2020). *Governance of Risk: Three Lines of Defence*. Retrieved from theiia.org: https://www.theiia.org/globalassets/documents/resources/the-iias-three-lines-model-an-update-of-the-three-lines-of-defense-july-2020/three-lines-model-updated-english.pdf

Chartered Institute of Internal Auditors. (2023). *Working with stakeholders*. Retrieved from Chartered Institute of Internal Auditors: https://www.iia.org.uk/resources/managing-internal-audit/working-with-stakeholders/

Che, L., Langli, J. C., & Svanström, T. (2018). Education, experience and audit effort. *Auditing*, 37(3), 91–115. DOI: 10.2308/ajpt-51896

Cooke, I. (2018). *IS Audit Basics: Innovation in the IT Audit Process*. Retrieved from ISACA: https://www.isaca.org/resources/isaca-journal/issues/2018/volume-2/is-audit-basics-innovation-in-the-it-audit-process

Cooper, D. J., & Robson, K. (2006). Accounting, professions and regulation: Locating the sites of professionalization. *Accounting, Organizations and Society*, 31(4-5), 415–444. DOI: 10.1016/j.aos.2006.03.003

DeFond, M. L., & Lennox, C. S. (2011). The effect of SOX on small auditor exits and audit quality. *Journal of Accounting and Economics*, 52(1), 21–40. DOI: 10.1016/j.jacceco.2011.03.002

Drogalas, G., Arampatzis, K., & Anagnostopoulou, E. (2016). The relationship between Corporate governance, internal audit and audit committee: Empirical evidence from Greece. *Corporate Ownership and Control*, 14(1), 569–577. DOI: 10.22495/cocv14i1c4art3

Ebaid, I. E. S. (2011), Internal audit function: an exploratory study from Egyptian listed firms. International Journal of Law and Management. Available at: https://www.emerald.com/insight/ content/doi/10.1108/17542431111119397/full/html#loginreload

Feng, M., Li, C., & McVay, S. (2009). Internal control and management guidance. *Journal of Accounting and Economics*, 48(2/3), 190–209. DOI: 10.1016/j.jacceco.2009.09.004

Gonthier-Besacier, N., Hottegindre, G., & Fine-Falcy, S. (2016). Audit quality perception: Beyond the 'role-perception gap'. *International Journal of Auditing*, 20(2), 186–201. DOI: 10.1111/ijau.12066

Grabis, C. (2022). *Five Project Management Best Practices for More Effective Audits*. Retrieved from Audit Board: https://www.auditboard.com/blog/project-management-best-practices-for-more-effective-audits/

Herath, H. S., & Herath, T. C. (2014). *IT security auditing: A performance evaluation decision model*. ScienceDirect.

IAASB. (2004). *International auditing and assurance standards board*. https://www.iaasb.org/consultations-projects/planning-audit-financial-statements

Initiative, I. D. (2020). *Engaging with Stakeholders for TAI Audits.* Retrieved from INTOSAI Development Initiative: https://idi.no/elibrary/professional-sais/tai-audit/1217-tai-audit-guide-chapter-5-engaging-with-stakeholders-for-tai-audits/file

ISACA. (2016). *CISA Review* (Manual 26th Edition). ISACA.

Jaleel, A. (2023). *ChatGPT and Leveraging Artificial Intelligence in Auditing*. ISACA.

Knechel, W. R., Krishnan, G. V., Pevzner, M., Shefchik, L. B., & Velury, U. K. (2013a). Audit quality: Insights from the academic literature. *Auditing*, 32(1, Supplement 1), 385–421. DOI: 10.2308/ajpt-50350

Kogan, A., Sudit, E. F., & Vasarhelyi, M. A. (2018). Continuous online auditing: A program of research. In Chan, D. Y., Chiu, V., & Vasarhelyi, M. A. (Eds.), *Continuous Auditing* (pp. 125–148). DOI: 10.1108/978-1-78743-413-420181006

Kolk, A., van der Veen, M. L., van Wateringen, S. L., van der Veldt, D., & Walhain, S. P. (1999). *KPMG International survey of environmental reporting 1999*. KPMG/ WIMM.

Kolodner, J. L. (1981, Spring). Towards an Understanding of the Role of Experience in the Evolution from Novice to Expert. *Journal of Accounting Research*, 19(1).

Kontiadis, I. Z. (2008). *Introduction to Social Administration and Social Security Institutions*. Papazisis Publications.

Kress, R., & Hildebrand, D. (2017). *How Analytics Will Transform Internal Audit* (Vol. 2). ISACA Journal.

Kuhn, J. R.Jr, & Sutton, S. G. (2010). Continuous Auditing in ERP System Environments: The Current State and Future Directions. *Journal of Information Systems*, 24(1), 91–112. DOI: 10.2308/jis.2010.24.1.91

Kuttybaeva, N., Raikhanova, G., Zhaparova, R., Kozhabatchina, G., & Akmolda, M. (2022, June 30). *Bulletin Of The Karaganda University Economy Series.* Retrieved from Technological audit in the system of optimization of innovative activity: https:// economy-vestnik.ksu.kz/index.php/economy-vestnik/article/view/667

Lee, A. (2022, September 2). *General information technology controls: IT risks auditors must be aware of.* Retrieved from Chartered Professional Accountants Canada: https://www.cpacanada.ca/business-and-accounting-resources/audit-and-assurance/ blog/2022/september/general-information-technology-controls-for-auditors

Leslie, D. A. (1985). *Materiality, the concepts and its applications in Auditing*. CICA.

Li, C., Peters, G. F., Richardson, V. J., & Watson, M. W. (2012). The consequences of information technology control weaknesses on management information systems: The case of Sarbanes-Oxley internal control reports. *Management Information Systems Quarterly*, 36(1), 179–203. DOI: 10.2307/41410413

Li, L., Qi, B., Tian, G., & Zhang, G. (2017). The contagion effect of low-quality audits at the level of individual auditors. *The Accounting Review*, 92(1), 137–163. DOI: 10.2308/accr-51407

Lindsay, J., Doutt, A., & Ide, C. (2019). *Emerging Technologies, Risk, and the Auditor's Focus*. Harvard Law School Forum on Corporate Governance.

Mainardi, R. (2011). Developing and Implementing a Practical Methodology. In Mainardi, R. (Ed.), *Harnessing the Power of Continuous Auditing: Developing and Implementing a Practical Methodology*. John Wiley & Sons, Incorporated.

Masli, A., Peters, G. F., Richardson, V. J., & Sanchez, J. M. (2010). Examining the potential benefits of internal control monitoring technology. *The Accounting Review*, 85(3), 1001–1034. DOI: 10.2308/accr.2010.85.3.1001

Mautz, R. K., & Mini, D. L. (1966). *Internal Control Evaluation and Audit Program Modification*. ProQuest.

McNair, C. J. (1991). Proper compromises: The management control dilemma in public accounting and its impact on auditor behavior. *Accounting, Organizations and Society*, 16(7), 635–653. DOI: 10.1016/0361-3682(91)90017-9

Mock, T. J., & Wright, A. (1992). An Exploratory Study of Auditor Evalyuation, Planning Judgements, revised version of a paper presented at the 1991 Annual Congress of the European Accounting Association, Maastricht, The Netherlands.

Onulaka, P. N. (2015). Internal and external audit effectiveness in fraud detection through continuous auditing. *International Journal of Management*, 6(10), 462–475.

PCAOB. (2007). *PCAOB: Public Company Accounting Oversight Board*. Retrieved from AS 2201: An Audit of Internal Control Over Financial Reporting That Is Integrated with An Audit of Financial Statements: https://pcaobus.org/oversight/standards/auditing-standards/details/AS2201

PCAOB. (2010). *PCAOB Public Company Accounting Oversight Board*. Retrieved from PCAOB Public Company Accounting Oversight Board: https://pcaobus.org/oversight/standards/auditing-standards/details/as-2101-audit-planning-2022

Rikhardsson, P., & Dull, R. (2016). An exploratory study of the adoption, application and impacts of continuous auditing technologies in small businesses. *International Journal of Accounting Information Systems*, 20, 26–37. DOI: 10.1016/j.accinf.2016.01.003

Ross, R., Pillitteri, V. Y., & Lefkovitz, N. (2020, October 1). *Selecting Security and Privacy Controls: Choosing the Right Approach*. Retrieved from NIST: https://www.nist.gov/blogs/cybersecurity-insights/selecting-security-and-privacy-controls-choosing-right-approach

Salka, T. (2014). The maturation of controls self-assessment. Available at: https://www.sans.org/reading-room/whitepapers/compliance/ maturation-controls-self-assessments-35307/

Santoro, G., Vrontis, D., Thrassou, A., & Dezi, L. (2018). The Internet of Things: Building a knowledge management system for open innovation and knowledge management capacity. *Technological Forecasting and Social Change*, 136, 347–354. DOI: 10.1016/j.techfore.2017.02.034

Schroeder, M. S., Solomon, I., & Vickrey, D. (1986). Audit quality: The perceptions of audit-committee chairpersons and audit partners. *Auditing*, 5(2), 86–94.

Spathis, C. (2007). Detecting Fraudulent Financial Statements by Using Continuous Auditing, Published in the Honorary volume for the peer Professor Aristotle Ignatiadis, Thessaloniki, Greece.

Stoel, D., Havelka, D., & Merhout, J. (2012, March). An analysis of attributes that impact information technology audit quality: A study of IT and financial audit practitioners. *International Journal of Accounting Information Systems*, 13(1), 60–79. DOI: 10.1016/j.accinf.2011.11.001

Suddaby, R., Cooper, D. J., & Greenwood, R. (2007). Transnational regulation of professional services: Governance dynamics of field level organizational change. *Accounting, Organizations and Society*, 32(4-5), 333–362. DOI: 10.1016/j.aos.2006.08.002

Sweeney, B., & McGarry, C. (2011). Commercial and professional audit goals: Inculcation of audit seniors. *International Journal of Auditing*, 15(3), 316–332. DOI: 10.1111/j.1099-1123.2011.00437.x

Teeter, R. A., Alles, M. G., & Vasarhelyi, M. A. (2010). The remote audit . *Journal of Emerging Technologies in Accounting*, 7(1), 73–88. DOI: 10.2308/jeta.2010.7.1.73

Vasarhelyi, M., & Halper, F. (2018). The continuous audit of online Systems1. In Continuous Auditing (Rutgers Studies in Accounting Analytics). Emerald Publishing. DOI: 10.1108/978-1-78743-413-420181004

Warming-Rasmussen, B., & Jensen, L. (1998). Quality dimensions in external audit services – an external user perspective. *European Accounting Review*, 7(1), 65–82. DOI: 10.1080/096381898336583

Woodroof, J., & Searcy, D. (2001). *Continuous audit: Model development and implementation within a debt covenant compliance domain*. Published in the International Journal of Accounting Information Systems. DOI: 10.1016/S1467-0895(01)00019-7

Chapter 2
Mitigating the Humans Risks to Cybersecurity Posture

Moksh Gupta
University at Buffalo, SUNY, USA

John Ryan
https://orcid.org/0009-0004-0136-4225
University at Buffalo, SUNY, USA

Tyler Boyer
https://orcid.org/0009-0002-5032-4639
University at Buffalo, SUNY, USA

ABSTRACT

This study addresses the critical field of information security risk mitigation introduced by humans. Recognizing and fixing risk factors resulting from human behavior is essential at a time when complex cyber threats plague digital environments. This research is significant because it acknowledges that human vulnerability plays a major role in information security breaches. Despite technological advances, insufficient training, malicious intent, and human error remain major obstacles. Organizations that ignore these factors risk devastating data breaches, financial ruin, and serious harm to their reputation. By addressing human-related vulnerabilities, companies can better protect their digital assets and ensure a more secure working environment. The research illustrates the importance of comprehensive training programs, strict security policies, and a culture of awareness to mitigate risks associated with human factors. Effective risk mitigation requires a multifaceted strategy that combines technology with human-centered strategies to safeguard against evolving cyber threats.

DOI: 10.4018/979-8-3693-4211-4.ch002

1. INTRODUCTION

As the rise of technology has taken over the world, there is continuously more data being stored online that needs to be protected. This also introduces the numerous ways that bad actors and hackers can attempt to gain access to this data through breaches due to weak security, whether that be technical or human error. Over time, it has been evident that the weakest link in information security is the human element involved in the company's efforts to protect its data. Since the mid 2000's researchers have noticed the increase in human error as a cause for incidents. For public companies from November 2004 to September 2008, the monthly ratio of human errors to incidents increased from ~27% to ~75%, while reaching as high as 97% in some months in between (Liginlal et al., 2009). This shows the extent of the issue in a time where information security was not nearly as talked about or important in any workplace. As time goes on, there are not many factors changing in the world of information security other than the amount of people using technology, the amount of data being stored, and the amount of attackers that want to cause an incident. The main issue we will look at here is the increase in users that will raise the probability of human error involved in the information security domain. Now more than ever, with the rise in remote work, emailing, conferencing, and remote desktops tools due to COVID-19, we have to find solutions to mitigate the amount of human error and incidents that happen too often. When creating an information security program there should be a balance between people, processes, and technology. Clearly the balance is skewed with the level of risk that humans introduce to the equation. The history of controls against human error in information security has evolved tremendously over the years, yet it still eludes the industry on how to reduce the amount of human error that causes it to be the weakest link in security. In today's digital era, cybersecurity plays a critical role in safeguarding information and systems from increasingly sophisticated cyber threats. Furthermore, these dangers leverage both technical and human vulnerabilities, warranting a multifaceted approach: utilizing advanced technology and comprehending human behavior. To bypass even the most complex security measures, attackers frequently take advantage of psychological tricks, human error, and social engineering. (Pfleeger & Caputo, 2012). Human Factor Vulnerabilities: In cybersecurity, human error continues to be a major risk despite advances in technology. Anytime employees and users share confidential information, click on malicious links, or disregard security procedures out of misunderstanding or negligence, they may inadvertently jeopardize security. Alongside technical measures, addressing these human elements calls for policies, awareness campaigns, and educational initiatives to foster a culture of security awareness (Pfleeger & Caputo, 2012). The emergence of technical solutions has not stopped the study of human factors from receiving insufficient attention. Saying that system security criteria will be met because users will behave in a secure manner as expected isn't always accurate. Since human security is an intangible and cannot be purchased, it will always be a crucial area of study. It follows that the importance of human elements in information security cannot be overstated. (Hughes-Lartey, Li, Botchey, & Qin, 2021). Recently, a lot of work-related duties have been finished at home or in coffee shops, disclosing sensitive information about the business and exposing it to hazards ranging from reputational damage to financial risk. Examining and assessing these threats has become imperative, as has talking about how an organization's culture and structure could create an environment that supports information security measures (Sidor-Rządkowska, 2022).

2. DATA LOSS PREVENTION

Companies have changed. Before their most prized possessions were their products or services, the crown jewel is now their data. Collecting data can help them make strategic informed decisions that can change the direction of the business. Companies will do anything to keep their data confidential. If this data is shared they could lose the advantage of surprise or if their data is PHI they could face major fines or legal action. Security teams spend as much time as they can looking forward to trying to be preventative to stop attackers, but this leaves them blind to what is happening behind them. A lot of data leaks could be from insiders just making mistakes and sending out the wrong information by accident. This raises the question of how can we stop data exfiltration from happening or how can we stop attackers from exporting our data if they can get into the system?

Companies can utilize a data loss prevention system. "Data Loss Prevention systems (DLP) aim to address the risk of data disclosure from insiders (and some malware as well). Their main idea is to observe and control the storage, movement, or handling of confidential data according to specified security policies" (Wuchner & Pretschner, 2012). These are systems that are designed to prevent accidents from happening. By controlling what information can leave the network, the system can catch people from emailing sensitive information, or stop attackers from leaving with massive amounts of data dumps. Many businesses use data loss prevention (DLP), a well-established technology, to assist their information security needs. DLP is a potent privacy-enhancing technology that can meet a variety of information-privacy requirements thanks to a number of important features. DLP is essentially a collection of integrated technologies that identify sensitive data and stop it from being used, released, or delivered uninvited to particular recipients or destinations, or stored in places that aren't allowed. (Stallings, 2020). Data loss prevention is a dynamic, continuous activity that necessitates regular organization effort and investment

(Emenike 2021). Current news articles highlight the problem's broad ramifications due to the rising use of SaaS, rising SaaS DLIs, and possible harm to organizations (Brignall, 2021; Carroll, 2021; Fung, 2021; Valinsky, 2021; Cluley, 2022; Gorelik, 2022). One of the most implemented DLPs is the one from Microsoft's Office 365.

They allow you to set policies on for users for the following:

show a pop-up policy tip to the user that warns them that they may be trying to share a sensitive item inappropriately block the sharing and, via a policy tip, allow the user to override the block and capture the users' justification block the sharing without the override option for data at rest, sensitive items can be locked and moved to a secure quarantine location for Teams chat, the sensitive information will not be displayed (Microsoft, 2021).

These types of policies can prevent the accidental sharing of information for users who are not aware of the sensitivity of the data. The system administrator can decide which rules to place, but either way, this gives them control over the data.

Microsoft allows the administrator to protect the user from themselves as well as stop adversaries trying to steal data. Microsoft endpoint protection comes with numerous features that can protect data. Administrators can audit and restrict different activities.

The first activity is "upload to cloud service or access by unallowed browsers" (Microsoft, 2021). This will look to see what kind of browser the user is using. If the browser the user is using is not approved the DLP will block the action and redirect to edge and if the action is still negative the system will block the action. Not all browsers are created equally, some have more security concerns than others, it is up to management to decide which browsers are approved and which are not. If you only allow windows systems in your environment, it should be a red flag if a user begins to use safari. By auditing this activity we can quickly end activities that could cause something bad from happening.

The next activity you can watch for is "copy to other applications" (Micsosoft, 2021). When we have confidential information, we want to keep it from escaping from where it is secure. This is useful because it can stop attackers from ex-filling information by emailing it out. Or stopping users make a small mistake where they didn't know that the information was confidential. Either way, we can block something bad from happening. This is another line of defense we can utilize to keep a breach from happening.

The next activity is "copy to USB removable media"(Micsosoft, 2021). There is a common security practice blocking all USB ports, which came from a cyber attack on the United States Military in 2008. What happened was "an infected flash drive that was inserted in a US military laptop at a base in the Middle East"(Netsurion, 2014). After this, the worm on the device quickly spread all over the US Central Command's network. To prevent this from happening again the US military barred systems from accepting removable media. However, this is not very feasible for the majority of organizations. Operations had to take the risk of using USBs because without them it can be hard for users to stay efficient. These USBs work both ways, you can put information and take it out. Endpoint protection can stop anyone from trying to copy info onto a USB and getting it out of the network. Two US printing companies were fined $130,000 for violating HIPAA after they unintentionally disclosed the health information of 56,000 residents of New Jersey State in a DLP-related incident. (Kolbasuk McGee, 2021).

Data Loss/Leakage Prevention (DLP) refers to the collective security procedures (controls) used by organizations to prevent the leakage of their sensitive and personal information (PII). (Tahboub and Saleh, 2014).

Everyone thinks of information leaving a network or a location by a hacker taking it out through a tunnel, emailing it out or storing data on a hard drive. But someone just printing out the documents just slips right under our radar. In Office 365 we can stop this from happening. We can add labels to our data and have them classified as protected. That way when someone tries to get information out of the network via a physical copy this will be stopped from happening. Additionally, data leaking is placed third among the top 10 cloud dangers (Khan and AlYasiri, 2016)

Remote desktop protocol has rapidly grown in the last few years, especially during the shift that came with the COVID-19 pandemic. Users "can connect a personal computer using the Internet at a cafe or public spaces. Using the smart office, it is possible to make a personal business environment to increase business efficiency"(Kim, 2014). This allows a user to be able to have their work desktop anywhere in the world. But this is also an entrance in a network. Any endpoint can turn into a disaster with or without intention. But with data loss protection we can still stop users from copying data to an RDP session.

The next big service that we can audit is whenever a user creates or renames an item (Micsosoft, 2021). We should not restrict this because our users need to work, but we should have logs for when they do this. We can have all these controls in a file that has "classified", but if we're not paying attention they can just make a new document and label it as "public" and retype the data, and our sensitive data is completely available to move around. This can cause a disaster, if it does we will be able to go back and look at the logs to see who could have let the data out and this will give us a start on how to control the leak. All of these controls are a great start in securing our data. From malicious users to users who just don't know any better, being able to stop the data from leaving is a great layer of defense and when stacked on top of other layers this is a great way of staying safe.

3. ROLE-BASED ACCESS CONTROL

Access control is crucial for every interaction that information security professionals and their users have, including both technological and physical. One specific access control technique is Role-Based Access Control (RBAC), which is a practical technique that only gives access to certain subjects depending on their role in the company. RBAC is a non discretionary access control which means that users do not have discretion regarding the group they are in or the access they are given. The way that this relates to human error caused incidents is this can help prevent unauthorized users from reading or writing different resources or data that they shouldn't be.

The way that RBAC works is that certain permissions are assigned to predefined roles or groups. A role could be any position in the organization, whether it be doctor, database administrator, or technician. These roles that are grouped together will have the same permissions no matter the individual. These permissions will be in an access control list (ACL) to keep track of who gets access to different data. Now once the roles and permissions have been established, you can develop a RBAC matrix that can map out the roles and each permission that role has based on the ACL. This will be useful if someone changes roles, or is terminated and should no longer have access to anything along with no role (Oracle 2024).

There are many benefits to the RBAC model that can enhance information security within an organization along with compliance of legal and regulatory rules. The enhanced compliance is important because one of the most key principles for a company is to abide by these local, state and federal rules that are set out to protect privacy. The reason that RBAC is useful for the compliance with these rules is that managers can manage the access to the data, and for more sensitive data, can prevent unauthorized access which would cause a legal issue especially with regulations such as HIPAA. The RBAC model can also create a separation of duties (SOD) which is an important concept that no one person has absolute control over a certain task. This is also an essential quality of RBAC as it mitigates the chances of an attack on a single account causing significant harm to the entire system itself.

Although RBAC seems to be an easy method of controlling access to data, the implementation of the model is an important process to be done by management in order for it to work to its full potential. The first step is to understand your organization and the needs of the business. You have to understand the technologies, job functions and processes that would utilize RBAC in order to enhance the security and protection of data. Next, which is critical to the model, is you have to define the roles in your organization that employees will fall under. This includes the tasks they are responsible for, what departments they are in, and what they should be authorized to be able to access or alter. When defining these roles, it is best to consider the practice of least privilege when granting this access which means that the employees will only be given the privileges that are absolutely necessary for this person to complete the tasks they are completing. Again, this means that if they do not need to have access they will not be authorized to access that data. It requires the insight and effort of a single entity in order to determine access levels.

4. TRAINING

As previously stated multiple times, the impact that employees have on information security in a company is enormous. Although there are a lot of technical controls that can be put in place to try to mitigate this impact, there can also be administrative controls set in place to also reduce this impact. This is where certain techniques such as training can play a role. Teaching the biggest risk factors in a company of how they get taken advantage of and proper internet safety techniques can truly reduce the amount of incidents that happen. Many malicious techniques that hackers or other bad actors utilize to target vulnerable employees such as phishing, pretexting and a business email compromise (BEC) attack, can be less likely to happen if you train your employees properly on the possibilities of these attacks and how to avoid falling for them. These social engineering techniques are common and should be taught to everyone in the organization.

Phishing attacks are one of the most common attack methods throughout the world. According to the Data Breach Investigation Report (DBIR) from Verizon, the majority of breaches (almost 40% of all breaches reported) were from phishing attacks alone. These attacks are a form of social engineering when the bad actor deceives the receiver into revealing sensitive information or installing malicious software onto their device. "Phishing attacks typically have three components that make them effective: the lure, hook, and catch" (Guilford, 2023). These attacks involve someone masquerading as someone else to convince the receiver to give them access or reveal information. "The e-mails look like messages sent to the victims, and the contents of the e-mails trick the sufferers into opening the E-mail" (Mahamood, 2023). "Due to growing risks online and associated costs of online deception in aging, there has been an increased attention on the investigation of age-related changes in susceptibility to phishing emails" (Pehlivanoglu, 2023, Lei, 2023). It is also by far the most common form of social engineering at an astounding ~80% of all incidents due to social engineering are due to phishing attacks. Knowing this information, there should be a heavy focus in your cybersecurity awareness training program. In order to implement this training, you first have to have these employees understand what a phishing attack is and what the attacker is trying to accomplish. Whether it be clicking on a suspicious link, giving out some information such as a personal email address or phone number, or anything other risky behavior through email, these should all be in the training for every employee. Once the training has been completed, and you believe your employees are aware of the risks and methods of phishing, you can even run simulated phishing attacks on your employees to not only test how the training has gone, but to also reinforce the training and help them catch on and recognize these attacks. This is not the only way to reinforce the training as you can have reminders around personal workstations and generally around the office. After a while, you can monitor the results of the training program and assess whether changes or improvements can be made in the future to further better the training and employees knowledge. The correct social awareness controls must be in place so the users are aware of these phishing attacks and can prevent them. "Attitudes toward the sharing of personal information online are critical because they allow phishing attempts to exist and succeed" (Lee, 2023). Mitigation

strategies to aid in the prevention of phishing risks include the following. "Follow security policies - adapt company policy to include specific security and anti-phishing training opportunities, especially for risky users and high-risk users" (Naqvi, 2023). Phishing education is education aimed at developing knowledge and user understanding.

Phishing training involves providing users practical and interactive experiences to simulate what risks to be aware of and a mock phishing email to be able to know the difference between phishing and real. "Simply reminding people to stop, think, and check can significantly reduce victimization rates because it helps break habitual responses and reliance on heuristics in evaluating information" (Robinson, 2023). These exercises and simulations can reorient how the users think after seeing an anomaly or something that is off in the email and take the correct steps while in a business work environment. Lastly, "Awareness interventions are commonly deployed as interruptions to users' regular workflow, to provide warnings and raise awareness about possible occurrences" (Sarker, 2024). "The broad and sweeping nature of AI impact means that many aspects of social engineering could be automated, potentially giving adversaries an advantage" (Jackson, 2023).

The other social engineering attacks that were mentioned earlier, can have similar training methods as phishing. The most important part of the training for the employees is that the information sticks with them. Again, this is the reason that the methods above are so important in the process of training. The simulated attack can make an employee make a mistake once, in a controlled circumstance, and hopefully make them realize and never make that mistake again. Being able to use specifically targeted phishing, such as the method of spear phishing, in the simulated attack can also prepare them for such real world attacks and make them comprehend the extent of what these attacks can go to obtain some information on how to get deeper into the company. There are certainly technical controls that can be put in place such as filters to prevent spam, phishing and malware from being received in business emails, but when it comes down to it, these aren't going to be 100% effective. The addition of training will complement these technical controls and provide defense in depth to produce the protection needed from these attacks.

Both the public and private sectors have historically depended on technology as the main line of defense against cyberattacks. But recent problems and patterns demonstrate how inadequate technology solutions are to counteract the changing threat landscape of cyberattacks. (Cranor & Garfinkel, 2005).

The realm of cyber threats is swiftly evolving, driven by technological progress and the increasing sophistication of cyber attackers. Techniques such as ransomware, phishing, and zero-day exploits exploit not only technical vulnerabilities but also human behaviors. Attackers often utilize social engineering tactics to bypass technological defenses by capitalizing on gaps in user awareness and actions (Byers, Wilson, & Bartlett, 2012).

The method of training is almost an essential practice in the business world in today's age. Without it, entire organizations can be attacked through the mistake of one employee who did not receive proper training. Senior management should be able to recognize the common threats to security and address this as soon as possible and should be considered just as important as technical controls. When implemented, it should never be forgotten and constantly assessed.

Cognitive Load: Managing Mental Effort in Security Practices

The mental strain necessary for digesting information and carrying out tasks is referred to as cognitive load. High cognitive load in cybersecurity might result in mistakes and protocol noncompliance. It is possible to lessen cognitive load and improve adherence to security measures by streamlining password regulations, providing clear instructions during security training, and automating regular updates. (Herley 2009).

Bias: Addressing Cognitive Biases in Security Decision-Making

Decisions on security are heavily influenced by cognitive biases including confirmation bias and overconfidence. Programs that raise awareness and provide simulations showing how prejudices can result in security breaches enable users to reduce risks and make well-informed decisions. (Fischhoff, 1982).

Heuristics are mental shortcuts for making decisions that might make daily decisions easier but come with cybersecurity hazards. Designing interventions that steer users toward safe behaviors and provide feedback on harmful acts is made possible by an understanding of these shortcuts. (Kumaraguru & Cranor, 2005).

Social Science Models: Using Frameworks to Assess Security Procedures

Social science models, such as the Health Belief Model, provide information about how people view and react to dangers. By modifying these models, one can customize instruction and outreach tactics to encourage users to embrace safe practices (Anderson & Moore, 2006).

5. PROTECTING DATA

The CIA triad stands for Confidentiality, Availability, and Integrity. Confidentiality is the right people should have access to things that they need. Access should be kept away from everyone else. Availability is you can get the information when you need it. Integrity is that the information you want has not been tampered with. This is the core of cyber security and this stands for every asset in an organization. Data being one of the most important assets can be broken down even more. Data can be categorized in three different states. There is data at rest, data in use, and data in transit. Data at rest is when your data is sitting in the hard drive not being used. Data in transit is when data is being moved around. This could be when data is being downloaded or transferred over a network. Data in use is when the data is actively being used, for example, you are using a word document, that data being pulled into the ram is data at use. All three of these states could be a target for attackers to get ahold of things they are not supposed to have.

Data in transit can be attacked with a simple man-in-the-middle attack. "The man-in-the-middle (MITM) attack exploits the fact that the HTTPS server sends a certificate with its public key to the Web browser"(Callegati et al., 2009). When you connect to a website you get a certificate from the site from a third party. That third party confirms the identity of the site, so you know who you are talking to. If an attacker can manipulate that certificate you can be anyone saying they are someone else. For example, we could think we are going to our bank website but we are talking to an imposter who is relaying our information to the site and relaying it back from the correct site. That way the victim does not know anything is wrong and the attacker is collecting all the traffic that is being sent between connecting parties.

For data in transit we can be trying to send an email to a customer or business partner, via email but if someone is between us we could never know. How do we stop this from happening if we encrypt our message? If we have encrypted all the attacker gets is useless, because they don't know what the message is. Only the right party should have the key to see the data in the clear. Data in transit has been greatly secured by transmitting everything with encryption.

The biggest issue in recent years comes from data at rest. With laptops and smartphones becoming essential, it has been easy for users to be able to work almost everywhere. But this is a double edge sword because people make mistakes, they leave devices in places or they are stolen. This is just part of human nature. People are busy. They could be working in a cafe and get a call and have to rush somewhere else and forget something. This will probably never stop. But the way we adapt to this is what makes a difference.

If we encrypt our devices, someone who comes across a laptop or a phone will not be able to access anything because they are locked out. This is great when used however that is not always the case. "44% encrypt laptops, 16% encrypt data on USB sticks and a mere 12% encrypt other types of mobile devices"(Solterbeck, 2006).

Laptops can use Bitlocker from Microsoft or Vilevault from Apple to encrypt these devices to stop some from ever getting in.

Smartphones are a different story, most can be broken into. If there is no password nothing is stopping an attacker. They don't even need physical access, if a user downloads a malicious app, an attacker has access. So how do we stop this from happening? With a mobile device management policy. The most secure is COBO, which stands for corporate-owned business only. We give users our phones which we are in control of. We can decide what they can download and other security settings. By setting policies, we can whitelist applications we need our users to work on and keep everything else out. This will keep attackers limiting attackers' ways into our users' devices.

One of the most important aspects of mobile devices management is the ability to remote wipe. "This feature allows the device owner to send a remote command to wipe the contents on the lost or stolen device"(Leom et al., 2016). This allows us to be able to remove data that has been placed in the wrong hands without wondering what will come from the lost device. Yes, we will lose the hardware but that is a lot cheaper than giving away the data to someone else.

6. SEPARATION OF DUTIES

Separation of duties is a great way to keep any organization secure or safe. Separation of duties is the principle that no user should be given enough privileges to misuse the system on their own (NIST, 2024). This policy makes sure no important changes or jobs are only done by one person. This can stop users from doing malicious activities, but also is another way to catch mistakes. By giving certain users different roles we can stop fraud from ever happening. For example, the user who makes changes to a payroll system should never be allowed to push out a paycheck. There is too much risk right there and that is asking for issues to arise. The bad employee may think they will never be caught, but we all know they will. But what we want is to minimize the amount they can steal. The goal is to not allow anything to be stolen. What we should have in place is a layer of escalation to have eyes on change the whole time. We should have one person make the change and have a superior confirm these changes. Then have someone else process the changes and have those confirmed before the payment is sent out the door.

This same methodology can be applied to any data in an organization. Whenever there is data that is going to be sent out and essentially public, there should be these checks in place. From Top secret to confidential, also PHI there should be these checks in place. Regardless of if they are just moving around the company to send to another country, we need these checks in place. There have been stories of a CEO getting phished, then the attacker tells the CFO to send money to an account. The CFO ends up sending the money to the attacker. If they would have followed this standard they would have stopped this attack. If the CFO would have had to confirm with someone besides just sending the money they could have stopped. They should have asked the CEO on a different channel if this is what they wanted.

7. GOVERNANCE AND MANAGEMENT

All of these security models and programs are extremely important steps when it comes to the security of information and data in an organization. But, all of these ideas and processes are somewhat futile without the proper governance and management applied to the organization and security of it. Governance when it comes to information security is the organizational management structure and strategies employed to ensure that IA and Cybersecurity efforts are aligned with business objectives. It gives clear assignments of responsibility and accountability, along with being consistent with compliance of laws and regulations. The management of the information security program is the formulation of relevant policies, procedures and guidelines that serve a goal of protecting enterprise assets. This is relevant for the allocation of resources, people and technology that need to be balanced in any information security program.

Technology is influencing every aspect of life, which raises the bar for security-related expectations and challenges to the highest levels of management. (Islam & Strafford, 2017; Alreemy et al., 2016; Dufva, 2019.) Technical expertise that is in line with the corporate strategy is a necessary component of an effective information security strategy, according to Kayworth and Whitten (2012). As a result, three main goals must be addressed by information security and cybersecurity strategies: Maintaining cultural fit, guaranteeing compliance, and striking a balance between information security and business needs (Kayworth & Whitten, 2012). For firms to ensure that decisions from senior management's strategy work are implemented appropriately, they must have established models, rules, and databases. (Gashgari et al., 2017; Alqurashi et al., 2017; Nicho 2018; von Solms & von Solms, 2009.)

Governance and management may be overlooked when it comes to information security as, again, people tend to think of the technology involved and some may even think about the people, but these processes are vital as well. This is the reason that there needs to be commitment and dedication from the board of directors and IT management to assure the governance and management of information security. The roles and responsibilities that these groups will be accountable for are the assignment of security responsibilities, overseeing IT system and project implementations, ensuring effective evaluation, selection, prioritization, and funding of IT security investments and much more in order to align IT and security to the specific business and strategy of the organization. Understanding how intentional organizational tactics can be used to support cyber security management in related engagements is crucial when viewing the field of cyber security management from an integrated perspective. This study provides insight into how a highly specialized sector might help cybersecurity's base beneficiaries as well as practitioners who specialize in the field.(Batra 2020). Governance also includes the documentation of policies, procedures, and standards that drive the governance activities in the information security program. The documentation of this sets the guidelines and "laws" of how things must be done around the organization for proper security. Documentation is truly important in the governance and management as it helps ensure the employees of the content of the security governance and makes sure that it is not ambiguous. Documentation can also help in ensuring employees are prepared for Business Continuity Plans, Disaster Recovery Plans, Incident Response Plans (Angafor et. al, 2020). The documentation is an underrated part of governance that is more important than people realize.

Relating this to the relevant topic of the risk that humans introduce into an organization, one of the principles of information security governance is that security related decisions should be based on risk itself. The board of directors, or management, has to truly assess the amount of risk that their employees impose on the organization. Without this assessment they are assuming this amount of risk and can either overstate or understate the true amount of risk that is present from the people of the company. There needs to be heavy involvement and understanding of risk for the upper management to make the proper decisions based on the true risk the company faces in order to align the governance and management of the information security program with the business goals and strategies in order to be successful in both fronts.

8. CASE STUDIES

Probably one of the most famous data extracts was the case of Edward Snowden. "Edward Snowden, the former CIA systems administrator who leaked information about classified NSA programs to the Guardian and the Washington Post"(Brownlee, 2016). Snowden leaked thousands of documents about mass surveillance from the US government. He was able to get these documents out of the system by uploading them to thumb drives. Because of his clearance and his system administration statutes he was able to pull files from the NSAs headquarters at Fort Meade, Maryland. This caused mass backlash to the NSA and what the government was doing to people around the world.

Regardless of the politics in this story, we should look at the atomic facts. A user pulled thousands of files and was able to upload them to a mobile USB but no one noticed. An organization such as the NSA should have had layers of security to prevent something like this, but they didn't and top-secret information was leaked.

If the NSA would have had data loss prevention in place this would have never happened. If the NSA had a proper system in place they should have had a group auditing the logs generated by all users, even sysadmins. They should have asked why was this person looking at this mass number of files and what did they need them for. If the logs would have gone to a separate server as read-only they could have seen this happening in life. Next is his extraction method.

He was able to pull massive amounts of data and upload them to USB drives. This was years after the pentagon incident so it's not like they have not seen issues with USBs before. They should have had policies that would not allow users to even be able to connect to the system.

Regardless of the thoughts on Snowden, the NSA should have had better controls in place to protect their data. If they would have used the policies from Office 365 they could have stopped this leak from ever happening.

In 2012 an ex-contractor for Howard University Hospital in DC reported that his car had been stolen. His vehicle contained his laptop. This device was unencrypted. On the device were the social security numbers of some of the patients. The download was against the hospital policy and HIPAA but regardless "Howard University Hospital in Washington, D.C., is notifying more than 34,000 patients about a data breach" (Anderson & Ross, 2021). The device has not to be found and the data has not been exposed yet.

If the company would have supported a company-owned business-only policy they would not be in this situation. They could have had the device encrypted using BitLocker or FileVault keeping the data secure. No one besides the contractor would be able to get access to the data. If the company would have better control policies set in place, IT would have been able to remotely wipe the device. This would not have solved all their issues, but they would be able to erase the data as long as it had not already been copied.

The company has since made changes where all devices are encrypted but they will still be punished for violating HIPAA.

A case that hits a little closer to home is what happened to Independent health in 2019. "Protected health information on more than 7,600 Independent Health members was accidentally emailed to a member in March"(Drury, 2021). The data contained PHI including names, providers, and claims. For independent health, they were lucky as you could get for a situation this bad. The unauthorized person who received the information was an Independent health member. The recipient notified Independent health and confirmed the email had been deleted. If the email had been sent to someone else this situation could have gone from bad to worse.

From the policies, we can use them and apply them to the case to see how this situation could have been prevented from ever happening in the first place. First, we would have been labeling this data as PHI. With this label, we would be able to detect when this information was trying to be sent to an authorized person. This could have been caught before it ever got out.

Next is they should have had separation of duties, more of a dual control system. Where when a user wants to send PHI it has to be overlooked by a superior. If someone else could have looked they could have seen that this email was going to someone who it is not supposed to be going to.

The next training, this may sound silly but if we could train all employees to double-check everything before you send, this could have never happened.

These are just three quick ways that if the right controls would have been in place this story would have never happened.

Case Study 1: Enhancing Password Security

The effect of simplifying password policies on user compliance and security was investigated in a study conducted in 2005 by Cranor and Garfinkel. The firm saw a large boost in compliance and a decrease in password-related security incidents by simplifying password requirements and giving users clear recommendations. This case study emphasizes how crucial it is to strike a balance between usability and security needs in order to improve security results. (Cranor & Garfinkel, 2005).

Case Study 2: Phishing Awareness Training

Kumaraguru and Cranor (2005) examined the efficacy of phishing awareness training initiatives in a case study. The study discovered that users' capacity to recognize and steer clear of phishing efforts was much enhanced by interactive training modules and lifelike simulations of phishing attacks. This data emphasizes how important effective and engaging training techniques are for raising user awareness and lowering the danger of social engineering scams. (Kumaraguru & Cranor, 2005).

Case Study 3: Cognitive Load Reduction in Security Tasks

Herley (2009) investigated the effects of reduced cognitive burden in security tasks. The company saw a drop in user errors and an increase in adherence to security measures by automating regular security updates and giving clear, simple instructions. In order to enhance user performance on security tasks, this case study highlights the significance of lowering cognitive load. (Herley, 2009).

9. CONCLUSION

Information security will continue to become more important as the world continues to become more technologically advanced, and the people involved in a company will have to continue to evolve with it. More attackers, and attack methods continue to rise in the everlasting fight to protect an organization's data and other sensitive information. This is a vital reason to continue to strengthen the knowledge and awareness of employees, along with other controls to mitigate their involvement in risk and safety of data. The overarching issue of humans being the largest risk and reasons for incidents and breaches, but over time we can try to get to a place where this is not the case and we can make the principal focus of security on the technical controls without having to worry about an employee in a random department of your organizations being the pathway for a hacker to attain access to your organizations systems.

Through the methods discussed prior, there is hope that companies can change the script on humans being the weakest link in security. As seen in the case studies, this is much more common than people are set out to believe and we have to use these real world examples to learn and move forward accordingly. Every incident due to human error could most likely have been avoided and in the future, we hope to reduce these errors year by year until we have another reason that's the weakest link in security. Strategic adaptability and Resilience: Resilience and strategic adaptability to new threats are essential components of effective cybersecurity solutions. This entails collecting proactive threat intelligence, assessing risks based on circumstances, and continuously monitoring and updating security protocols. Agility is a necessary skill for organizations to quickly adapt their defenses and incident response strategies in response to emerging threats and vulnerabilities. (Vance, Siponen, & Pahnila, 2012).

REFERENCES

Alqurashi, E., Wills, G., & Gilbert, L. (2013). A viable system model for information security governance: Establishing a baseline of the current information security operations system. *IFIP International Information Security Conference*, 245-256. DOI: 10.1007/978-3-642-39218-4_19

Alreemy, Z., Chang, V., Walters, R., & Wills, G. (2016). Critical success factors (CSFs) for information technology governance (ITG). *International Journal of Information Management*, 36(6), 907–916. DOI: 10.1016/j.ijinfomgt.2016.05.017

Anderson, H., & Ross, R. (n.d.). Stolen laptop: Breach affects 34,000. Healthcare Information Security. Retrieved December 17, 2021, from https://www.healthcareinfosecurity.com/stolen-laptop-breach-affects-34000-a-4647

Anderson, R., & Moore, T. (2006) The Economics of Information Security https://www.researchgate.net/publication/216757755_The_Economics_of_Information_Security

Angafor, G. N., Yevseyeva, I., & He, Y. (2020). Game-based learning: A review of tabletop exercises for cybersecurity incident response training. *Security and Privacy*, 3(6), e126. DOI: 10.1002/spy2.126

Basset, G. (2021). *Data Breach Investigation Report*. Verizon.

Batra, A. (2020) Cyber security management: Creating governance, risk, and compliance framework. I-Manager's Journal on Software Engineering, 14(4).

Brignall, M. (2021) Npower withdraws mobile app after hackers steal personal details https://www.theguardian.com/business/2021/feb/27/npower-mobile-app-hackers-personaldetails-gas-electricitycustomers?utm_term=b609f7eaeca6965c550e347f83bac052&utm_campaign=GuardianTodayUK&utm_s ource=esp&utm_medium=Email&CMP=GTUK_email

Brownlee, K. (2016). The civil disobedience of Edward Snowden. *Philosophy and Social Criticism*, 42(10), 965–970. DOI: 10.1177/0191453716631167

Callegati, F., Cerroni, W., & Ramilli, M. (2009). Man-in-the-middle attack to the HTTPS protocol. *IEEE Security and Privacy*, 7(1), 78–81. DOI: 10.1109/MSP.2009.12

Carroll, R. (2021) Ransomware attack disrupts Irish health services. The Guardian. https://www.theguardian.com/world/2021/may/14/ransomware-attack-disrupts-irish-healthservices?utm_term=bcbaa56dfd395c672786d3b14913fd95&utm_campaign=GuardianTodayUK&utm_so urce=esp&utm_medium=Email&CMP=GTUK_email

Cluley, G. (2021) Ransomware is the biggest threat, says GCHQ cybersecurity chief https://www.tripwire.com/state-of-security/security-data-protection/ransomware-biggest-threat-saysgchq-cybersecurity-chief/?utm_source=The State of Security Newsletter&utm_medium=email&utm_campaign=FO-06-21- 2021&utm_content=httpswwwtripwirecomstateofsecu

Drury, T. (n.d.). Bizjournals.com. Retrieved December 17, 2021, from https://www.bizjournals.com/buffalo/news/2019/05/10/independent-health-mistakenly-emailed-information.html

Dufva, M. (2019, December 31). Teknologia sulautuu kaikkeen. Megatrendit 2020. Sitran selvityksiä, 162. Sitra. https://www.sitra.fi/julkaisut/megatrendit2020/

Emenike, S. U. (2021). Data loss prevention in a remote work environment https://urn.kb.se/resolve?urn=urn:nbn:se:his:diva-20203

Ferraiolo, D. F., Kuhn, D. R., & Chandramouli, R. (2007). *Role-based access control.* Artech House.

Fischhoff, B. (1982) For Those Condemned To Study the Past: Heuristics and Biases in Hindsight.https://www.researchgate.net/publication/248628593_For_Those_Condemned_To_Study_the_Past_Heuristics_and_Biases_in_Hindsight

Fung, B. (2021) 'Hackers breach Electronic Arts, stealing game source code and tools', https://www.cnn.com/2021/06/10/tech/electronic-arts-hack/index.html

Garfinkel, S., & Cranor, L. (2005) Security and Usability https://www.oreilly.com/library/view/security-and-usability/0596008279/

Gashgari, G., Walters, R. J., & Wills, G. (2017). A Proposed Best-practice Framework for Information Security Governance. *Proceedings of the 2nd International Conference on Internet of Things, Big Data and Security*, 295-301. DOI: 10.5220/0006303102950301

Gorelik, M. (2022). Log4j Exploit Hits Again: Vulnerable VMWare Horizon Servers at Risk. https://blog.morphisec.com/log4j-exploit-hits-again-vulnerable-vmware-horizon-servers-at-risk

Guilford, M. (2023). Systemic Risk Analysis of Human Factors in Phishing (Doctoral dissertation, Old Dominion University).

Herley, C. (2009) So long, and no thanks for the externalities https://dl.acm.org/doi/10.1145/1719030.1719050

Hughes-Lartey, K., Li, M. E., Botchey, F., & Qin, Z. (2021) Human factor, a critical weak point in the information security of an organization's Internet of things. https://pubmed.ncbi.nlm.nih.gov/33768182/

Islam, M., & Stafford, T. (2017). Information Technology (IT) integration and cybersecurity/security: The Security Savviness of Board of Directors. 23rd Americas Conference on Information Systems (AMCIS 2017): A Tradition of Innovation.

Jackson, K. A. (2023). A Systematic Review of Machine Learning Enabled Phishing. arXiv preprint arXiv:2310.06998.

Kayworth, T., & Whitten, D. (2012). Effective Information Security Requires a Balance of Social and Technology. *MIS Quarterly Executive*, 9(3), 163–175. https://ssrn.com/abstract=2058035

Khan, N., & Al-Yasiri, A. (2016). Identifying Cloud Security Threats to Strengthen Cloud Computing Adoption Framework. *Procedia Computer Science*, 94, 485–490. DOI: 10.1016/j.procs.2016.08.075

Kim, C. (2014). Design and Implementation Smart Office System Based on Remote Desktop Protocol (RDP). The Journal of the Institute of Internet, Broadcasting and Communication.

Kolbasuk McGee, M. (2021) Record Number of Major Health Data Breaches in 2021 https://www.govinfosecurity.com/record-number-major-health-data-breaches-in-2021-a-18327

Kumaraguru, P., & Cranor, L. (2005) Privacy Indexes: A Survey of Westin's Studies https://www.semanticscholar.org/paper/Privacy-Indexes%3A-A-Survey-of-Westin%27s-Studies-Kumaraguru-Cranor/e47618a4355991aee3a2fd94c5e8adc1058f4a88

Learn about data loss prevention - Microsoft 365 compliance. Microsoft 365 Compliance | Microsoft Docs. (n.d.). Retrieved December 16, 2021, from https://docs.microsoft.com/en-us/microsoft-365/compliance/dlp-learn-about-dlp?view=o365-worldwide

Learn about Microsoft 365 endpoint data loss prevention - microsoft 365 compliance. Microsoft 365 Compliance | Microsoft Docs. (n.d.). Retrieved December 17, 2021, from https://docs.microsoft.com/en-us/microsoft-365/compliance/endpoint-dlp-learn-about?view=o365-worldwide

Lee, Y. Y., Gan, C. L., & Liew, T. W. (2023). Thwarting Instant Messaging Phishing Attacks: The Role of Self-Efficacy and the Mediating Effect of Attitude towards Online Sharing of Personal Information. *International Journal of Environmental Research and Public Health*, 20(4), 3514. DOI: 10.3390/ijerph20043514 PMID: 36834209

Lei, W., Hu, S., & Hsu, C. (2023). Unveiling the process of phishing precautions taking: The moderating role of optimism bias. *Computers & Security*, 129, 103249. DOI: 10.1016/j.cose.2023.103249

Leom, M. D., Choo, K.-K. R., & Hunt, R. (2016). Remote wiping and secure deletion on mobile devices: A Review. *Journal of Forensic Sciences*, 61(6), 1473–1492. DOI: 10.1111/1556-4029.13203 PMID: 27651127

Liginlal, D., Sim, I., & Khansa, L. (2009). How Significant Is Human Error as a Cause of Privacy Breaches? an Empirical Study and a Framework for Error Management. *Computers & Security*, 28(3-4), 215–228. DOI: 10.1016/j.cose.2008.11.003

Mahamood, A. F., Ramli, A. J., Yakob, T. K. T., Ali, E., & Affandy, H. B. (2023). Analysis the types and impacts of phishing attacks on internet users. *Journal of Global Business and Social Entrepreneurship*, 9(26).

Naqvi, B., Perova, K., Farooq, A., Makhdoom, I., Oyedeji, S., & Porras, J. (2023). Mitigation strategies against the phishing attacks: A systematic literature review. *Computers & Security*, 132, 103387. DOI: 10.1016/j.cose.2023.103387

NBCUniversal News Group. (2013, August 26). How snowden did it. NBCNews.com. Retrieved December 17, 2021, from https://www.nbcnews.com/news/world/how-snowden-did-it-flna8c11003160

Netsurion. (2014, January 16). Looking back: Operation buckshot yankee & agent.btz. Netsurion. Retrieved December 16, 2021, from https://www.netsurion.com/articles/looking-back-operation-buckshot-yankee-agent-btz

Nicho, M. (2018). A process model for implementing information systems security governance. *Information and Computer Security*, 26(1), 10–38. DOI: 10.1108/ICS-07-2016-0061

NIST. (2024), Separation of Duty, Computer Security Resource Center, Assessed from https://csrc.nist.gov/glossary/term/separation_of_duty

Oracle (2024), Configuring Advanced Role-based Access Control, Retrieved online from https://docs.oracle.com/cd/E28280_01/admin.1111/e16580/rbac.htm

Pehlivanoglu, D., Shoenfelt, A., Hakim, Z. M., Heemskerk, A., Zhen, J., Mosqueda, M., ... Ebner, N. C. (2023). Phishing vulnerability compounded by older age, APOE4 genotype, and lower cognition.

Pfleeger, S., & Caputo, D. (2012). Leveraging behavioral science to mitigate cyber security risk. https://www.researchgate.net/publication/257006498_Leveraging_behavioral_science_to_mitigate_cyber_security_risk

Ribeiro, L., Guedes, I. S., & Cardoso, C. S. (2024). Which factors predict susceptibility to phishing? An empirical study. *Computers & Security*, 136, 103558. DOI: 10.1016/j.cose.2023.103558

Robinson, J. (n.d.). Reducing Employee Phishing Risk with Mindfulness Training. Center for Cybersecurity and Data Intelligence, 937, 229-1929.

Sarker, O., Jayatilaka, A., Haggag, S., Liu, C., & Babar, M. A. (2024). A Multivocal Literature Review on challenges and critical success factors of phishing education, training and awareness. *Journal of Systems and Software*, 208, 111899. DOI: 10.1016/j.jss.2023.111899

Sidor-Rządkowska, M. (2022) Human - the weakest or the strongest link? The role of organisational culture in ensuring security of remote work https://www.jomswsge.com/Human-the-weakest-or-the-strongest-link-The-role-of-organisational-culture-in-ensuring,156776,0,2.html

Solterbeck, A. (2006). Protecting data at rest and in Motion. *Network Security*, 2006(9), 14–17. DOI: 10.1016/S1353-4858(06)70424-X

Stallings, W. (2020). Data loss prevention as a privacy-enhancing technology, Journal of Data Protection & Privacy, 3(3), 323-333.

Tahboub, R., & Saleh, Y. (2014) Data leakage/loss prevention systems (DLP). *2014 World Congress on Computer Applications and Information Systems, WCCAIS 2014*, 1–6. DOI: 10.1109/WCCAIS.2014.6916624

Valinsky, J. (2021) McDonald's hit by data breach. https://www.cnn.com/2021/06/11/business/mcdonalds-data-breach/index.html

Vance, A., Siponen, M., & Pahnila, S. (2012) Motivating IS security compliance: Insights from habit and protection motivation theory. https://psycnet.apa.org/record/2012-12998-008

von Solms, S. H. & von Solms, R. (2009). Information security governance. Springer Science+Business Media. DOI: 10.1007/978-0-387-79984-1

Wuchner, T., & Pretschner, A. (2012). Data loss prevention based on data-driven usage control. 2012 IEEE 23rd International Symposium on Software Reliability Engineering. DOI: 10.1109/ISSRE.2012.10

Chapter 3
Bridging the Gap: A Comparative Study of CIS and NIST Cybersecurity Frameworks

Atish Kumar Dash
University at Buffalo, SUNY, USA

Shashank Shivananda
University at Buffalo, SUNY, USA

Raghvendra Singh
University at Buffalo, SUNY, USA

Manish Gupta
University at Buffalo, SUNY, USA

ABSTRACT

The Critical Security Controls (CIS) and National Institute of Standards and Technology Cybersecurity Framework are both important for increasing organizational cybersecurity, with each catering to certain demands and implementation approaches. The CIS Controls, which were initially announced in 2008, are organized into Implementation Groups and provide a prioritized approach suitable for companies with varying levels of cybersecurity maturity. Also, the NIST Cybersecurity Framework was established in 2014 and employs a risk-based framework focusing on six essential function. This framework includes technology like risk assessment tools, continuous monitoring systems, and incident response platforms. While the CIS Controls give specific, practical actions for immediate adoption, the NIST Framework focuses on overall risk management and compliance with larger regulatory requirements, providing a holistic, customized approach for improving cybersecurity resilience.

DOI: 10.4018/979-8-3693-4211-4.ch003

OVERVIEW OF CIS CONTROLS V8

CIS is a framework that was developed by the Center for Information Security (CIS) in 2008. This framework helps organizations follow the standards to effectively defend against cybersecurity attacks and threats. It covers various programs such as CIS Cyber Marketplace, CIS Benchmarks, and communities. Through these programs, CIS works with various private organizations, government and academics to educate and guide to follow the best practices of cybersecurity. Currently, version 8 of CIS is running in the market a.k.a CIS V8. By following the CIS Controls, organizations can establish a baseline level of security and reduce the likelihood of successful cyber-attacks (Center for Internet Security, 2021).

CIS has its presence across the globe and its standards cover most of the organizations irrespective of size, country or operation. So, this framework is focused on mitigation and defense. The CIS has a set of step-by-step practical guides for adoption as well as implementation.

It also encompasses the documentation, which is written by cyber tech experts, which could be easily understood by the tech and non-technical people. The CIS also covers the threats that are common in cyberspace. The latest version of the CIS Controls, which are guidelines for cybersecurity, has made things easier to grasp. They have divided the controls into three Implementation Groups (IGs). By just implementing Implementation Group 1 (IG1), it covers 15 out of (The 18 CIS Controls, 2021). The CIS Controls, also known as Critical Security Controls, were developed because of cross-sector collaboration and extensive study (Center for Internet Security, 2021). This framework provides organizations with guidelines for enhancing their information security alignment, with a focus on high-priority initiatives that can mitigate typical cyber threats (SANS Institute, 2008). Understanding the origins of the CIS Controls necessitates an examination of their fundamental studies along with input from diverse organizations and experts. In 2008 SANS Institute published Consensus Audit Guidelines which are like CIS controls. The CAG project brings up cybersecurity professionals from industries, schools, universities and government to identify the most crucial areas that organizations can work on to enhance security. The goal was to create a set of safeguards based on actual attack data that would offer a sensible, data approach to cybersecurity. The concluding guidelines stressed real and practical steps that firms may take to defend themselves contrary to common and serious cyber threats. The set of principles evolved into the "20 Critical Security Controls" which formed the starting point for the CIS Controls. This framework enables enterprises to adhere to the criteria required to effectively fight against cybersecurity assaults and threats. It encompasses a variety of projects, including the CIS Cyber Marketplace, CIS Benchmarks, and Communities.

It covers various programs such as CIS Cyber Marketplace, CIS Benchmarks and communities. Through these programs, CIS works with various private organizations, government and universities to educate and guide to follow the best practices of cybersecurity. Currently, version 8 of CIS is running in the market a.k.a CIS V8. By adhering to the CIS Controls, companies may create a starting point of security and lower the chance of successful cyberattacks.

CIS has its presence across the globe and its standards cover most of the organizations regardless of size, country, or operation. So, this framework is focused on mitigation and defense. The CIS has a set of step-by-step practical guides for adoption and implementation.

It also encompasses the documentation, which is written by cyber tech experts and could be easily understood by tech and non-technical people. The CIS also covers the threats that are common in cyberspace. The latest version of the CIS Controls, which are guidelines for cybersecurity, has made things easier to grasp. They have divided the controls into three Implementation Groups (IGs), with just implementing Implementation Group 1 (IG1), which covers 15 out of the 18 CIS Controls. Controls are steps that help to manage risks and each control can be broken down into smaller tasks called safeguards. Safeguards are measurable actions that help to ensure what is being done is necessary to stay safe and in control.

The three IG groups are IG1 also known as Central Cyber Hygiene, IG2 (includes IG1), and IG3 (includes IG1 & IG2). IG1 focuses primarily on small IT companies, with the primary goal being to maintain operational continuity in the face of downtime restrictions. The data sensitivity in this group typically lies around financial information at a low level. In IG1, it emphasizes solutions that are more feasible to implement with little cyber expertise. This ensures the reduction of non-targeted and general cyber-attacks. This strategy guarantees that cybersecurity measures remain both practical and accessible, even in the face of resource constraints.

In IG2, people oversee and safeguard IT infrastructure. IG2 provides support to several departments with varying risk profiles according to their missions and job functions. Small business organizations could face difficulties adhering to regulations. IG2 can tolerate brief outages in service and often handle and keep sensitive customer or company data. If a breach happens, losing the public's trust is a serious worry.

Individuals in an IG3 have several areas of expertise, such as risk management and testing for penetration. They deal with private information that is governed by regulations and laws. Their key objectives are to preserve sensitive information and keep systems operating. The breach into IG3 might lead to serious issues for all parties involved. Defending the attackers and minimizing the effect of surprise attacks are the main goals of the security measures for IG3.

Figure 1. The top 5 cyber-attacks and IG1 CIS safeguards control percentage

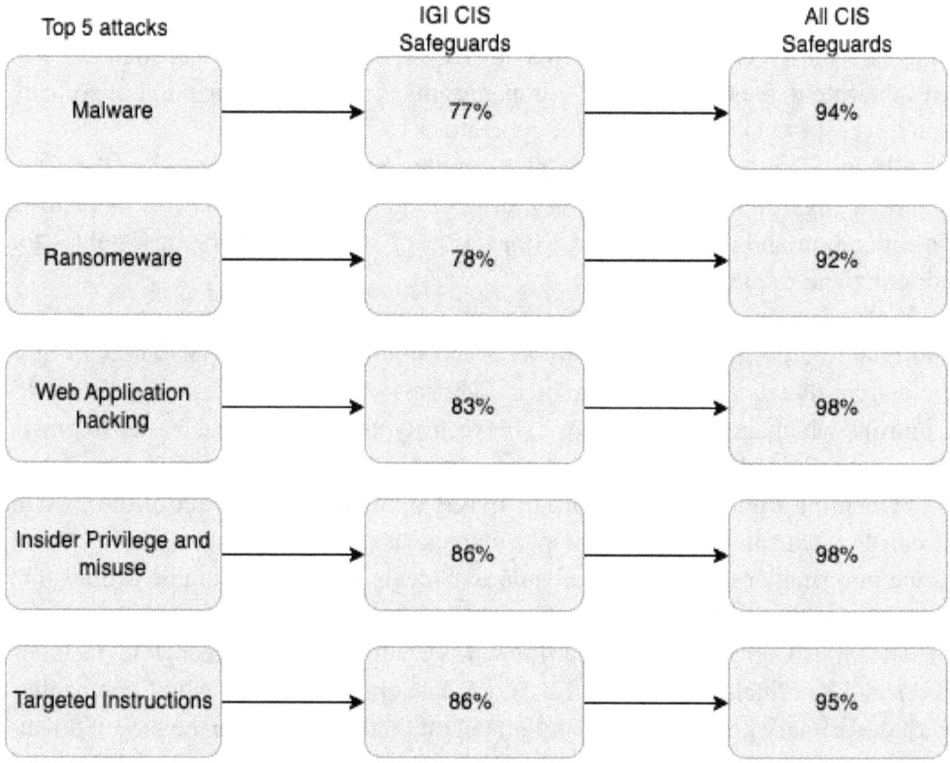

The 18 CIS controls are as follows:

Inventory and Control of Enterprise Assets, Inventory and Control of Software Assets, Data Protection, Secure Configuration of Enterprise Assets and Software, Account Management, Access Control Management, Continuous Vulnerability Management, Audit Log Management, Email and Web Browser Protections, Malware Defenses, Data Recovery, Network Infrastructure Management, Network Monitoring and Defense, Security Awareness and Skills Training, Service Provider Management, Application Software Security, Incident Response Management, Penetration Testing

BACKGROUND OF NIST CSF

As the world moves toward digital technologies, along with considering the growing number of computing and digital devices, there has been a significant increase in the number of cyber-attacks. Small to medium and large businesses and governments have primarily been affected by these. This coincides with the widespread usage and growth of technology. Further, organizations are expected to spend billions to ward off such cyber-attacks (Dowdy, 2012). Additionally for such businesses, especially for-profit organizations, some of these attacks have also led to the erosion of confidence for their customers and key shareholders (Esteves et al., 2017). Hence, considering the stakes it is imperative that organizations focus on achieving their business goals but also prioritizing enhancing their cybersecurity objectives, which ought to be in alignment with their business objectives.

As a result, it is imperative for businesses to manage their cybersecurity risks in an effective manner. This is usually achieved by adopting certain frameworks, which are a set of guidelines or best practices. One such framework that is widely used is the NIST Cybersecurity Framework (NIST CSF) is amongst one of the widely used frameworks. The National Institute of Standards and Technology (NIST) was founded in 1901. It is a part of the U.S. Department of Commerce. Its major purpose is to enhance the industrial competitiveness of the U.S. across the globe. In terms of the historical context, the development of this framework was kicked off after the then-president Mr. Barack Obama signed the Presidential Executive Order 13636, to enhance the innovation and competitiveness of the US across the world (The White House, 2013). The National Institute of Standards and Technology (NIST) released version 1.0 of the framework in 2014 to provide a high-level perspective for organizations to tackle and manage their cybersecurity risks. After several iterations as well as workshops, the NIST CSF v2.0 was released for public comments on February 26, 2024 (National Institute of Standards and Technology, 2024). Its overall purpose is to serve as a guide for businesses and organizations, large or small, to focus on understanding and managing their cybersecurity risks in an effective manner (Federal Trade Commission, 2022).

The NIST CSF v2.0 is essentially a set of best practices, covering 6 primary functions: Govern, Identify, Protect, Detect, Respond, and Recover., for organizations recommended by the NIST. Expounding on the different 6 core functions, when we touch on the first function Govern, we can observe that this forms the starting point for any organization to understand on a high level what their overall cybersecurity risk management strategy should be and what are the different policies they can work to complement their overall business strategy and goals. All the above core 6 functions are both interdependent and interrelated to each other, helping to create a common underlying platform, often being showcased as a wheel, which informs the overall cyber planning for any organization, whether small or large.

Further, the CSF 2.0 consists of the following major components: CSF core, CSF Organizational Profiles, and CSF Tiers. The CSF core functions were discussed in the previous paragraphs. The CSF Organizational Profile comprises the Current and Target Profile for the organization in order to find the current gaps in their cybersecurity landscape and address them to achieve their Target Profile risk management objectives through an effective creation and implementation of an action plan. This process is started by creating an Organization Profile first and consequently following the aforementioned steps. Lastly, considering the NIST CSF Tiers, these ensure that organizations are in alignment with the previously discussed Current and Target Profiles. This serves as a benchmark for organizations as they move through their journey, step by step, of enhancing their cybersecurity risk posture. Hence, in summary, these major 3 components of the NIST CSF v2.0 help organizations to enhance their cybersecurity posture by focusing on outcomes, as-is current and target state, and finally best management practices (National Institute of Standards and Technology, 2024).

Now, there are several other frameworks as well that are widely used across various industries and organizations to manage their cybersecurity risk and enhance their security posture. These include frameworks such as CIS Controls, COBIT by ISACA, NIST 800-53, etc (Amiruddin et al., 2021). Additionally, there has also been research and comparisons made between the closely related, NIST Special Publication 800-53 to the ISO 27001 Information security standard (Roy, 2020). Cyber risk planning and management can thus help organizations achieve their business goals, primarily when IT/IS strategies are aligned with the business strategy of the organization. However, in this chapter we will focus primarily on covering both NIST CSF v2.0 and CIS Controls v8. Additionally, we will also be covering the scope and applicability of the NIST CSF v2.0 along with the challenges and future trends of adopting the framework.

SCOPE AND APPLICABILITY

Cis Controls V8 Framework

The CIS Framework is an extensive collection of industry best practices designed to help businesses strengthen their cybersecurity posture. Its scope is vast, including an extensive spectrum of security tasks and requirements, making it appropriate for a variety of businesses, irrespective of size or business. The framework is divided across 18 comprehensive control areas, covering everything from fundamental asset management to sophisticated response to incidents and penetration testing.

Prioritization is one of the most important parts of CIS Controls. The controls are organized into three implementation groups (IGs) that address varying degrees of an organization's security maturity and accessibility to resources. IG1 focuses on basic controls that are simple to apply, making it suited for small and medium-sized businesses (SMEs) with minimal resources. IG2 and IG3 provide more extensive controls for businesses with more complicated environments and resources, such as major corporations and government agencies.

The CIS Controls are very adaptable and may be used in a variety of technical situations, including physical systems, cloud-based services as well as hybrid scenarios. This versatility allows enterprises to keep a consistent safety record across various types of IT systems. Furthermore, the CIS Controls are compatible with other major cybersecurity frameworks and standards, including the (NIST Cybersecurity Framework National Institute of Standards and Technology 2024, May 1) and ISO/IEC 27001, which makes it simpler for companies to achieve regulatory compliance and incorporate the best practices into their existing security programs.

In addition, the CIS Controls cater to unique demands across numerous sectors. For example, financial services businesses can use the safeguards to secure money transfers and protect sensitive client data, whereas healthcare institutions can use them to protect patient data and comply with standards such as HIPAA (Rights, O. F. C., 2022). Government entities can safeguard essential infrastructure and assure the quality of public services, while universities can secure scholarly research and provide safe virtual learning environments. This industry-specific applicability highlights the system's broad relevance and efficacy in improving cybersecurity across several industries.

National Institute of Standards and Technology: Cybersecurity Framework V2.0

Considering the realm of digital technologies and cyber security, as we covered earlier, there are several frameworks, guidelines, and best practices to tackle such risks. Some of these frameworks, such as (Amiruddin et al., 2021) ISO/IEC 27001, CIS Controls, and COBIT, also offer valuable guidelines that can be tailored to specific industry sectors or specific organizations. However, the NIST CSF framework, across its several versions, has been leveraged by various industry sectors, including small, medium, and large businesses, universities, non-profits, and government partners. Its flexible and expansive scope stand as its core strengths. Some of NIST's priority research areas include industry sectors such as energy, healthcare, manufacturing, environment, etc. (Boehm, 2013). This universality, along with seamless integration with existing standards and frameworks, helps organizations to adopt a holistic approach to cybersecurity risk management.

In terms of the pertinence of the NIST CSF, there exists current research on the applicability of this framework to enhance the cybersecurity risk posture of local governments (Ibrahim et al., 2018). The approach presented in the research can be used to find measurable metrics which are applicable to the different Framework Core Functions. Additionally, one of the advantages of NIST CSF is the consideration of the Target Profile which enables organizations to conduct a thorough self-assessment (National Institute of Standards and Technology, 2024). Furthermore, research has also been conducted with respect to mapping the commonly used MITRE ATT&CK Matrix/Framework to the NIST CSF using a tool called "Cyber Threat Dictionary." This commonly showcases the flexibility of the NIST CSF in terms of being usable in comparison with several other popular frameworks (Kwon et al., 2020).

The CSF has demonstrated itself as being crucial for various organizations, supporting and proactively helping them to manage their cybersecurity risks and issues. It permits organizations to tailor their cybersecurity approaches over time, enabling them to advance their capabilities. Moreover, CSF 2.0 covers its domain past defending basic framework to include organizations over all divisions. This form places a newly discovered accentuation on administration, highlighting the significance of educated decision-making in cybersecurity technique definition and execution. It underscores that cybersecurity is an essential endeavor that warrants consideration from senior leadership along with other key concerns like budgetary soundness and reputation management. Thus, CSF has proven indispensable for numerous organizations, aiding them in proactively addressing and mitigating cybersecurity threats. CSF 2.0 represents an evolution from its predecessors, offering a comprehensive suite of adaptable resources. It allows organizations to tailor their cybersecurity approaches over time, accommodating shifting needs and evolving capabilities.

Comparing Cis V8 and NIST V2.0

The CIS Controls and the NIST CSF have specific qualities that make them appropriate for various organizational objectives. The CIS Controls are very restrictive and particularly aimed at IT and cybersecurity professionals searching for precise, actionable controls. Smaller businesses or those who have yet to begin with cybersecurity will find them extremely helpful. Conversely, the NIST CSF serves companies across all sizes and industries and is more expansive and strategic. Larger businesses with strict risk management guidelines and those operating in regulated sectors will find it especially useful.

Both frameworks are updated on a regular basis, however the CIS Controls are supported by a community-driven approach that guarantees they remain relevant to the most recent dangers. The NIST CSF, although being updated on a regular basis, is inspired by a larger range of standards and recommended practices, giving a broader strategy that may incorporate multiple elements of cybersecurity (Center for Internet Security, 2023; National Institute of Standards and Technology, 2018).

The goal of the CIS Controls is to offer a set of prioritized, implementable guidelines for defending data and IT infrastructure from cyberattacks. Their simple, prescriptive nature makes them perfect for small to medium-sized companies with limited cybersecurity resources. Even those with less understanding of cybersecurity can use these controls since they offer quick, quantifiable security-enhancing activities (Center for Internet Security, 2023). In contrast, the NIST Framework is more expansive and strategically oriented, aiming to be flexible and expandable to suit businesses of all sizes and industries, including infrastructures.

Because of its risk-based approach, it is particularly helpful for larger companies in regulated industries with demanding risk management requirements (National Institute of Standards and Technology, 2018).

Implementing the CIS Controls may be relatively simple for firms that value clear instructions and concrete processes. The tiered implementing group (IG1, IG2, and IG3) enable businesses to begin with fundamental controls and graduate to more complex ones as their abilities develop. This organized strategy enables enterprises to gradually improve their safety record without becoming overwhelmed by the variety of safeguards (Center for Internet Security, 2023).

Yet, the NIST CSF necessitates a more in-depth awareness of the organization's risk environment, as well as a greater level of planning effort. Its adaptable and risk-based approach needs a thorough risk assessment and a customized implementation strategy. Organizations must determine and assign priority to their specific risks before putting in place procedures to successfully handle them. This sophistication can be difficult, but it provides for a highly tailored security approach (National Institute of Standards and Technology, 2018).

The NIST CSF's risk management emphasis and flexible framework enable extensive customization. The framework's notion of profiles allows businesses to customize it to their own requirements and conditions. A profile depicts the results based on an organization's business needs, risk tolerance, and assets, allowing them to match their cybersecurity efforts with their company's goals and regulatory obligations (NIST, 2018). The CIS Controls, while prescriptive, provide some flexibility via their implementation groups. Organizations may tailor controls according to their complexity, scope, and security maturity, which makes it easier to begin with the fundamentals and progress in the future (Center for Internet Security, 2023).

The NIST CSF's broad and holistic approach makes it compatible with various cybersecurity norms and best practices. It incorporates multiple other standards, including the international standard ISO/IEC 27001, COBIT, and others, to provide a unified framework that can support a wide range of cybersecurity programs and activities. This integration feature makes the NIST CSF a useful tool for enterprises wanting to align their cybersecurity efforts with other current standards (National Institute of Standards and Technology, 2018). While comparatively limited in scope, the CIS Controls can be used in conjunction with additional standards and frameworks. Organizations can employ the precise and controls given by CIS as an operational guide within the larger strategic environment of a framework such as NIST CSF or ISO/IEC 27001.

As discussed in the previous sections, in recent years, there has been a surge of companies experiencing internal system breaches. This has affected not only small organizations but also several mid-to-large organizations such as Sony Pictures, Home Depot, JPMorgan Chase, Yahoo, Target, etc. (Esteves et al., 2017). It has also been seen that such breaches can often even remain undetected for months. Thus, it is imperative for organizations of varying sizes to adopt relevant cybersecurity frameworks. This enables them to manage and thwart such rapidly increasing risks in the current technology landscape. Organizations adopting such best practices can not only better defend themselves against such attacks but also add value to their customers and shareholders.

The NIST CSF is considered to be quite comprehensive, expansive, and adaptable, especially with respect to its implementation, in managing and mitigating cybersecurity threats. One of its major strengths lies in its adaptability. The framework integrates some of the best industry practices. Additionally, it facilitates forming a common language or understanding for organizations of all sizes as well as industry sectors. Furthermore, the framework's scalability ensures that organizations tailor their guidelines to their specific needs, and thus promote a proactive approach toward improving their risk posture.

Additionally, the comprehensive structure of NIST CSF v2.0, whilst integrating industry best practices and standards, enhances its applicability. The six core functions—Govern, Identify, Protect, Detect, Respond, and Recover—ensure a holistic approach toward managing cyber risks (National Institute of Standards and Technology, 2024). It offers various sectors such as healthcare organizations a structured approach to safeguarding patient data. It can be implemented by such organizations and tailored to ensure security measures for electronic health records, medical devices, and communication networks (Kandasamy et al., 2022). This highlights the importance of NIST CSF, and thus demonstrates its ability to address cybersecurity challenges across a wide range of sectors in diverse contexts.

Furthermore, Higher Education Institutions (HEIs) can also be a good candidate to adopt the NIST CSF to address their cybersecurity risks. This research proposes a Cybersecurity Maturity Assessment Framework for such HEIs (Almomani et al., 2021).

Additionally, NIST has demonstrated its versatility by being applicable in IoT implementations across mobile and wireless communications. This includes areas like smart-connected transportation and smart-connected parking, which support a range of research projects (Webb & Hume, 2018). By integrating NIST standards, these projects can ensure robust cybersecurity measures, enhancing the reliability and security of emerging technologies and smart infrastructure.

While the NIST CSF v2.0 offers several benefits, which were covered earlier; there are also certain challenges as well as drawbacks when considering its usage and implementation, specifically from a skill and talent gap perspective. Issues such as retaining skilled talent, a shortage of dedicated cybersecurity personnel, and a lack of cybersecurity expertise among leadership further can complicate implementation of this framework (Deloitte Inc., n.d.). Successful deployment of the NIST CSF requires personnel, either internally or externally sourced, to manage, maintain, monitor, respond, reevaluate, and improve cybersecurity controls continually. Additionally, Gartner predicts that by 2025, lack of human intervention as well as talent would lead to over half of the cyber incidents ahead (Gartner Inc., 2023). Additionally, according to the current literature, it has been observed that there is a lack of cost-benefit analysis in the guidance of the NIST CSF (Gordon et al., 2020), and the literature mentioned provides a logical basis for considering the cost-benefit analysis of cybersecurity investments. As presented, below is a comparison Table 1 showcasing a comparative analysis between the NIST CSF v2.0 and the CIS Controls v8 cybersecurity frameworks across several aspects.

Table 1. Comparison between CIS and NIST CSF v2.0

Feature/Aspect	CIS Controls v8	NIST CSF v2.0
Purpose	It provides a set of guidelines and prescriptive actions for organizations to enhance their cybersecurity posture.	It provides a comprehensive and expansive policy framework for organization of all sizes to manage their cybersecurity risks.
Framework Components	18 Controls categorized into three Implementation Groups (IG1, IG2, IG3).	Six Core Functions: Gover, Identify, Protect, Detect, Respond, Recover.
Scope	Primarily technical and operational controls for IT systems.	Broad, including governance, risk management, and operational processes.
Intended Audience	IT and security professionals within organizations.	Organizational leadership, risk managers, and security professionals.
Adoption	Widely adopted by small to medium-sized enterprises (SMEs).	Considered and leveraged by organizations of all sizes.
Compliance and Benchmarking	Often used for internal benchmarking and compliance with other standards.	Framework for establishing a baseline of cybersecurity practices, facilitating communication and assessment.
International Applicability	Primarily used in the United States but recognized globally.	Recognized and used globally, with some regional adaptations.
Third Party Risk Management	Addresses third-party risk within certain controls (e.g., Control 15: Service Provider Management).	Comprehensive approach to third-party risk management, integrated into the Identify function.

CHALLENGES AND FUTURE TRENDS

Cybersecurity is always one of the challenging fields. Implementing a framework in the organization is not an easy task. Cybersecurity is growing as technology is advancing. The CIS V8 framework is crafted in such a way that it can efficiently tackle the growing cyber-attacks with the ease of cyber tools. Even after implementation of the framework, there will be many things to consider in order to attain a high level of data protection and security.

The key issue is that organizations allocate very small amounts of budget towards cybersecurity. Only a small percentage of an organization's budget is devoted to cybersecurity. Figure 2 shows the organizational budget allocation, this is based on the report from Deloitte (Deloitte Development LLC., 2023).

Figure 2. Cybersecurity insights 2023: Budgets and benchmarks for financial services institutions, Deloitte Development LLC

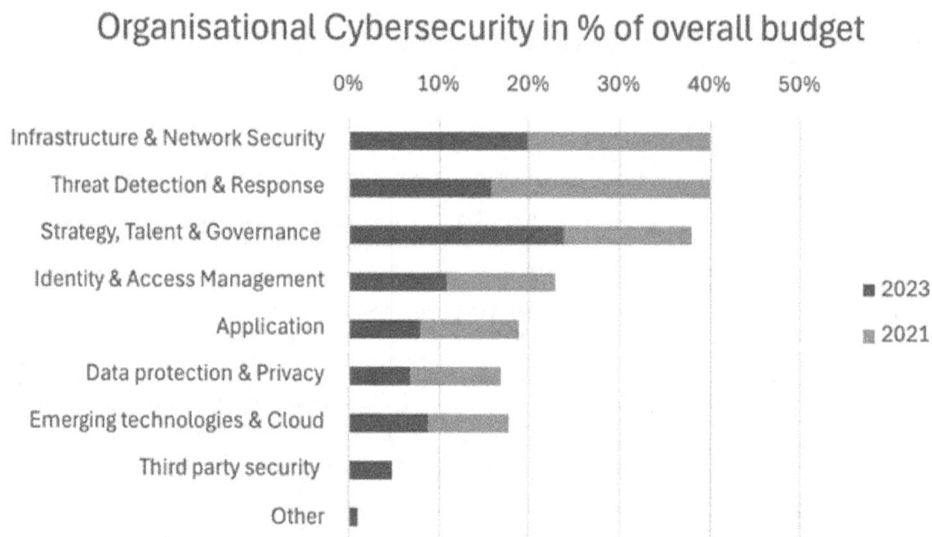

The implementation of comprehensive security measures, such as the CIS Controls V8, which necessitate substantial financial resources, is complicated by this underinvestment. Implementing the CIS framework, meeting the standards in a mid-sized or large organization requires having to create a full-fledged plan that the security team will implement in phases. It gives a reliable security posture, but implementing CIS controls seamlessly requires investment. Also, the cybersecurity industry is facing a significant skill gap of cyber professionals, so the implementation would meet all the requirements, standards and be error proof.

Another serious challenge is Integrating CIS Controls V8 with the current IT and security systems is a challenge for many organizations. It will take a great deal of time, energy and resources to integrate these systems and add new controls.

CIS Controls V8 offers a powerful collection of preventive measures to lessen and stop cyberattacks. Because these controls have their foundation in real-world data and expert remarks on cybersecurity, the most prevalent and serious risks are taken care of. This framework has been upgraded with additional defenses against emerging tactics and attack methods employed by cybercriminals. This ongoing upgrading procedure guarantees that defenses against the most recent threats continue to be effective and pertinent. There are special security risks associated with moving to cloud and hybrid systems, including breaches of information, misconfigurations, and unauthorized access.

CIS Controls V8 offers detailed instructions with an emphasis on secure configuration, ongoing monitoring and access control for safeguarding cloud infrastructure and services. Due to the unpredictable nature of cloud systems, resources and settings can change frequently these controls aid organizations in managing security threats.

CIS Controls V8 offers more thorough instructions on safeguarding cloud resources as an increasing number of enterprises shift to cloud environments. Security best practices for cutting-edge technologies like artificial intelligence (AI), machine learning, and the Internet of Things (IoT) have been incorporated into CIS V8. With the advent of these technologies come new ways to attack, and this framework attempts to reduce the related risks by offering workable security solutions. It is imperative to tackle the distinct security obstacles linked to cloud computing, including but not limited to breaches of data, configuration errors, and access management.

With the increase in smartphone and remote work usage, CIS V8 incorporates more controls and standards for safeguarding mobile devices and apps. This is critical for securing the organizational data that is accessed and saved on mobile devices.

The CIS Risk Identification and Evaluation Method (CIS RAM) - helps an organization justify investments for fair adoption of its CIS controls, defines their permissible level of risk, prioritizes and implements the CIS controls appropriately and helps to demonstrate the response. CIS RAM will continue to grow, giving organizations more advanced resources for quantitatively assessing and controlling cybersecurity risks. This helps rationalize investments in cybersecurity through demonstrable risk reduction outcomes. CIS Controls V8 is rapidly being linked to multiple regulatory frameworks (such as NIST, PCI DSS, and HIPAA) to assist enterprises expedite their compliance processes. This trend is expected to continue, which will make it easier for businesses to certify compliance with multiple regulations using a single set of controls.

CONCLUSION

The Center for Internet Security (CIS) and the National Institute of Standards and Technology (NIST) are the two prominent frameworks for improving organizational cybersecurity attacks. Although they differ in implementation, both these frameworks tend to strengthen cyber defenses, methodology and different use cases. CIS controls are developed through the joint efforts of experts from business and government. The CIS controls, first published by the SANS Institute in 2008 as the Consensus Auditing Guidelines (CAG), are designed to address real-world cyber threats by using real attack data. This concept has led to the "20 Critical Security Controls," the most recent version being CIS Controls v8. This version divides controls into three Implementation Groups (IGs) based on organizational size and capabilities: IG1 (Basic Cyber Hygiene) for small and medium-sized enterprises that have little knowledge of IT, IG2 for companies with more complicated IT environments, and IG3 for businesses with advanced cybersecurity requirements. Each control within these categories is divided into sub-controls or safeguards, with thorough instructions for execution.

The NIST Framework came into existence in 2014, which was designed to be flexible and applicable to organizations of various sizes. It mainly focuses on six core functions like Govern, Identify, Protect, Detect, Respond, and Recover.

These functions cover a comprehensive approach to manage cyber threats and risks, covering from understanding to mitigating the risks and implementing the security measures. This framework has various tiers to help organizations to assess their cyber practices and areas of improvement.

CIS Controls are especially helpful for firms seeking precise, step-by-step instructions to strengthen their cybersecurity since they are highly prescriptive and actionable. Small and medium-sized enterprises and organizations with little resources and experience in cybersecurity are especially well-suited for them. These firms may more easily comply with regulatory obligations and be ready for cybersecurity audits thanks to this tiered approach, which helps them prioritize measures based on their unique needs. The CIS Controls' practicality enables enterprises to rapidly achieve noticeable changes.

On the other hand, the NIST is extremely adaptable and thorough, made to fit the particular requirements of any kind of company. With its strategic approach that is ideal for complex IT environments and high cybersecurity threats, it is especially advantageous for major organizations and critical infrastructure sectors. Organizations may better incorporate cybersecurity into their larger risk management procedures by utilizing the NIST CSF's risk management emphasis. Due to its widespread acceptance and recognition around the globe, it is an invaluable foundation for businesses that operate in several legal countries.

In conclusion, the CIS Controls are perfect for smaller businesses or those with minimal cybersecurity experience since they provide specific, doable actions that are intended for real-world implementation. On the other hand, the NIST CSF is more appropriate for bigger businesses with more complicated requirements since it offers an adaptable, high-level framework focused on risk management. Although they address distinct needs and situations, both paradigms are crucial for improving organizational cybersecurity.

REFERENCES

Almomani, I., Ahmed, M., & Maglaras, L. (2021). Cybersecurity maturity assessment framework for higher education institutions in Saudi Arabia. *PeerJ. Computer Science*, 7, e703. https://peerj.com/articles/cs-703/. DOI: 10.7717/peerj-cs.703 PMID: 34604525

Amiruddin, A., Afiansyah, H. G., & Nugroho, H. A. (2021a). Cyber-risk management planning using NIST CSF v1.1, NIST SP 800-53 rev. 5, and CIS controls V8. *2021 International Conference on Informatics, Multimedia, Cyber and Information System (ICIMCIS)*. https://doi.org/DOI: 10.1109/ICIMCIS53775.2021.9699337

Boehm, J. (2014, November). NIST–Working with Industry To Accelerate Innovation. In 2014 ERC. https://peer.asee.org/25216.pdf

Center for internet security (CIS) releases CIS critical security controls V8 to reflect evolving technology, threats. (2021, December 1). CIS. https://www.cisecurity.org/about-us/media/press-release/center-for-internet-security-cis-releases-cis-controls-v8-to-reflect-evolving-technology-threats

Cis - Center for Internet Security. (2024, May 23). CISO Global. https://www.ciso.inc/capabilities/strategy-risk-solutions/managed-compliance-security-offering/cis-center-for-internet-security/#:~:text=CIS%20Critical%20Security%20Controls%20Version,management%20for%20future%20cyber%20defense

Cybersecurity Framework, N. I. S. T. 2.0: Resource & Overview Guide. (2024). https://nvlpubs.nist.gov/nistpubs/SpecialPublications/NIST.SP.1299.pdf

Dowdy, J. (2012). *The cyber-security threat to us growth and prosperity. Cyberspace: A New Domain for National Security*. https://www.mckinsey.com/kz/~/media/mckinsey/dotcom/client_service/aerospace%20and%20defense/cybersecurity_threat_to_growth_and_prosperity.pdf

Esteves, J., Ramalho, E., & De Haro, G. (2017). To improve cybersecurity, think like a hacker. *MIT Sloan Management Review*. Retrieved May 30, 2024, from https://sloanreview.mit.edu/article/to-improve-cybersecurity-think-like-a-hacker/

Freeze, D. (2021, April 27). *Cybercrime To Cost The World $10.5 Trillion Annually By 2025. Cybercrime Magazine*.https://cybersecurityventures.com/cybercrime-damage-costs-10-trillion-by-2025/

Gartner. (2023, February 22). *Gartner predicts nearly half of cybersecurity leaders will change jobs by 2025. Gartner. Retrieved May 30, 2024, from*https://www.gartner.com/en/newsroom/press-releases/2023-02-22-gartner-predicts-nearly-half-of-cybersecurity-leaders-will-change-jobs-by-2025

Gordon, L. A., Loeb, M. P., & Zhou, L. (2020b). Integrating cost–benefit analysis into the NIST Cybersecurity Framework via the Gordon–Loeb Model. *Journal of Cybersecurity*, 6(1), tyaa005. Advance online publication. DOI: 10.1093/cybsec/tyaa005

IC3 Annual Report and Fraud Flyer. (2024, March 18). https://www.ic3.gov/Media/Y2024/PSA240318#:~:text=In%202023%2C%20the%20IC3%20received,result%20of%20frauds%20and%20scams

Ibrahim, A., Valli, C., McAteer, I., & Chaudhry, J. (2018). A security review of local government using NIST CSF: A case study. *The Journal of Supercomputing*, 74(10), 5171–5186. DOI: 10.1007/s11227-018-2479-2

Kandasamy, K., Srinivas, S., Achuthan, K., & Rangan, V. P. (2022). Digital Healthcare - cyberattacks in Asian organizations: An analysis of vulnerabilities, risks, NIST Perspectives, and recommendations. *IEEE Access : Practical Innovations, Open Solutions*, 10, 12345–12364. DOI: 10.1109/ACCESS.2022.3145372

Keller, N. (2013). Cybersecurity framework. https://www.nist.gov/cyberframework

Kwon, R., Ashley, T., Castleberry, J., Mckenzie, P., & Gupta Gourisetti, S. N. (2020). *Cyber threat dictionary using Mitre ATT&CK matrix and NIST Cybersecurity Framework Mapping. 2020 Resilience Week.* RWS. DOI: 10.1109/RWS50334.2020.9241271

Lance Spitzner. (2024, May 29). SANS Institute. https://www.sans.org/white-papers/SANS-2021-Survey-OTICS-Cybersecurity/

Liu, H., & Staff in the Office of Technology. (2022, October 6). *Understanding the NIST cybersecurity framework.* Federal Trade Commission. https://www.ftc.gov/business-guidance/small-businesses/cybersecurity/nist-framework

National Archives and Records Administration. (2013). *Executive Order -- Improving Critical Infrastructure Cybersecurity*. National Archives and Records Administration. https://obamawhitehouse.archives.gov/the-press-office/2013/02/12/executive-order-improving-critical-infrastructure-cybersecurity

NIST cybersecurity framework. (2024b, May 1). NIST. https://www.nist.gov/itl/smallbusinesscyber/nist-cybersecurity-framework-0

NIST history. (2019, November 15). NIST. https://www.nist.gov/history

OCR. (2022, January 19). *Your rights under HIPAA*. HHS.gov. https://www.hhs.gov/hipaa/for-individuals/guidance-materials-for-consumers/index.html

Öğüt, H., Raghunathan, S., & Menon, N. (2011). Cyber security risk management: Public policy implications of correlated risk, imperfect ability to prove loss, and observability of self-protection. *Risk Analysis*, 31(3), 497–512. DOI: 10.1111/j.1539-6924.2010.01478.x PMID: 20807381

Roy, P. P. (2020). A high-level comparison between the NIST Cyber Security Framework and the ISO 27001 Information Security Standard. *2020 National Conference on Emerging Trends on Sustainable Technology and Engineering Applications (NCETSTEA)*. https://doi.org/DOI: 10.1109/NCETSTEA48365.2020.9119914

The 18 CIS controls. (2021b, October 28). CIS. https://www.cisecurity.org/controls/cis-controls-list

The Changing Faces of Cybersecurity. (n.d.). Deloitte Canada. https://www2.deloitte.com/ca/en/pages/risk/articles/the-changing-faces-of-cybersecurity.html

The NIST Cybersecurity Framework (CSF) 2.0. (2024). https://nvlpubs.nist.gov/nistpubs/CSWP/NIST.CSWP.29.pdf

Webb, J., & Hume, D. (2018). Campus IOT collaboration and governance using the NIST Cybersecurity Framework. *Living in the Internet of Things: Cybersecurity of the IoT*. Advance online publication. DOI: 10.1049/cp.2018.0025

Chapter 4

Safeguarding Financial Integrity Utilizing Sarbanes-Oxley for IT Audits in Modern Corporations

Anjali
University at Buffalo, SUNY, USA

Raghvendra Singh
University at Buffalo, SUNY, USA

Pranith Shetty
CISCO, USA

ABSTRACT

This study digs into the critical intersection between the Sarbanes-Oxley Act (SOX) and corporate audits of information technology (IT). SOX, which was initially intended to improve financial transparency, has had a significant impact on IT controls, data security, and reporting accuracy. The study delves into SOX regulations, particularly Section 404, as they apply to IT, necessitating strong internal controls, data integrity, and secure record-keeping processes. This chapter highlights the strategic application of SOX for comprehensive IT audits using real world case studies and practical insights. It emphasizes the interdependence of financial and IT controls, highlighting how SOX serves as a foundation for maintaining the integrity of electronic data and safeguarding enterprises' economic well-being.

DOI: 10.4018/979-8-3693-4211-4.ch004

INTRODUCTION

On July 30, 2002, President Bush signed The Sarbanes-Oxley Act of 2002 (Public Law 107–204, 2002), a United States federal law, aka the 'Public Company Accounting Reform and Investor Protection Act' (in the Senate) and 'Corporate and Auditing Accountability and Responsibility Act' (in the House) and commonly called Sarbanes–Oxley, Sarbox or SOX. It is named after sponsors U.S. Senator Paul Sarbanes (D-MD) and U.S. Representative Michael G. Oxley (R-OH) (Act, S. O., 2002). Among other things, SOX amends the Securities Exchange Act of 1934 (Public Law 112-158, 2012) and the Securities Act of 1933 (Public Law. 117–263, 2022). It set new or enhanced standards for all U.S. public company boards, management, and public accounting firms. This Act was legislated in connection to the issues that arose from fraudulent accounting practices, such as the Enron, Tyco, and WorldCom scandals.

The questions about governance in American corporations that were raised in relation to these events are threatening to rock investor confidence in the financial markets. These scandals had eroded public confidence in financial reporting and accounting practices and called for an urgent need to be addressed by the lawmakers. SOX act rushed on technologies for reinforced oversights, responsibilities, and transparency; basically, recalibrating the integration between financial reporting and IT auditing practices (Šimková, 2005). The Sarbanes-Oxley Act focuses on transparency and accountability of information; it introduces new requirements with respect to providing financial information disclosure by the companies. Formerly, U.S. public companies were required to provide disclosure information concerning certain occurrences, such as incorporation and, thereafter, in any efforts made at raising capital through the public markets.

Previous studies have accounted for how the Act has been widely considered the most far-reaching securities legislation since the Securities Acts of 1933 and 1934 (Alexander et al., 2013). It not only imposes additional disclosure requirements, but more importantly, proposes substantive corporate governance mandates, a practice that is unprecedented in the history of federal securities legislation (Zhang, 2007). SOX promised improved corporate governance and more accountability for financial actions of senior corporate officers and oversight of public accountants. Post-SOX, entrenched firms increased risky and value-enhancing investments. These investments were financed by reductions in financial slack and dividend payouts and by lower cost of debt. The specific mechanism driving the positive changes in corporate policies of entrenched firms is the SOX requirement of an independent compensation committee (Pryshchepa, 2021). Initial business responses to SOX varied from acceptance (Melancon, 2002; Miller & Pashkoff, 2002) to concern (Desmond, 2002; Evers, 2002; Kahn, 2003) with many of these points continuing to echo 10 years (Coates & Srinivasan, 2014) after the passing of the SOX legislation (Gordon & Jamal, 2018).

The Sarbanes-Oxley established new or improved standards of corporate accountability and penalties that may be used by corporate wrongdoers. It has 11 titles laying out rules for the responsibilities of auditors and corporations, rules of disclosure relating to financial issues, and harsher penalties for 'white-collar' crimes. Sections 302 and 404 (Gupta et al., 2016) of this act are of particular interest to IT executives. They target the internal company controls aimed at ensuring the accuracy of the information appearing in financial statements.

This paper articulates the historic impetus for the SOX, tracing its conceptualization to its contemporary operational fame and usage amongst industry standards underlining its significance for redefining the fiduciary obligations of organizations. The analysis presented here evidently places at the forefront the significance of Section 404 of SOX in explaining the complex relationship between statutory compliance and the integrity of financial informatics. SOX 404 costs - internal labor costs, external consulting and technology expenses, and auditor attestation charges. Based on a sample of companies that voluntarily disclosed SOX 404 cost information during the period from January 2003 to September 2005, it was observed that the mean (median) total compliance costs for Section 404 is \$2.2 (\$1.2) million (Krishnan et al., 2008).

From a multidisciplinary review for SOX after 10 years, it's clear that while the direct costs of the Act were substantial and fell disproportionately on smaller companies, costs had fallen over time. Research about indirect costs such as loss of risk taking in the U.S. was inconclusive. Financial reporting quality appeared to have gone up after SOX but research on causal attribution is weak (Coates & Srinivasan, 2014). Findings of Emarald Insight also corroborates to the fact that over the long run (10-15 years) after SOX adoption, there is a significant positive change in conservatism as compared to during the previous similar period (Kim et al., 2019).

The study dissects layers of nuanced enforcement of the act, situating it within the large perspective of governance of IT and the threat of ethical economic practice. This directly applies to the software systems that a company uses for controlling, transmitting, and calculating the data utilized in financial reports. Misinformation is punishable by fines up to 5 million dollars and/or up to 20 years imprisonment.

In the unfolding narrative, we unpack the impetus in the back of SOX's stringent compliance requirements and its ripple results across IT governance and risk management strategies. This advent will help readers to look into the fabric of SOX, providing a structured overview which is technically informed, charting the course of a legislative measure which has turn out to be synonymous with the governance of financial data.

BACKGROUND TO SARBANES-OXLEY ACT

To understand SOX, we must first know of the Enron debacle that unfolded in the early 2000's. Enron was a very old and reputable company in the energy sector, but it was eventually exposed as a massive financial fraud. This essentially meant they were falsifying their financial statements. They employed accounting tricks to inflate their profits and set up complex partnerships to hide their debts, presenting an illusion of solid financial health. Many investors believed Enron was a sound investment and bought shares, but when the truth came out, Enron collapsed, causing its stock price to plummet. The bankruptcy of Enron in 2001, with its $62 billion in assets, was the largest in U.S. history, to that point (McLean & Elkind, 2013). It resulted in over four thousand employees losing their jobs, retirement savings, and medical benefits. The average severance pay awarded was $4,500 (McLean & Elkind, 2013). The Enron crisis was a massive corporate disaster. In June 2002, then one of the largest international accounting firms, Arthur Andersen all but collapsed when it was found guilty of obstruction of justice in connection with Enron. With the debacle of Enron, and its auditing firm, Arthur Andersen, the revelation of the two connected occurrences pointed out the necessity of legislation in order to avoid this from happening in the future. (Eichar, 2009). Weak internal control at Enron; abuse of off-balance sheet entities and conflicting interests with their external auditors, Arthur Andersen, who literally created the largest accounting scandal in the United States are the issues that the Sarbanes-Oxley Act deals with.

The response of lawmakers to the collapse of Enron was "immediate and far-reaching" in an effort to "deter future fraud and increase the accountability" of corporate executives and boards, hence, Congress passed the Sarbanes-Oxley Act in July of 2002 . Section 404 of SOX requires the establishment of ICFR and that the management thereof be enforced. Additionally, independent auditors are required to attest to and report on the effectiveness of those ICFR (404-b) (Eichar, 2009; Buckberg et al., 2003). These requirements met with widespread approval from individual and institutional investors. In contrast, the business community viewed the new rules as overly burdensome, arguing that they imposed compliance costs without commensurate benefits (Hochberg et al., 2009). Smaller firms that shoulder proportionally heavier fixed costs of compliance were therefore being alerted to this issue (Holmstrom & Kaplan, 2009). The U.S. Securities and Exchange Commission (SEC, 2003) issued guidance for Section 404(a) requirements, and the Public Company Accounting Oversight Board (PCAOB) had implemented Auditing Standard No. 5 for 404(b) requirements.

SOX impacts corporate governance and financial practices extensively, with Sections 302 and 404 particularly affecting information technology systems within corporations. Section 302, in particular, mandates that senior corporate officers be personally certifying the accuracy of financial information and, in so doing, require strong internal controls and reporting methods. (Stephens, 2008). This has culminated in the integration of comprehensive frameworks like COBIT (Control Objectives for Information and Related Technologies) and ITIL (Information Technology Infrastructure Library) to guide compliance. Technological advancement also has placed automation in the control assessment, improving accuracy in the compliance report through continuous monitoring and real-time systems (Stephens, 2011; Gong et al., 2009).

Section 404 mandates the annual assessment of such controls, really acting like pace for stringent measures of data integrity and security, including effective access controls and encryption. This has given rise to specialized IT audit software that would streamline the compliance process and facilitate giving the necessary audit trails, hence the documentation and assessment of the IT controls over financial reporting (Klamm & Watson, 2009). Overall, the evidence is consistent with a causal link between Section 404 compliance and improvements in the quality of the firms' information environment. Specifically, 80% of respondents ascribe some benefits to Section 404 compliance. Large fractions of respondents cite a positive impact of compliance on the quality of their firm's internal control structure (73%), their audit committee's confidence in the ICFR (71%), the quality of their firm's financial reporting (48%), and their firm's ability to prevent and detect fraud (47%) (Alexander et al., 2013)

The perceived benefits of compliance are higher when the information environment of the firm improves by following SOX, as captured by lower equity betas and higher stock liquidity (Ashbaugh-Skaife et al., 2009). The role of IT in compliance is no longer in the regime of acting as a supporting mechanism; it has transformed into a pivotal constituent of strategic corporate governance. Post-SOX, IT governance changes its role to close integration with corporate strategies towards effective management of risks and, from the business perspective, creation of value. This goes to amplify the importance of emerging technology in cloud computing, artificial intelligence, and blockchain, etc., on a day-to-day growing need for automation and security of process factors for compliance. Big data analytics plays a very crucial role not only in predictive risk management but also in the process of compliance monitoring (Chambers & Payne 2011).

Results from a survey of 173 public and private companies reveal that internal audit function size is positively associated with: (1) better audit committee governance, (2) greater organizational experience of the chief audit executive, (3) missions involving IT auditing, (4) the use of sophisticated audit technologies, (5) the use of a staffing model in which internal audit is used for rotational leadership development, (6) organization size, and (7) the number of foreign subsidiaries that the organization possesses (Anderson et al., 2012). The impact of SOX on organizational ethics can be assessed by analyzing how formal codes of ethics have changed since its enactment. The role of corporate codes of ethics as modes of formal organizational discourse is demonstrated by numerous studies that have examined codes in order to increase understanding of their terms, content, purpose, function, and effects (Farrell & Farrell, 1998).

Section 404, for example, requires corporations to maintain and evaluate the efficiency of their internal controls over financial reporting. This requires meticulous documentation of financial operations and assessments to ensure the correctness of the financial statement. The function of independent external auditors in examining these controls and financial reporting is crucial. SOX also mandated that CEOs and CFOs guarantee the accuracy and completeness of financial reports, making them personally accountable for any inaccuracies. Furthermore, it imposes restrictions on non-audit services offered by external auditors in order to avoid conflicts of interest. It requires the formation of audit committees comprised of independent directors to ensure independent scrutiny (Hoitash & Hoitash, 2009).

The Act has far-reaching consequences for information technology (IT) and data security since businesses must protect electronic documents and maintain secure data retention standards. The Act not only encourages financial transparency and honesty, but it also makes businesses accountable for financial reporting and governance. Finally, SOX serves as a precaution against corporate fraud and a cornerstone of investor confidence in the integrity of financial markets. (Coates, 2007; Squires & Squires, 2003)

The Sarbanes-Oxley Act is the most significant change to U.S. securities act since 1934. The Act's congressional sponsors, Representative Michael G. Oxley and Senator Paul Sarbanes, both of them believe that the legislation is helping to restore investors' confidence and deter fraud. The main objective of SOX is to protect investors. In addition, service purchases for large-scale information technologies involve significant strategic business risks for customer organizations (such as the exploitation of vendors, the loss of strategic advantage, and vendor failure) (ALTINAY, n.d.).

Ultimately, IT systems should be able to adapt to regulatory change and business conditions. This will be done through continuous education and training of IT personnel on the latest compliance mandates, technologies, and best practices. Application of the current research and case studies gives companies an applied understanding and theoretical framework to help them enhance their effectiveness of IT controls in curbing financial fraud and guaranteeing transparency in the way financial reporting is done. This constant adaptation and improvement in the practice of IT audit and compliance underscores a lasting influence that SOX has in the refinement of corporate accountability and integrity in financial disclosures (Leech & Leech, 2011).

PERILS OF NON-COMPLIANCE

Inadequate financial controls can lead to data breaches and cybersecurity concerns, putting sensitive financial information at risk. Weak financial controls and noncompliance with the Sarbanes-Oxley Act (SOX) can also pose significant risks to businesses and the financial ecosystem. Failure to follow SOX laws can result in erroneous financial reporting, which can harm an organization's reputation and financial soundness. Companies risk inaccurate financial information without strong internal controls, which can mislead investors, lose shareholder trust, and cause stock prices to fall. The lack of strict governance measures raises the potential of corporate fraud, exposing businesses to criminal and civil penalties, including fines and jail for key executives (Webb, 2008)

THE ELEVEN TITLES OF SARBANES OXLEY

Title I: Public Company Accounting Oversight Board

The establishment of the PCAOB introduced a new level of oversight for public company audits. The Board plays an important role in regulating the activities of auditors, ensuring Compliance with established standards and ethical practices. One action that the PCAOB can take is issuing restatements when companies need to correct errors in a financial statement. Former PCAOB board member James Kaiser mentions that in 2006, the PCAOB had to look at over 1,800 restatements, while in 2019, they only reviewed 85 (Eckstein, 2021). This shows the increase in the quality of audits that have occurred since SOX was implemented.

Title II: Auditor Independence

This title set restrictions on the types of services auditors could provide to clients, aiming to prevent conflicts of interest. The SEC mentions the requirements for auditor rotation and approval after five years, ensuring that auditors remain impartial and independent. There is also a timeout period of five years (Stimson, 2005).

Title III: Corporate Responsibility

Senior executives are required to confirm the accuracy of financial reports personally, increasing accountability. This title emphasized the role of senior management in encouraging a culture of compliance and integrity within organizations. A former vice president and chief financial officer mentioned that the act of signing on the financial reports every quater was a stark reminder of the ownership and responsibility for those important disclosures (Eckstein, 2021).

Title IV: Enhanced Financial Disclosures

This title introduced more stringent requirements for financial disclosures, aiming to increase transparency and investor confidence. It mandated detailed reporting of figures such as off-balance sheet transactions and stock transactions of executives (Alexander et al., 2013).

Title V: Analyst Conflicts of Interest

Aimed at improving the integrity of securities research and preventing conflicts of interest. It established codes of conduct for securities analysts and required disclosure of knowable conflicts of interest, such as if the analyst owned stock in the company being analyzed.

Title VI: Commission Resources and Authority

This title expanded the powers and resources of the Securities and Exchange Commission (SEC), enabling it to regulate the securities industry more effectively. It included provisions to enhance the SEC's ability to supervise corporate disclosures and eliminate fraudulent activities in the securities markets.

Title VII: Studies and Reports

This title includes several of the reports and studies required to create SOX. These studies were aimed at continually improving the regulatory framework and adapting to emergent challenges in financial reporting and auditing.

Title VIII: Corporate and Criminal Fraud Accountability

Known as the "Corporate and Criminal Fraud Accountability Act of 2002," this title is designed to protect investors by enhancing the accuracy and reliability of corporate disclosures. It introduced severe criminal penalties for changing or destroying financial records and provided protections for whistleblowers who report fraudulent activities. SOX even gives whistleblowers the ability to sue their employer if that company retaliates against them.

Title IX: White-Collar Crime Penalty Enhancements

This title significantly increased the penalties for white-collar crimes to deter corporate fraud. It included provisions that improved the sentencing guidelines and penalties for those convicted of fraud-related crimes. Fines of up to five million dollars or a prison sentence of up to 20 years are penalties that could possibly be sentenced to executives who partake in white-collar crime.

Title X: Corporate Tax Returns

This brief but significant section requires the CEO of a company to sign the company's tax return, guaranteeing that corporate tax filings are subject to the same level of accountability as other financial reports. This requirement was designed to increase the responsibility of senior corporate officers and reduce the occurrence of corporate tax fraud.

Title XI: Corporate Fraud and Accountability

Known as the "Corporate Fraud Accountability Act of 2002," this title deals with penalties for fraud by corporate officers and issues connected to the destruction of evidence in fraud investigations. It reinforces the legal penalties for corporate fraud, aiming to discourage misconduct and hold executives accountable for the reliability of financial reporting.

IT Audit Procedures Before the Sarbanes-Oxley Act

Focus and Scope

IT audits concentrated mostly on operational efficiency and security before Sarbanes-Oxley, and while compliance and governance were still checked, they were a much smaller part of the audit. This meant technical evaluations of hardware and software had the most importance, assessing performance and reliability rather than compliance. Data integrity checks were routine, ensuring the accuracy and consistency of data in IT systems, particularly those related to financial transactions. However, due to companies not adhering to compliance, some companies abused the system and hid decreasing stock prices (WorldCom) and massive amounts of debt (Enron) (Baxter, 2021).

Regulatory Environment

The regulatory environment was not as strict as it is now, as there was no legal mandate for compliance in IT operations. Companies mostly followed best practices and guidelines for their regulations. Many companies followed frameworks like COBIT for best practices in IT governance, but there was no legal obligation to adhere to such standards. Even today, many companies use the COBIT framework to suit their needs. At the time, the focus for most companies was more on adherence to internal policies and procedures rather than external regulations.

Internal Controls

Companies were expected to have internal controls, but they were not as thoroughly tested or documented as they would be post-SOX (Baxter, 2021). Operational controls had more emphasis placed on them compared to internal controls related to financial reporting.

Audit Reporting

Audit reports were technical in nature, discussing system performance, uptime, and security vulnerabilities. There was less attention paid to the broader context of how IT systems supported overall business objectives and regulatory compliance. Recommendations by auditors were often focused on technical improvements and efficiency enhancements (Charles et al., 2010).

External Audit Reliance

External auditors reviewed previous IT audits, primarily to understand the technical environment of a company rather than to assess compliance. IT audits were seen as a separate domain from financial audits, and so there was less crossover than the audits of today.

CHANGES IN AUDIT PROCEDURES AFTER THE SARBANES-OXLEY ACT

Increased Focus on Internal Controls

IT audits became integrated with the concept of strong internal controls for financial reporting after the numerous scandals that affected companies such as Enron and Tyco. The role of the IT department in safeguarding financial data became a primary focus, with audits thoroughly assessing controls around financial applications and databases.

Documentation and Testing

SOX requires detailed documentation and regular testing of controls. This led to IT audits having a more organized approach where controls are assessed on how well they are documented, implemented, and maintained. IT departments have to work closely with auditors to ensure that every control is where it needs to be and that they are functioning as intended.

Section 404 Compliance

Compliance with Section 404 became a central aspect of IT audits, linking IT operations directly to corporate financial health. Section 404 requires companies to create and maintain internal controls for financial reports, and they must document, test, and maintain the controls to make sure they are compliant. The IT department's role has now expanded to make sure that systems and processes comply with this section.

INTEGRATION WITH FINANCIAL AUDITS

IT audits were no longer separate assessments but were integrated into the framework of financial auditing. Understanding and assessing IT controls became a critical component of evaluating a company's financial integrity.

Auditor Independence

SOX mandated a clear segregation between auditing and consulting services, affecting how IT audit services were conducted and reported. Auditors were required to maintain a higher degree of independence from the companies they audited, reducing conflicts of interest (McConnell & Banks, 2003).

Enhanced Reporting Requirements

Reports from IT audits became more comprehensive, focusing on how IT controls impact compliance and financial reporting. Auditors began identifying and reporting on issues in IT controls that could affect the integrity of financial reporting.

Risk Management and Continuous Monitoring

IT audits started to include an emphasis on ongoing risk management and the need for constant monitoring of IT controls. This shift emphasized an active approach to IT governance, with a focus on continuous improvement and compliance. Companies needed to be able to perform efficient risk assessments to determine their scope, as otherwise, they would face an increase in costs related to compliance when testing programs that should not be included within the scope (Mehta, 2010).

Increased Scrutiny and Penalties

The increased penalties under SOX led to a more cautious and thorough approach to IT audits. Companies became more cautious in maintaining IT controls aware of the legal and financial penalties of non-compliance.

Impact on IT Governance

The Sarbanes Oxley Act (SOX) has significantly impacted how companies handle their IT governance. This act requires corporations to be responsible and transparent in their governance practices, particularly when managing information technology (IT) systems. Adhering to the Sarbanes Oxley Act (SOX) means IT professionals must meet demands by providing transparent and timely information while safeguarding valuable company resources. Compliance with this act has shifted from being an obligation to becoming a competitive advantage, shaping businesses' focus on IT governance and controls. The act prioritizes enhancing governance by implementing oversight and management mechanisms reinforcing corporate responsibility. It mandates that executives in companies are accountable for developing, evaluating, and overseeing the effectiveness of controls related to financial reporting and disclosure. The IT department plays a role in establishing an internal control environment. (Damianides, 2005)

Sections 302 and 404 of the Sarbanes Oxley Act (SOX) highlight the importance of organizations establishing IT controls that ensure the reliability of information and uphold ethical standards. This regulation has also led corporations to reassess and strengthen existing controls, improving efficiency. The Sarbanes Oxley Act (SOX) has impacted reporting and IT governance. It has led to the adopting of control frameworks like COSO for reporting and COBIT for IT governance. These frameworks help companies ensure compliance and enhance their internal control systems, giving management and boards of directors confidence. SOX has transformed IT governance from a support function to a strategic asset in achieving business objectives and maintaining corporate integrity as it strengthens the connection between IT and business strategy while fulfilling compliance obligations. (Damianides, 2005)

To fully understand the pressures on IT operations, it is crucial to acknowledge the substantial influence of SOX on IT governance. Over the past decade, various legislative measures, such as HIPAA, have required businesses to safeguard information through encryption and protection measures. However, SOX goes beyond these data security regulations by mandating IT governance practices that prevent errors in reporting for public companies. The development of IT governance is a response to the need for regulation and oversight of processes involved in creating, integrating, and maintaining information systems within organizations. The rise of publicized IT issues and increased use of communication among businesses has prompted the adoption of formal standards for IT governance. (Leih, 2009)

Regulatory measures such as SOX, Basel II in Europe, and the Clinger-Cohen Act in the USA have shaped the evolution of IT governance. The importance of IT management in business strategy and risk management has pushed IT governance ideas to the forefront. Currently, board-level executives rely on IT leadership for policy decisions within organizations. Managing IT has become a part of executives' responsibilities. (Leih, 2009)

According to Delbaere and Ferreira (2007), laws and regulations that impact IT governance can be categorized into four domains: data and network security, data and network integrity rules, procedures and processes, and record retention and accessibility. While most regulations have focused on data protection, recent legislation has started exerting an influence on the management of IT companies. The Clinger-Cohen Act of 1996 has particularly affected U.S. Government agencies by requiring them to adopt techniques for managing their IT portfolios and implementing strategic IT planning similar to those utilized by public or private corporations. On the other hand, Basel II primarily affects financial institutions by implementing risk management regulations. In addition to the Sarbanes Oxley Act

(SOX), which mandates controls for financial reporting, these measures highlight the vital relationship between financial reporting and information technology (IT), significantly impacting IT governance in numerous public companies. (Leih, 2009)

Various legal constraints have prompted the evolution of IT governance, expanding its focus from data security to encompass a role in strategy and risk management. This trend reflects a growing recognition of the role that IT plays in ensuring business integrity and operational efficiency.

Risk Management

One of the areas that SOX heavily emphasizes is Enterprise Risk Management (ERM), which has resulted in changes in how businesses approach risk. This law mandates that companies adopt a structured approach to managing risks beyond traditional financial risks to encompass operational and regulatory concerns. Such a thorough evaluation of risks is crucial for ensuring accurate reporting—a fundamental goal of SOX. (Morrison, 2004)

SOX also underscores the integration of risk management into governance as an aspect. This integration requires identifying, analyzing, and managing potential risks related to financial reporting. As a result of SOX, organizations have elevated the importance of risk management within their decision-making processes—ensuring that risk considerations are a part of corporate governance. (Spicer, 2006)

Operational risk management has gained prominence under the provisions outlined by SOX. The Sarbanes Oxley Act has affected how companies manage risks. These risks include losses due to inadequate internal procedures, systems, or external events. To comply with SOX requirements, companies must have procedures to identify, monitor, and control these risks. This focus ensures that operational risks are recognized and effectively managed to prevent errors and misstatements. (Morrison, 2004)

Moreover, SOX has highlighted the importance of internal control systems in risk management. Internal controls are implemented to ensure the accuracy and completeness of reporting. SOX mandates the establishment of internal control measures. It requires management to evaluate and report on their effectiveness annually. This requirement has fostered a systematic approach to internal controls, strengthening firms' risk management frameworks. (Spicer, 2006)

SOX has also significantly impacted the audit function and internal controls. The legislation has expanded auditors' responsibilities in the risk management process by reviewing controls and financial reporting. This enhanced audit role is a check and balance mechanism in governance and risk management structures, promoting greater accountability and transparency in financial reporting. (Morrison, 2004)

In conclusion, the Sarbanes Oxley Act has changed risk management practices. SOX has fostered transparency, accountability, and awareness of risks within companies by integrating risk management into the core of governance. It emphasizes the importance of risk and internal control systems. The lasting impact of this legislation is significant as it has reshaped how businesses perceive and handle risks, safeguarding the interests of investors and the public from wrongdoing. (Spicer, 2006)

Evolving Role of IT Auditors

Ever since the Sarbanes Oxley Act (SOX) was passed in 2002, the role of IT auditors has experienced growth. Initially, their focus was mainly on complying with financial reporting requirements. However, SOX brought about a shift by emphasizing the importance of controls for financial reporting, with IT playing a crucial role in this aspect. As a result, IT auditors had to expand their knowledge beyond IT controls and understand how these controls interact with reporting processes. (Teck-Heang & Md. Ali, 2008)

With technology becoming complex and playing a role in operations, the role of IT auditors has become even more essential in evaluating the effectiveness of internal controls. They are responsible for assessing reliability of information systems and ensuring the accuracy of the data they generate. This requires them to dive into data processing and ensure that systems governing transactions function correctly. Thanks to SOX standards, IT auditors' responsibilities have expanded significantly, placing them at the forefront of ensuring compliance and maintaining integrity. (Ajao et al., 2016)

Moreover, as technologies like cloud computing, big data, and AI emerge, IT auditors must have an understanding of these technologies to identify potential risks and effectively govern their settings. This shift reflects the evolving landscape of business and the growing reliance on technology for tasks within companies. Consequently, IT auditors now serve not as compliance officers but as advisors assisting organizations in navigating the complexities of technology when it comes to financial reporting and compliance (Feliciano & Quick, 2022).

Furthermore, in light of Sarbanes Oxley, the role of IT auditors has expanded beyond evaluations of IT controls to encompass an understanding of how technology impacts financial reporting and controls. This change mirrors the environment and the increasing importance of technology in ensuring integrity throughout financial processes.

ETHICAL CONSIDERATIONS IN SOX AND IT AUDITING

The information system process that facilitates the reporting of an organization's financial reporting has to undergo standardized internal and external supervision. SOX mainly aims to improve corporate responsibility, better accuracy, and reliable reporting and should counter any unethical practices in the business (Orin, 2008). It has significantly affected how corporate boards and managers approach financial disclosure and the internal IT system that facilitates the same.

Ethical Frameworks

SOX underscores the need for ethics in the corporate world and mandates a code of ethics for the top leadership to have transparent and honest conduct in reporting. Some of the ethical considerations in IT auditing in the context of SOX are integrity, privacy, transparency, and objectivity (Anand, 2008). For instance, auditors must ensure the confidentiality of the company's data if they have access to important and sensitive information. Any leakage or breach of confidentiality can affect the business operation and competitiveness of the firm in the marketplace. So, it is vital to have a framework to ensure not only the non-audit employees but also the internal audit and external audit team follow guidelines that do not violate the firm's confidential policy.

Another discussion that happens when it comes to ethical practices is the role of government. As a regulator, government agencies can have access to various information and business practices of the firm. These agencies have to ensure that there is no data compromise from their side. In many countries, firms might not have the chance to counter the government's action regarding violations. This would seriously impact their business. So, it is crucial to ensure that the government also follows strict guidelines to ensure firms are not affected by unethical practices.

Challenges and Solutions

One of the critical challenges in this area is a conflict of interest of the parties involved. For instance, there is a conflict of interest when auditors face pressure to ignore the issues in favor of the company being audited. This could be mitigated by making sure auditor independence is maintained and the right penalties are done for an ethical violation. Ethical practices in IT auditing can play a crucial role in developing a fair business environment in an economy.

While implementing SOX in an organization, there could be challenges related to how effective the IT controls are in supporting the provisions of the act. The challenges in designing and implementing effective IT controls that facilitate ethical practices in an organization are many. One, historical evidence suggests that attempts to impose any ethical behavior in corporate financial reports have usually failed. For more than a century, the United States' aim to enforce transparency and integrity has not been successful. While there have been initial advantages that exist for the short term, the corporation and its auditors try adapting new ways to hide financial results and defraud shareholders, customers, and suppliers. Penalties and civil proceedings did not deter the repetition of the crime. Moreover, criminal proceedings for federal white-collar crime did not result in harsh penalties. Also, it is a misconception that advanced electronic systems for reporting limit the chance of unethical behavior. There are three weaknesses in IT systems: 1) Internal control systems are created on the assumption that they are invalid.2) Internal control systems are difficult to design and implement to manage today's complex business environment 3) internal audit is less significant at a time when the system is becoming more sophisticated. Oftentimes IT control may provide opportunities for different types of unethical behavior. One of the cases that illustrates this is the HealthSouth employees case where the employees were able to enter small amounts of transactions but on a larger scale, and they did so by taking advantage of the limit of transaction amount an auditor can check. Without loopholes in IT systems, this fraud would not have happened. So, sometimes poorly designed internal IT controls also negatively impact the firms' reporting. SOX, even though it has made good contributions to overall ethical practices in organizations, sometimes fraudulent activity occurs if IT controls are not effective for a particular firm or business. (Rockness, 2005)

GLOBAL EFFECT OF SOX ACT

Influence Beyond the United States

The SOX act passed in US Congress had implications not just for domestic companies but also for global firms, which had a similar need for stringent regulation for reporting their data. Many foreign companies listed on US stock exchanges had to comply with the same requirement. This made foreign companies follow the same in their country of incorporation as well. It has inspired many foreign governments to adopt similar or modified versions of the SOX Act to improve corporate governance in respective countries (Duarte et al., 2013).

Impact on International Businesses

For international businesses, following the SOX rules was challenging due to variability in the regulatory and legal environment in their respective jurisdictions. The act had rules that were more suitable for the companies operating in the US environment. Compliance costs have significantly increased for many international companies compared to domestic companies due to this.

Global Best Practices

The global influence of SOX has made a pathway to have a unified approach to corporate governance standards and information reporting. It paved the way for adopting IT auditing practices that can help firms comply with financial reporting requirements worldwide. The increased role of IT in financial reporting and strong internal controls have improved the reliability of the financial information provided by companies. This, in a way, made it easier for many foreign firms to form business relationships as there is data transparency. If there were no reliable data and standard financial reporting practices, then companies would have to invest more in reviewing their stakeholders' data.

Criticism of SOX on International Business

The Sarbanes model had conflicts with many nations' cultural as well as governance values. One of the key implications for international companies was section 404 of the act, where publicly traded companies have to maintain internal policies and necessary control mechanisms. Sometimes, compliance was difficult due to contradictory regulatory systems existing in the foreign country. For example, in the US, there is a set of procedures that motivates the employee to whistle-blowing, and at the same time, in Europe, there is a restriction on whistle-blowing. This created a dilemma for many institutions in the beginning. For compliance with two legal requirements, companies had to invest large amounts of capital, including IT spending. Higher compliance was burdensome for many foreign companies. Due to this, many companies had left the US listing in the initial stages. This had an impact on the business of those players who exited the US listing. (Lanois, 2007)

Overall, Sarbanes-Oxley Act had a great positive impact on financial reporting transparency over the last decades; it also had a lot of ramifications in terms of compliance cost and extraterritorial application, which affected global companies, especially firms that had strong business relationships with the United States. Many of the foreign companies have improved their relationship with US partners, and some of them could not survive due to stringent regulations.

Since, SOX has been passed by the US government, there has been advent of many software tools that help companies implement the various sections of SOX efficiently and in a hassle free manner. Listed below are few software tools with the detailed explanation of how they implement various sections of SOX.

HyperProof

Hyperproof, a cloud-based GRC audit software, is designed specifically for managing ongoing compliance operations at scale. With pre-built framework templates to get started quickly, automatic evidence collecting and testing, task management to expedite team communication, and audit preparedness to guarantee that one is always ready for the auditor. Hyperproof adds efficiency to compliance. With the power of Hyperproof, one can eliminate repeated compliance tasks and instead focus on strategic endeavors. To align the company with the Sarbanes-Oxley Act (SOX), Hyperproof can be a useful tool in several ways.

Centralized administration of evidence: By offering a unified platform for managing and storing all evidence associated with the IT controls, Hyperproof eases the strain of manual document gathering and guarantees consistent readiness for audits.

Control mapping and testing: Hyperproof assists in automating testing processes and mapping your IT controls to pertinent SOX sections, which reduces effort and improves accuracy while saving time.

Risk assessment and reporting: One can manage the status of remediation efforts, identify and rank SOX-related risks, and provide thorough reports for both internal and external stakeholders with Hyperproof's risk register and reporting tools.

Ongoing observation: Hyperproof interfaces with several systems to offer instantaneous or very instantaneous insights into IT setup, permitting the ongoing observation of SOX-critical controls and anticipatory detection of possible problems.

Cooperation and communication: Hyperproof makes it easier for internal teams and external auditors to work together, which promotes improved communication and streamlined audit procedures.

Clear audit trail and documentation: Hyperproof maintains an automated log of all modifications made to evidence and controls, which is necessary for SOX compliance. Here are some specific ways Hyperproof can be used for different SOX sections:

Section 302 - Management's Responsibility for Financial Reports: Hyperproof assists with tracking remedial actions for found control vulnerabilities, creating reports for management review, and documenting and upholding internal control over financial reporting.
Section 404 - Internal Control Over Financial Reporting: One can automate control testing processes, create, implement, and test internal controls with Hyperproof's assistance, and monitor progress toward SOX compliance.
Section 802 - Public Company Accounting Oversight Board: By keeping audit trails, fostering effective contact with external auditors, and documenting one's internal control system.

One reason would be that when measuring the costs of a program, it can be difficult to get an accurate accounting. Salaries and benefits for those in a compliance department or doing compliance-related tasks are easy enough to determine, as are the costs for new compliance-related software and technologies or consultants and lawyers to design and implement new training programs. But outside of that, those in compliance often fail to accurately calculate the costs of what they are asking employees to do as part of a compliance program. For example, every hour of yearly compliance training an employee is required to undergo costs a company money in real labor dollars, not to mention opportunity costs. The same is true for every form that is necessary to fill out or guidance to be read to meet a compliance obligation. Moreover, to get a truly accurate cost calculation, one must measure the labor and other resources it takes to fix compliance violations that are discovered. Few companies take this comprehensive approach to compliance costs, and even fewer regulators and academics recognize it. (Haugh & Bedi, 2023)

StandardFusion
It drastically enhances the company's SOX compliance posture by utilizing Hyperproof's capabilities. This will lower risks, save time and money, and guarantee more transparency and accurate financial reporting. StandardFusion is a platform devoted to resolving actual information security issues, and it may assist your company in meeting all of its GRC requirements. Similar to Hyperproof, StandardFusion can help the company comply with the Sarbanes-Oxley Act (SOX) in a number of ways. How to do it is as follows:
Compliance with SOX for IT General Controls (ITGCs): StandardFusion provides pre-built ITGCs that save manual implementation time and guarantee uniform compliance throughout your IT ecosystem. StandardFusion automates a number of SOX control testing processes, increasing productivity and freeing up staff for more difficult jobs.

Gap analysis and remediation tracking: To ensure continual improvement, StandardFusion finds holes in the SOX compliance and offers a platform for managing and recording remedial efforts.

Centralized evidence repository: StandardFusion reduces the possibility of missing documents and streamlines audits by centrally storing all SOX-related data.

Real-time insights and continuous monitoring: StandardFusion gives proactive access to real-time information about the IT environment, enabling one to spot and resolve possible SOX compliance problems before they become serious.

Thorough audit reports: StandardFusion produces thorough audit reports that satisfy SEC and PCAOB regulations, guaranteeing openness and confidence among stakeholders.

Section 302: StandardFusion facilitates management's accountability for SOX compliance by aiding in the documentation and upkeep of internal control over financial reporting.

Section 404: StandardFusion makes it easier to comply with Section 404 regulations by automating control testing and supplying proof of internal control over financial reporting. Section 404 deals with management's evaluation of internal controls. It mandates that each organization's annual report include an 'internal control report' that (1) states management's responsibility for creating and sustaining a sufficient internal control framework and processes for financial reporting and (2) includes an evaluation of the performance of internal control structures and procedures for financial reporting as of the close of the organization's fiscal year. External auditors must verify and report on management's evaluation of internal controls. This attestation must adhere to the PCAOB's guidelines for attestation engagements. (Braganza, 2006).

Section 802: By enhancing contact with external auditors, StandardFusion's audit trail and reporting features assist in meeting PCAOB reporting standards.

Onspring

As a full-featured GRC (Governance, Risk & Compliance) platform, Onspring can help to comply with Sarbanes-Oxley (SOX) in a number of ways.

Control Catalog and Mapping: With Onspring, One can track the efficacy of financial and IT controls, centralize them, and map them to pertinent SOX sections. This exemplifies a documented internal control environment and helps with effective control management.

Automated Control Testing: To decrease human labor and increase testing precision, Onspring offers automated testing capabilities for a number of SOX controls. In addition to increasing the control environment, this can save time and resources.

Risk Assessment and Mitigation: With Onspring, one can pinpoint and rank the risks that have the potential to affect SOX compliance. With the help of its risk assessment tools, the company can create mitigation plans and monitor their advancement, exhibiting proactive risk management.

Workflow Automation: Control testing, tracking remediation, reporting, and other SOX compliance workflows are all automated using Onspring. This increases productivity, lowers error rates, and guarantees that jobs are completed on time.

Centralized Evidence Management: Onspring maintains a single repository for all SOX-related evidence, such as remediation records, test results, and control documents. This lowers the possibility of missing documentation and streamlines audits.

Continuous Monitoring: By offering real-time insights into a company's financial and IT systems, Onspring makes it possible to continuously monitor possible problems with SOX compliance. This enables the corganization to take proactive measures to resolve issues before they worsen.

Pre-built SOX Templates: To ensure compliance with SOX regulations, Onspring provides pre-built templates and workflows. Doing so can guarantee that one is adhering to best practices and can save time.

Reporting and Audit Trail: Onspring maintains an accurate audit trail for SOX compliance by automatically monitoring all modifications made to data and controls. Comprehensive reports are produced by its reporting tools for both internal and external stakeholders.

PCAOB and SEC Compliance: By meeting PCAOB and SEC regulations, Onspring's features and reporting capabilities boost stakeholder confidence and transparency.

Section 302: The risk assessment and control management solutions from Onspring assist management in carrying out their obligation to ensure the accuracy of financial reporting.

Section 404: Effective internal control over financial reporting is supported by Onspring's automated control testing, continuous monitoring, and reporting features.

Section 802: To ensure compliance with PCAOB reporting standards and to promote effective communication with external auditors, Onspring offers audit trail and reporting options.

SafetyCulture

SafetyCulture can indirectly support Sarbanes-Oxley (SOX) compliance in a number of ways, especially with regard to Section 404 of the Act, which addresses internal controls over financial reporting, even if it isn't specifically designed to do so. SafetyCulture assists in the identification and management of operational risks, particularly those that may have an influence on financial reporting. One can lessen the possibility of monetary losses and misstatements by taking proactive measures to address safety dangers and occurrences.

Data Integrity and Traceability: SafetyCulture's data gathering and reporting tools can offer an audit trail of safety-related actions that are documented, proving openness and conformity to protocols. This could be an important proof of internal financial reporting controls.

Compliance Management: By lowering the possibility of fines and penalties, SafetyCulture can assist in managing adherence to pertinent safety standards, which may have an indirect effect on financial reporting.

Incident Reporting and Investigation: SafetyCulture makes it easier to report and look into safety problems in real-time, which enables prompt correction and reduces the possibility of financial damages. This indicates a robust system of internal control.

Documentation and Training: SafetyCulture offers resources for training staff members and recording safety protocols. By promoting uniformity and adherence to internal controls, these measures can lower the possibility of mistakes or omissions in financial reporting.

SafetyCulture assists companies in creating a culture of safety, which can improve risk management practices across all departments, including finance. Indirectly, this can support SOX compliance by lowering risks that could impact financial reporting. There is growing evidence that employers are realizing that maintaining exceptional safety performance helps them obtain contracts and keep clients. Furthermore, in response to the Sarbanes-Oxley Act of 2002, a law requiring corporate accountability to shareholders, management is expected to control safety and health risks, not only because companies have a moral obligation to protect workers but also because companies have a financial obligation to avoid financial disaster. (Crossman, 2008)

Continuous Improvement: SafetyCulture's data analysis tools can help with continuous process improvements in safety and, in the long run, strengthen internal controls over financial reporting by spotting trends and patterns in safety occurrences.

CASE STUDIES AND TYING SECTIONS

Enron

The Enron scandal occurred in the early 2000s, impacting the American energy corporation known as Enron Corporation. Enron was previously regarded as one of the most successful companies in the United States but eventually faced bankruptcy due to extensive accounting fraud and corporate misconduct. Established in 1985, Enron swiftly grew to become one of America's most respected corporations operating in sectors such as energy, natural gas, and communications. To manipulate its records and inflate profits while concealing debt, Enron executed a network of financial transactions. It utilized off-balance sheet partnerships called special purpose entities to keep debt off its statements. Enron employed an accounting practice called mark-to-market accounting. This technique allowed them to record income value as if it had already been earned. Unfortunately, this method led to an overestimation of Enron's profitability.

As the truth about Enron's position emerged, the company experienced a sharp decline in its stock price. Numerous employees were laid off. Investors suffered losses amounting to billions of dollars. On December 2nd, 2001, Enron filed for bankruptcy. This event marked one of the largest bankruptcies in U.S. History at that time. As a result of the collapse, the accounting firm Arthur Andersen, which served as Enron's auditor, was dissolved.

Connection

Section 302 requires CEOs and CFOs to certify the accuracy of their companies' financial statements. Their responsibility is to ensure that these statements are free from errors and provide a representation of the company's financial position. This rule was established in response to concerns raised by Enron's practices and aims to hold top executives accountable for maintaining reporting accuracy. (Li, 2010)

WorldCom

Another notable corporate scandal that occurred in the 2000s involved WorldCom, a significant telecommunications company in the United States at that time. The scandal exposed instances of accounting practices and financial misconduct, ultimately contributing to the downfall of the company. WorldCom, headquartered in Clinton, Mississippi, experienced growth throughout the 1990s through mergers and acquisitions. By the 2000s, it had become one of the largest players in the telecommunications industry. Similar to Enron's situation, WorldCom also engaged in accounting fraud with an aim to artificially boost earnings and hide issues.

The corporation made the mistake of classifying general expenses as capital expenditures, which resulted in spreading costs over a period and showing higher reported profits. WorldCom's management, led by CEO Bernard Ebbers, was responsible for treating costs associated with line charges as assets of expenses. This tactic allowed WorldCom to inflate its assets and report profits more than it actually earned. The accounting scandal at WorldCom was enormous. Caused billions of dollars in losses. Despite experiencing setbacks, the company still managed to record profits through fraudulent means. This scandal ranks among the largest and most egregious commercial scandals in US history.

Eventually, the irregularities were exposed, leading to WorldCom's filing for bankruptcy on July 21, 2002. At that time, it became the largest bankruptcy case in US history. The bankruptcy had far-reaching consequences impacting employees, shareholders, and the telecommunications industry as a whole.

Connection

In connection with this issue, Section 404 of the Sarbanes Oxley Act (SOX) mandates corporations to establish and maintain controls for financial reporting purposes. Management is required to evaluate and report on the effectiveness of these controls. During the WorldCom scandal, the company engaged in accounting fraud by capitalizing on costs that should have been treated as expenses. Compliance with SOX Section 404 helps organizations prevent acts by implementing robust internal controls. WorldCom's failure to adhere to these guidelines highlights the role of internal controls in preventing financial inaccuracies. (Lyke & Jickling, 2002)

Arthur Andersen

The Arthur Andersen controversy is closely tied to the Enron scandal as they were the accounting firm for auditing Enron's statements. Arthur Andersen, being one of the five audit and accounting firms globally, faced consequences due to its association with Enron. This scandal not only led to the downfall of Arthur Andersen but also added to the overall aftermath of the Enron debacle. For years, Arthur Andersen served as Enron's auditor, conducting audits and providing consultancy services. However, despite Enron's involvement in irregularities and fraudulent activities, Arthur Andersen failed to identify and report these issues, raising concerns about the effectiveness of their auditing processes.

As investigations into Enron operations progressed, it came to light that Arthur Andersen had deliberately destroyed a number of documents relevant to Enron's audit. This raised suspicions about cover-ups and obstruction of justice through document deletion. In March 2002, the US Department of Justice charged Arthur Andersen with obstructing justice by disposing of documents related to their audit on Enron. The destruction of records was carried out with intent to impede investigations into Enron's misconduct, according to the indictment.

The indictment and subsequent legal battles had consequences for Arthur Andersen. The company experienced a loss of business, and its reputation suffered damage. In June 2002, Arthur Andersen was declared guilty of obstructing justice, effectively ending the firm's career as an accounting firm. The scandal involving Arthur Andersen had an impact on the accounting industry, leading to increased scrutiny of the relationships between audit firms and their clients. It raised concerns about conflicts of interest when an auditing firm provides both auditing and advisory services to the client.

Connection

In connection with this, Section 201 of the Sarbanes Oxley Act (SOX) restricts auditors from offering non-audit services to their audit customers. This provision aims to ensure auditor independence and objectivity. Arthur Andersen faced allegations regarding compromised independence as an Enron auditor. The company was accused of both auditing and consulting for Enron, which created a conflict of interest. SOX Section 201 addresses this concern by placing limitations on auditors' ability to provide non-audit services to their audit clients. Section 802 of SOX criminalizes actions that obstruct, impede, or influence an investigation by altering, destroying, hiding, falsifying, or creating entries in any record, document, or tangible object.

CONCLUSION

This comprehensive study delves into the impact of the Sarbanes Oxley Act (SOX) on governance, specifically focusing on IT audits. SOX, enacted in response to scandals, brought about significant changes in terms of corporate responsibility, transparency, and financial integrity. It mandates documentation, testing, and reporting to ensure financial statements with a particular emphasis on robust internal controls within the realm of IT. The reach of this act extends beyond U.S. Borders as it establishes standards for governance and IT audit procedures. Numerous case studies demonstrate that SOX has bolstered the role of IT audits by integrating them into the financial IT auditing process and enhancing governance practices. Not only has this act curbed misconduct, but it has also reinforced the connection between financial accuracy, IT governance, and ethical conduct within corporations. In this way, it plays a role in promoting stability and inspiring investor confidence.

REFERENCES

Act, S. O. (2002). Sarbanes-oxley act. *Washington DC*. https://citeseerx.ist.psu.edu/document?repid=rep1&type=pdf&doi=1e106d64c637d9c4c3860d6cbde5db7392689d94

Ajao, O. S., Olamide, J. O., & Temitope, A. A. (2016). Evolution and development of auditing. *Unique Journal of Business Management Research, 3*(1), 032-040.

Alexander, C. R., Bauguess, S. W., Bernile, G., Lee, Y. H. A., & Marietta-Westberg, J. (2013). Economic effects of SOX Section 404 compliance: *A corporate insider perspective.Journal ofAccounting and Economics*, 56(2-3), 267–290. DOI: 10.1016/j.jacceco.2013.09.002

Altinay. (n.d.). https://www.researchgate.net/profile/Aysenur-Altinay/publication/325546334_THE_IMPORTANCE_OF_SOX_COMPLIANCE_FOR_AMERICAN_COMPANIES_125/links/5b151ce0a6fdcc4611e2a3a9/THE-IMPORTANCE-OF-SOX-COMPLIANCE-FOR-AMERICAN-COMPANIES-125.pdf

Anand, S. (2008). Information security implications of Sarbanes-Oxley. *Information Security Journal: A Global Perspective, 17*(2), 75-79. DOI: 10.1080/19393550801953372

Anderson, U. L., Christ, M. H., Johnstone, K. M., & Rittenberg, L. E. (2012). A post-SOX examination of factors associated with the size of internal audit functions. *Accounting Horizons*, 26(2), 167–191. DOI: 10.2308/acch-50115

Ashbaugh-Skaife, H., Collins, D. W., Kinney, W. R.Jr, & LaFond, R. (2009). The effect of SOX internal control deficiencies on firm risk and cost of equity. *Journal of Accounting Research*, 47(1), 1–43. DOI: 10.1111/j.1475-679X.2008.00315.x

Baxter, C. (2022). The Impact of SOX on the Industry 20 Years Ago and Today. *ISACA Journal*, (1). https://www.isaca.org/resources/isaca-journal/issues/2022/volume-1/the-impact-of-sox-on-the-industry-20-years-ago-and-today

Braganza, A., & Desouza, K. C. (2006). Implementing section 404 of the Sarbanes Oxley Act: recommendations for information Systems organizations.

Buckberg, E., Foster, T. S., Miller, R. I., & Werner, A. (2003). Recent Trends in Securities Class Action Litigation: Will Enron and Sarbanes-Oxley Change the Tides. *NERA Economic Consulting*. https://www.nera.com/image/6143.pdf

Chambers, D., & Payne, J. (2011). Audit quality and accrual persistence: Evidence from the pre-and post-Sarbanes-Oxley periods. *Managerial Auditing Journal*, 26(5), 437–456. DOI: 10.1108/02686901111129580

Charles, S. L., Glover, S. M., & Sharp, N. Y. (2010). The association between financial reporting risk and audit fees before and after the historic events surrounding SOX. *Auditing*, 29(1), 15–39. DOI: 10.2308/aud.2010.29.1.15

Coates, J. C.IV. (2007). The goals and promise of the Sarbanes–Oxley Act. *The Journal of Economic Perspectives*, 21(1), 91–116. DOI: 10.1257/jep.21.1.91

Coates, J. C., & Srinivasan, S. (2014). SOX after ten years: A multidisciplinary review. *Accounting Horizons*, 28(3), 627–671. DOI: 10.2308/acch-50759

Crossman, D. C. (2008). *The impact of safety culture on worker motivation and the economic bottom line* (Doctoral dissertation, Capella University).

Damianides, M. (2005). Sarbanes-Oxley and IT governance: New guidance on IT control and compliance. *Information Systems Management*, 22(1), 77–85. DOI: 10 .1201/1078/44912.22.1.20051201/85741.9

Desmond, N. (2002). Repeal the Sarbanes-Oxley tax now! *Business 2.0, 3*(December), 75.

Duarte, J., Kong, K., Siegel, S., & Young, L. (2014). The impact of the Sarbanes–Oxley Act on shareholders and managers of foreign firms. *Review of Finance*, 18(1), 417–455. DOI: 10.1093/rof/rft008

Eckstein, E. (2021, May 24). 5 key Takeaways After 20 Years of Sarbanes-Oxley. Saint Joseph's University. https://www.sju.edu/news/5-key-takeaways-after-20-years-sarbanes-oxley

Eichar, S. W. (2009). Sarbanes Oxley Act of 2002: Will it Be Effective in Preventing Another Enron Scandal? *Accountancy*, 130(1311), 13.

Farrell, H., & Farrell, B. J. (1998). The language of business codes of ethics: Implications of knowledge and power. *Journal of Business Ethics*, 17, 587–601.

Feliciano, C., & Quick, R. (2022). Innovative information technology in auditing: Auditors' perceptions of future importance and current auditor expertise. *Accounting in Europe*, 19(2), 311–331. DOI: 10.1080/17449480.2022.2046283

Gong, G., Ke, B., & Yu, Y. (2009). SOX-mandated internal control deficiency disclosure under Section 302 and earnings quality: Evidence from cross-listed firms. DOI: 10.2139/ssrn.1028620

Gordon, I. M., & Nazari, J. A. (2018). Review of SOX in the business ethics literature. *Managerial Auditing Journal*, 33(5), 470–502. DOI: 10.1108/MAJ-08-2017-1629

Gupta, P. P., Sami, H., & Zhou, H. (2018). Do companies with effective internal controls over financial reporting benefit from Sarbanes–Oxley sections 302 and 404? *Journal of Accounting, Auditing & Finance*, 33(2), 200–227. DOI: 10.1177/0148558X16663091

Haugh, T., & Bedi, S. (2023). Valuing Corporate Compliance.

Hochberg, Y. V., Sapienza, P., & Vissing-Jørgensen, A. (2009). A lobbying approach to evaluating the Sarbanes-Oxley Act of 2002. *Journal of Accounting Research*, 47(2), 519–583. DOI: 10.1111/j.1475-679X.2009.00321.x

Hoitash, R., & Hoitash, U. (2009). The role of audit committees in managing relationships with external auditors after SOX: Evidence from the USA. *Managerial Auditing Journal*, 24(4), 368–397. DOI: 10.1108/02686900910948206

Holmstrom, B., & Kaplan, S. N. (2009). The state of US corporate governance: What's right and what's wrong? In *US Corporate Governance* (pp. 26–47). Columbia University Press. DOI: 10.7312/chew14856-002

Kahn, J. (2003). Blowing it. *Fortune*, 148(3), 42.

Kim, M. S., Dandu, J., & Iren, P. (2019). The effect of SOX on audit quality. *Journal of Financial Crime*, 26(3), 897–909. DOI: 10.1108/JFC-08-2018-0088

Klamm, B. K., & Watson, M. W. (2009). SOX 404 reported internal control weaknesses: A test of COSO framework components and information technology. *Journal of information systems, 23*(2), 1-23. *Retrieved from Journal of Information Systems*, 23(2), 1–23.

Krishnan, J., Rama, D., & Zhang, Y. (2008). Costs to comply with SOX Section 404. *Auditing*, 27(1), 169–186. DOI: 10.2308/aud.2008.27.1.169

Lanois, P. (2007). Between a Rock and a Hard Place: The Sarbanes-Oxley Act and Its Global Impact. *University of Pennsylvania Journal of International Law*, 5(4), 1–19.

Leech, T., & Leech, L. (2011). Preventing the next wave of unreliable financial reporting: Why US Congress should amend Section 404 of the Sarbanes–Oxley Act. *International Journal of Disclosure and Governance*, 8(4), 295–322. DOI: 10.1057/jdg.2011.18

Leih, M. J. (2009). *Regulatory impact on IT governance: A multiple case study on the Sarbanes-Oxley Act*. The Claremont Graduate University.

Li, Y. (2010). The case analysis of the scandal of Enron. *International Journal of Business and Management*, 5(10), 37. DOI: 10.5539/ijbm.v5n10p37

Lyke, B., & Jickling, M. (2002, August). WorldCom: The accounting scandal. In *Congressional Research Service Report for Congress, August* (Vol. 29, pp. 1-6).

McConnell, D. K.Jr, & Banks, G. Y. (2003). How Sarbanes-Oxley will change the audit process. *Journal of Accountancy*, 196(3), 49. https://www.journalofaccountancy.com/issues/2003/sep/howsarbanesoxleywillchangetheauditprocess.html

McLean, B., & Elkind, P. (2013). *The smartest guys in the room: The amazing rise and scandalous fall of Enron*. Penguin.

Mehta, A. (2010). An approach toward Sarbanes-oxley ITGC Risk assessment. *ISACA Journal, 5*, 15. https://www.isaca.org/resources/isaca-journal/past-issues/2010/an-approach-toward-sarbanes-oxley-itgc-risk-assessment

Melancon, B. C. (2002). A new accounting culture. *Journal of Accountancy*, 194(4), 27.

Miller, R. I., & Pashkoff, P. H. (2002). Regulations under the sarbanes-oxley act. *Journal of Accountancy*, 194(4), 33–37.

Morrison, A. D. (2004, July). Sarbanes-Oxley, corporate governance and operational risk. In *Proceedings of the Sarbanes-Oxford Conference held at Said Business School,* University of Oxford (Vol. 22).

Orin, R. M. (2008). Ethical guidance and constraint under the Sarbanes-Oxley Act of 2002. *Journal of Accounting, Auditing & Finance*, 23(1), 141–171. DOI: 10.1177/0148558X0802300108

Pryshchepa, O. (2021). Disciplining entrenched managers through corporate governance reform: Implications for risk-taking behavior. *Corporate Governance*, 29(4), 328–351. DOI: 10.1111/corg.12370

Public Law 107–204, 1. (2002, July 30). Retrieved from https://www.govinfo.gov/content/pkg/PLAW-107publ204/pdf/PLAW-107publ204.pdf

Public Law 112-158. (2012, August 10). Securities Exchange Act Of 1934. Retrieved from https://www.nyse.com/publicdocs/nyse/regulation/nyse/sea34.pdf

Public Law 117–263. (2022, December 23). Ecanctment: Securities Act of 1933.

Rockness, H., & Rockness, J. (2005). Legislated ethics: From Enron to Sarbanes-Oxley, the impact on corporate America. *Journal of Business Ethics*, 57(1), 31–54. DOI: 10.1007/s10551-004-3819-0

SEC. (2003, January 22). Commission Adopts Rules Strengthening Auditor Independence. Commission adopts Rules Strengthening Auditor Independence. https://www.sec.gov/news/press/2003-9.htm

Šimková, E. (2005). Impact of the Sarbanes-Oxley Act on the system of internal controls and IS audit. *Systémová Integrace*, (3), 92-111. https://scholar.archive.org/work/vahyopbrgveoro6aa74ef6ojke/access/wayback/http://www.cssi.cz/cssi/system/files/all/simkova.pdf

Spicer, R. L. (2006). *Enterprise risk management and Sarbanes-Oxley Compliance: a model of convergence in accounting audit practice*. Capella University.

Squires, S. E., & Squires, S. (2003). *Inside Arthur Andersen: shifting values, unexpected consequences*. FT Press.

Stephens, N. M. (2008). *Corporate governance quality and internal control reporting under Sox*. The University of Arizona.

Stephens, N. M. (2011). External auditor characteristics and internal control reporting under SOX section 302. *Managerial Auditing Journal*, 26(2), 114–129. DOI: 10.1108/02686901111095001

Stimson, W. A. (2005). Sarbanes-Oxley and ISO 9000. *Quality control and applied statistics, 50*(4), 409.

Teck-Heang, L. E. E., & Ali, A. M. (2008). The evolution of auditing: An analysis of the historical development. *Journal of Modern Accounting and auditing, 4*(12), 1.

Webb, E. (2008). Sarbanes-Oxley compliance and violation: An empirical study. *Review of Accounting and Finance*, 7(1), 5–23. DOI: 10.1108/14757700810853824

Zhang, I. X. (2007). Economic consequences of the Sarbanes–Oxley Act of 2002. *Journal of Accounting and Economics*, 44(1-2), 74–115. DOI: 10.1016/j.jacceco.2007.02.002

Chapter 5

Identifying Opportunities in the Enhancement of an Organization's Third-Party Risk Posture

Abinash Jena
https://orcid.org/0009-0001-5103-2956
University at Buffalo, SUNY, USA

Annie Bhardwaj
University at Buffalo, SUNY, USA

Rajdeep Murmu
University at Buffalo, SUNY, USA

Prarthana Seeralan
University at Buffalo, SUNY, USA

Manish Gupta
University at Buffalo, SUNY, USA

Raj Sharman
https://orcid.org/0000-0001-5838-7330
University at Buffalo, SUNY, USA

ABSTRACT

As organizations increasingly rely on third-party entities, managing third-party risks has become crucial for overall risk governance. This chapter explores third-party risk management (TPRM), highlighting past events, challenges, opportunities in due diligence, and evolving strategies for safeguarding organizational interests in a complex, interconnected business landscape. The study reviews the current state of TPRM, recent security breaches, and challenges in managing third-party risks. It identifies common pitfalls and gaps in existing frameworks, focusing on due diligence processes, risk assessment, and mitigation techniques. Insights into various third-party risks, including cybersecurity vulnerabilities, data privacy concerns, and regulatory compliance, are provided through an extensive literature review and case analyses. Additionally, the chapter examines the role of technology, agreements, and

DOI: 10.4018/979-8-3693-4211-4.ch005

key indicators in enhancing TPRM practices, aiming to streamline risk assessments and response mechanisms.

INTRODUCTION

In the last few years organisations have shown a large dependency on third-party vendors because outsourcing the work is helping companies to be more efficient and productive, thereby generating more revenue and clients (Rasner, 2021). So, outsourcing has become the newly accepted way of performing the job and it will continue to grow in the coming years. Therefore, the risks associated with third parties will play an important role in framing the security posture of any organisations in future (Rasner, 2021). The security posture and maturity of a firm managing third party risks is majorly governed by the complexity or simplicity of the policies and the procedures that a company is governed by. The challenges associated with vendor relationships in the threat landscape is impacted by the role played by external entities, suppliers, and service providers and effectively handling the third-party risks will depend on a comprehensive all-round approach to ensure risks are mitigated that will ensure business continuity and help compliance with laws and regulations (Jaeger, 2018).

A malicious agent has a better chance of stealing protected data of an organization by going after third party service providers. So, the process of managing vendor risks plays a big role in deciding the strength and posture of a firm in managing cyber risks. In the current scenario, as per statistics, an average company is connected with 600 vendors in some way or the other. A recent statistic showed that three nation-state APT attacks that took advantage of holes in supply chain cybersecurity occurred at the end of 2020 in a single month (Rasner, 2021). Vietnam and Mongolia were the targets of two of them. Even though more victims are being found, the damage and extent of the SolarWinds Orion exploit are still unknown, but it has affected significant government systems and well-known technology companies worldwide. It is obvious that the supply chain is being targeted and weaponized by the advanced persistent actors, or hackers. They security posture of third parties is the weakest link to their actual targets.

On the contrary, managing third party risks have not been given priority in the pecking order. There is lack in collaboration in the cybersecurity and the third-party risks management team and the objective has never been consistent with the goals of the company (Medrano, 2022). Performing security mitigation operations in different silos doesn't help the firm rather weaken the security state. The same thing occurs when a firm try to be compliant to avoid regulatory fines rather than managing the vendor risks to avoid breaches because just being compliant doesn't necessarily means the company cannot be breached through third parties. The secure and successful organisations do not only comply to regulations but also put the extra effort in addressing the potential risks that could adversely impact the organisations. So, there is lack of awareness in majority of companies about the severity of risks and outcomes associated with third parties which led to inadequate risk mitigation approaches thereby reducing the security state of a company. In terms of performing due diligence, as per a study in Ponemon Institute, only 40 percent of the organisations perform any kind of cybersecurity due diligence (Klein, 2007). This data shows that there is lack of expertise in the field of Third-Party Risk Management and companies need to show will to tackle vendor risks. Therefore, addressing these gaps require a comprehensive and a structured approach which will need to create a risk management framework, investment in resources, training and awareness, and a commitment to continuous improvement.

LITERATURE REVIEW

Historical Perspective

Third-party risk is the set of risks that include challenges and opportunities in managing risks relating to external service providers, distributors, partners, and other parties (Warren, 2014).There are different challenges in the proper third-party risk management, such as unclear ownership of responsibilities, reactive approach, and the complexity of global supply chains. It lays much emphasis on the role of internal audit in filling such gaps through objective assessments, evaluation of compliance with regulations and policies and identification of improvement areas.

As organizations depend more on cloud service providers for important infrastructure and services, they should also consider and manage well third-party risks which arise from such compliance. Some of the security issues of cloud computing are data breach, data loss, traffic hijacking, and insecure interfaces (Kashyap & Sharma, 2015). The risks, however, cause direct threats, but also implications for third party relationships and security of shared cloud environments. An organization should have a conducted its thorough research and diligence work as it selects a cloud service provider and that measures put in place are in line with the industry standards and best practices.

In order to simplify risk assessment methods, this includes developing service and third-party risk evaluations. The key role of internal audit in TPRM including, monitoring activities, assurance on governance and risk management effectiveness, and integration between business units and TPRM teams. Internal auditors are expected to assess program governance, risk escalation processes, and documentation completeness (Rose & Frio, 2017).

In 2017, the high-profile data breaches that happened at Yahoo, Equifax and SEC, which accent the need for improving third party risk assessment to all organizations. The Opus and Ponemon Institute's study gives worrying statistics. According to the studied companies, the report shows that 56% of companies experience third-party breaches while 84% do not have inventory or oversight of third-party relationships (Mont, 2017). It is critical to know about third-party relationships, borrowing controls, and adapting risk assessments according to the nature of the partnership.

Resilience based approach underlines the need to handle end to end services considering a balance of investments between protection and sustainability, on selecting the critical activities and cybersecurity requirements and establishing consistent processes. The resilience-based roadmap goes for the assignment of prioritization roles, implementation of repeatable procedures, implementation of requirements tracking approach, balancing proactive and reactive activities, and reframing of long-term alliance relationships as all-encompassing entities (Haller & Wallen, 2016). It works on partnership between external and internal bodies, utilizes collaborative risk management approach and also applies NIST CSF, to effectively manage risks with third parties (National Institute of Standards and Technology (NIST), n.d.).

Polling by Opus Global, RapidRatings, and Deloitte shows significant risk management challenges in companies that go beyond risks stemming from their direct suppliers (Jaeger, 2018). Among the major findings was lack of knowledge regarding risks from fourth- and nth-party connectivity, personnel and financial issues, the need of measurable data to support budget allocation, the role of automation in monitoring and auditing third-party connections, the vitality of centralized risk management to enhance productivity and service quality, the need for collaboration across business functions for efficient risk management and to share information.

The main features of the General Data Protection Regulation (GDPR) are individual rights expansion, the need for data protection officers, privacy by design, privacy impact assessments, and data breach notifications according to the analysis of the program's impact on third-party risk management (European Union, n.d.). GDPR has an effect on third party interactions by imposing additional obligations on organisations like data controllers and processors. Risk management from third parties can realize GDPR compliance by a five-step process which covers data mapping, policies and contractual documents, a thorough risk assessment, audits, remediation, and ongoing monitoring (Andreisova, 2020).

Current State of Research

Nowadays the companies are aware of the cybersecurity because the modern businesses are reliant on the outside organisations, so fortification of security inside company's internal network is not enough because the dependencies carry the hackers' new opportunities for the attack. With the highest cybersecurity measures in place, the organization's data, clients, and reputation are at risk even third parties (Keskin et al., 2021).

Financial industry is usually the true target of virtually any cyber-attack, and the vendors are typically its source (Bronson, 2022). Vendors are most frequently attacked because they are easier targets of infiltration allowing attackers to pivot to the network of the original target organization. Shortcomings in vendor vetting during the onboarding, a lack of understanding of third-party risk, being oblivious to active risk detection, a lack of periodic assessment of the existing vendors, and unfamiliarity with creating information security policies and procedures are the five typical weaknesses of third-party risk management.

In 2022, nearly two thirds of health care organizations suffered a data breach via remote access, contributed by third parties. 1 in 3 data breaches in healthcare and 1 in 5 all breaches are the responsibility of healthcare affiliates. For effective patient data protection, a TPRM program should be in place throughout the whole business relationships, i.e., vendor selection, onboarding, and termination phases. Managed security service providers pick up vendor assessments to maintain the aligned groundwork for all vendors evaluated (Adams, 2023).

Superannuation companies outsource many accountings and also cybersecurity services from the third parties, but the outsourcing has many create complexities and hazardous transactions. By thorough vendor due diligence, clear contractual agreements, and regular compliance check-ups, superannuation organizations are to guarantee the long-term stability and member safety (Bronson, 2022, Keizer, 2022, Keskin et. Al., 2021). The digital era redefined the financial industry where cybersecurity becomes a very leitmotif of the third-party partnerships. Superannuation organisations must plan for the cybersecurity protocols, have a business continuity plan and it must also follow both industry-specific and general regulatory standards. Employee awareness and constant improvement are very central to the TPRM success (Dawodu, 2024). A symbiosis of cybersecurity and accounting could possibly be one of the many ways to deal with complex risks much better and achieve the resilience. Success in the finance industry has always relied on the risk management.

Common Risk Management Frameworks for TPRM

Risk management has become crucial as it helps in the identification of risks, evaluation of risks, prevention or minimization of the identified risks. There are different approaches that are used by conceptual frameworks such as COSO-ERM, NIST CSF, ISO 31000, and COBIT (Efe, 2023). Even though all these frameworks are designed to facilitate the management of risks, they have varying scopes and approaches as well as their suitability in specific industries.

Strategy and performance are the two fundamental components of Enterprise Risk Management (ERM) according to the 2004 ERM framework update by the Committee of Sponsoring Organizations of the Treadway Commission (COSO). Performance, Strategy and Objective Setting, Governance and Culture, Performance is included in the five areas of the updated framework. Performance is the determination, evaluation and the reporting of those vulnerabilities that will put at the risk the strategic objectives and the business' goals. Governance creates the organizational voice. Culture is associated with morality and risk concepts. Risk appetite and Strategy and Objective Setting are tied to the Strategy. The new paradigm suggests that risk management is a talent and a way of thinking which can help with the decisions and not a bad that needs to be eradicated. Internal auditors should be retrained on the matter and every risk response should be considered during the situation analysis (Anderson, 2017).

The International Organization for Standardization created the ISO 31000: 2009 Risk Management Standard which is very famous and widely used in the engineering project community (Murphy & Yates, 2009). The framework includes 11 risk management principles with a revised definition of risk that stresses the aspects of decision making, value creation, uncertainty handling and organisation, timeliness and systematicity. Risk management guidelines are applauded in terms of how comprehensive they are, advising that implementing them is of more importance than just the risk manager activities (Olechowski et al., 2016).

The classical notion and the procedural logic are the foundation of ISO 31000 risk management system. It defines a systematic process of risk assessment, analysis, and selection. The framework heavily stresses the importance of continuous communication, documentation, and measure review. Risk management process must be reviewed periodically to accommodate new hazards in addition to changes in internal and external environments. An ISO 31000 risk management system enhances a company s efficacy as it identifies and promotes awareness of its main hazards (Lalonde & Boiral, 2012). It specifies the duties for the organizations e.g. coming up with mitigation plans, informing the participants and ensuring the availability of resources. One of the major objectives of the standard is to make risk management systems fit to each company situation, considering the position of stakeholders, politics, and culture. Nevertheless, some obstacles, which may be, the absence of systems, inappropriate use, insufficient funding, and inadequate involvement of human resource may most likely prevent implementation of ISO 31000.

In 2013, President Obama ordered NIST to build security guidelines for online networks used by critical infrastructure organization (Sargent, 2012). Centred on voluntary technology neutral guidelines for information security the Framework document is relevant to the water supply, chemicals manufacture, utilities, healthcare, and agriculture industry. A paradigm has gotten global attention and accepted by organizations like Intel and the University of Pittsburgh (Scofield, 2016). Cybersecurity outcomes are standardized and thus, the exchange of information about cyber threats on critical web resources is facilitated. The Core, Implementation Tiers, and Profile combine the three parts of the framework. Organizations employing the Framework are to identify those areas where improvements can be made by mapping their current information protection mechanisms against those illustrated in the document (Zivkov et al., 2015). Repeatedly, this analytical routine is done. The framework shows firms on how to handle the objectives of data and information retention, security, and continuity of operations in total.

Developed by ISACA, the COBIT 5 framework is an all-embracing frame that addresses all the critical business, security, and risk concerns pertaining to the cloud computing by integrating various approaches and standards such as TOGAF, PMBOK, COSO, and ITIL. Two viewpoints are provided by COBIT 5: risk function and risk management. Regarding risk management, a company's daily risk reporting, risk identification, analysis, and optimisation is of prime importance (Nicho et al., 2017). The aim of the risk function perspective is to develop and maintain an effective framework by which the risks are governed and managed. This perspective encompasses the following processes: establishing and monitoring governance framework, delivering benefits, managing the stakeholders, managing the costs, managing the human resources, managing relationship, managing quality and knowledge, monitoring the performance and conformance, monitoring the internal control systems, and adhering to regulations (Akbar Khrisna, 2014).

TPRM CONCEPTS AND FRAMEWORK

TPRM Concepts

Identification and Categorization of Third-Party Risk

This stage involves the creation of a detailed inventory or list of third parties – suppliers, contractors, business partners – whom the first party engages for its business and shares information systems and resources at all levels. A detailed list of services provided by the third parties, the level of integration with the primary organization's network, and the degree of access to information need to be mentioned for effective identification and tracking of third parties. It is crucial to periodically update this list for continuous visibility.

Furthermore, based on the business requirement, these third parties can be categorized based on multiple categories, some of which could be the degree of regulatory compliance, financial strength and stability, and access to data and systems. Categorization of third parties enables systematic prioritization of a group of third parties while carrying out risk assessments as needed.

Risk Assessment and Due Diligence

Currently, thorough assessments evaluate the risks associated with every third-party association, employing due diligence to ensure the third party's reliability and adherence to the organization's security standards. A comprehensive risk assessment necessitates the identification of potential hazards, their probability, and the potential outcomes for each third-party connection. Validating the provided information from the third party and assessing their expertise and history form integral components of due diligence. Ultimately, establishing a protocol for regularly reviewing and overseeing interactions with third parties is essential for businesses.

Risk Mitigation and Control

After the identification of the organization's exposure to risks in the previous stage, policies, and controls must be put in place to mitigate them. According to National Institute of Standards and Technology (NIST) Special Publication 800-30, risk mitigation is defined as prioritizing, evaluating, and implementing the necessary controls that are derived from the risk management process (Blank & Gallagher, 2012). In terms of third-party risk management, risk mitigation and control strategies may include multiple methods like incorporating necessary contractual clauses, performing continuous or regular oversight, installing data protection methods, proactively responding to incidents, and transferring some risk via risk insurance.

Usually, a risk mitigation workflow includes the following stages:

- Risk flagging and score designation.
- Evaluation of risk against your organization's risk appetite.
- Treatment and control validation in the scope of the desired residual risk level.
- Continual monitoring for increased risk levels (e.g., data breaches) (Moog, 2022)

Continuous Monitoring and Risk Optimization

In today's constantly evolving business environment, companies need to continuously review, monitor, and adjust their risk management plans to minimize potential risks associated with third-party interactions.

The ongoing risk tracking is also a critical element of a third-party vendor risk management approach at the strategic level. While ongoing monitoring is a subcategory of continuous monitoring, it migrates the risk profile of systems to more of a time-oriented format which prompts real-time alerts to management about changes in vulnerabilities/ processes to allow for more timely decisions regarding third party risk. (Cochran, et al., 2017) The key steps involved in implementing a continuous improvement framework include establishing clear goals and objectives, defining key metrics and key performance indicators, collecting and analysing data from third parties at periodically, implementing strategies to improve processes and monitoring and evaluating third parties risk postures.

Frameworks for TPRM

Effective third-party risk management (TPRM) frameworks are crucial for organizations to navigate the complex landscape of cybersecurity threats and data privacy concerns. These frameworks serve as a structured approach to mitigating risks associated with third-party relationships, offering guidance on due diligence and due care. The choice of a TPRM framework depends on various factors, including company structure, risk profile, operations, size, and location. This paper explores key TPRM frameworks, such as ISO 27036 and NIST 800-SP, shedding light on their components and relevance to different industries. Additionally, it discusses the foundational practices and baseline controls outlined in NIST SP 800-161, emphasizing the importance of incorporating these practices to ensure robust TPRM strategies. The upcoming revision of NIST 800-161 is also anticipated to address evolving cybersecurity challenges and industry developments. Therefore, third-party relationships play a pivotal role in organizational operations (Keskin et al., 2021). However, these relationships expose companies to various risks, including cybersecurity threats and data privacy breaches. To navigate these challenges, organizations adopt Third-Party Risk Management (TPRM) frameworks, mirroring the approach taken for cybersecurity frameworks. This section delves into the significance of TPRM frameworks, their adaptability based on organizational factors, and the regulatory guidance that underpins their adoption. These TPRM frameworks provide organizations with a systematic approach to identifying, assessing, and mitigating risks associated with third-party relationships. The choice of a framework is contingent upon factors such as company structure, risk profile, operational scope, size, and geographical location.

ISO 27036 stands out as a comprehensive four-part standard offering guidance on the assessment and handling of security risks within the supply chain and third-party relationships. Focusing on business-to-business relationships, ISO 27036 covers information technology outsourcing, cloud services, professional services, hardware, software, and telecommunications. The four parts of ISO 27036 provide detailed insights into security requirements, guidelines for information system supply chain security, and specific considerations for cloud services (Rasner, 2021).

NIST 800-SP, specifically Special Publication 800-161, addresses supply chain risk management (SCRM) practices for federal information systems and organizations. Published in 2015, this document outlines the risks associated with information and communications technology (ICT) products and services in the supply chain. It provides federal agencies with guidance on identifying, assessing, and mitigating ICT supply chain risks. The document emphasizes the integration of SCRM into overall risk management activities, incorporating a multi-tiered approach.

NIST SP 800-161 establishes foundational practices and baseline controls essential for effective TPRM. These practices include risk management hierarchy, organization governance, consistent processes for determining impact levels, risk assessment processes, and quality and reliability programs. The baseline controls encompass a wide range of aspects, including access control, awareness and training, audit and accountability, security assessment and authorization, configuration management, contingency planning, and more. Adopting these practices and controls ensures a robust TPRM strategy (Rasner, 2021). Since its initial publication in 2015, NIST SP 800-161 has undergone changes in methodology, risks, and technology. An upcoming revision, prompted by feedback and industry developments, is expected to address evolving cybersecurity challenges. Although a specific release date for Revision 1 is pending, the attention it is likely to receive, especially in light of recent supply chain security incidents, underscores the importance of staying abreast of advancements in TPRM frameworks. So, these are the anticipated enhancements expected in the revised NIST 800-161 framework (Boyens, et al., 2022).

The **NIST Special Publication 800-53** (NIST SP 800-53) holds a crucial role in shaping resilient cybersecurity practices, with its influence extending to third-party risk management (TPRM). Developed by NIST, a non-regulatory branch of the U.S. Department of Commerce, SP 800-53 offers a comprehensive set of security controls and guidelines to strengthen federal agencies' information systems. However, its impact goes beyond government entities, as organizations globally adopt its principles as a foundation for securing their systems. SP 800-53's core consists of adaptable and customizable security controls organized into families, enabling organizations to tailor cybersecurity strategies based on their unique needs and risk profiles. When applied to TPRM, SP 800-53 provides a structured approach to assess and manage risks associated with third-party relationships (NIST, 2020).

PCI DSS (Payment Card Industry Data Security Standard) controls are pivotal in managing third party risks. PCI DSS controls establish precise requirements for storing, processing, and transmitting payment card data. In TPRM, these controls mandate that third-party vendors adhere to stringent security measures akin to the primary organization, crucial for upholding cardholder data integrity and confidentiality across the supply chain. Secondly, TPRM practices leveraging PCI DSS controls involve assessing the security stance of third-party vendors in handling payment card data. This encompasses evaluating their PCI DSS compliance, conducting regular security assessments, and ensuring vendors implement safeguards against data breaches. By integrating PCI DSS controls into TPRM frameworks, organizations create a robust, standardized approach to managing and monitoring payment card data security across their third-party ecosystem. This proactive strategy prevents breaches, safeguards sensitive information, and ensures continuous compliance with industry standards (Council, 2023b). Specific to third-party risk management, PCI DSS Requirement 12: Tackle Information Security through Organizational Policies and Programs, section 12. 8: Risk management to information assets related to third party vendor is declared in terms of third party vendor service provider (TPV) that TPV is accountable for the protection of the data in accordance with the PCI DSS regulations and also check compliance. Third parties are expected to demonstrate compliance to the 12 requirements of the PCI DSS, and this is where internal controls assessment and an on-going monitoring comes in useful (Lang, 2024).

The **COBIT (Control Objectives for Information and Related Technologies)** framework constitutes a thorough collection of guidelines governing the governance and management of enterprise information and technology. This framework offers a structured set of controls, processes, and best practices designed to align IT with business objectives. In the realm of third-party risk management (TPRM), COBIT assumes a pivotal role in aiding organizations to institute robust controls for the mitigation and management of risks linked to their external partners (ISACA, 2019).

COBIT's controls are applied in TPRM in several key areas:

Risk Identification and Assessment (APO12, APO13): COBIT controls facilitate organizations in identifying and assessing risks linked to third-party engagements. APO12 oversees overall risk management, while APO13 specifically targets security risk management. Through these controls, organizations can systematically evaluate potential risks introduced by third parties, encompassing aspects such as data security, compliance, and business continuity.

Compliance with Policies and Regulations (EDM03, EDM05): Ensuring compliance with internal policies and external regulations is crucial in TPRM. COBIT controls within EDM03 and EDM05 offer guidance on optimizing risk with stakeholder transparency. This involves aligning third-party activities with organizational policies and regulatory requirements, fostering a transparent and compliant environment.

Information Security (DSS01, DSS04): COBIT's controls for information security (DSS01) aid organizations in defining and implementing policies and procedures to safeguard information. DSS04 concentrates on continuity management, ensuring third parties have measures for addressing disruptions. These controls contribute to establishing a secure environment for data managed by third parties.

Change Management (BAI05): Managing changes introduced by third parties is vital for a secure IT environment. COBIT's BAI05 control guides organizations in managing organizational change, ensuring that third-party alterations align with business objectives and do not introduce new risks.

Monitoring and Performance Evaluation (MEA01, MEA03): Continuous monitoring and evaluation of third-party performance and compliance are integral to effective TPRM. COBIT controls under MEA01 and MEA03 provide a framework for ongoing assessment, allowing organizations to monitor third-party activities, evaluate performance, and ensure adherence to external requirements.

To summarise, the COBIT framework controls provide a thorough set of guidelines for organizations to proficiently handle third-party risks. Incorporating these controls into their TPRM processes enables organizations to strengthen their risk assessment capabilities, guarantee regulatory compliance, and uphold a secure and resilient IT environment in partnership with external collaborators (Costic, 2019).

Hence, effective TPRM frameworks are indispensable for organizations aiming to navigate the intricate landscape of cybersecurity threats and data privacy concerns associated with third-party relationships. The adaptability of these frameworks, as seen in ISO 27036 and NIST 800-SP, allows organizations to tailor their approach based on their unique characteristics. Foundational practices and baseline controls, as outlined in NIST SP 800-161, serve as pillars for a robust TPRM strategy. As the landscape evolves, ongoing revisions, such as the anticipated NIST 800-161 Revision 1, will play a crucial role in enhancing TPRM frameworks to address emerging challenges and industry developments.

DETAILED CASE STUDY ANALYSIS

Security breaches involving third parties in the supply chain have been in the news very often. These kinds of incidents date back to the early days of the Internet. With the rise in the involvement of third parties in the daily business transactions of organizations, these vendors have become frequent and sometimes easy targets to break into the network and pivot toward the first party. According to a Forrester report published in 2021, 55% of security professionals reported experiencing an incident or breach that involved third-party service providers in the previous 12 months (Forrester Research, 2021).

In the next section, we highlight some of the major supply chain attacks that have transpired in the last 15 years. These instances serve to underscore the various pathways that can be taken by malicious agents to infiltrate the network of targeted organizations, leveraging the vulnerabilities of third-party infrastructure or processes. We have covered companies operating in different industries with significant market leadership in their own right. The Target and Home Depot breaches created major headlines during the middle of the last decade. Nowadays, the vetting of cybersecurity practices of third-party service providers is much more commonplace than they were during the times these events took place (Fazzini, 2019). The three other events that we have discussed are much more recent that have taken place or have been reported after the onset of the COVID-19 pandemic. Two of these are attributed to companies – Okta and SolarWinds – which develop IT and cybersecurity solutions for their clients. However, the incidents provide two contrasting perspectives concerning the relationship of the aforementioned companies in their respective third-party partnerships. We also look into the data breach of KeyBank, which as of December 2023, is considered to be within the top 20 US banks based on asset valuation (Bond, 2023). The case puts a spotlight on unsecure practices by partners while storing and handling sensitive customer information of a company.

Target

One of the most infamous examples of cyber risks in the last decade due to third-party engagements would be the Target data breach. It's a typical case of cyber risks hidden within the supply chain of the first party that occurred in 2013. The magnitude of the breach can be understood from the fact that credit card unions had to shell out over 200 million dollars simply to reissue cards (Shu et al., 2017). The concerned attackers successfully conducted a phishing attack and stole the network credentials of Fazio Mechanical Services, which was a supplier of HVAC systems. This company did not have the necessary level of compliance with legal and industry standards. The threat actors then pivoted toward Target's vendor portal, from which they went on to install a custom software BlackPOS on Target's point-of-sale system. It was used to exfiltrate unencrypted PIN code data from the POS systems.

There were a few ways this could have been prevented – one of which is the use of network segmentation to restrict Target's POS machine from third-party access. There was also a lack of oversight as far as Target's security team was concerned as they reportedly chose to ignore alerts by their intrusion detection systems concerning the exit pathways that the attackers intended to utilize for extracting data (Keskin et al., 2021). Had the security team acted on those alerts, the data exfiltration could have been prevented. Another way that is relevant to our topic of discussion is the process of ensuring that Target's vendor with access to its networks has its security posture aligned with Target's information security requirements. The right stipulations in Target's contracts with Fazio Mechanical Services could have been the key. It could have forced the third party to ensure high-security standards and prevent Target's network credentials from being stolen in the first place.

Home Depot

Just one year after the Target incident, Home Depot, an American multinational home improvement retail corporation, reported a credit card data theft, with attackers stealing over 50 million credit card numbers of customers and their email addresses. Just like the Target breach, stolen credentials from a third-party vendor were used to breach Home Depot's network. This was again a case of insufficient monitoring by the security team and an absence of a proper network segmentation and vendor vetting process. A SANS whitepaper on the incident mentions that Home Depot was lacking in effective monitoring capabilities and the oversight of identities and access for third-party service providers (Hawkins, 2015). This further demonstrates the benefit of the least privilege principle in managing information security practices in an organization. Internal access to resources should be blocked for third-party vendors by default and only minimal accesses should be granted to perform the tasks that they are contracted to perform. After the attack, the company implemented measures to continuously monitor and manage accesses provided to third parties. Furthermore, it implemented scanning tools that enabled continuous vulnerability and malicious movement monitoring on the organizational network and POS network. It also segmented its networks to prevent third parties from being able to access its POS network (Keskin et al., 2021). According to a company announcement, Home Depot began following the National Institute of Standards and Technology Cybersecurity Framework. It also hired a full-time Chief Information Security Officer in 2015. It also appointed a Data Security and Privacy Governance Committee. The committee provides oversight at the enterprise level and handles governance over data protection and cybersecurity. The committee shares reports to the company Audit Committee and Board periodically (Jones, 2020).

Okta

In January 2022, Okta, a publicly traded identity and access management company, was breached by the infamous Lazarus$ group. The attack was attributed to a third party, Sykes Enterprise, that provides customer support services. The group used a widely available password-grabbing tool to infiltrate Sykes' systems. They gained sufficient privileges to deactivate the security scanning tools, thus eliminating the chances of a timely intrusion detection (Newman, 2022). Thereafter the hacking group gained access to Okta's internal network impacting 366 corporate customers. They gained superuser access to Okta's admin panel which could have been used as a route to breach servers of clients that use its authentication solutions (Sharma, 2022). This incident highlights the need for solid third-party risk management strategies and solutions to help them closely monitor third-party security risks and mitigate breaches as soon as possible. Okta has publicly claimed that it had detected suspicious activity on a Sykes employee's Okta account on January 20 and 21 and had shared information with Sitel, the parent organization of Sykes Enterprise. However, that was not enough as it subsequently faced data theft. A more comprehensive approach to third-party management could have given Okta greater visibility into Sykes' cybersecurity posture, including the credentials and sensitive customer data at risk. (Bradbury, David, 2022)

It should also be noted that customer support service companies are great targets for malicious actors simply because they often possess extensive access to the organizations for which they offer customer service support. In this case, the hackers infiltrated Sykes's network for a duration of five days before they were identified and expelled (Shapira, 2022). In such scenarios, it is important to perform a risk-based prioritization concerning the monitoring of the security standards and postures of third-party vendors.

KeyBank

KeyBank faced a massive data breach in July 2022 when malicious actors stole personal data from its mortgage holders. The breach was attributed to one of its third-party partners, Overby-Seawell Company, which is an insurance service provider and facilitates a real-time insurance monitoring tracking system for companies in the banking and financial industry. (Bajak, 2022) The attackers were able to remotely breach into the internal network of Overby-Seawell and steal personal data of KeyBank's clients including Social Security Numbers, phone numbers, and policy numbers. According to a federal lawsuit, the stolen personal information has the potential to be utilized for fraudulent activities, leading to additional harm to customers' finances, property, credit, and reputation (Shapira, 2022). This incident highlights the risk of involving outsourcing companies to handle or store the personal information of customers. In this case, even though there is no indication that KeyBank's data security systems were inadequate, it can be deemed to have been negligent in entrusting sensitive consumer data to its (Console and Associates, 2022). A proper mechanism of oversight is necessary to understand the third party's data safety practices and hold it accountable for the security of sensitive data. One way is to periodically engage reputed independent auditing companies to evaluate the protocols and practices that the third party employs to safeguard the primary organizations' data.

SolarWinds

SolarWinds Inc. develops network management software, the primary product being Orion. It is a key vendor to thousands of companies across the globe. The importance of SolarWinds as a vendor is such that over 18,000 companies' networks were breached in 2020 through this incident, as attackers utilized the software update infrastructure to push malware to its customers.

The degree of success is attributed to the fact that the malware was introduced through an update originating from SolarWinds' servers and was digitally signed by a valid digital certificate bearing its name (Williams, 2020). Hence, the trust and reputation that SolarWinds has gained from its customers became a crucial factor for the deployment of the malware into thousands of companies' systems. Another factor that played an important role in the success of the attack was the nature of the malware. The attack was finally discovered by an employee of a customer belonging to the cybersecurity sector. The employee noticed suspicious activity regarding multi-factor authentication with an additional phone being registered for another employee without the knowledge of the company (Keskin et al., 2021). With the malware executed, the threat actors could pivot in multiple directions, with some customers of SolarWinds discovering that their MS Office 365 and Azure Cloud services had become targets of the attack.

This incident highlights that all third-party vendors, irrespective of their reputation and size, can be breached. Large organizations might have better information security hygiene in place than their smaller counterparts. However, they also provide better returns for malicious actors once breached as they hold the keys to the networks of many customers.

CROSS CASE ANALYSIS

All these incidents throw light on the perils that third parties introduce to an organization's business and information technology landscape. Businesses need to understand that despite adhering to appropriate cyber policies and procedures, the risk of vulnerability persists if a supplier becomes compromised. Supply chain vulnerabilities can arise from vendors who have access to organizational networks, third parties employing insufficient data storage methods, and suppliers with generally inadequate cybersecurity practices (F.Keskin et al., 2021). On the other hand, as businesses intensify their scrutiny of supply chain risks, it becomes crucial for third-party vendors to embrace robust cybersecurity measures. These suppliers need to acknowledge their potential impact on larger clients' security and proactively safeguard against potential threats. Neglecting to enforce these safeguards may lead to cybersecurity weaknesses, diminished client confidence, and business losses. By adhering to strong digital policies and practices, third-party vendors can demonstrate the organization's dedication to security, earning trust from both existing and potential clients.

Data Encryption and Security Measures play a pivotal role in fortifying third-party risk management. By encrypting sensitive data exchanged with external partners, organizations bolster their defense against unauthorized access. This process involves converting information into a coded format that is decipherable only with the appropriate encryption key. Concurrently, the implementation of robust cybersecurity measures, including multi-factor authentication and secure data transmission protocols, is imperative. Multi-factor authentication adds an extra layer of identity verification, enhancing access controls. Secure data transmission protocols, such as HTTPS, safeguard data in transit. A report by the Information Systems Audit and Control Association (ISACA) underscores the critical role of encryption in mitigating data breaches, emphasizing its role as a cornerstone in securing sensitive information (Joy, 2018). This proactive approach contributes significantly to reducing the risk of data compromise and unauthorized access during third-party interactions.

In addition to closing the cybersecurity gaps in their IT landscape, certain organizations are additionally investing in cybersecurity insurance to transfer some of the risk to their insurance companies. Cybersecurity insurance generally covers a business's liability for a data breach that encompasses sensitive customer information, including SSNs, credit card numbers, account numbers, health records, etc. In addition to closing the cybersecurity gaps in their IT landscape, certain organizations are additionally investing in cybersecurity insurance to transfer some of the risk to their insurance companies. Cybersecurity insurance generally covers a business's liability for a data breach that encompasses sensitive customer information, including SSNs, credit card numbers, account numbers, health records, etc. (Nationwide, n.d.). In all the security incidents that have been mentioned in the previous sections, regular audits of the information security practices of third parties can play a critical role in detecting anomalous behaviour. Conducting risk-based independent audits would have drawn attention to the deficiencies in the security posture of the third parties. The audit observations would have made these parties answerable to the customers whose data they use or networks they have access to for conducting business. An increase in information security capabilities does not guarantee the prevention of cybersecurity attacks but can deter them or minimize the damage through vigilance and early response.

CHALLENGES IN TPRM

Loss of control is the most fundamental and defining challenge in managing third-party risks. Businesses that rely on third parties, whether they are suppliers, contractors, consultants, or providers of critical infrastructure, give up some control over the assets, people, and processes on which they rely. This holds true no matter how strong or well-drafted the contract or agreement is. Outsourcing implies that the organization is reliant on third-party entities that may or may not share its approach to resilience and cybersecurity or may have a lower level of security capability. Of course, third parties approach resilience based on their own business interests, priorities, and financial circumstances. A major impediment in every case is that much of the information needed to make accurate decisions and manage risk is held by a third party. Failures have an immediate effect on the organizations that rely on them. Third-party risk management is a challenge for all organizations (Bronson, 2022). Smaller businesses may find it difficult to persuade larger vendors to meet their needs or to provide adequate information about the supplier's cybersecurity capabilities. Larger companies may have more resources than smaller companies, but they frequently must manage relationships with hundreds of vendors. Third-party risk management can quickly become time-consuming and complicated. The risk of relying on third parties exists everywhere.

Identifying and quantifying critical third parties is a major issue for many organizations, particularly those with multiple services or products. Thousands of third-party vendors may need to be evaluated, necessitating a substantial investment in resources just to track and manage them. The list of suppliers must be updated on a regular basis to reflect significant changes for tracking to be effective. Such changes include changes in the relative importance of the third party, the organization's requirements for the third party, the organizational services, and products it supports, contract changes, location changes, administrative changes, and changes in second or third tier suppliers and subcontractors (if tracked). Many different parts of an organization are affected and involved in third-party risk management (Keizer, 2022). Getting internal stakeholders to understand and participate in risk management is a critical issue. Many procurement and purchasing departments, for example, continue to disregard the importance of evaluating third-party cybersecurity capabilities and including relevant requirements and clauses in contracts. To manage third-party risks, some institutions employ business rules. They may, for example, prohibit the hosting or processing of certain types of data outside of the organization. One disadvantage of this approach is that it may not provide enough flexibility for implementing new technologies and innovating in novel ways. Institutions may become overly reliant on a smaller supplier who is the sole source for a particular item or provides a significant competitive advantage but lacks robust cybersecurity capabilities. Third-party risks frequently include a collection of threats that extend beyond the scope of the organization's risk management activities. Some companies are overly concerned with risks. When hosting data in the cloud, for example, most organizations request attestations or other evidence of cybersecurity capability from the vendor (Wallen, 2016). However, information and communications technology support almost every supplier for a given organization, not just those explicitly focused on data processing and storage. Because of the breadth and complexity of these dependencies, a more comprehensive cybersecurity risk assessment than is typically performed may be required. Furthermore, some businesses fail to recognize their broader external reliance on critical infrastructure and public services. External dependencies management is a broader approach to third-party risk that takes into account the entire range of external or third parties.

BEST PRACTICES IN TPRM

Organizations these days need to work with multiple external suppliers and third parties. It's important to make sure that any business partner has its act together in terms of governance, risk, and compliance. If they don't, their actions (or lack thereof) could become a high risk. Third-party risk Management is putting a spotlight on the policies, procedures, risks, and controls of external entities. So external relationships are integral to modern business operations, providing efficiency and flexibility but also exposing organizations to a myriad of risks (Abrahams, et al., 2024). Effective third-party risk management (TPRM) involves identifying, assessing, and mitigating these risks to safeguard the integrity and security of business processes. This comprehensive analysis delves into the various risk mitigation techniques employed in TPRM.

It is important for an organization to monitor or verify the activities of its partners to ensure they are operating following agreed-upon cybersecurity hygiene practices. This is the basis of the principle of Trust but Verify in the context of third-party risk management. Monitoring third parties and inspecting their means of operations are increasingly important for not only good corporate governance but for safeguarding the information technology and assets of the first party. Organizations need to pay a great deal of attention to third-party risk, and they need to implement an effective third-party lifecycle management mechanism that reduces inefficiencies to drive out as much risk as possible (Bhattacherjee, 2023).

Effective Third-Party Contract and Relationship Management

In the realm of third-party risk management, robust contractual protections serve as a cornerstone in mitigating potential risks and fostering secure collaborations. These contracts play a pivotal role in delineating the terms, conditions, and responsibilities of all parties involved, establishing a comprehensive framework that governs the relationship. Clear and precise contractual language becomes especially crucial when outlining data protection measures and security protocols to safeguard sensitive information shared with third parties. The organizations with meticulously crafted contracts experience a tangible reduction in risks associated with third-party engagements. Additionally, these contracts serve as a crucial tool in dispute resolution, providing a predefined mechanism for addressing issues and discrepancies that may arise during the business relationship. Therefore, investing in the development and enforcement of robust contractual protections emerges as a strategic imperative for organizations seeking to fortify their third-party risk management strategies. We have deep dived into different types of agreements in later part of paper that a company should be certain when managing third party risks. Robust contractual and relationship management practices with third-party providers are essential to manage third-party risks and involve a comprehensive procedure. These include –

- Developing and Drafting Contractual Agreements with Third-Party Providers

Clearly defined roles, responsibilities, deliverables, terms, and conditions are keys to ensuring compliance with the organization's business requirements, risk postures, and appetite by third-party service providers. These contracts usually explain the liabilities, penalties, and compliance requirements to engage with the organization for business transactions.

- Establishing Service Level Agreements and Expectations

Service Level Agreements assist in setting the benchmark as far as service requirements are concerned. They specify the performance metrics, standards of service, response times, turnaround times, and other measurable yardsticks. Contracts are usually created specifying service level agreements and punitive damages when these service levels are not met by the third party (Cezar et al., 2014).

- Enforcing Compliance with Contractual Obligations

Regular audits and assessments of third-party service providers are essential elements of monitoring for compliance with contractual obligations both in terms of service delivery and security hygiene. In their paper, Hussain & Al-Mourad (2014) describe the importance of third-party auditors contracted by the first party to verify the adherence of service providers to service levels and security agreements.

- Periodically Reviewing and Updating Contracts

Contractual agreements must be periodically reviewed and modified to conform to evolving business needs and the rising cybersecurity threat landscape. This ensures that the agreements remain relevant over time. Contracts should be dynamic, and an outdated contract is the same as not having any contract at all (Di Bernardo, 2014).

Having a Robust Incident Response and Remediation Plan

Given the nature and frequency of cybersecurity events in recent times, it is critical to have a well-documented incident response procedure in any organization that values its information assets. When it comes to managing third-party risks, there are certain areas of an organization's business process that come under the purview of related third parties and their IT ecosystems. Hence, it is crucial to involve these suppliers and business partners who can proactively help respond to incidents. Hence, the incident response process should include protocols for notifying the third-party provider and determining their contribution to the incident in case of an issue. As part of the remediation of incidents, the events should be logged to understand the shortcomings of current practices, realign the vendor and partner responsibilities, revise controls set up in the third-party landscape, and if possible, provide suggestions to the partners to fortify their controls to ensure the incidents are not repeated. (Spampinato et al., n.d.)

So, incident response planning is a critical component of third-party risk management, ensuring organizations can effectively navigate and mitigate potential incidents. Developing thorough response plans involves formulating communication strategies, establishing dedicated incident response teams, and coordinating efforts to contain and resolve issues swiftly and having an incident response plan is key to mitigating disruptions in the heat of the moment and will help firms be better prepared for when incidents do occur (Wilkinson, 2022). The significance of crisis response planning cannot be overstated, particularly in its role in enhancing organizational resilience against the diverse impacts of third-party risks. By anticipating and preparing for potential crises, organizations can minimize the impact on operations, reputation, and customer trust. This proactive approach, supported by scholarly research, underscores the strategic importance of crisis response planning as an integral aspect of comprehensive third-party risk management strategies.

Having a Strong Insurance Coverage

Insurance coverage emerges as a pivotal element in third-party risk management, offering financial protection against potential breaches or incidents. Organizations recognize the significance of tailoring insurance policies to address the unique challenges posed by third-party relationships. According to a comprehensive study conducted by the Risk Management Society (RIMS) in 2021, insurance serves as a vital risk transfer mechanism. This mechanism proves invaluable in mitigating the substantial financial repercussions that may arise from incidents involving third parties. (RIMS, 2021) RIMS emphasizes the strategic role of insurance in alleviating the economic burden associated with third-party risks.

Effective KRI's Management

Measuring Key Risk Indicators (KRIs) entails a systematic procedure of assessing and quantifying the specified risk indicators. KRI measurement is crucial for enterprises to identify risk exposure, monitor changes over time, and implement informed risk-mitigation decisions. (Medrano, 2022). Metrics from Key Risk Indicators (KRIs) is critical in enabling proactive risk management for organisations by providing with insights into potential risks and early signals before risks escalate. Organizations can build a proactive risk management strategy that is responsive to the evolving threat landscape, anticipates challenges, and allows for effective risk mitigation by leveraging KRI data in different ways. Regular reviews and adjustments based on KRI insights contribute to a risk management framework that is more resilient and adaptable. An effective KRI helps in early identification of risk which allows organisation to address critical risks before they escalate by providing timely response. It also strengthens the company's security posture by allowing them to anticipate for potential adverse conditions and help them develop response plan and strategies, thereby improving the preparedness for the future risks.

Moreover, the accurate KRI metrics can be incorporated in dynamic risk assessment program for a firm by managing and updating risk profiles based on the current values of KRIs. So, KRIs help firms to synchronize taking risks with the objectives of the company and evolving outside variables making sure the organization's tolerance for risk is still reasonable and applicable. Organizations can develop a proactive risk management strategy that is adaptable to the changing threat landscape, foresees difficulties, and enables efficient risk mitigation by utilizing KRI data in these ways. A more flexible and resilient risk management framework is the result of regular reviews and modifications based on KRI insights (Davies et al., 2006). Refer Table 1 for improvement guidelines.

Role of Business Agreements in Managing Third Party Risks

Several business agreements are essential to the security posture of the organisation and keeping expectations clear from the beginning. Together, the contracts provide a thorough framework for handling third-party risks during the business partnership. Organizations must customize these agreements to meet their unique requirements and adhere to industry regulations. In order to adjust to evolving risks and modifications in the business environment, regular reviews and updates are also required.

The degree of service that a third party is expected to provide is specified in the **Service Level Agreements (SLAs)**. Performance indicators, service accessibility, reaction times, and other crucial factors are included in this. SLAs aid in setting precise standards for the calibre and dependability of services rendered by outside parties (Palachuk, 2018). They provide a framework for assessing and controlling risks related to performance. Service Level Agreements are essential contracts that specify the duties, obligations, and performance standards between a company and its outside suppliers. Details about service availability, response times, security precautions, and other KPIs are usually included in these agreements. SLAs hold contractors responsible for fulfilling predetermined standards and help set clear expectations.

Organizations frequently sign extensive **Contractual Agreements** with third parties in addition to SLAs (Taylor, 2017). The legal and commercial aspects of the relationship are outlined in these contracts, along with data protection provisions, indemnity agreements, confidentiality requirements, and dispute resolution procedures. Well-written contracts lay the foundation for efficient risk mitigation and offer a legal framework for controlling third-party risks.

According to **General Data Protection Regulation (GDPR)** - Article 28, now a days, Data Processing Agreements are essential for any organization handling personal data. These contracts specify the conditions under which a third party may process personal data and are intended to guarantee adherence to data protection laws. DPAs specify the data handling procedures, security measures, and mutual obligations for safeguarding sensitive information.

Businesses frequently demand that third parties have Business Continuity and Disaster Recovery (BCDR) plans in place to mitigate the risk of operations disruptions. The actions that third parties will take to guarantee service continuity in the event of a disaster or major disruption are outlined in BCDR agreements (Organisation, 2019). These contracts are essential for preserving operational resilience and reducing the effect of unanticipated circumstances.

Organizations are increasingly including **Cybersecurity Agreements** in their dealings with third parties due to the growing threat of cyberattacks. These agreements are primarily concerned with making sure that third parties follow strict cybersecurity guidelines, carry out routine security audits, and promptly report any security incidents (Lewis, 2020). Cybersecurity agreements are especially crucial for sectors of the economy where data integrity and confidentiality are vital.

OPPORTUNITIES IN THIRD-PARTY DUE DILIGENCE

The meaning of *Due Diligence* varies depending on the context and sector. Its meaning in real estate is different from its meaning in law or for that matter, in other sectors like banking. However, if we must define due diligence in a simple yet overarching manner, it is essentially the actions that we can reasonably expect people or parties to take to safeguard themselves and their interests. When an individual buys a product online from an e-commerce platform, he/she looks for customer reviews, which can be argued as a form of due diligence he/she carries out before investing in the product. Usually, when businesses are involved, due diligence follows a process that involves risk and compliance checks, investigations, reviews, or audits to verify facts and information about a subject.

In this paper, we will be concentrating on the practice of Third-Party Due Diligence, which is the process of taking a risk-based approach to vetting vendors, distributors, and service providers to identify any causes of alarm signalling a risk to the company (HyperComply, 2022). In addition to vetting new suppliers before they are onboarded into the first party's list of suppliers, it's crucial to maintain a level of due diligence for existing vendors and implement a system of ongoing monitoring.

The Need for Due Diligence

Due diligence is essentially an investigation conducted by a business before entering a financial transaction or signing a contract with a third party. It is an important step that involves thoroughly researching and analysing the subject to ensure that the business is making an informed decision. This is a crucial aspect of any business deal that cannot be overlooked. The primary goal of due diligence for a business is to obtain knowledge of potential risks associated with the third party before entrusting it with sensitive information and systems. According to a Gartner study, among the 256 legal and compliance leaders interviewed, 80% agreed that third parties perform new-in-kind technology services for a business, which mainly include services beyond a company's core business. These third parties are increasingly comprised of start-ups and innovators (Gartner, 2019). This further highlights the need for a proper due diligence mechanism to reduce risk and prioritize the organization's security.

With the regulatory environment becoming stricter in the realms of information security and data privacy, an organization would prefer third parties to be compliant with regulations to minimize its exposure to risks of legal sanctions or fines.

Due diligence is a critical aspect of any deal, playing a pivotal role in the success of both parties in carrying out the operations in scope which is part of the entire value chain of the first party. However, there are a number of obstacles in the due diligence process that can result in costly surprises, missed synergy goals, and overspent integration budgets. Apart from synergies, insufficient vetting of third-party IT environments can lead to information breaches resulting in further tangible costs in monetary terms and intangible losses like reputation and market shares.

In the next few sections, we aim to identify common gaps in the due diligence process and provide strategies to strengthen the process. By addressing these issues, organizations can enhance the effectiveness of their due diligence efforts, obtain synergistic benefits, and reduce the attack surface from cybersecurity threats.

Gaps in Due Diligence

The importance of due diligence before and during an engagement with third parties cannot be stressed enough. However, certain gaps exist as far as actual practices in the industry are concerned. These challenges creep up during the initial due diligence and contracting phases and lead to security issues that threaten business activities in the future.

- Lack of Holistic View in Due Diligence - Organizations often face challenges when vendors drive due diligence, as the focus tends to be on the vendor's core competencies, neglecting a holistic view. This myopic approach can lead to an inadequate understanding of the environment, especially concerning information security which is crucial in today's businesses. Issues in binding the scope of engagement with third parties prevent a focussed due diligence of the vendors. Vague statements around scope contribute to misunderstandings, affecting costs and user perceptions that can derail the success of the engagement.
- Communication Challenges - Effective communication becomes critical during due diligence to manage service-related expectations, combat staff uncertainty down the line, and secure buy-in at all levels of third-party engagement. Inadequate communication may result in the withholding of critical information that may jeopardize business activities during adverse events like data breaches. Poor governance throughout the engagement life cycle is a common reason for disputes and relationship breakdowns which need to be assessed while conducting due diligence of vendors. Failure to precisely define the service scope during due diligence can lead to disputes and ultimately operational disruptions (Coetzee & Lessing, 2004).
- Access to Information and Data - Much of the information pertinent to the assessment of non-financial risk of a third-party service provider may be held on-site rather than the headquarters office. This is particularly true in the initial stages of the project, when reporting hierarchies related to the engagement may not yet have been formalized. Furthermore, without inspecting the situation on the ground and engaging with stakeholders other than project staff or contractors, the materiality of certain issues in the realm of unsafe IT practices may be difficult to evaluate. According to a survey conducted by Deloitte across 170 participating organizations, 69.5% of respondents claimed that periodic visit to third-party locations is the most effective way of gaining assurance over third parties (Park & Sen, 2016). The lack of a valid reason should be considered a red flag for future engagements with the third party. In other cases, collecting relevant data for due diligence can be challenging due to time constraints.

• Insufficient Benchmarking and Evaluation - Organizations often overlook the importance of benchmarking IT costs and competencies before outsourcing a portion of their business to third parties (Gartner Group, 1999). Additionally, vendors may fail to confirm and understand customer expectations, leading to misalignments in service delivery. The size of the third-party service provider presents different challenges during benchmarking and evaluation. When initiating business with a relatively new organization that has not yet faced independent audits, it becomes difficult to validate the security controls to ensure they align with the first party's security posture.

Some of the major breaches that we highlighted earlier showcase the need for important background checks during due diligence. The KeyBank breach is a perfect example of an organization without enough insights into the IT security posture of one of its most important third-party partners. IT due diligence could have enabled the bank to initiate a demand for secure practices especially when dealing with the sensitive financial and personal information of customers.

Steps to Strengthen Third-Party Due Diligence

Confidence is crucial in establishing third-party relationships, yet it alone isn't sufficient. Corporations and their global extensions frequently engage with identical third parties without acknowledging the potential risks involved. Companies must acknowledge the potential risks associated with these third-party relationships. They must enhance their understanding of the supply chain's visibility and bolster their monitoring efforts. There are a few steps an organization can take to perform this, as mentioned below:

- **Leveraging information from both external and internal sources**
  Although internal screening evaluations, onboarding procedures, risk assessments, and ongoing monitoring are vital components of third-party due diligence, sourcing information from external sources is equally crucial. Many organizations currently consider validating their potential third-party relationships utilizing external data outlets such as sanction lists and media coverage of known security incidents and breaches. Independent security assessments of the concerned third-party service provider can be leveraged to determine the vulnerabilities of the IT landscape of the third party like patching issues and the absence of secure coding practices.
- **Using a Risk-based Approach to Due Diligence**

A pivotal step that precedes contractual agreements is the screening of third parties during onboarding. A comprehensive but well-defined screening process should be in place that provides input on the significance of the third-party relationship. Factors such as the nature of the business, access to sensitive information and IT infrastructure, business continuity, expenditure, and financial aspects are crucial for assessing a third party. Implementing a risk-based segmentation is paramount for thorough due diligence. A streamlined segmentation during the onboarding phase aids in structuring subsequent steps for third-party due diligence. A risk-based segmentation enables an organization to direct attention to higher risk third parties to effectively prioritize limited resources. A risk-based classification of third parties should be performed (Deloitte Development LLC., 2019) according to the terminologies that the first-party organization is comfortable with.

- **Due Diligence Checklist**

  To ensure a thorough IT due diligence process, a comprehensive checklist is essential to identify any integration area that can pose a risk to the organization. A checklist ensures a method to keep track of the process areas that need to be investigated so that no area is missed. An organization must include items in the checklist to evaluate the security, reliability, scalability, availability, performance, and integration efforts (Roehl-Anderson, 2010). The checklist can help in driving a rigorous due diligence process. Its must be documented properly and updated with the evolving technological landscape to aid in future due diligence processes.

- **Balancing Technology and Human Insights**

  The screening process of a third party against databases and sanctions lists can be automated. For a burgeoning population of third-party entities involved in an organization, this is highly critical to manage due diligence processes. However, the outputs of algorithms alone cannot provide the entire story without the right human insights into factors like local jurisdictions, business environments, the nature of the industry, and other social aspects. Technology can be leveraged for resource-intensive repetitive tasks involved in tracking and monitoring the activities of third-party entities. These automated monitoring outputs feed into the subsequent analysis to take necessary decisions and timely actions.

- **Establish a well-defined escalation process.**

  Even though the implementation of due diligence procedures from the third party's initial onboarding to ongoing monitoring help to reduce potential dangers, residual risks exist for any organization. As a result, the implementation of an escalation structure assumes paramount importance in expediting the resolution of difficulties and streamlining the decision-making process (Metricstream, n.d.). The involvement of upper management is crucial to resolve issues due to compliance or during incidents. When third parties involved has heavy integration with the organization's IT infrastructure, the involvement of the CXOs in the IT Security and Risk verticals becomes critical.

- **Continuous Due Diligence**

  Information technology remains an evolving sector with new paradigm shifts in the way data is processed, transported, and stored. Such evolutions bring about changes in the threat landscape. Sometimes, a change in the IT landscape of a third-party service provider and not the organization itself can raise security issues.

  Hence, IT due diligence remains essential. Once engagements with the vendors are initiated, the first-party team gains a deeper insight into the actual state of the third-party technology. Hence, all assumptions considered, and key decisions taken during the pre-deal due diligence require revalidations (Roehl-Anderson, 2010).

By addressing gaps and challenges in the due diligence process, organizations can enhance their ability to achieve synergies in business operations with their third-party partners enabled by secure integration in IT resources of all the parties.

CONCLUSION

Role of IS Audit in Third-Party Risk Management

The role of periodic information systems audits is essential to keep an organization's digital assets safe as audits act as the Third Line of Defence. Its responsibility encompasses reporting to the board and audit committee, while also ensuring that regulators and external auditors are assured of the effectiveness of the control culture in both design and operation within the organization (Deloitte, 2020).

The introduction of the right to audit clause within the service level agreement authorizes the first party to conduct audits of the vendor and establishes the financial and other responsibilities and incentives for each party concerned. In certain cases, expanded service level agreements incorporate provisions like the host's auditing rights, detailing aspects such as audit scope, process, frequency, and potential triggers for unscheduled audits. (Raval & Shah, 2017). This sets the tone for the effective monitoring of third-party security practices by the first party.

In the dynamic landscape of business, adherence to regulatory standards is paramount for mitigating risks associated with third-party relationships. Regular compliance audits verify third-party vendors' adherence to contractual agreements and compliance standards and involve examining financial practices, data security practices, and overall compliance of operations (Abrahams, et al., 2024). This proactive approach acts as a shield against legal repercussions and financial penalties that may arise from non-compliance. Audits play an important role in ensuring the alignment of an organization's procedures and protocols with the regulatory frameworks. By doing so, organizations not only reduce operational and reputational risks but also foster a culture of responsibility and integrity in their external partnerships.

THOUGHTS AND REFLECTIONS

On a closing note, the research paper has cast light on the critical significance of Third-Party Risk Management (TPRM) in today's increasingly interconnected business landscape. As organizations continue to rely heavily on third-party vendors and service providers to support their operations and drive proficiency, the need to effectively manage third-party risks has become supreme for ensuring business resilience, protecting sensitive data, and maintaining regulatory compliance.

The analysis presented in this paper highlights the multifaceted nature of third-party risks, ranging from cybersecurity vulnerabilities to data privacy concerns and regulatory compliance challenges. Recent incidents and breaches due to lapses in security by third parties serve as absolute reminders of the potential consequences of inadequate risk management practices in vendor relationships. The interconnected nature of modern supply chains and business ecosystems further amplifies the need for robust TPRM strategies to mitigate risks effectively.

One of the key findings of the research is the lack of prioritization and awareness surrounding third-party risks within many organizations. Despite the growing threat landscape and increasing regulatory scrutiny, a significant portion of companies still lack comprehensive TPRM frameworks and fail to perform adequate due diligence when engaging with third-party vendors. This gap in understanding and preparedness leaves organizations vulnerable to a wide range of risks, including data breaches, regulatory fines, and reputational damage.

Furthermore, the research has identified common challenges and pitfalls in current TPRM practices, such as siloed approaches to security mitigation, lack of collaboration between cybersecurity and risk management teams, and a compliance-driven mindset that overlooks proactive risk management strategies. Addressing these challenges requires a holistic and structured approach to TPRM, encompassing the development of robust contractual agreements, investment in resources and training, and a commitment to continuous improvement.

Moving forward, organizations must prioritize TPRM as an integral component of their overall risk governance framework. This entails fostering closer collaboration between different departments, including cybersecurity, risk management, procurement, and legal, to ensure alignment of objectives and a unified approach to managing third-party risks. Moreover, organizations must invest in technologies and tools that enable proactive risk monitoring, threat detection, and incident response capabilities to mitigate risks effectively.

In conclusion, the research underscores the importance of proactive and comprehensive TPRM strategies in safeguarding organizational interests, enhancing business resilience, and maintaining trust and confidence among stakeholders. By addressing the gaps and challenges identified in this paper and adopting a proactive stance towards TPRM, organizations can strengthen their security posture, mitigate risks effectively, and thrive in today's dynamic and interconnected business environment.

REFERENCES

Abrahams, T. O., Farayola, O. A., Kaggwa, S., Uwaoma, P. U., Hassan, A. O., & Dawodu, S. O. (2024). Reviewing third-party risk management: Best practices in accounting and cybersecurity for superannuation organizations. *Finance & Accounting Research Journal*, 6(1), 23.

Adams, M. (2023). Third-party risk management critical to protecting against cyberattack.

Akbar Khrisna, H. (2014). Risk Management Framework With COBIT 5 And Risk Management Framework for Cloud Computing Integration.

Anderson, D. (2017). COSO ERM: Getting risk management right: Strategy and organizational performance are the heart of the updated framework.

Andreisová, L. (2020). Analysis of the Impact of the GDPR on Third-Party Risk Management Programs and Related Recommendations for Domestic as Well as International Corporate World.

Bajak, F. (2022). *KeyBank: Hackers of third-party provider stole customer data*. AP News.

Bhattacherjee, S. (2023, April 20). *Third-Party Risk Management Lifecycle: A Strategic Approach*. Retrieved from SignalX: https://signalx.ai/blog/third-party-risk-management-lifecycle/

Blank, R. M., & Gallagher, P. D. (2012). *NIST Special Publication 800-30 Guide for Conducting Risk Assessments*. National Institute of Standards and Technology, US Dept. of Commerce. Gaithersburg: National Institute of Standards and Technology.

Bond, C. (2023, December 6). *20 Biggest Banks in America*. Retrieved from US News & World Report: https://www.usnews.com/banking/articles/biggest-banks-in-america

Boyens, J., Smith, A., Bartol, N., Winkler, K., Holbrook, A., & Fallon, M. (2022). *Cybersecurity Supply Chain Risk Management Practices for Systems and Organizations*. NIST Special Publication-NIST SP 800-161r1.

Bradbury, D. (2022). *Okta's Investigation of the January 2022 Compromise*. Okta.

Bronson, H. E. (2022). Five Common Shortcomings of Third-Party Management Programs in Financial Organizations and Recommended Risk Management Strategies.

Cezar, A., Cavusoglu, H., & Raghunathan, S. (2014). Outsourcing Information Security: Contracting Issues and Security Implications. In *Management Science* (pp. 638-657). Institute for Operations Research and the Management Sciences.

Cochran, B., Gundrothu, S., Hill, J., Johar, G., Shawn, M., Manley, A., & Ward, P. (2017). *Continuous Monitoring of Third Party Vendors: Building Best Practices*. Shared Assessments.

Coetzee, D., & Lessing, N. (2004). Information technology: Manaement Issues in the Due Diligence and Contracting Phase of Outsourcing Contracts. *Journal of Contemporary Management*, 16-30.

Console & Associates. (2022, August 30). *KeyBank Announces Third-Party Data Breach Following Incident at Third-Party Vendor, Overby-Seawell Company*. Retrieved from JDSUPRA: https://www.jdsupra.com/legalnews/keybank-announces-third-party-data-8464347/

Costic, L. (2019). *COBIT Focus Area: Information & Technology Risk*. ISACA.

Council, P. S. (2023b, December 1). Retrieved from PCI Security Standards Council – Protect Payment Data with Industry-driven Security Standards, Training, and Programs.: https://www.pcisecuritystandards.org/document_library/?document=third-party-security-assurance

Davies, J., Finlay, M., McLenaghen, T., & Wilson, D. (n.d.). *Key Risk Indicators – Their Role in Operational Risk Management and Measurement*. Retrieved from 2006

Dawodu, S. O. (2024). Reviewing third-party risk management: best practices in accounting and cybersecurity for superannuation.

Deloitte. (2020). *Modernizing the three lines of defense model An internal audit perspective*. Retrieved from Deloitte: https://www2.deloitte.com/us/en/pages/advisory/articles/modernizing-the-three-lines-of-defense-model.html

Di Bernardo, M. (2014). *Contingent contracts: A tool for facilitating the negotiation and managing risks. the case of an international sale of goods from Portugal to Brasil*. Retrieved from Repositório da Universidade NOVA de Lisboa (RUN): http://hdl.handle.net/10362/17437

E, B. H. (2022). Five Common Shortcomings of Third-Party Management Programs in Financial Organizations and Recommended Risk Management Strategies.

Efe, A. (2023). *A comparison of key risk management frameworks: COSO-ERM, NIST RMF, ISO 31.000*. COBIT.

European Union. (n.d.). *GDPR.EU*. Retrieved from GDPR: https://gdpr.eu/

Fazzini, K. (2019, December 23). *In a decade of cybersecurity alarms, these are the breaches that actually mattered.* Retrieved from CNBC: https://www.cnbc.com/2019/12/23/stuxnet-target-equifax-worst-breaches-of-2010s.html

Forrester Research, Inc. (2021). *Predictions 2022: Cybersecurity, Risk and Privacy.* Forrester Research, Inc.

Gartner. (2019). *Stay Ahead of Growing Third- Party Risk.*

Haller, J., & Wallen, C. M. (2016). Anaging third party risk in financial services organizations: A resilience-based approach.

Hawkins, B. (2015). *Case Study: The Home Depot Data Breach.* SANS Institute.

Hussain, M., & Al-Mourad, M. B. (2014). Effective Third Party Auditing in Cloud Computing. *2014 28th International Conference on Advanced Information Networking and Applications Workshops.* IEEE.

ISACA. (2019). Retrieved from ISACA: https://www.isaca.org/resources/news-and-trends/newsletters/atisaca/2019/volume-23/applying-cobit-to-vendor-risk-management

Jaeger, J. (2018). Reducing third-party risks with eyes wide open: Recent analyses show that many companies don't have adequate visibility into their third parties, and even less so their third parties' third parties and beyond (so-called Nth parties).

Jones, D. (2020, November 25). *Home Depot codifies data reforms in $17.5M breach settlement with states.* Retrieved from Cybersecurity Dive: https://www.cybersecuritydive.com/news/home-depot-data-breach-settlement/589736/

Joy, J. (2018). *Toward Encrypted and Private Databases.* ISACA.

Kashyap, R. K., & Sharma, S. (2015). Security challenges and issues in Cloud Computing – The way ahead.

Keskin, O. F., Caramancion, K. M., Tatar, I., Raza, O., & Tatar, U. (2021). Cyber Third-Party Risk Management: A Comparison of Non-Intrusive Risk Scoring Reports. *Electronics (Basel)*, 10(10), 1168. DOI: 10.3390/electronics10101168

Klein, A. (2007). Building an Identity Management Infrastructure for Today...and Tomorrow. *Information Systems Security : ... International Conference, ICISS ... : Proceedings*, 16(2), 74–79. DOI: 10.1080/10658980701250083

Lalonde, C., & Boiral, O. (2012). Managing risks through ISO 31000: A critical analysis.

Lang, S. (2024, April 2). *Meeting PCI DSS Third-Party Service Provider Requirements*. Retrieved from Prevalent: https://www.prevalent.net/compliance/pci-dss/#:~:text=The%20PCI%20DSS%20and%20Third%2DParty%20Service%20Provider%20Management&text=The%20standard%20applies%20to%20all,place%20to%20secure%20cardholder%20data

Lewis, D. J. (2020). *The Cyber Defence Review*. Retrieved from Private Actors' Roles in International Cybersecurity Agreements – Unlearned Lessons.

Medrano, D. (2022). *Third-Party Key Risk Indicators – What Management Should Consider.*

Mont, J. (2017). Recent data breaches impart third-party risk lessons: The data breaches at Yahoo, Equifax, and the SEC send a collective warning to organizations everywhere to improve their own third-party risk assessment.

Moog, M. (2022, August 5). *Eight Steps to Manage the Third-Party Lifecycle*. Retrieved from ISACA: https://www.isaca.org/resources/news-and-trends/isaca-now-blog/2022/eight-steps-to-manage-the-third-party-lifecycle

Murphy, C. N., & Yates, J. (2009). *The International Organization for Standardization*. ISO. DOI: 10.4324/9780203884348

National Institute of Standards and Technology (NIST). (n.d.). *Cybersecurity Framework*. Retrieved from NIST: https://www.nist.gov/cyberframework

Nationwide. (n.d.). *Business solutions center What is cyber insurance?* Retrieved from Nationwide: https://www.nationwide.com/business/solutions-center/cybersecurity/what-is-cyber-insurance

Newman, L. H. (2022, March 28). *Leaked Details of the Lapsus$ Hack Make Okta's Slow Response Look More Bizarre*. Retrieved from Wired: https://www.wired.com/story/lapsus-okta-hack-sitel-leak/

Nicho, M., Khan, S., & Rahman, M. (2017). Managing Information Security Risk Using Integrated Governance Risk and Compliance.

NIST. (2020). NIST-NIST SP 800 53 Rev. 5.

Olechowski, A., Oehmen, J., Seering, W., & Ben-Daya, M. (2016). *The professionalization of risk management: What role can the ISO 31000 risk management principles play?*

Palachuk, K. W. (2018). *Service Agreements*. Great Little Book Publishing Co., Inc.

Park, K., & Sen, S. (2016). *Third-party governance and risk management The threats are real.* Deloitte TTP.

Rasner, G. C. (2021). *Cybersecurity and Third-Party Risk.* John Wiley & Sons, Inc.

Raval, V., & Shah, S. (2017). Third-party Risk Management. *ISACA Journal Third-party. Risk Management*, 13–18.

Risk Assessment Special Interest Group (SIG). (2012). *Information Supplement: PCI DSS Risk Assessment Guidelines.* PCI.

Roehl-Anderson, J. (2010). *IT Best Practices for Financial Managers*. John Wiley & Sons, Inc.

Rose, M., & Frio, D. (2017). A smarter approach to third-party risk: adopting a focused, collaborative strategy can help improve management of outsourced service providers.

Sargent, J. F. (2012). The Obama Administration's Proposal to Establish a National Network for Manufacturing Innovation.

Scofield, M. (2016). Benefiting from the NIST cybersecurity framework.

Shapira, E. (2022, December 20). *The 4 Most Notable Third-Party Data Breaches of 2022 (So Far)*. Retrieved from Panorays: https://panorays.com/blog/the-4-most-notable-third-party-data-breaches-of-2022-so-far/

Sharma, A. (2022, March 22). *Okta investigating claims of customer data breach from Lapsus$ group*. Retrieved from Bleeping Computer: https://www.bleepingcomputer.com/news/security/okta-investigating-claims-of-customer-data-breach-from-lapsus-group/

Shu, X., Tian, K., Cambrione, A., & Yao, D. (2017, January 18). *Breaking the Target: An Analysis of Target Data Breach and Lessons Learned.* Retrieved from https://arxiv.org/pdf/1701.04940.pdf

Spampinato, L., Morris, D., & Curcurito, M. (n.d.). *Third-Party Incident Management (TPIM): How to Balance IRPs with Third Parties*. Retrieved from Wolf & Company, P.C.: https://www.wolfandco.com/resources/insights/third-party-incident-management-how-balance-irps-third-parties/#:~:text=The%20TPIM%20process%20involves%20identifying,to%20incidents%20that%20may%20arise

Taylor, R. T. (2017). *Contract Law*. Oxford University Press.

Wallen, J. H. (2016). *Managing third party risk in financial services organizations: A resilience-based approach.* Carnegie Mellon University.

Warren, P. D. (2014). Closing the gaps in third-party risk management: internal audit can add value by assessing risk around the organization's business relationships.

Wilkinson, B. (2022). *Improving Third-Party Incident Response Starts with a Solid Incident Management Foundation*. Prevalent.

Williams, J. (2020, December 15). *What You Need to Know About the SolarWinds Supply-Chain Attack*. Retrieved from SANS: https://www.sans.org/blog/what-you-need-to-know-about-the-solarwinds-supply-chain-attack/

Zivkov, E., Nerandzic, B., & Kuzmanovic, B. (2015). A Correlation Between the Function of Controlling and the Process of Risk Management in the Company.

Chapter 6
Ensuring Sustenance of Innovation:
Emerging Audit Practices for Healthcare Industry

Monal Gupta
University at Buffalo, SUNY, USA

Khan Yasin
University at Buffalo, SUNY, USA

ABSTRACT

Questions have been posed over the effectiveness of these audits in improving hospital systems, giving rise to new trends and practices in healthcare audits. Since most hospitals are in the constant chime to improve the quality and length of their patients' lives, there is an impetus to not only innovate medical practices but also improve risk management and internal audit functions to ensure controlled and sustained adoption. Internal audit trends will generally improve healthcare institutions' quality of care and operations. It leads to better data analytics tools, improved information systems, leveraging new technology, addressing evolving management needs, dealing with relationships with third-party providers carefully, and complying with new regulations. The research is critical to ensure as the healthcare industry continues to leverage new technologies and data tools to ensure better quality care to their patients and society, risks are effectively managed.

DOI: 10.4018/979-8-3693-4211-4.ch006

1. INTRODUCTION

Auditing involves a series of processes in healthcare, such as assessment, evaluation, and patient care improvement, following a systematic formula. It involves weighing the modern practices in contrast to the set standards in the healthcare system. These practices form a crucial fragment in clinical governance that focus in provided quality and patient-centric care. Auditing helps healthcare institutions determine whether they are running their business in an appropriate approach. It evaluates several patient care aspects, such as the structures, processes, and results of care practices in the organization. Mouchantaf, et. al (2021) looked at the efficiency of security risk management (SRM) in the healthcare industry, which also examines how staff feel about several critical success factors (CSFs), such as team member autonomy, corporate security tactics, company maturity, open dialogue, encouragement from executive management, holistic company views, security repair, and development of human resources. Zafar et., al (2014) reviewed partnership among stakeholders to maximize the safety of patients using active risk reduction plan by unifying phrases, operations, and standards of care. Teoh and Cheong (2008) offer methods to put ERM programs into behavior, involving evaluation of risks, role an explanation, and formulation of strategies. at attempt to improve care for patients & decrease administrative procedure times, the case study examines the introduction of enterprise resource management (ERM) at Singaporean hospital. Vilakazi, & Adebesin (2023) conducted a systemic literature review of threats to healthcare data and mitigation strategies and found that virtualization and cloud computing provide risks related to cybersecurity to medical information, and mobile phones offer potential. Errors by humans, dependence on external IT services, and an absence of policies make up the obstacles to overcome. Encrypting information, blockchain technology, and user instruction were suggested as examples of remedies (Martinez et., al, 2023). In addition, unique situations such as increased reliance on human performance (Nifakos, et. al, 2021) and during pandemic times (Sendelj & Ognjanovic, 2022; Sardi, et.al, 2020) present unique challenges in risk management practices.

Healthcare systems are susceptible to the ever-changing dimensions of society, such as technology. It, therefore, calls for healthcare auditors to be on their toes for such trends for quality improvement. Some of these emerging auditing practices include; artificial intelligence, soft controls, and third-party risk management (TPRM). Other scholars, such as (Yaqoob et al., 2019), introduced blockchain as an algorithm for addressing risk management, especially involving third parties. This research paper will give a profound insight into the trending auditing activities in healthcare, as mentioned in this paragraph.

2. ARTIFICIAL INTELLIGENCE

Artificial intelligence (AI) rapidly evolves in several business settings and healthcare systems. Adoption of AI can help upgrade financial procedures, improve reliability, and foster corporate expansion in the quickly changing economy (Bogdan et al. 2023).It assesses risks and provides probable solutions. AI has made a big impact on the accounting and auditing sector in recent years. Internal audits in healthcare integrate clinical governance, manage risks, and transform management processes. (Dunn and Hollander 2017) focus on the impact of AI on auditing by redeveloping AI systems in auditing based on identified benefits and restrictions. By supporting honest and transparent information, Nguyen et al. (2022) further emphasizes the advantages of AI technology for the auditing process. (Bunker, 2021) describes AI as a trend that would be predominant among internal auditors as different organizations, tremendous and small, are moving towards automated programs. A 2019 survey by Gartner revealed a significant increase of organizations adopting AI for auditing by 270% over four years (Gartner, 2019), and International Data Corporation (IDC) predicts that the global expenditure on AI will be approximately $97.9 billion in the year 2023. Furthermore, rather than being concerned about AI replacing their jobs, accountants and professionals should welcome new technology as a vital instrument to improve client support. Professionals can guarantee a long-lasting and sustainable career with the right training and abilities in AI. (Ding et al. 2023; Firoiu et al. 2023a)

Thanks to developments in cognitive machine technologies, particularly in the creation and use of artificial intelligence (AI), many professions have experienced significant transformations (Li 2018). AI eliminates all human errors (Zemankova, 2019), making it crucial for quality improvement in the healthcare realm. AI technologies are steadily defining their position in healthcare; it has proved their role in refining patient care and extending their services to the administration level on decision-making matters and problem-solving within the facility. AI technologies come in handy during diseases diagnosis equated to humans, and it is just a matter of time until these techs replace human medics. Advancements in technologies supporting healthcare is critical in ensuring modernization applications and data protection (Ozturk and Yildibasi, 2020; Queiroz et al., 2021; Sharma and Kshetri, 2020).

2.1. Machine Learning

Machine Learning (ML) in the medical world has witnessed significant progress over the decades. There are preliminaries to address healthcare needs to advance patient care, ease medics' workload, restructure healthcare practices, and encourage medics. Image-based triage development has enabled computer vision translation and seconds the reader: this is one of the significant successes in healthcare ML (Zhang et al., 2022). Electronic Health Records (EHRs) are also substantial medical advancements and play a crucial role in disease and pandemic prediction. Several ML software platforms are securing places in hospitals. In 2018, the United States Food and Drug Administration (FDA) sanctioned IDX-DR used to sense diabetic retinopathy emerging as the first ML software approved for clinical use. Chatbot triage organizations such as Babylon have collaborated with the United Kingdom National system, and Viz.ai has employed their triage tools in over 100 US hospitals.

As ML tools occupy clinics, the problem changes from development to deployment. While trying to mitigate the gap in model development versus deployment, a new trend arises: data importance. (Zhang et al., 2022) argue that multi-institutional, diverse, well-labeled, and extensive datasets play crucial roles in driving performance in the real world, equating to model optimization, and are essential for mitigating biases. Obtaining rich datasets is a daunting task due to patient privacy, limitations to access clinical data, and diversity in organizational data frameworks. Most of the challenges related to ML deployment arise from data, that is, how to upload data to the model, enhance workflow incorporation, and establish timely medical predictions.

2.2. Generative Models

Over the years, Generative Adversarial Networks (GANs) have emerged as some of the significant advances in deep learning. GANs are crucial in healthcare in that they augment data sets, reconstruct images, curb issues regarding privacy-restricted and uneven datasets, and undertake image modality translations and image reconstruction (Xu et al., 2019). GANs can establish numerous synthetic yet accurate data. GANs have two networks, the generator and the discriminator. The generator tries to comprehend data distribution derived from various samples and create new samples from that distribution. On the other hand, the discriminator tries to differentiate the natural and synthetic data (Figure 1).

Figure 1 GAN Model

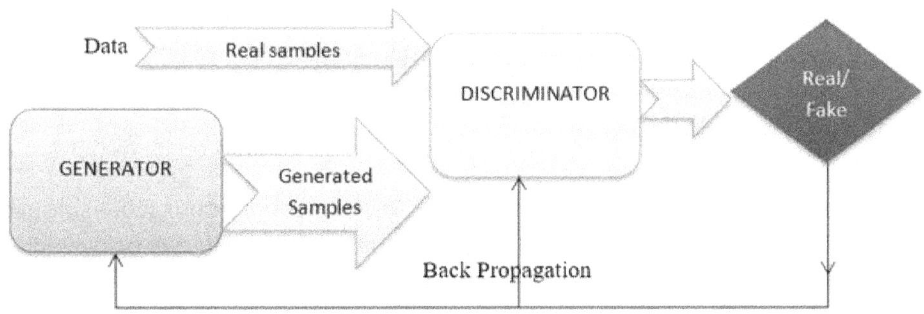

As time passed, new GANs emerged to overcome the challenges of the first GAN and boost its performance and functionalities. Some of these original GAN challenges included low-quality images and unsteady teaching. The table below highlights the GAN models and their applications in healthcare (Table 1).

Table 1. GAN models

Model	**Application**
GAN original	Multifarious
Wasserstein-GAN & Wasserstein-GAN-GP	Open-ended image synthesis Disease modeling
Conditional GANs, e.g., CGAN,pix2pix, cycle GAN, auxiliary GAN	Image-to-image translation, lesion detection, anonymity, data augmentation, and data segmentation
Deep Convolution GAN	Data augmentation and Class Balance
LAP-GAN and PRO-GAN	Unconditioned picture synthesis
Self-Attention GAN and BigGAN	Conditioned picture synthesis

Augmenting Datasets

Most deep-learning tools for medical-image segmentation accomplishments and performance reach the physician level. The success of these deep-learning tools depends on diverse, heterogeneous, and balanced datasets. This aspect cuts across all domains, but when it applies to healthcare, it becomes restrictive, as obstacles hamper comprehensive data collection. For example, accessing standardized medical records is cumbersome, even exacerbated since hospital records represent a particular patient population or hospital. The data becomes unreliable since it can overrepresent the patients' population or a common disease. Imbalanced and invariable datasets contributed to model failure and biases. To curb these challenges, it is crucial to employ standard data-manipulation systems such as flipping, translation, and picture scaling (Wang & Perez, 2017). GANs can solve these challenges. GANs are crucial in enhancing training data and thus augment model performance. Convolutional Neural Network (CNN) used for liver lesions classifications, trained using synthetic and accurate data, enhanced model performance by 10% equated to the one trained using only traditional data (Frid-Adar et al., 2018).

GANs and Patient Privacy

When establishing clinical datasets, patients' privacy is compromised—sharing or exposing patient records while creating multi-institutional datasets bridges privacy and thus poses a risk to the individual. Upholding privacy protocol does not guarantee privacy protection; in some instances, patient features can be leaked from the model. GANs data have no attribution to an individual patient and thus provide a solution to privacy invasion since GANs synthesize data as a representation of the patient population (Zhang et al., 2022). GANs are patient-anonymization technologies that create synthetic data used in model training. While models using only synthetic data perform below par (Zhang et al., 2022), blending with 10% of actual data significantly augments the model performance. Consequently, using GANs synthetic data in image-segmentation model training accomplished a 95% accuracy as the model using accurate data (Zhang et al., 2022). Therefore employing synthetic datasets for creating a model can curb privacy protection-related problems.

GANs Image-to-Image Translation

Image-to-image translation is one of the significant roles of GANs. It occurs between several image modalities, such as positron emission (PET), computed tomography (CT), T1 images, T2 images, and Magnetic Resonance Images (MRI). The movement of images between modalities mitigates the expensive and time-consuming image acquisition procedures. It is also crucial in cases where images are unavailable, such as imaging people with metal implants. There are two practical approaches to image-to-image translation: paired (using pix2pix) and unpaired image (using Cycle GAN) training. Pix2pix creates synthetic computed tomography (CT) images to establish the correct pelvis dose that is MR-based. With paired MR images and angiography, pix2pix underwent modifications to create a model forT1 and T2 MRIs to examine vascular structures (Zhang et al., 2022).

Regarding 3D multimodal clinical images and mobile organs, it is complex to get paired images as they lack cross-modality paired records: Cycle GAN deals with scenarios of unpaired images. Most of the challenges facing unpaired image translation are that it is difficult to ascertain prediction accuracy. There are also geometric distortions that injure anatomical structures; according to (Zhang et al., 2022), one can mitigate this issue by using two backup maps to curb synthetic data invariances.

GANs are crucial in ensuring balance in datasets and upholding patient privacy. GANs are the future of healthcare; however, training volatility and low image quality affect GANs hampering their adoption in clinical settings for image translation and segmentations. GANs also face challenges regarding their approval for clinical practices since they are few. Despite this, GANs have made significant improvements to already existing models. These advances may create the basis for approving GANs in the healthcare realm.

2.2.1. Federated Learning

Regarding multi-institutional datasets, there is central model training in that data obtained from several institutions are accumulated in one server. However, this centralized training represents a portion of critical medical data that would be important while developing a model. Most jurisdictions and legal bodies demand that patient records should stay local. Federated learning involves using decentralized data together in the instrumentation of one server.

While centralized training involves moving medical data from different points to a central server for model training, in federated learning, clinical data does not move (Zhang et al., 2022). Every location with training data receives a model copy for training, and once updated, they all send it back to the central server. Other subsequent pieces of training follow, repeating the same procedure until the model training ends. No clinical data leaves its location, thus alleviating issues breaching patient privacy protocols. It also reduces data accumulation costs and speeds up the training datasets scaling process in scope and diversity. There are two applications of federated learning: cross-silo and cross-device learning.

2.2.2. Cross-Silo Learning

Cross-silo is a form of federated learning which mitigates the inadequacies of centralized training (Li et al., 2020). Some of the recent cross-silo applications include creating a segmenter for Covid-19 chest-C lesion, facilitating the creation of 'digital twins,' and leveraging electronic health records to foresee admission to hospital because of heart conditions. Some of the latest efforts include gauging the model design limitations and approaches to improve their performance and mitigate federated learning deployment challenges such as privacy breaches and data heterogeneity (Sheller et al., 2019).

Federated learning models often face domain shifts equated to centralized learning. Despite this, the federated learning model can accomplish up to 99% success as centralized learning, and evidently, there is a need to deploy it in healthcare sectors (Zhang et al., 2022). While federated learning upholds patients' privacy, there are still risks of breaches. While institutions give information on model updates during training, sensitive patient data can reveal seepage into other parties or servers. There are two approaches to curb such privacy breaches sparse vector approach (Lyu et al., 2017) and careful parameter sharing (Hitaj et al., 2017).

Another concern of federated learning is dealing with data that are not identically distributed or independent (non-IID data). Healthcare records partly face this challenge since the high dominance of diseases in some hospitals equated to others, thus bringing label-distribution skew. Secondly, institution-specific data collection approaches can cause inconsistencies in labels and figures. Non-IID data cause glitches in popular algorithms such as FedAvg from converging in federated learning. To address this issue, there is a need to reframe data to ensure uniformity and uphold data heterogeneity, that is, consensus and pluralism.

Cross-Device Learning

As competent techs gain popularity, sensor technology advances, and mass production becomes cheaper; healthcare data will increase (Zhang et al., 2022). 'Smart' software can create troves of consistent and diverse data to teach ML models and establish personalized health intuitions for each operator. It will therefore heighten issues of accumulating massive data into a central server for training and aggravate privacy concerns. Cross-device is a form of federated learning launched to address the issues of massive data created from decentralized devices and installed in several other devices, such as Apple's Siri used in voice recognition.

Using cross-device learning in training clinical models is among the trends in healthcare. This training approach has outdone the non-federated learning by at least 5.3% (Zhang et al., 2022). For instance, during the FedHealth pre-training process, the human-activity-recognition dataset used 80% of the data before its deployment to local institutions for the actual training and summed up (Chen et al., 2020). The summed-up model Later goes back to the consumer and is personalized using user-specific data. Model personalization mitigates global models' problems and disparities in users' probability distributions.

2.2.3. Federated Learning Opportunities and Challenges

Looking at the performance and the promises federated learning holds for healthcare in the coming years, federated learning will witness its implementation in the healthcare sector. Integrating federated learning in healthcare institutions will call for harmonization among institutions during the model training process. Healthcare data will have to undergo standardization before training progresses. It could be problematic owing to the disparities in institutions on data collection and labeling techniques. Recent data pre-processing channels can be employed in developing multi-organizational training datasets; in federated learning, the roles shift from the central server to the local institutions. Successful deployment of federated learning requires streamlining of these processes among all institutions.

Challenges facing federated learning include the failure of model developers to examine the data at the development stage. Data scrutiny is crucial to detect mislabeled data and emerging trends. Tools using GANs to develop synthetic data to represent actual data and population statistics are helpful: federated analytics is an example of such a tool. It is unclear if tools designed for cross-device learning could still be helpful in cross-silo settings while still upholding patient privacy. Consequently, deploying federated learning requires resilient frameworks. Such software is patented, and those free are predominantly for carrying out research.

Implementing federated learning to meet its expectations calls for proper coordination and time. Many federated learning problems are solved through frameworks that can mitigate privacy breaches, issues with non-IID data, and those that augment model aggregation. On the other hand, participating health institutions should possess an up-to-date infrastructure to facilitate model training, data uniformity, and effective communication between local institutions and the server. Some trends include Federated Tumor Segmentation Initiative, which trains models on lesion segmentation in over 29 healthcare institutions globally. This initiative aims to establish a universal model aggregation algorithm and even out training data from different institutions. NVIDIA collaboration is another initiative that trained models for mammography classification. The mentioned initiates provide blueprints for federated learning for healthcare.

2.3. Natural Language Processing (NLP)

Crucial clinical data, such as the patient's symptoms and disease severity, are not recorded in structured information fields but are clinician-generated texts. Natural Language Processing (NLP) is one AI application that comes in handy in interpreting these clinical data.NLP involves deep learning crucial for speech recognition in healthcare. It converts unstructured clinician-generated texts to structured data that can be used for crucial clinical decisions, health surveillance, and quality control (Doan et al., 2014). NLP enables clinicians to comprehend and classify medical data. NLP systems are designed to evaluate unstructured patients' clinical notes, providing profound insight into quality improvement for better outcomes. NLP relieves medics from the daunting task of feeding in Electronic Health Records and provides a patient-centric service. Computer-Assisted Coding (CAC) is a common NLP application that captures medical procedure data and diagnosis and maximizes claims. NLP is, in many ways taking healthcare to a new level.

NLP centers on text and discourse analysis to derive meaning from these words. Some of the accomplishments of NLP include picture captioning, machine translation, and generating texts. Algorithms such as Recurrent Neural Networks (RNNs) are operational at processing time series, texts, dialogues, and language, making it crucial for this field of study (Esteva et al., 2019). EHRs are growing ubiquitous over time. Healthcare data in sizeable clinical organizations can obtain over 10 million medical transactions from patients in 10 years, and one hospitalization can produce over 150,000 health records (Esteva et al., 2019). The prospective benefits of the mentioned data can have significant implications for healthcare advancements.

Establishing deep learning models requires a series of steps. The first step involves raw data accumulation from various organizations to ensure the system created is inclusive. The accumulated data undergo standardization and is analyzed across patients, making it suitable for model training (Esteva et al., 2019). It enables medics to establish patients' diagnoses, patients' symptom lists, and probable medical interventions. Up-to-date, many organizations use supervised learning to make predictions using structured data such as demographics, lab outcomes, and vitals. While recognizing the vitality of unstructured data, researchers and scholars employ unsupervised and semi-supervised techniques such as auto-encoders. Auto-encoders involve training networks to establish good representation through compression and reconstruction of unlabeled information: this is useful in diagnosis predictions (Esteva et al., 2019).

Medical Information Mart for Intensive Care (MIMIC) datasets are valuable in sepsis40 predictions entailing ICU patients. The coming generations will foresee advances in speech recognition automation and clinical virtual assistants who can accurately transcribe patients' visits. ICU patients offer a substantial amount of data equated to non-ICU patients; however, this is just a minute representation of the general patient population. It is, therefore, uncertain about deriving the efficiency of such models created from data that generalizes the larger patient population.

With a medic's 11-hour workday, they spend 6 hours feeding in EHRs: this is a daunting task and hampers them from offering patient-centric care (Esteva et al., 2019). RNN language translation model uses a technique to translate speech to text from one language to another. It would mitigate the challenges of language barriers in healthcare settings. Employing RNNs on EHRs could be easy to carry out medical transcriptions. The major challenge would be extracting an accurate transcription from the clinical conversation classifying and analyzing all the medical entities, and summarizing the entire dialogue.

However promising these algorithms are to the future of healthcare, few healthcare settings have deployed these models for clinical practice. Future considerations should include unstructured EHRs while developing NLP models (Figure 2). For example, medics always ignore clinical notes while establishing predictive models. RNNs are currently setting significant predictive results by blending structured and unstructured EHRs using a semi-supervised approach. Combining both data allows learning across a vast patient population using diverse EHRs, outperforming the traditional methods in carrying out clinical tasks such as determining readmission rates and death, predicting diagnoses, and establishing the length of hospital stay.

Figure 2. NLP diagnosis prediction using both structured and unstructured EHRs

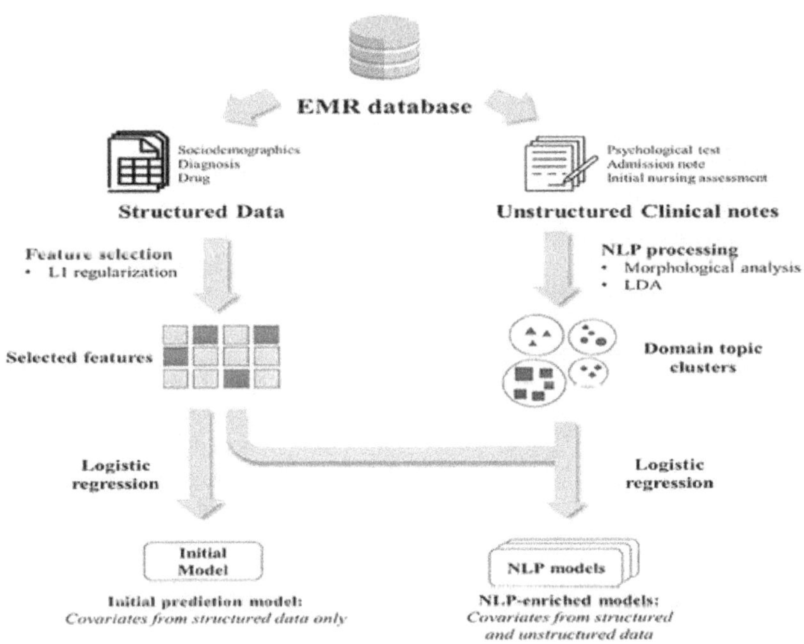

Soft controls involve organizational culture and understanding workers' and management behaviors. In healthcare, patient outcomes rely on medics' behaviors and managerial skills (Figure 3). Following the relevant legislation and partly because of scandals, for example, SBM offshore, Vestia, SNS Reaal, and Rabobank, among others, soft controls have become critical for administrative authorities, auditors, and business settings as a whole (Combee et al., 2015). Internal auditors put considerable emphasis and attention on the hard controls, such as the design and operation effectiveness and frameworks, while cultural and moral aspects (soft controls) are barely addressed. Considering the significant implications of human behavior controls, it is absurd to overlook these soft aspects. Ignoring these aspects does not reveal the extent of the audit being in "control."

Hard controls have a direct influence on the workers' conduct. Soft controls, on the other hand, intervene in a worker's performance, that is, their personality and opinions (convictions), thus influencing their integrity, values, loyalty, and honesty (Combee et al., 2015). Below is a diagram (Figure 5) explaining the relationship between hard controls and a soft control.

Figure 3. Soft controls vs. hard controls

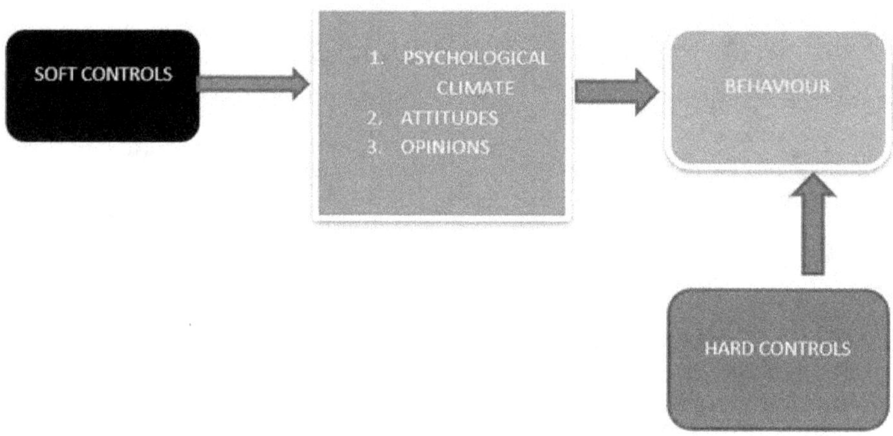

While hard controls supervise individual behaviors through explicit measures, soft controls monitor the attitudes of company workers through values and conventions. Soft controls employ social influence approaches, stress the need for shared values in an organization, and influence employees' conduct at work (Chtiouia & Thiéry-Dubuissonb, 2011). Soft controls in an auditing environment form a basis of discipline among colleagues; organizational culture comprises shared values among members of an organization incorporated unconsciously concerning the organizational objectives. Several aspects define individuals' attitudes concerning organizational goals and values, including economic values (generating profits), corporate values, and social values. People act based on their ideologies and their manager's values: working environments affect people's values.

Corporate culture is a soft control tool exercised on workers. Individuals incorporate solid values and beliefs, avoid authority orders, and perform their duties accordingly. Consequently, ethical contribution in carrying out soft control is vague; however, there is a connection between integrities and employees' willingness to perform well (Chtiouia & Thiéry-Dubuissonb, 2011). The code of ethics provides workers (medics in case) with behavioral orientation. One can view this as a form of soft control; it may seem coercive due to several sanctions, but it helps realize organizational goals and promotes ethical behaviors. An organization cannot establish a robust working environment unless they ensure no employee creates a humiliating context for other workers. Involving administrative authorities in selecting and deploying an ethics program could influence managerial. Carrying out soft controls using an ethics program could have pernicious implications: it may weaken over time, motivating workers to employ their moral judgments in new situations, leading to this politicization and skills atrophy (Chtiouia & Thiéry-Dubuissonb, 2011).

It is crucial to comprehend if soft controls have capacities lacking in hard controls. Soft controls are essential in behavioral control, especially in ambiguous and unpredictable situations. Using hard controls in behavioral monitoring proves its efficiency in predictable conditions. Hard controls cannot handle the complexities in companies with their rigid nature; it can be cumbersome to adapt to likely changes and shifts that organizations could experience. While organizations cannot establish rules to cover all situations, it makes hard control limited. Therefore, creating an implicit soft control model is crucial to managing workers in unpredictable events. Due to managerial influence, the workers would have a series of unstated rules and norms. These unstated rules promote a shared philosophy guiding the organization's conduct and decision-making processes. It should create an environment of confidence and loyalty where it would be impossible for hard controls.

The discussion above on soft controls shows they have significant promises for healthcare auditing practices. While technical advances ease medics' workload, physicians also need behavioral control to help them handle unpredictable situations while working with different patients. Doctors must establish a code of conduct because AI algorithms would not handle behavioral controls for the organization's success. Having common philosophy and shared values is crucial for any company.

3. THIRD-PARTY RISK MANAGEMENT

Healthcare organizations struggle to detect, respond, heal, and shield themselves against third-party threats and data breaches. Current methodologies to mitigate third-party risks are unsuccessful: this failure has negative implications for the economy (Angle, 2022). The approaches fail for various reasons, including the absence of automated third-party risk management approaches for digital clinical applications (over-reliance on manual techniques), carrying out risk assessments is costly, and takes time. Healthcare organizations barely deploy third-party assessment controls. Third parties handling EHRs are rapidly growing due to the changing complexities of healthcare data. Healthcare providers depend on third parties for data management and AI medical application (infrastructure). As EHRs grow complex, so does their management and thus requiring more third parties. Third parties are responsible for 50% of healthcare data breaches owing to data stewardship challenges since the infrastructure belongs to third parties, and hospitals barely manage their data (Angle, 2022).

"Muddling Through"

Muddling is a dangerous risk management approach, yet many healthcare organizations find themselves in this trap. There is adequate proof that United States healthcare organizations are short of a structured cyber-resilience strategy. Healthcare organization barely invest on cyber security: the complexities that come with operating cyber security lead to establishment of an ineffective approach. A third of healthcare executives procure cybersecurity software blindly (Abraham et al., 2019).

Healthcare industries tend to be too trusting and overlook the overlying risk until hackers disclose these loopholes. Criminal healthcare cyber-attacks have augmented by approximately 125% over the past five years: a Los Angeles-based hospital had to part with a ransom of $17,000 Bitcoin to a hacker who had seized their system controls (Abraham et al., 2019). Often, the patient would receive medical bills for the procedure they did not undergo: a hacker used a victim's credential to procure a mobility scooter, among other medical equipment. Healthcare data breaches cost organizations approximately $400 for each stolen record; this is relatively higher than banks and retail enterprises, which are roughly $215 and $165, respectively (Abraham et al., 2019). Cyber attackers like Wannacry and Petya have kept organizations on their toes to establish comprehensive cyber security strategies. The hurdles in deploying cyber security software make it cumbersome for organizations to shift to a stable state.

Most healthcare organizations are unprepared to handle cyber-attacks. Its complex nature forces healthcare executives to assume and employ an if-it-ain't-broke-don't-fix-it attitude (Abraham et al., 2019). The extensive adoption of Internet of Things (IoT) applications has expanded cyber-attack surfaces and thus increased vulnerabilities (Cartwright, 2023). IoT devices serve different purposes, including monitoring patients remotely, alerting medics on device malfunction, assessing patients" hospital stay, and providing health education (Abouzakhar et.al, 2017). IoT applications are susceptible to attacks equated to traditional computers and, if left unpatched, become vulnerable to potential attacks (Abraham et al., 2019). To worsen the situation, IoT vendors tend to install weak security measures like poor encryption conventions, which barely meet traditional standards. Healthcare datasets are honey pots for cyber-attacker due to the continuous sharing of EHRs across different devices and locations: IOTs could be the future of healthcare, but it exposes healthcare to new vulnerabilities such as denial-of-service attacks, stolen password, and loss of confidential data that could be liable for blackmail (Abraham et al., 2019). A substantial percentage of EHRs applications are cloud-based, which broadly increases the attack surface since any can access EHRs in the cloud, creating more security challenges. It is cumbersome for healthcare executives to ensure that third parties guarantee the security of EHRs. Huraizah et. al (2019) presented an IoT Security risk-management system for healthcare, the author brings emphasis to the dangers related to IoT technology in the healthcare sector and offers an approach for reducing these hazards. The model, which aims at providing a safe IoT environment in obedience with quality performance indicators, is broken down into three sections: Healthcare IoT Risk Management, the Healthcare Achievement Index for Accountability (HPIA), and installation phases.

There are many security legal frameworks with intersecting objectives and sanctions. Deciding on a suitable framework poses a major dilemma for health organizations. Despite the advancements in security frameworks, healthcare organizations still lag in deploying these systems and do not use risk-based tools. The National Institute of Standards and Technology (NIST) has a robust risk-based cybersecurity framework that can detect potential risks, and healthcare organizations should try to adopt this framework. It is crucial to note that Ransomware shuts patient care and not IT: one cannot look at the security risk but the business risk it poses.

In the United States, there are numerous laws on cyber security, such as the Omnibus law, the 1996 Health Insurance Portability and Accountability Act (HIPAA), the 2015 Cyber Disclosure Act, and the Gramm Leach-Bliley Act of 1999 (Abraham et al., 2019). Health organizations must comply with these rules, despite being ambiguous, setting data security expectations. For example, currently, HIPAA does not entail having a certification (gold standard) other than for organizations to observe the security controls list. Federal health organizations are delegated to comply with HIPAA guidelines, while their private counterparts have the autonomy to choose controls that suit their framework. The Healthcare sector does not require certification for cyber security control: this would influence an organization to comply with the required standard.NIST's role is to ensure compliance but meeting these standards exhausts companies' resources to arrive at "a "secure enough" state. Experts comprehend that "secure enough" is barely enough, given the security breaches experienced by federal bodies like National Security Agency (Abraham et al., 2019). Even staying up to speed with federal laws is a daunting task. Compliance cannot promise resilience to cyber security.

IT functions can establish measures for companies to identify, prevent, and recuperate from attacks. Ineffective IT functions would provide loopholes for cyber security attacks: for instance, if hospitals do not update inventories of vital data. It is crucial to note the open ports on the network: some companies still have ex-third parties on their networks. Such organizations barely monitor the networks and lack knowledge of who is on their network traffic, and cannot ascertain the security of their IT environment. Advancement encryption protocols and penetration tests do not mitigate cyber-attack risks: a mature IT is crucial for cyber resilience, which is the ability to prevent attacks and recover quickly from attacks (Abraham from attacks. Establishing an operational cybersecurity framework is costly and time-consuming. The annual IT budget is very low; other companies cut on this budget while others lack formal security frameworks.

The implications of cyber-attack can be massive such as losing reputation, exposure of confidential data, lawsuits, bankruptcy, operation interference, and business shutdown in every case. Therefore, profound insight into the negative implications of cyber-attacks is crucial for achieving cyber resilience. Healthcare administrative authorities should be part of setting these strategies; unfortunately, this is never the case in most healthcare facilities as IT is always an afterthought lacking resources to curb attacks. Such companies are ignorant, and operating on ignorance could cause panic when they experience an attack. Executive management must be proactive in understanding company vulnerabilities, partake in security-review discussions, and establish a security committee. A survey established approximately 40% of authorities is cognizant of cyber-attack protocols (Abraham et al., 2019). It explains the poor investment in IT functions. Recently investments in cyber security are augmenting courtesy of current attacks; however, they do not have a strategy (Abraham et al., 2019).

4. MITIGATING CYBER SECURITY ATTACKS

Hospitals must comprehend their tolerance abilities before establishing mitigation strategies, whether they are offering patient-centric care or upholding patient privacy. Organizations should have zero tolerance for failure to report any security breaches, shutting down the hospital portal five minutes after an attack and deploying forensic analysts to determine the severity (Chaudhary, 2018). Ascertaining tolerance levels is crucial while developing a cyber-security model as it enhances clarity. Comprehending cyber-security threats involves profiling the fundamental business function, all operational units, and the enterprises" procedures. After that, the company should prepare an inventory comprising all vulnerable assets and the individuals liable for handling these assets. The company will then ascertain the rate of risk impact of each asset. Determining the severity of each threat may vary from one organization to another depending on the dataset they feel is vital, like hospitals (EHRs) and banks (financial encryption codes) (Chaudhary, 2018).

Valuing cyber-security hazards include approximating the costs based on different breach scenarios. This estimation is important in ascertaining the investment cost required for developing and deploying security frameworks. The Healthcare sector must contemplate the negative implication, including patient relocation, sanctions, paying ransom, reputation, revoking of permits, federal penalties, business closure, and extra costs relating to retrieving lost data, installing new security frameworks, and buying new equipment (Cram et al., 2020). The company should start budgeting on data backups, cyber-security training, screening cloud service suppliers, robust security frameworks, continuous data monitoring, AI enabled systems, and highly trained personnel. Typical emergency response procedures are reactionary and might not foresee possible hazards. To help with preemptive incident response (IR), cyber security intelligence (CTI) can offer details on newly identified threats. He et. al. (2022) present investigation uses of CTI advisories alongside a proactive detection and response approach based on NIST to combat ransomware threats like WannaCry. To move from reactive to proactive defense against cyber threats, the report emphasizes how critical it is to integrate CTI into IR procedures in the healthcare industry. Cyberattacks are targeted towards health care firm's supply chain (Tully, 2020; Wong, 2014); where newer technological products present newer risks and required different protection methods (Suman, 2021; Services, 2023).

For institutions to enhance safety and protect critical patient data, SIEM implementation is important. The study (Elsami et. al, 2017) emphasizes the importance of data security, compliance with regulations, and privacy, integrity, and accessibility in information security. In the interest of properly minimizing dangers, it also covers attacks such as ransomware or a need for current security procedures. The overall goals of the research are to guide future institution SIEM deployments and promote security in the medical sector. SIEM systems have increased in use because of on-demand options, and they help companies in discovering and submitting problems for investigation. Sajedi (2018) focused on data hiding techniques like watermarking, stenography, and encryption to safeguard medical facilities from privacy invasions. Patient privacy is necessary due to advances in electronic interaction and surveillance in healthcare. To safeguard healthcare facilities, a few safety precautions are required, including restricted access and data hiding. It has been recommended that one employs reputable third parties and specific techniques to prevent DoS attacks on mobile devices (Sajedi, 2018).

Communication function is vital in every sector, and healthcare is no exception. The success of developing and deploying cyber-security frameworks relies on effective communication. It ranges from involving the senior faculties to deploy the necessary resources to educating several stakeholders to uphold confidentiality. Despite the complexities associated with cyber securities, effective communication must have clarity, be personalized, and be candid (Chaudhary, 2018). Lack of cognizance and comprehension, it might be cumbersome to mobilize support from stakeholders and enhance a hands-on cyber-security culture (Cram et al., 2020). Communication is crucial in that: the boards need to understand the cost of keeping the hackers at bay, managers need to understand how to operate without obstruction from tight security procedures such as two-factor authentication that consumes time from offering patient care, and technicians want to understand the type of controls crucial for organizations protection (Cram et al., 2020). A cyber-security consultant must conduct a series of interpersonal and multilevel communication in different departments.

5. BLOCK CHAIN IN THE MEDICAL REALM

Blockchain is one of the emerging auditing practices in healthcare (Attaran, 2020). Bitcoin became the first blockchains digital currency. Blockchain is in its initial stages; however, it has grasped the attention of society, scholars, and domain experts from numerous sectors such as finance, education, economics, government, healthcare, the Internet of Things (IoT), and manufacturing. With applications including clinical trials, drug counterfeiting, online patient access, automated health claims adjudication, sharing patient medical data, public health care management, online patient records, automated health claims adjudication, and precision medicine, it significantly benefits the health care industry (Ali et al., 2021; Balasubramanian et al., 2021; Sharma et. al; McGhin, 2019). Blockchain's ledger technology holds substantial promises for the healthcare sector (Massaro, 2021; Yaqoob et al., 2019; Wamba et al., 2020; Hopkins, 2021).).

Its diverse nature, toughness, tamper-free, confidentiality, digital currency, decentralization, safety, and harmony created through cryptographic algorithms, can mitigate contemporary healthcare issues. Blockchain has a decentralized ledger comprising a series (chain) of time-stamped authentic transaction blocks connected cryptographically (Dwivedi et al., 2019. When users generate a transaction private key digitally signs the transaction and disseminates it to its network. Each network user ensures block validation through unanimity protocol creation. The authenticated block then attaches to the chain the restructured ledger duplicates across permission network users (Agbo & Mahmoud, 2020). The consensus protocol would replace centralized healthcare authority and third parties. Blockchain has three categories; the first is a digital currency, which focuses on digital payment models without involving intermediaries (third parties), and decentralization applications on automated smart contracts. The third category focuses on societal welfare is crucial in the transmission of confidential public data in the government, education, and healthcare, such as healthcoin and learningcoin (Daniel et al., 2017).

5.1. Blockchain and Healthcare

Blockchain would solve the problem of EHRs management. Different healthcare stakeholders such as medics, payers, administration, and payers obtain and share EHRs across and this. Data provenance is crucial for EHRs" authenticity. Data management is unavoidable, and medics can achieve decentralized communication through information duplication across validated network nodes minus third parties. Real-time data updates and monitored EHRs access augments fraud detection, settling claims, and curbing counterfeit drugs in the market (Yaqoob et al., 2019) (Figure 4). Blockchain would lessen the time-consuming and costly data transmission procedures for medical research and patient supervision.

The decentralized ledger is helpful in instances of incompatible fragmented EHRs, enhancing coordination and patient care (Dwivedi et al., 2019). A synchronized system allows fast data transmission and patient notification and boosts positive market competitiveness. Centralized systems are prone to insecurities, failures, and vulnerabilities. Claim adjudication endure series of compilation: blockchain's interoperability nature can address this issue. Common immutable prescriptions facilitate medication harmony for improved patient care.

Figure 4. Blockchain decentralized ledger (Yaqoob et al., 2019)

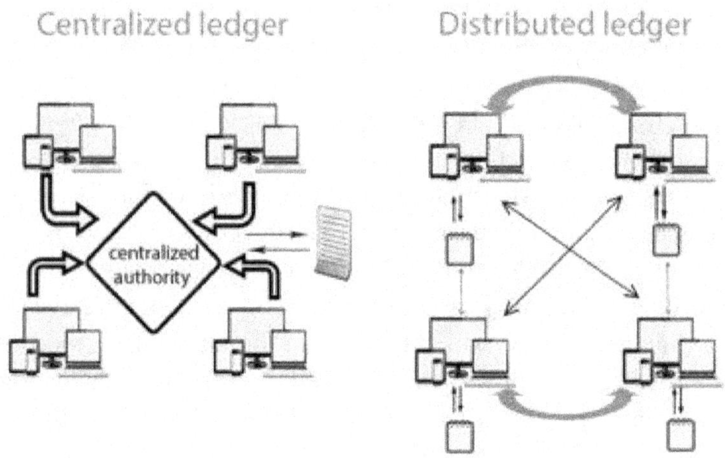

Healthcare data are prone to security breaches and might affect patient privacy and the hospital's reputation including fraud (Abbas et al., 2020) and need attention for resolution (Tortorella et al., 2021).

Blockchain's immutability ensures transparency through cryptographic codes that decrypt certain data and guarantee patient-controlled access (Yaqoob et al., 2019). Patients hold their health records and have the capacity to cancel and grant access to other stakeholders, such as medics and researchers. Security issues are due to dependence on a centralized authority. Altering transaction in a blockchain-based requires extraordinary computational power and consensus mechanism making it impossible. Data provenance is crucial for EHRs blockchain's time-stamped and authenticated data can relieve payers from perilous monetary loss. One can also trace data origins, avoid data snooping, and enhance data accuracy through time-stamped blocks; authorities can also track drug production and supply procedures to detect fake drugs in the market courtesy of data provenance. Digital currency ensures transparency in healthcare financial transactions.

6. LIMITATIONS

Blockchain technology holds substantial promises in the healthcare sector but has limitations. Blockchain-based healthcare systems adopt sensory devices on patients; they may suffer storage problems due to the heavy load computation. Additionally, blockchain transaction processes are time-consuming and take several days to finish one transaction. Bitcoin blockchain carries out seven transactions in a second. In comparison, Visa executes 2000 transactions and Twitter (5000) in seconds. Such slow speed limits the blockchain's scalability (Agbo & Mahmoud, 2020). Blockchain-based healthcare systems would have problems with speed and scalability. Blockchain operates on a consensus mechanism, and malicious miners can flood the network and scrap blocks from scrupulous miners and may take hold of valuable data or coins. Therefore, blockchain systems are prone to 51% security attacks (Yaqoob et al., 2019). Blockchain's transparent nature provides another challenge to confidentiality breaches. A patient's EHRs and biomedical applications are sensitive, and transparency would imply that everyone would access all sensitive information. Consequently, blockchain-based cloud limits data access controls to uphold EHRs' confidentiality and security.

Another blockchain-related problem is the issues of anonymity as blockchain hash value conceals identity; criminals take advantage of the blockchain obscurity and commit fraud. Blockchain suffers a series of fraud hype as cyber-attackers use Ransomware, seize company networks, and demand ransom. People can procure illicit drugs from the Dark Web using cryptocurrencies. Blockchain also poses environmental unsustainability issues in that the energy cost for transacting one bitcoin could power two American households in a day: making it expensive.

7. CONCLUSION

Healthcare systems are susceptible to the ever-changing dimensions of society, such as technology. It, therefore, calls for healthcare auditors to be on their toes for such trends for quality improvement. These emerging trends include AI algorithms such as machine learning and natural learning processes. Soft controls replace traditional hard controls and complement areas hard controls cannot handle, such as unpredictable events. While the healthcare sector relies on auditors for quality improvement, they might experience risks from third parties, which call for mitigations. Blockchain provides solutions for third-party risks, such as the decentralized nature that resolves vulnerabilities and insecurities with third parties. It also ensures data transmission processes are smooth, secure, and interoperable. However, blockchain transparency exposes patients' confidential data, which there is a need to establish a system that would uphold patient privacy and effective information transmission across different stakeholders.

REFERENCES

Abbas, K., Afaq, M., Khan, T. A., & Song, W. C. (2020). A blockchain and machine learning- based drug supply chain management and recommendation system for smart pharmaceutical industry. *Electronics (Basel)*, 9(5), 852. Advance online publication. DOI: 10.3390/electronics9050852

Abouzakhar, N., Jones, A., & Angelopoulou, O. (2017). Internet of things security: a review of risks and threats to healthcare sector. IEEE International Conference on Internet of Things (iThings) and IEEE Green Computing and Communications (GreenCom) and IEEE Cyber, Physical and Social Computing (CPSCom) and IEEE Smart Data (SmartData) (pp. 373-378). IEEE. DOI: 10.1109/iThings-GreenCom-CPSCom-SmartData.2017.62

Abraham, C., Chatterjee, D., & Sims, R. R. (2019). Muddling through cybersecurity: Insights from the U.S. healthcare industry. *Business Horizons*, 62(4), 539–548. DOI: 10.1016/j.bushor.2019.03.010

Agbo, C. C., & Mahmoud, Q. H. (2020). Blockchain in healthcare. *International Journal of Healthcare Information Systems and Informatics*, 15(3), 82–97. DOI: 10.4018/IJHISI.2020070105

Ali, M., Jaradat, A., Kulakli, A., & Abuhalimeh, A. (2021). A comparative study: Blockchain technology utilization benefits, challenges, and functionalities. *IEEE Access : Practical Innovations, Open Solutions*, 9(1), 12730–12749. DOI: 10.1109/ACCESS.2021.3050241

Angle, J. (2022). Third-Party Vendor Risk Management 2. Research Gate. https://www.researchgate.net/publication/362135483_Third-Party_Vendor_Risk_Management_2

Attaran, M. (2020). Blockchain technology in healthcare: Challenges and opportunities. *International Journal of Healthcare Management*, 15(1), 1–14. DOI: 10.1080/20479700.2020.1843887

Balasubramanian, S., Shukla, V., Sethi, J. S., Islam, N., & Saloum, R. (2021). A readiness assessment framework for blockchain adoption: A healthcare case study. *Technological Forecasting and Social Change*, 165, 120536. DOI: 10.1016/j.techfore.2020.120536

Bogdan, V., Rus, L., Gherai, D. S., Florea, A. G., & Bugnar, N. G. (2023). A Streamline Sustainable Business Performance Reporting Model by an Integrated FinESG Approach. *Sustainability (Basel)*, 15(24), 16860. DOI: 10.3390/su152416860

Bunker, R. (2021, January 25). Emerging trends in internal audit for 2021. Barclay Simpson UK. https://www.barclaysimpson.com/blogs/a-new-era-emerging-trends-in-internal-audit-for-2021-12525151636

Cartwright, A. J. (2023). The elephant in the room: Cybersecurity in healthcare. *Journal of Clinical Monitoring and Computing*, 37(5), 1–10. DOI: 10.1007/s10877-023-01013-5 PMID: 37088852

Chaudhary, P. (2018). Mitigating cyber attacks through security models and networking protocols. *International Journal on Computer Science and Engineering*, 6(8), 925–929. DOI: 10.26438/ijcse/v6i8.925929

Chen, Y., Qin, X., Wang, J., Yu, C., & Gao, W. (2020). FedHealth: A Federated Transfer Learning Framework for Wearable Wealthcare. *IEEE Intelligent Systems*, 35(4), 83–93. DOI: 10.1109/MIS.2020.2988604

Chtiouia, T., & Thiéry-Dubuissonb, S. (2011). Hard and Soft Controls: Mind the Gap! Tawhid Chtiouia and Stéphanie Thiéry-Dubuissonb. *International Journal of Business*, 16(3), 290–302.

Combee, J., Dijkman, M., Ockels, G., Wortel, R., & Vries, B. D. (2015). Discussion paper Soft controls. What are the Starting Points for the Internal Auditor? The institute of internal auditors in Netherlands. https://www.iia.nl/SiteFiles/Publicaties/IIA_Bro%20A4%20Soft%20Controls%20Engels%2002.pdf

Cram, W. A., Proudfoot, J. G., & D'Arcy, J. (2020). Maximizing employee compliance with cybersecurity policies. *MIS Quarterly Executive*, 183–198. DOI: 10.17705/2msqe.00032

Daniel, J., Sargolzaei, A., Abdelghani, M., Sargolzaei, S., & Amaba, B. (2017). Blockchain technology, cognitive computing, and healthcare innovations. *Journal of Advances in Information Technology*, 194-198, 194–198. Advance online publication. DOI: 10.12720/jait.8.3.194-198

Ding, R., Shen, S., Zhu, Y., Du, L., Chen, S., Liang, J., Wang, K., Xiao, W., & Hong, Y. (2023). Evolution, Forecasting, and Driving Mechanisms of the Digital Financial Network: Evidence from China. *Sustainability (Basel)*, 15(22), 16072. DOI: 10.3390/su152216072

Doan, S., Conway, M., Phuong, T. M., & Ohno-Machado, L. (2014). Natural language processing in biomedicine: A unified system architecture overview. *Methods in Molecular Biology (Clifton, N.J.)*, 1168, 275–294. DOI: 10.1007/978-1-4939-0847-9_16 PMID: 24870142

Dunn, C. L., & Hollander, S. (2017). The impact of artificial intelligence on auditing. *Current Issues in Auditing*, 11, A1–A12.

Dwivedi, A., Srivastava, G., Dhar, S., & Singh, R. (2019). A decentralized privacy-preserving healthcare blockchain for IoT. *Sensors (Basel)*, 19(2), 326. DOI: 10.3390/s19020326 PMID: 30650612

Esteva, A., Robicquet, A., Ramsundar, B., Kuleshov, V., DePristo, M., Chou, K., Cui, C., Corrado, G., Thrun, S., & Dean, J. (2019). A guide to deep learning in healthcare. *Nature Medicine*, 25(1), 24–29. DOI: 10.1038/s41591-018-0316-z PMID: 30617335

Firoiu, D., Ionescu, G. H., Cojocaru, T. M., Niculescu, M., Cimpoeru, M. N., & Călin, O. A. (2023b). Progress of EU Member States Regarding the Bioeconomy and Biomass Producing and Converting Sectors. *Sustainability (Basel)*, 15(19), 14128. DOI: 10.3390/su151914128

Frid-Adar, M., Diamant, I., Klang, E., Amitai, M., Goldberger, J., & Greenspan, H. (2018). GAN-based synthetic medical image augmentation for increased CNN performance in liver lesion classification. *Neurocomputing*, 321, 321–331. DOI: 10.1016/j.neucom.2018.09.013

Gartner. (2019, January 21). Gartner survey shows 37 percent of organizations have implemented AI in some form. https://www.gartner.com/en/newsroom/press-releases/2019-01-21-gartner-survey-shows-37-percent-of-organizations-have

He, Y., Maglaras, L., Aliyu, A., & Luo, C. (2022). Healthcare security incident response strategy-a proactive incident response (ir) procedure. *Security and Communication Networks*, 2022, 2022. DOI: 10.1155/2022/2775249

Hitaj, B., Ateniese, G., & Perez-Cruz, F. (2017). Deep models under the GAN. *Proceedings of the 2017 ACM SIGSAC Conference on Computer and Communications Security*. DOI: 10.1145/3133956.3134012

Hopkins, J.L. (2021). An investigation into emerging industry 4.0 technologies as drivers of supply chain innovation in Australia. Computers in Industry, 125. doi: . compind.2020.103323DOI: 10.1016/j

Li, X., Gu, Y., Dvornek, N., Staib, L. H., Ventola, P., & Duncan, J. S. (2020). Multi-site fMRI analysis using privacy preserving federated learning and domain adaptation: ABIDE results. *Medical Image Analysis*, 65, 101765. DOI: 10.1016/j.media.2020.101765 PMID: 32679533

Li, Z. (2018). The impact of AI on the field of accounting: Preventing fraud and generating positive effects on accounting information quality. *Journal of Accounting and Finance*, 32, 78–92.

Lyu, M., Su, D., & Li, N. (2017). Understanding the sparse vector technique for differential privacy. *Proceedings of the VLDB Endowment International Conference on Very Large Data Bases*, 10(6), 637–648. DOI: 10.14778/3055330.3055331

Mar, V. (2021, April 2). Technology trend 2021: Artificial intelligence a necessity in healthcare. Techment. https://www.techment.com/technology-trend-2021-artificial-intelligence-a-necessity-in-healthcare/

Martínez, A. L., Pérez, M. G., & Ruiz-Martínez, A. (2023). A Comprehensive Review of the state-of-the-art on security and privacy issues in Healthcare. *ACM Computing Surveys*, 55(12), 1–38. Advance online publication. DOI: 10.1145/3571156

Massaro, M. (2021). Digital transformation in the healthcare sector through blockchain technology. Insights from academic research and business developments. *Technovation*, 120.

McGhin, T., Choo, K. K. R., Liu, C. Z., & He, D. (2019). Blockchain in healthcare applications: Research challenges and opportunities. *Journal of Network and Computer Applications*, 135, 62–75. DOI: 10.1016/j.jnca.2019.02.027

Mouchantaf, R., Auth, D., Moride, Y., Raine, J., Han, S. Y., & Smith, M. Y. (2021). Risk Management for the 21st Century: Current Status and Future Needs. *Drug Safety*, 44(4), 409–419. DOI: 10.1007/s40264-020-01033-z PMID: 33565024

Nguyen, A., Smith, J., & Johnson, L. (2022). The positive impact of AI technology on the auditing process to enhance information transparency. *Journal of Accounting and Auditing*, 45, 112–128.

Nifakos, S., Chandramouli, K., Nikolaou, C. K., Papachristou, P., Koch, S., Panaousis, E., & Bonacina, S. (2021, July). Influence of Human Factors on Cyber Security within Healthcare Organisations: A Systematic Review, (in eng). *Sensors (Basel)*, 21(15), 28. DOI: 10.3390/s21155119 PMID: 34372354

Ozturk, C., & Yildibasi, A. (2020). Barriers to implementation of blockchain into supply chain management using an integrated multi-criteria decision-making method: A numerical example. *Soft Computing*, 24(19), 14771–14789. DOI: 10.1007/s00500-020-04831-w

Queiroz, M. M., Fosso Wamba, S., De Bourmont, M., & Telles, R. (2021). Blockchain adoption in operations and supply chain management: Empirical evidence from an emerging economy. *International Journal of Production Research*, 59(20), 6087–6103. DOI: 10.1080/00207543.2020.1803511

Sajedi, H. (2018). Applications of data hiding techniques in medical and healthcare systems: A survey. *Network Modeling and Analysis in Health Informatics and Bioinformatics*, 7(1), 6. DOI: 10.1007/s13721-018-0169-x

Sardi, A., Rizzi, A., Sorano, E., & Guerrieri, A. (2020). Cyber Risk in Health Facilities: A Systematic Literature Review. *Sustainability (Basel)*, 12(17), 7002. Advance online publication. DOI: 10.3390/su12177002

Sendelj, R., & Ognjanovic, I. (2022). Cybersecurity Challenges in Healthcare. Stud Health Technol Inform, 300, 190–202. DOI: 10.3233/SHTI220951

Services, D. O. (2023). Health Industry Cybersecurity Practices: Managing Threats and Protecting Patients.

Sharma, L., Olson, J., Guha, A., & McDougal, L. (2021). How blockchain will transform the healthcare ecosystem. *Business Horizons*, 64(5), 673–682. DOI: 10.1016/j.bushor.2021.02.019

Sharma, R., & Kshetri, N. (2020). Digital healthcare: Historical development, applications, and future research directions. *International Journal of Information Management*, 53, 302–309. DOI: 10.1016/j.ijinfomgt.2020.102105

Sheller, M. J., Reina, G. A., Edwards, B., Martin, J., & Bakas, S. (2019). Multi-institutional deep learning modeling without sharing patient data: A feasibility study on brain tumor segmentation. Brainlesion: Glioma, Multiple Sclerosis, Stroke and Traumatic Brain Injuries, 92-104. DOI: 10.1007/978-3-030-11723-8_9

Suman, M. J. (2021). Dentistry 4.0 technologies applications for dentistry during COVID-19 pandemic. Sustainable Operations and Computers, 87-96.

Teoh, S., & Cheong, C. (2008). Implicit Enterprise Risk Management: An IT Healthcare Adoption Case Study. ACIS 2008 Proceedings - 19th Australasian Conference on Information Systems. 1011-1018.

Tortorella, G. L., Fogliatto, F. S., Sunder, M., Cawley, V., Vergara, A. M., & Vassolo, R. (2021). Assessment and prioritisation of healthcare 4.0 implementation in hospitals using quality function deployment. *International Journal of Production Research*, 60(10), 1–23. DOI: 10.1080/00207543.2021.1912429

Tully, J. S., Selzer, J., Phillips, J. P., O'Connor, P., & Dameff, C. (2020). Healthcare Challenges in the Era of Cybersecurity. *Health Security*, 18(3), 281–231. DOI: 10.1089/hs.2019.0123 PMID: 32559153

Vilakazi, K., & Adebesin, F. (2023). A Systematic Literature Review on Cybersecurity Threats to Healthcare Data and Mitigation Strategies. *EPiC Series in Computing*, 93, 240–251. DOI: 10.29007/hf15

Wamba, S. F., & Queiroz, M. M. (2020). Blockchain in the operations and supply chain management: Benefits, challenges, and future research opportunities. *International Journal of Information Management*, 52, 102064. DOI: 10.1016/j.ijinfomgt.2019.102064

Wang, J., & Perez, L. (2017). The effectiveness of data augmentation in image classification using deep learning. arXiv.org. https://arxiv.org/abs/1712.04621v1

Wong, A. J. (2014). Healthcare Cybersecurity Risk Management: Keys To an Effective Plan. *Biomedical Instrumentation & Technology*, 26–30. PMID: 24848146

Xu, F., Zhang, J., Shi, Y., Kang, K., & Yang, S. (2019). A fast low-rank matrix factorization method for dynamic magnetic resonance imaging restoration. 2019 5th International Conference on Big Data Computing and Communications (BIGCOM). DOI: 10.1109/BIGCOM.2019.00014

Yaqoob, S., Murad, M., Talib, R., Dawood, A., Saleem, S., Arif, F., & Nadeem, A. (2019). Use of blockchain in healthcare: A systematic literature review. *International Journal of Advanced Computer Science and Applications*, 10(5). Advance online publication. DOI: 10.14569/IJACSA.2019.0100581

Zafar, H., Ko, M. S., & Clark, J. G. (2014). Security Risk Management in Healthcare: A Case Study. Communications of the Association for Information Systems, 34. DOI: 10.17705/1CAIS.03437

Zakaria, H., Abu Bakar, N. A., Hassan, N. H., & Yaacob, S. (2019). IoT Security Risk Management Model for Secured Practice in Healthcare Environment. Procedia Computer Science, 161, 1241-1248. DOI: 10.1016/j.procs.2019.11.238

Zemankova, A. (2019). Artificial intelligence in audit and accounting: Development, current trends, opportunities and threats - Literature review. *2019 International Conference on Control, Artificial Intelligence, Robotics & Optimization (ICCAIRO)*. DOI: 10.1109/ICCAIRO47923.2019.00031

Zhang, A., Xing, L., Zou, J., & Wu, J. C. (2022). Shifting machine learning for healthcare from development to deployment and from models to data. *Nature Biomedical Engineering*, 6(12), 1330–1345. Advance online publication. DOI: 10.1038/s41551-022-00898-y PMID: 35788685

Chapter 7
IS Auditing in Modernizing Legacy Systems Using Salesforce

Lokesh Bollini
University at Buffalo, SUNY, USA

Rajesh Vishwanatham
https://orcid.org/0009-0007-1440-1779
University at Buffalo, SUNY, USA

Sai Kiran Reddy Ponnavolu
University at Buffalo, SUNY, USA

Raghvendra Singh
University at Buffalo, SUNY, USA

ABSTRACT

The evolution of technology has increased the complexity of software systems. Legacy systems pose challenges due to their monolithic architecture. To stay competitive, businesses need to modernize these systems, particularly by migrating to cloud platforms. This transition is complex, requiring careful consideration of business needs, technical capabilities, and organizational culture. Financial institutions face issues like inflexibility, high maintenance costs, and limited analytical capabilities. This chapter explores modernization strategies such as upgrading components, integrating new technologies like Salesforce, or forming strategic partnerships. Salesforce, with its cloud-based architecture, offers improved data governance, regulatory compliance, cost savings, and better decision-making. The research highlights the importance of modernization to overcome legacy system limitations and emphasizes

DOI: 10.4018/979-8-3693-4211-4.ch007

Salesforce's potential in driving organizational success in the digital era.

INTRODUCTION

In the 1990s, companies employed many COBOL programmers and consultants to address issues connected to Y2K. There were an estimated 120 billion lines of source code being maintained in 1990, mostly in COBOL and FOR- TRAN. Since 1990, there has been a huge increase in computers for business process support. One estimate is that roughly 250 billion lines of source code are now being maintained and that this number is increasing all the time (Seacord, 2003).

Since funding is rarely available for initiatives to delete unnecessary code, information systems often grow over time. For instance, the average Forty 100 firm updates, patches, and performs other maintenance on 35 million lines of code annually, adding only 10% to that total. Because of this, the quantity of code that these companies maintain doubles every seven years. Legacy systems are vital but out-of-date software applications that support the main business operations of an organization. These are powered by old hardware and software, which presents problems including inadequate reliability and safety threats. Because these systems are intricately linked to vital functions, updating or migrating them can be dangerous and difficult. Moving these systems to cloud settings becomes critically necessary, though, as companies must continue to be responsive to market developments and remain competitive.

Deploying to the cloud offers plenty of advantages, including enhanced maintainability and reliability because the service provider manages system maintenance and updates, and scalability, which allows resources to be changed according to demand without requiring large upfront investments. Additionally, cloud platforms provide better interoperability with contemporary applications and may significantly reduce operating costs by lowering the costs of maintaining legacy systems and physical infrastructure.

Despite these benefits, there are significant risks associated with the migration process, such as possible privacy and data security breaches, system outages during the transfer, and an increased dependency on cloud hosting companies. Organizations frequently choose a phased migration approach, use hybrid models that maintain essential operations on-premises, or engage the aid of IT professionals with experience in cloud migrations in order to reduce these risks. This systematic approach guarantees that business activities are least disrupted during the move and that cloud technologies are optimally utilized. Software modernization is a challenging and complex exercise (Knoche & Hasselbring, 2021). It involves multi-domain considerations such as business aspects, technical capability, economic features, and organizational culture (movska & Lago, 2017), (Pianini & Neri, 2021). A legacy system is a mission critical system that supports the core business process of the organization with the restriction of outdated hardware, software, and resources to maintain. These systems often have monolithic software architecture, which does not consider modularity as a design principle (Walker et al., 2020) and the systems work in silos (Ganesan & Chithralekha, 2016). Due to the years of usage, development, and improvement, legacy application's size and complexity are increasing, making the disadvantages of legacy monolith architecture outweigh its advantages (Kazanavičius & Mažeika, 2019). From the business perspective, existing core functionality systems developed using the latest technologies are defined as legacy systems if the system does not satisfy new business requirements and is unfit for the future needs of the organizations (Khadka et al., 2012). Researchers have proposed various legacy to cloud migration frameworks. Approaches such as industrial domain-driven (Walker et al., 2020), architecture-driven modernization (Fazal-Baqaie et al., 2016), horseshoe reengineering model (Fernández-Medina et al., 2015), and dependency graph (Corbetta et al., 2018) help the migration execution process. However, from our initial observation, end-to-end migration frameworks are still limited (Yadav et al., 2020), and little work has been done to evaluate them. For this reason, it is difficult to assess the quality of these migration frameworks. Thus, we initiate a systematic literature review (SLR) to further investigate this area from a quality perspective.These systems often have a monolithic software architecture, which does not consider modularity as a design principle (Walker et al., 2020) and the systems work in silos (Ganesan & Chithralekha, 2016). Due to years of usage, development, and improvement, legacy application's size and complexity are increasing, making the disadvantages of legacy monolith architecture outweigh its advantages (Kazanavičius & Mažeika, 2019). From a business perspective, existing core functionality systems developed using the latest technologies are defined as legacy systems if the system does not satisfy new business requirements and is unfit for the future needs of the organizations (Khadka et al., 2012).

Researchers have proposed various legacy to cloud migration frameworks. Approaches such as industrial domain-driven (Walker et al., 2020), architecture-driven modernization (Fazal-Baqaie et al., 2016), horseshoe reengineering model (Fernández-Medina et al., 2015), and dependency graph (Corbetta et al., 2018) help the migration execution process. However, from our initial observation, end-to-end migration frameworks are still limited (Yadav et al., 2020), and little work has been done to evaluate them. For this reason, it is difficult to assess the quality of these migration frameworks. Thus, we initiate a systematic literature review (SLR) to further investigate this area from a quality perspective.

A lot of banks and other financial companies run on old systems that were often built decades ago using out of date technologies like domino applications. These methods may not have done what they are supposed to do, but they are now becoming more and more problematic. Some problems with these systems are that they don't allow for much flexibility, high keeping costs and not much options or not doing any analytics activities.

These limitations have negative impact on various business operations. Sometime data is inaccessible and difficult to analyse and makes decision making capabilities in a low way to help customers. Business operations slow down or block the work because of old and outdated infrastructure and manual process resulting in high costs. However, these challenges can put organizations less competitive when compared evolving market.

To address these issues, banks and financial organizations are looking into the possible ways to modernize. Replacing legacy systems with modern platforms like salesforce like upgrading specific components or integrating them with these technologies are most efficient options taken into consideration. Strategic merging can also help in accessing to new technology and expertise. By adopting innovation, organizations can overcome the limitations of legacy systems improves data management, streamline operations, and enhance decision making.

Improved data management and more effective operations are made possible by the incorporation modern technologies. Platforms such as Salesforce, for example, can give powerful CRM solutions that deliver insightful data about the habits and preferences of customers, allowing for more individualized service and focused marketing campaigns. Additionally, by automating more repetitive tasks, these platforms reduce mistake rates and free up human resources for more intricate decision-making procedures.

Moreover, strategic combinations are being explored as a rapid and efficient means of gaining access to new technology and skills. Financial institutions can bypass the methodical and expensive process of modernizing outdated systems by acquiring or merging with tech-forward companies. This allows them to instantly take advantage of cutting-edge technology infrastructure and creative cultures. In addition to improving operational capabilities, this strategy gives these companies an advantage over competitors that are also utilizing the power of digital transformation. All things considered, the deliberate modernization of legacy systems not only reduces current inefficiencies but also gives banks and other financial organizations the resources they need to spur future growth and development.

LITERATURE REVIEW

Legacy Systems

Legacy systems are the backbone of businesses since they refer to any business-critical software systems that are no longer being modified and whose failure can have a substantial impact on the enterprise's daily operations.

Legacy systems Evolution is the process of replacing, re-developing, reusing, or moving software components and platforms when old maintainer techniques no longer meet the desired target system. Desktop applications that are based on a client-server architectural pattern can be considered legacy systems if they are still in use among large enterprise organizations such as universities. The reason is that client-server solutions have many limitations with respect to extensibility and the adaptation of new emerging e-business requirements. Thus, a system can be considered a legacy system in one context, but not in another, smaller (B. Y. Alkazemi, 2013).

The major goal of software modernization is to reduce maintenance costs and increase flexibility, allowing businesses to efficiently meet market demands while maintaining a competitive advantage. Software systems typically evolve in three phases: maintenance, modernization, and replacement. When business requirements change from the original planned usage, maintenance actions are begun to ensure the system's continuing functionality. As the software system matures and maintenance becomes difficult and expensive, modernization becomes an essential step. In some circumstances, the modernization process may result in a complete replacement of the outdated system. (M'baya, 2017).

Legacy systems are an interesting field of study, attracting scholars that investigate multiple challenges, methodologies, approaches, and guidelines linked to legacy systems. The focus on legacy system modernization has grown fast, with academics looking for to connect existing systems with the most recent advances in technology. Legacy systems are defined differently by different scholars, although they are typically described as old, critical, and fundamental information systems that have been in operation for a long time. These systems are frequently capable of addressing some business requirements, but they may not comply with evolving architectural standards. Legacy systems are information systems that use technology, programming languages, and standards from a previous generation or period of innovation.

Legacy systems are comprised of six interconnected elements: application software, supporting software, system hardware, application data, business processes, and rules or policies.

Legacy systems are important because they are widely used by major businesses, especially the public sector, to provide mission-critical services. Despite being old and possibly outdated, legacy systems are dependable in sustaining daily operations and serve a critical role in continued service delivery, with users familiar and operations running smoothly. These systems are key corporate assets, containing years of business rules, coding, data, user experience, updates, and additions required for everyday operations. Legacy systems are important contributors to information flow and business administration, as their source codes include essential business logic and requirements for possible system upgrades.

Despite their significance, obstacles like as maintenance difficulties, outdated technology, and limits on addressing increasing needs make the upgrading of legacy systems complex yet difficult task (Razali, 2013).

Legacy Systems and Challenges

A legacy system is old but still operational information system; it also refers to any business-critical system that resists modification and has a high failure rate. (Crotty, 2017). (Plennert, 2018) In the context of legacy systems, phrases such as technical debt, code stench, code decay, and software ageing are used. (Gholami, 2017) Legacy systems are also obsolete computer systems that require a lot of maintenance and are difficult to integrate with newer technologies. The core of a legacy system is the application, which can quickly become obsolete due to the rapid advancement of technologies. (Stojkov, 2021) A legacy system is an out-of-date monolithic system that cannot be upgraded to the most recent version. According to this notion, (Abu Bakar, 2020) all new systems eventually become legacy. Legacy systems are made up of the applications, programmes, and technology that power them. (Tapia, 2020) reveal that legacy applications frequently use monolithic architecture design techniques and rely on obsolete technology and infrastructures. (Kotusev, 2019) feels that the layered nature of various legacy systems increases the architectural diversity and complexity of IT platforms. (Eitelhuber, 2018) also stated that there are occasions when adding new or editing current functions is not possible. The term legacy is used by the next generation of developers and administrators for a variety of reasons; either the development approach, the programming language used in the systems, or the technology operating these systems is old (Johann, 2016). (Alija, 2017) believes that legacy systems play a role in evolving systems to meet the needs of the business, which include new capabilities, upgrades to comply with new rules, and enhancement patches. (Greenhalgh, 2019) In many circumstances, legacy systems do not meet the purchase policies of IT organisations. Finally, legacy software and applications do not adhere to IT standards and norms.

Time Constraints. Completing modernization within the timeframe specified emerged as the most major challenge, driven by many challenges inherent in older systems, such as a lack of resources, including specialists and documentation. Respondents indicated anxiety about running out of funds and time, which was mostly due to a dearth of individuals with legacy system expertise. The lengthy duration of these projects frequently results in departures from earlier plans, causing additional delays. Participants described their experiences with legacy modernization projects that took longer than expected, with initial expectations for a three-year modernization extending to a five-year timeline. A lack of resources was noted as a contributing factor, with a significant 63.6% of respondents reporting that time restrictions were regularly encountered in legacy system modernization initiatives, reflecting both challenging and extremely challenging cases.

Data Migration. Data migration is the transfer of data from one system to another. Data migration varies from data movement, data integration, and traditional ETL (extract, transform, and load) in that it migrates to a new environment, is a one-time procedure, and ensures consistency of usage. Data migration efforts have a low success rate, however not as bad as comparable software projects. The time it takes to conduct a data migration when just considering the extract and load phases is a function of the size of the data objects, the speed in the transferring media, and the degree of parallelism. (Velimeneti, 2016)

Addressing Soft Factors of Modernization. In this study, Murer defines soft factors in modernization as non-technological components such as people, communication, and organizational business values (Murer, 2011). The issues noted by practitioners focus around three important soft elements. First, there is the challenge of successfully explaining the rationale and implications of legacy system upgrading. This problem is strongly related to the second soft element, which is obtaining funds from high management. Informants frequently reported that a lack of understanding among upper management about the modernization issue impedes money allocation for the process. The communication challenge also includes articulating the effects of modernization, notably in terms of return on investment (ROI). Top management's preference for short-term ROI presents a challenge, according to one expert, who stated that once an investment is made, there is an expectation of speedy returns. To address these issues, practitioners emphasize the significance of establishing appropriate business cases that describe the existing cost, migration cost, new total cost of ownership, and expected ROI. Business cases in this scenario may incorporate soft components such as increased maintenance or performance because they directly represent business value. The report divides the challenges into three categories: Predicting ROI of modernization, Difficult to communicate consequences of modernization, and Funding modernization projects, (Murer, 2011) with survey respondents citing varied levels of difficulty in each. Notably, a considerable portion of respondents find estimating ROI and ensuring funding for modernization is particularly difficult, emphasizing the need of addressing these soft elements in the modernization process.

Lack of knowledge. The informants cited a lack of understanding about legacy systems as a major difficulty in the modernization process. Modernization needs a wide range of skills, including knowledge of database environments, operating systems, middleware, enterprise services bus architecture, and business functionality translation. When attempting to comprehend the complexities of the old system, a lack of understanding becomes even more of an issue. Organizations can acquire insights into needs and speed up the creation of a new system by reverse engineering and rigorously documenting existing systems. The poll results echoed these thoughts, with 60.7% of respondents describing a lack of expertise as “challenging” or “very challenging” in the context of legacy system modernization. (Khadka et al., 2014)

Legacy Systems and Maintenance

Maintaining outdated systems is becoming increasingly costly. According to (Tantry et al., 2017), organisations must modernise their old systems to new platforms such as the cloud to save maintenance and operating costs. (Attaran, 2017) stated that the cost benefits of cloud computing force certain organisations that use traditional systems to reinvest in themselves. (Usman Sana, 2021) said that cloud computing provides significant chances to perform cost-effective workflows without the need for any setup. Some businesses rely on old systems to conduct their operations but cannot afford to keep them running, creating a barrier to agility and competitiveness. (Rosas, 2017).

According to the Accountability Office, legacy systems technicians that maintain older systems are uncommon. As a result, they are in high demand and therefore more expensive (GAO, 2019). According to (Stevenson, 2020), as software evolves, IT workers must preserve its integrity even as the system and its underlying components grow in scope and size. According to (Alexandrova, 2019), legacy systems are generally critical for organisations, and even minor failures can be disastrous.

Upgrading obsolete legacy systems needs several steps, such as software platform migration, replacement, redesign, and reuse. The main advantages of this move are lower maintenance costs and greater flexibility in this growing technology. Furthermore, selecting the best modernization approach for making sound decisions cannot be done on the spur of the moment. A preliminary analysis and assessment based on numerous factors, such as software value, risk analysis, and cost estimation, is required to evaluate methods. This method will make hybrid modernization plans and decisions for specific system components harder. For example, you could choose to convert code for one component while updating the user interface for another. As a result, deciding on the best modernization strategy is difficult because there are so many variables to consider. Furthermore, early research and evaluation of software systems is required for a successful modernization endeavour. Any evolution exercise must involve system evaluation since it provides us with a comprehensive grasp of the legacy system. The beginning status of the legacy transformation must be determined before developing the programme. A lot of issues arise currently, including increased maintenance costs, a lack of experienced staff for outdated systems, and working with capable partners (M'baya, 2017; Khabouze, 2022).

Auditing in Legacy Systems

Considering increasing security breaches and compromises, almost 70% of the 2019 HIMSS Cybersecurity Survey respondents are still exploiting some legacy systems. The survey concludes that the continued use of legacy systems raises grave concerns regarding the vulnerability of the healthcare ecosystem. But this can be applied to any other industry.

Legacy system auditing presents a unique set of challenges due to outdated technology, low transparency, and a high potential of risk and fraud. Inefficient processes, erroneous assessments, and impaired data integrity can all result in problems. Organisations that complete risk assessments, develop detailed audit plans, leverage specialised technologies, focus on data analysis, improve access controls, address security concerns, and consider modernization can be successful in overcoming these issues.

Table 1. Risk assessments and detailed audit plans

Quality	Addressing the User Needs	The application meets the main requirements and specifications of the users. More than 90% of the users agree with the solution. Updating procedures are carried out at a regular interval to meet the expectations of users. A specific change management team, solution designing team is responsible for the specifications addressing users' requirements.
	User- Friendly	Easy navigation capabilities make application utilization at ease
	Compliance	Law and regulations reviewed at each stage so that applications are compliant with GDPR and PIM Laws
	Effectiveness	Applications are designed in such a way that offering zero downtime with adequate clustering process storing the applications at different servers in a different zone so that workload balancing maintained across all applications.
Security	Consistency	Maintaining different environments for every application to maintain security standards. Access control list is maintained and documented at every environment. Proper controls are placed to ensure application do not violate the security guidelines and maintain security standards.
	Integrity	Since the applications are traditional based applications until and unless user authorization is not provided to access the applications. So, integration is not a considerable issue unless anonymous access has been granted at the application level.
	Reliability	Root cause analysis procedures are in place to ensure the failures have been addressed with no repetition in the near future and also SLA are placed to expedite the issue depending on business criticality.
Readability	Auditability	The application is being tested at different stages and proper audit controls are used in test the efficiency of the application. Once concern is update are made at more frequently since changes of business requirement are properly not in place.
	Evolution	Team which manages the changes are performed by few people because of outdated technology and limited expertise.

Basic Strategies and Activities for Modernization of Legacy Software

A standard LSA modernization plan is required for efficient information technology (IT) management in businesses that rely substantially on software applications for mission-critical activities (Srinivas, 2016). In the current study, LSA modernization is defined as a set of both managerial and technical activities for replacing or transforming software using modern technology in a cost-effective manner that does not disrupt the business service, in order to make the software not only reusable but also more valuable, profitable, reliable, and extend the functionality of the existing LSA's output (Norfolk, 2014); (Zheng, 2013). The goal is to improve the application's functionality, interoperability, performance, and reusability while preserving the business service that the program supports (Norfolk, 2014). Software application modernization includes both software maintenance, which involves changes made after delivery to correct, adapt, improve, or detect and correct potential flaws (Zheng, 2013), and software migration, which involves switching from one operating environment to another (Srinivas, 2016).

Legacy Software Modernization: Maintaining and Updating Old Systems

Software continues to evolve throughout its lifetime, with changes ranging from minor bug fixes to complete rebuilds. This evolution can be broadly categorized into three main activities: maintenance, modernization, and replacement.

Maintenance. Keeping the System Running Smoothly, maintenance involves making small, incremental changes to the system, such as fixing bugs or adding minor features. These changes typically don't alter the overall structure of the code and are essential for keeping the system running smoothly. Modernization: Breathing New Life into Old Systems, modernization involves more extensive changes than maintenance, but still aims to preserve a significant portion of the existing system. This can include restructuring the code, improving functionality, or adding new features to keep the system up-to-date and relevant. Replacement: Starting from Scratch, replacement involves rebuilding the system from scratch, either all at once (big bang approach) or incrementally. This is the most drastic option and is usually only considered when the existing system is no longer viable or cannot be easily modernized.

Modernization Approaches: White vs. Black Box

Modernization strategies can be further classified into two categories based on the level of system understanding required: black-box and white-box.

Black-box modernization involves wrapping the legacy system with a new layer that hides the complexity of the old code and provides a modern interface. This approach requires minimal knowledge of the internal workings of the system and is a good option for preserving existing functionality while making it more accessible and compatible with new technologies.

White-box modernization, also known as software reengineering. This requires an initial reverse engineering process to gain an understanding of the internal system operation. The system's components and relationships are recognized and represented at a higher level of abstraction (Chikofsky, 1990)

Wrapping: A Powerful Modernization Technique

Wrapping is a powerful technique used in both black-box and white-box modernization. It involves creating a wrapper around the legacy system that intercepts its inputs and outputs, translating them to a format that is compatible with the new environment. This allows the legacy system to be integrated with new systems and technologies without modifying the original code. Wrapping techniques provide a low-risk short-term solution, promising a quick turnaround and minimal changes to the existing legacy platform (Canfora et al., 2008)

The Reengineering Process

Reengineering is a broader process that encompasses both wrapping and other techniques for modernizing legacy systems. It typically involves three phases:

Reverse engineering. Understanding the existing system by analysing its code and creating documentation. Reverse engineering needs the same knowledge and infrastructure as forward engineering. Reverse engineering ''just" applies the forward transformations backwards, i.e. in reverse. (Mehlich, 2000)

Restructuring. Applying various techniques to improve the code's structure and organization. Dividing broad functions into smaller, more targeted ones is one way that restructuring can be implemented. Because of its modularity, developers can change some elements of the code without impacting other pieces. Furthermore, refactoring methods that involve changing variables' names or giving them more descriptive names can greatly increase the maintainability of code.

Forward engineering. Forward engineering is the process of writing new code to include extra features or functionalities into an already-existing software system. It's similar to adding a new wing to your house; you're expanding it with additional features without drastically altering the current structure. Forward engineering starts with clearly defined requirements that outline the desired features and functionalities.

Modernization in Action: Beyond Black and White

While black-box and white-box approaches might suggest wrapping as an alternative to reengineering, it often becomes a valuable tool within the reengineering process itself. Wrapping can be performed at different levels of abstraction, requiring varying degrees of understanding of the legacy code.

For example, some wrapping techniques require minimal knowledge of the internal workings of the system, while others benefit from a deeper understanding of the wrapped interfaces, class hierarchy, or object interrelations. This might involve some level of reverse engineering for better comprehension.

Additionally, after wrapping, forward engineering can be applied to the wrappers to extend the functionality of the legacy system, add safety features, or implement new features using new technologies.

Legacy Modernization Techniques

One of the main difficulties of software evolution is that all artefacts produced and used during the entire software life cycle are subject to changes, ranging from early requirements over analysis and design documents, to source code and executable code. These alterations span from the early stages of requirements to the development of analysis and design documents, source code, and finally, the executable code. This dynamic inherently gives rise to several specialized fields within the realm of software evolution. These include, among others, the evolution of requirements, architectural changes, data transformations, runtime adjustments, and the evolution of language paradigms. Additionally, the discourse on the modernization of legacy systems, emphasizing that such modernization can occur at distinct levels, encompassing functional aspects, data transformations, and enhancements to user interfaces. This underscores the evident need for a diverse array of modernization techniques tailored to each level and facet within the broad landscape of software evolution.

Within the expansive domain of legacy software modernization, various methodologies and techniques come into focus, with some standing out prominently:

Challenges With Salesforce for Legacy Modernization

Common mistakes in change management include postponing the implementation of change, which is often motivated by the belief that more time leads to better judgments, even though time is a main impediment. Slow progress stymies performance: businesses must be aligned on goals and take quick action to generate value, not complete consensus. A cohesive change strategy is critical; poorly designed initiatives frequently fail. Implementing effective project management procedures is critical for preventing chaos. It is critical to use proper indicators to track progress; negative signals during transformation can indicate beneficial gains. Providing appropriate training is critical for learning new skills. Addressing personal concerns is critical for gaining employee participation; unclear projects meet increased resistance. Adjusting reward systems to encourage change is required since current systems maintain the status quo. Effective communication, including open talks with relevant stakeholders, helps to sustain change efforts. Leadership is essential; committed leaders expertly negotiate resistance to ensure successful change implementation (Pritchett, 2017).

Cognitive elements and proposals on how to help adoption. People frequently express distrust towards technology. Individuals frequently must change their attitudes about technology to welcome new breakthroughs. Doubts may arise over efficacy of groupware products in improving a company's success. Increased communication and groupware training are required to address these challenges (Orlikowski, 1993).

Structural elements and proposals for easy adoption. Individuals may be unwilling to invest time in learning or using the Salesforce CRM system if non-chargeable hours are not authorized. The reward system should not be a hindrance to system installation. In a highly competitive setting, individuals may be discouraged from sharing information or skills to keep an advantage. Organizing group trainings could be the first step in creating a more collaborative and transparent culture. It is critical to transition away from a competitive and individualistic culture to foster cooperative use of groupware solutions. A lack of clear rules and standards governing software usage and duties can lead to a wide range of work habits and decreased motivation during the early phases of system adoption. It necessitates the implementation of new workplace practices. Insufficient comprehension of the system may cause concerns about personal accountability and data security. To overcome these difficulties, more training and education regarding the device and its use are required.

A Study About Salesforce CRM Implementation in Scandinavian Business

The major concern is the involvement of top leadership in execution. Senior management should oversee and manage the implementation process. Following closely is the importance of inspiring staff to support the CRM deployment. Implementing a new system necessitates greater effort from employees, but the results will be worthwhile in the long run.

To position the CRM system as a new component that improves the company's ability to serve clients efficiently, emphasizing its dynamic character in which data must be constantly updated. Furthermore, it is critical to encourage clients to regularly supply accurate data to the CRM system (Ramaseshan & Mattson, 2007).

Automated Migration. A pivotal technique involving the migration of languages, databases, and platforms using software tools such as automated parsers and converters. Notable instances include the migration of legacy applications and associated data from antiquated databases to contemporary relational databases, along with program restructuring practices like dead code elimination and GOTO elimination. Importantly, automated migration implies a transformation process characterized by algorithmic precision, devoid of the necessity for human intervention in the transformation process.

Re-hosting. An approach that entails the relocation of legacy applications to a different platform, while preserving the intrinsic business logic and data. Re-hosting is frequently employed in conjunction with other modernization techniques, notably automated migration.

Package Implementation. A strategy involving the substitution of legacy applications with pre-existing commercial-off-the-shelf (COTS) packages. COTS software is generally a software that is not developed inside the project but acquired from a vendor and used "as-is", or with minor modifications (Li, 2006). This strategy focuses around constructing a portfolio incorporating the most advantageous packages available from external vendors. However, it comes with the caveat that the reuse of existing legacy business logic is not feasible. Furthermore, some degree of reengineering or customization of packages, coupled with the rewriting of business logic, may be entailed in this process.

Reengineering/Re-architecting. Acknowledged as the most efficient modernization technique, this methodology operates by extracting requirements from existing legacy applications and subsequently redeveloping them on contemporary platforms utilizing new technologies. A prominent example is the adoption of modern technology along with innovative architectural paradigms, such as the embrace of Service-Oriented Architecture through systematic reengineering.

SOA Integration. An approach that revolves around exposing the business logic and data embedded within legacy programs as well-defined and reusable services. A straightforward means of addressing legacy modernization is the encapsulation of existing application interfaces through Service-Oriented Architecture (SOA) wrappers. This results in the creation of SOA services that can be seamlessly integrated into a new platform, while the underlying implementation remains anchored in the existing legacy code (Malinova, 2010).

Salesforce as a Solution

Salesforce is one of the largest cloud computing technologies, which is available on cloud, no need to install any software for it. Now a day's cloud computing is fastest growing technology. It is observed that businesses and individuals are moving their data to the cloud because fault-tolerant data storage is becoming more important. As large number of data nodes used in the cloud storage system, the probability of some data nodes failure increases. (Ghonge & Wasekar, 2019)

With a growth of technologies, data and the need of sharing and analysing the data became increasingly important. Enterprise companies require a reliable way of moving the data between different systems. There are many out-of-the-box products which provide integration solutions. However, not in all cases such products justify the price or fulfil the requirements. That is the time when custom integrations must be built.

In today's digitally driven world, business face a stark reality is that it limits agility, productivity, and competitiveness. Businesses must cope with this harsh truth with highly competitive environment. The maintenance costs of the outdated systems are high, they do not have any vital capabilities and they have difficulty integrating with more recent technology. As a result, they pose substantial obstacles to organizational expansion. Salesforce, the most popular cloud-based customer relationship management platform, is becoming increasingly popular among businesses as a strong solution for updating their legacy systems. This is because many organizations see the vital need for transformation.

Burden of Legacy Systems

Many companies still use legacy system, which are relics of a bygone period. These cumbersome platforms are frequently constructed using an outdated technologies and do not possess the adaptability and scalability that are necessary to accommodate the ever-changing requirements of modern businesses. The inability to adapt to changing circumstances results in efficiency, the waste of resources, and ultimately missed opportunities. However, older systems frequently have difficulty integrating with recent technologies and applications, which results in the formation of data silos that limit interaction and make it more difficult to make decisions.

Data Management in a Centralized Way

Salesforce is a consolidated data management platform that provides businesses with an all-inclusive way to combine contact, opportunity, lead, and case data. The 360-degree perspective of customers provided by this unified repository enables sales and customer support teams to better comprehend the needs, preferences, and interactions of their customers. By letting companies customize communications, marketing plans, and sales tactics according to specific client profiles, the platforms promote individualized interactions. Salesforce improves the client experience by guaranteeing prompt issue resolution and streamlined sales procedures through effective lead management, opportunity tracking and contact and case management. salesforce's integration capabilities facilitate the smooth transfer of data between several departments, promoting teamwork and a cohesive approach to customer relationship management.

Automated Workflows. SFA, or sales force automation, is the use of technology to support routine sales operations. Users utilize these technologies to complete administrative and other repetitive activities. Sales representatives can work more effectively when manual activities that are routine and repetitive are converted to automated ones through SFA. Applications like calendaring tools and quarterly automated sales reporting are essential components of sales technology, for instance (Agnihotri, 2010).

Salesforce's ability to automate repetitive operations, such as lead generation, opportunity management and service case resolution has a significant impact on operational efficiency that extends beyond data management.in order to ensure that sales teams concentrate on the most promising prospects and speed up the conversion process, the platform uses automation tools to streamline the lead scoring routing and nurturing processes. Salesforce's automated tools in opportunity management make it easier for opportunities to go through different phases of the sales pipeline and give sales reps timely alerts, updates and remainders. This improves forecasting accuracy and shortens the sales cycle, enabling businesses to strategically allocate resources and make well-informed decisions.

Moreover, salesforce's automation powers are applied in service case resolution through automated case routing which quickly routes service requests to the relevant teams or individuals. This shortens reaction times and increases client satisfaction by promptly resolving issues. Automating routine procedures frees up the personnel from laborious, manual duties so they may concentrate on higher-value work like interacting with clients and supporting strategic objectives. In addition to raising staff morale, this transforming effect encourages an inventive and flexible organizational culture, setting up companies for long-term success in a competitive market.

Exceptional insights and analytical capabilities. Salesforce is a standout choice for businesses looking for powerful analytics and reporting tools to have a deep understanding of their operations. The platform provides a visual depiction of crucial metrics and performance trends, enabling users to monitor KPI's and generate customisable reports and dashboards with its powerful reporting features. This provides an overview of organizational health and improves data comprehension while promoting agile decision making. Businesses can identify trends and take use of cutting-edge capabilities, such predictive modelling using tools like einstein analytics, Organizations may predict future trends, take preventative measures, and find hidden insights in their data by using this machine learning-driven strategy.

Additionally, by helping businesses to consistently track KPI's pinpoint areas for development, and streamline processes, salesforce's reporting and analytics solutions support a culture of continuous improvement. The availability of real-time data and actionable insights facilitates efficient departmental communication, enabling efforts to be aligned with corporate objectives and ultimately leading to business success. Salesforce is a key source for companies dedicated to data-driven intelligence and strategic growth because of its analytics-focused development, which improves decision making processes and equips companies to adapt dynamic environments.

Cloud Based Scalability

Through this adoption of cloud computing, salesforce rescues the requirement for expensive upgrades to both its hardware and software. Long term flexibility and adaptability are ensured by this cloud-based platforms inherent capacity to readily scale to match the expansion of businesses and their ever-changing requirements. With public and private clouds becoming more and more popular, an increasing number of businesses and organizations are utilizing the cloud. Although there are many cloud service providers, AWS, Amazon, and Google Cloud continue to lead the market. For small and medium-sized businesses, the largest obstacle is the expense of cloud adaption. Thus, it's critical to think about why making a cloud investment is required. Another crucial concern is cloud data security (Marańda W, 2022)

Seamless Integration. Salesforce integrates seamlessly with a vary array of third-party applications, spanning ERP systems, marketing automation tools, and specialized tools like MuleSoft and Apigee. This comprehensive integration dismantles data silos and creates a unified digital ecosystem. This allows for enhanced collaboration, streamlined workflows, and powerful automation capabilities.

MuleSoft's platform acts a central integration hub, connecting salesforce to various applications through pre-built connectors and custom integrations. MuleSoft has the capability to process messages in batches. It splits the large messages into individual records that are processed asynchronously within batch jobs (Seth, 2018). This facilitates seamless data exchange and real-time synchronization, enabling business to automate complex processes and acquire important insights from aggregated data. This is made possible by the seamless flow of data and the synchronization of activities in real-time. Through its emphasis on API management and security, Apigee can supplement MuleSoft's collection of features.

By leveraging MuleSoft and Apigee alongside salesforce integration, organization have opportunity to reap tremendous benefits by utilizing MuleSoft and Apigee. The Data flow between different applications may be streamlined, routine processes and workflows can be automated, important insights can be gained through the consolidation of data, salesforce functionality can be extended, and collaboration and partner integrations can be improved. In the end, these linkages give organization the ability to create a single digital environment that not only drives efficiency but also stimulates creativity and prepares the road for success in the current competitive landscape.

Modernization Benefits

When old systems are modernized with salesforce there are a magnitude of benefits that have a significant impact. Organizations can expect to see is: A better customer experience can be achieved by providing customers with personalized experiences and consistent touch point across all channels resulting in customer satisfaction and loyalty. Increased Efficiency and Productivity: The automation of processes and the streamlining of workflows free up time and resources for employees, enabling them to concentrate on tasks that provide value to the organization resulting in productivity and efficiency. Reduced costs: Eliminating costly hardware and software maintenance costs, in conjunction with a gain in efficiency, leads to significant cost reductions thanks to the combination of these two factors. Agility and scalability: Since salesforce hosted in the cloud, it ensures that business is ready to adjust to the ever-changing demands of the market and to the expansion that lies ahead. Security Features: Salesforce provides a comprehensive set of security measures that safeguard sensitive data and ensure compliance with pertinent industry requirements.

Modernization Challenges

Here are problems to take into consideration, even though the benefits of modernization cannot be denied. These include,

Figure 1. Illustration of HET's Branching Structure

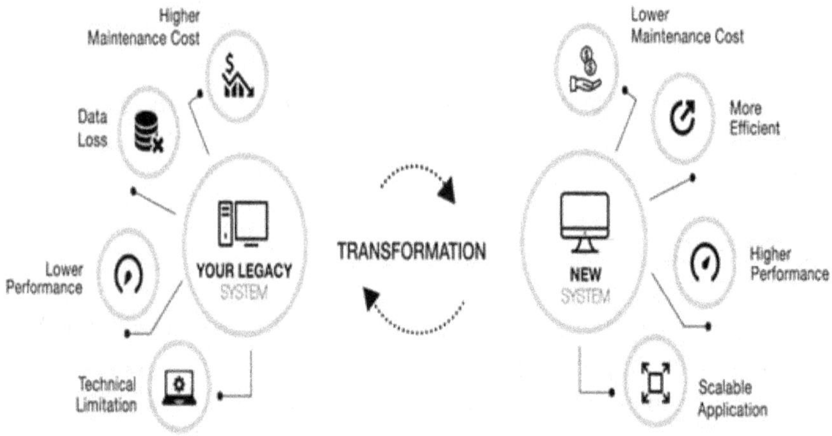

Note: Figure shows how transformation of legacy system to Salesforce system happens.

Data Migration. It is a process that involves careful preparation and execution in order to successfully move massive amounts of data from legacy system to salesforce. System Integration: The process of integrating salesforce with pre-existing systems can be an intricate one that requires specialized technical knowledge. Change Management: To successfully encourage people to accept new processes and technology. It is necessary to have efficient communication, training, and support procedures in place. Making a modernization a successful Journey: It is important for firms to adhere to the following main tactics to ensure a smooth and successful journey toward modernization. Planning and Preparation: Establishing a committed team to oversee the process is an important part of planning and preparation. This includes defining the project's goals, scope, budget, and timeframe in a clear and concise manner. Engaging Employee: Employees should be kept informed and involved throughout the process. Concerns should be addressed, and full training should be provided in order to motivate adoption and develop confidence. Professional Assistance: Use of experience of skilled salesforce consultants or implementation partners to manage the technological complexity the assure successful execution.

Why Salesforce

Salesforce.com has been audited and shown promising results in integration with cloud services. The audited application has a degree of safety of SL = 97%. Given that the assumed degree of risk is RL = 2 and that the application is not considered sensitive, the minimal safety level required for one domain to be compliant is: 95%.

The sole non-compliant domain is Portability and Interoperability, which has a safety level of 94.62%. This signifies that the effort necessary to perform the required upgrade for compliance is insignificant because the difference till the minimal safety level is very modest. The average degree of compliance for the ten compliant domains is 97.7%. We may conclude that the audited service cloud is a safe service, with a level of safety of 97%, demonstrating the high-performance security and control systems in place to provide transparency, privacy, availability, and required performance. Salesforce.com was compliant in majority of the domains in the architecture we audited, resulting in a 90.9% compliance rate. As previously stated, the gap between the safety level on the non-compliant domain and the minimal safety level necessary for compliance is modest, so salesforce.com is classified as a safe, controllable, and high-performance cloud service in the overall evaluation.

By referencing this case study, we can infer that Salesforce has the necessary security controls, audit controls which are basic requirements in integrating legacy systems. (Georgiana Mateescu, 2015).

IMPLEMENTATION STRATEGIES

Parallel Cutover Strategies

To successfully upgrade from a legacy system to salesforce required careful consideration. With a controlled and progressive transition, the parallel cutover method ensures that data integrity is maintained while simultaneously reducing the chances of disruption. This approach involves running both systems simultaneously, allowing users to learn the new platform at their own pace and facilitates a more seamless adoption process.

However, running two systems simultaneously also presents challenges increased management complexity, data synchronisation issues and possibility of user resistance. It is possible to mitigate these issues and assure a successful transition by utilizing a shadow system, dual data entry and organized rollouts at various stages.

Below are some parallel cutover strategies for modernizing legacy system to salesforce".

Phased Rollout

Phase1 – Pillot Migration. Transitioning from a legacy system to salesforce require meticulous planning. The phased rollout approach provides a regulated and effective way to accomplish a successful migration. To minimize disturbance and guarantee a seamless transition for all stakeholders, this technique entails moving users and departments gradually.

Phase 2 – Gradual Expansion. Moving a smaller workflow or group of users to salesforce is the first step in the process. This pilot migration allows for through testing and refinement of the new system before broader adoption. Pilot group members can offer insightful comments on the functionality and usability of the system guiding future development and improvement.

Phase 3 – Decommission the legacy system. Based on the learnings from the pilot phase, additional users or departments are gradually migrated to salesforce. Consequently, this guarantees that migration will prioritize essential user groups and functions, thereby ensuring that core activities will continue uninterrupted. Through the process of incremental scaling the migration process, organisations can solve any unanticipated issues and adapt the approach as needed.

Phase 4 – User Adoption. Once the migration is successful to salesforce and all the users are comfortable with the new salesforce platform, the legacy system will be decommissioned. The completion of this final stage signifies the completion of migration process and enables enterprises to have full control over the leverages and benefits of salesforce.

Phase 5 – Flexibility and Customization. The Phased rollout strategy offers several advantages over other migration approaches. This strategy encourages user adoption and ultimately results in a successful transition because it reduces disruptions to a minimum and guarantees the preservation of data integrity. Additionally, flexibility of the phased rollout enables organisation to adjust the process to their own needs and complexities ensuring a migration a smooth and efficient experience.

Dual Entry

Transitioning from legacy systems to salesforce is accomplished through the use of a data centric method known as the dual entry strategy. Users are required to enter data into both systems for a certain amount of time. This allows for comprehensive data validation and ensures that no essential information is lost during the transition.

Benefits of Dual Entry. This strategy provides a number of various advantages. The process of importing into both systems allows for the identification and correction of any potential inconsistencies or errors that may occur prior to the complete shift to salesforce. This enhances data accuracy and minimizes the risk of data loss or inconsistencies. In addition, the dual entry procedure helps to build confidence in the new platform by ensuring that the data submitted is accurate and comprehensive before relying solely on salesforce. Finally, it provides a comprehensive audit trail of all data entries, enabling organizations to track changes and identify any potential issues, invaluable for troubleshooting and maintain data integrity.

Dual Entry Implementation. Implementing dual entry involves defining the data scope, setting the validation period, establishing data synchronization, and training users on the process and data validation procedures are all necessary steps. On the other hand, it is essential to consider the potential difficulties, which may include an increase in the amount of work of users, the possibility of data inconsistencies and an increase in the amount of administrative overhead.

Challenges of Dual Entry. When it comes to maintaining the integrity of data during the conversion of legacy systems, the dual entry technique is an approach that is quite beneficial. This strategy helps firms limit the risk of data loss and enable a smooth transition to salesforce by offering a rigorous data validation process and extensive audit trail.

Data Synchronization

A smooth salesforce-legacy system transition requires data synchronization. Real time or near real time data interchange between platforms ensures data availability across platforms. Users may operate easily in each system, with changes automatically reflected in the other. However, careful planning and execution are essential to data integrity and process consistency.

Benefits of Data Synchronization. Data Synchronization has many advantag es. Firstly, it lets user operate in either system or obtain updated data regardless of platform, improving the user experience. This boosts workflow and user pleasure. Second, preserving data integrity across all platforms reduces data duplication and inconsistencies, ensuring reliable information for informed decision-making. Last,

Realtime synchronization allows both systems to update data instantly, promoting transparency and real-time decision-making.

Data Synchronization Implementation. Effective data synchronization involves careful consideration of numerous elements. Identifying important and frequently updated data pieces that need synchronization. Data volume and latency determine the best synchronization strategy, such as real-time data pipelines or batch processing. Data integrity and consistency are also ensured by precise mapping rules between the legacy system and salesforce. Before and after deployment, synchronization must be tested and monitored to assure data accuracy and seamless operation.

Challenges in Data Synchronization. Data synchronization is challenging. This requires technical skills and specialized tools. If poorly conceived and implemented, the procedure may introduce data mistakes or inconsistencies risking data integrity. Finally, real-time synchronization may affect system performance, requiring careful optimization and resource allocation.

Shadow System

The term "shadow system" refers to the sequential user adaption behaviour that occurs at the system level through the expansion and adaptation of the basic framework of effective use (Haag, 2015). Implementing salesforce through shadow system is a risk-free and efficient method that does not require any disruptions to daily operations. The process entails establishing an isolated salesforce environment that replicates the operation of the legacy system. This results in numerous advantages:

Reduced Risk. User training and testing of the new system can occur in a secure environment, ensuring that no disruptions to their current workflow occur. This facilitates the timely detection and resolution of any problems prior to their implementation in production.

User Adoption. By providing users with an opportunity to familiarize themselves with salesforce, the adoption rate can be significantly improved.

Transition. The seamless transition from the shadow system to production minimizes disruption and ensures a smooth user experience.

Improved Data Quality. By cleaning and migrating data in the shadow system, you can ensure data quality in the production environment.

How A Shadow System Works

Creating a replica. To start creating a shadow system, a copy of the legacy system must made and placed inside the salesforce environment. In addition to moving data, this replication includes moving workflows and procedures from the old system to salesforce. In order to ensure that information is correctly transferred and in line with the new environment's structure, data mapping is an essential component of this phase. The Objective is to create in salesforce a mirrored version of the features found in the legacy system.
Test and refine. After the replica is installed the shadow system goes through testing so that users can assess its functionality and offer comments. Finding any inconsistencies, inefficiencies, or opportunities for improvement requires careful attention to detail throughout this testing and refinement phase. In order to evaluate the systems efficacy, users actively interact with it by modelling real world scenarios. User feedback enables the shadow system to be improved, adjusted and fine-tuned iteratively before moving on to the production environment.
Migrate data and users. Upon successful testing and refinement, moving users and data to the production environment is the next step. The process of data migration guarantees the smooth movement of replicated information from the shadow system to the active salesforce environment. User accounts, permissions and the access privileges are moved over to salesforce at the same time. The migration process must be executed meticulously to avoid data discrepancies and disruptions in user access during the transition.
Decommission the legacy system. Once the migration is complete, legacy system will be decommissioned. The legacy system is deactivated after the migration is finished and all parties are satisfied with the shadow system functionality. Decommissioning the process of formally retiring or stopping the old system to mark the end of the migration to the new salesforce environment. Organization usually stops providing access to the legacy system during this period and reroute users and procedures to the fully functional salesforce solution. Decommissioning signals the official transition to a more sophisticated and effective system, simplifies operations, and gets rid of redundancy.

Key Considerations of the Shadow System

Data Mapping. The proper installation of the shadow system depends heavily on the data mapping. For a precise and thorough data conversion great care must be taken while mapping data between the legacy system and salesforce. In order to reduce the possibility of data loss or inconsistencies during the transfer, the mapping procedure entails aligning data fields, structures and formats between the two systems. Effective data mapping requires a deep comprehension of the links and interaction between data.

User Training. User adoption and skill play a major role in a shadow system's effectiveness. It is essential to give users enough training on the new salesforce system and related operations. The Features of the shadow system, navigational protocols, and any modifications to business processes should all be covered in training sessions. Users with adequate training facilitate a more seamless transition, increase efficiency, and reduce the possibility of mistakes or disturbances when adjusting to the new system.

Change Management. Developing a thorough change management strategy is necessary to address concerns and guarantee a smooth transition. Anticipating and handling user, stakeholder and organizational opposition to change are all part of change management. Effective change management involves resolving user concerns integrating stakeholders in the decision-making process, and clearly communicating the benefits of the shadow system. An effective change management strategy promotes an adaptable culture and helps cultivate a positive attitude toward the transition.

Testing and Validation. Before migrating to the production environment, thorough testing and validation of the shadow system are imperative. To find and fix any problems, errors, or inconsistencies in the system, extensive testing scenarios must be carried out. Data integrity, system functionalities, user interface and the shadow system's general performance should all be tested. Validation guarantees that the system satisfies business requirements is in line with the intended goals and runs without a hitch in a real-world setting. Thorough testing increases the shadow system's dependability and reduce the chance of disruptions.

Benefits of Parallel Cutover

Reduced Risk. When compared to other cutover approaches parallel cutover method significantly lowers the chance of disruptions of data loss, which is one of its main advantages. Organizations are able to detect and resolve problems in real time by running both new and old systems simultaneously. By taking this proactive measure, the risk associated with system cutover is eventually reduced since it lessens the likelihood of significant failures and guarantees a more seamless transition.

Improved Data Quality. Dual entry and ongoing data synchronization between old and new systems are made easier by parallel cutover. This continuous synchronization helps ensure that data migrate correctly, which significantly improves the quality of data. By ensuring that the data in the new system corresponds precisely with the data in the legacy system, organizations can lower the possibility of errors and inconsistencies.

User Adoption. Users can learn and adjust to the new system at their own pace thanks to the flexibility provided by parallel cutover. A more comfortable and less disruptive user experience is fostered by this gradual transition. Which improves user acceptance, until they are ready to completely adopt the new system, users can carry on using the well-known old one. This strategy reduces resistance to change and increases user happiness.

Greater Flexibility. Parallel cutover gives business more freedom to customize the transition process to their own needs and solve particular difficulties. Parallel cutover enables for flexibility, I contrast to other cutover techniques that could have inflexible structures. Organizations can alter the transition's scope, timing and order to better suit their unique operational challenges and business requirements.

Continuous Business Operations. Since the new and legacy systems are running concurrently, parallel cutover permits continuous business operations. Organizations can continue their usual business operations without major disruptions or downtime thanks to this continuity. The stability and continuity of client service are enhanced by the capacity to conduct simultaneous operations.

Real-time Issue Identification. Organizations can detect and resolve problems in real-time by running two systems simultaneously. By taking a proactive stance, possible problems can be resolved quickly. Lessening the impact on operations. By enabling the company to react quickly to unforeseen problems, real-time issue identification helps to improve the cutover process's overall efficiency.

Challenges of Parallel Cutover

Increased Complexity. During a parallel cutover, managing two systems at once adds a new layer of complexity. To make sure that both systems function properly, more people and technological resources are required. The organization must invest additional efforts in managing the complexities of managing two operations, keeping lines of communication channels, dealing with and coordinating with several tasks.

Data Synchronization Challenges. The maintenance of consistent data across both systems requires careful planning and execution, which is one of the challenges associated with data synchronization. One of the critical challenges in a parallel cutover is ensuring consistent data synchronization between the old and new systems. This requires proper planning and implementation to prevent inconsistencies or problems with data integrity. When working with massive datasets or intricate data structures, the complexity increases. For organizations to successfully synchronize data and reduce the possibility of errors or inconsistencies, they require strong strategies and tools.

User Resistance. There is a possibility that some users will be resistant to change and required more training and support. Introducing changes often faces resistance from users from the old system. Users may be reluctant to adopt new systems during a parallel cutover because they are habituated with the current procedures and are resistant to change.it will take more work to overcome this reluctance in the form of user education, support systems, and persuasive messaging that emphasizes the advantages of the new system. The success of the cutover depends on resolving user concerns and making sure the transition goes smoothly.

Testing Challenges. To make sure that both systems operate well together and produce reliable results, parallel cutover necessitates extensive testing. Validating the synchronization of data between the old and new systems in addition to the new system's features is part of testing in a parallel environment. it might be difficult and time –consuming to manage extensive test scenarios, spot and fix any inconsistencies and guarantee a seamless transfer.

Extended Timeline. Conducting parallel operations is inevitable that the cutover procedure will take longer when concurrent processes are carried out. Maintaining two systems at once necessitates close cooperation and could lengthen the changeover period overall. This delay may lead to higher expenses, possible disruptions to regular business operations and the requirement for ongoing efforts to guarantee a smooth transition.

Resource Intensiveness. The parallel cutover approach requires more personnel organizational effort, and technological infrastructure. Effectively allocating and managing these resources become extremely difficult. The demands of adopting a new system must be balanced with continuous operations for organizations, which may put a strain on existing resources.

Coordination and Communication. The need for seamless coordination and communication is heightened during a parallel cutover. Ensuring that all stakeholders are well-informed tasks are synchronized, and potential issues are addressed promptly becomes a challenging aspect. Miscommunication or lack of coordination can lead to disruptions and negatively impact the success of the cutover process.

Dependency on Legacy systems. Until the full transition is finished, operating in parallel mode necessitates a dependent on the legacy system. There may be difficulties with this dependency, particularly if the previous system had flaws or limits.to minimize any negative effects on operations and guarantee a seamless transition, organization must carefully manage this time.

CONCLUSION

Salesforce transforms outdated processes and gives businesses access to previously unattainable levels of productivity and efficacy. Its broad features, intuitive interface, and cloud-based architecture simplify processes, improve data accessibility, and promote smooth cooperation. This translates into real advantages in terms of security cost savings, agility, and data insights. Salesforce provides sophisticated auditing mechanisms for data correctness and integrity in addition to its primary functions. Comprehensive data change history, workflow insights, data access tracking and code execution details are provided by features including field Audit trail, Process Builder audit trail, Data import Audit trail, and apex audit trail. Organizations benefit from improved data governance regulatory compliance, and lower fraud and mistake risks as a result. Salesforce is a potent tool for modernizing legacy systems. Organization is given the agility, confidence, and competitive edge they need to manage the digital landscape thanks to its cloud-based architecture, many functionality, and sophisticated auditing methodologies. Organizations may reach new heights of success and realize their greatest potential by embracing salesforce. Salesforce stands as a powerful tool for modernizing legacy systems and unlocking unprecedented efficiency and effectiveness. Its cloud-based architecture, rich feature set, and advanced auditing techniques empower organizations to navigate the dynamic digital landscape with agility, confidence, and a competitive edge. By embracing the transformative power of Salesforce, organizations unlock new levels of success and achieve their full potential in an ever-evolving world.

REFERENCES

Abu, K., & Razali, R. (2013). A preliminary review of legacy information systems evaluation models. *International Conference on Research and Innovation in Information Systems (ICRIIS)*. DOI: 10.1109/ICRIIS.2013.6716728

Abu Bakar, H. K., Razali, R., & Jambari, D. I. (2020). A guidance to legacy systems modernization. *International Journal on Advanced Science, Engineering and Information Technology*, 10(3), 1042. DOI: 10.18517/ijaseit.10.3.10265

Agnihotri, R. (2010). *Effective Sales Force Automation and Customer Relationship Management: A Focus on Selection and Implementation*. Business Expert Press. DOI: 10.4128/9781606491287

Alexandrova, A., & Rapanotti, L. (2019). Requirements analysis gamification in legacy system replacement projects. *Requirements Engineering*. Advance online publication. DOI: 10.1007/s00766-019-00311-2

Alija, N. (2017). Justification of Software Maintenance Costs. *International Journal of Advanced Research in Computer Science and Software Engineering*, 7(3), 15–23. DOI: 10.23956/ijarcsse/V7I2/01207

Attaran, M. (2017). Cloud Computing Technology: Leveraging the Power of the Internet to Improve Business Performance. *Journal of International Technology and Information Management*, 26(1), 112–137. DOI: 10.58729/1941-6679.1283

Baxter, I. D., & Mehlich, M. (2000). Reverse engineering is reverse forward engineering. *Science of Computer Programming*, 36(2-3), 131–147. DOI: 10.1016/S0167-6423(99)00034-9

Canfora, G., Fasolino, A. R., Frattolillo, G., & Tramontana, P. (2008). A wrapping approach for migrating legacy system interactive functionalities to Service Oriented Architectures. *Journal of Systems and Software*, 81(4), 463–480. DOI: 10.1016/j.jss.2007.06.006

Chikofsky, E. J., & Cross, J. H. (1990). Reverse engineering and design recovery: A taxonomy. *IEEE Software*, 7(1), 13–17. DOI: 10.1109/52.43044

Corbetta, S., Meeus, W., Cappe, E., Catthoor, F., & & Fritsch, A. (2018). Proof-of-Concept HARPA Measurement-Based Platform Modelling. Harnessing Performance Variability in Embedded and High-performance Many/Multi-core Platforms: A Cross-layer Approach.

Crotty, J., & Horrocks, I. (2017). Managing legacy system costs: A case study of a meta-assessment model to identify solutions in a large financial services company. *Applied Computing and Informatics*, 13(2), 175–183. DOI: 10.1016/j.aci.2016.12.001

Cusumano, M. J. (n.d.). *Modernizing Legacy Systems: Software Transformations in the Cloud.*

Efremovska, A., & Lago, P. (2017). From Legacy to Cloud: Risks and Benefits in Software Cloud Migration. *In Software Architecture for Big Data and the Cloud* (pp. 147-165).

Eitelhuber, T. W., Thackray, J., Hodges, S., & Alan, J. (2018). Fit for purpose - developing a software platform to support the modern challenges of data linkage in Western Australia. *International Journal of Population Data Science*, 3(3). Advance online publication. DOI: 10.23889/ijpds.v3i3.435 PMID: 32935016

Fowler, M. (2021). *Application integration.* Martinfowler.com. https://martinfowler.com/tags/application%20integration.html

Ganesan, A. S., & Chithralekha, T. (2016). A Survey on Survey of Migration of Legacy Systems. *Proceedings of the International Conference on Informatics and Analytics* (pp. 1-10). DOI: 10.1145/2980258.2980409

GAO. (2019). *Agencies Need to Develop Modernization Plans for Critical Legacy Systems*. U.S. Government Accountability Office. https://www.gao.gov/products/gao-19-471

Gholami, M. F., Daneshgar, F., Beydoun, G., & Rabhi, F. (2017). Challenges in migrating legacy software systems to the cloud — An empirical study. *Information Systems*, 67, 100–113. DOI: 10.1016/j.is.2017.03.008

Greenhalgh, T., Wherton, J., Shaw, S., Papoutsi, C., Vijayaraghavan, S., & Stones, R. (2019). Infrastructure Revisited: An Ethnographic Case Study of how Health Information Infrastructure Shapes and Constrains Technological Innovation. *Journal of Medical Internet Research*, 21(12), e16093. DOI: 10.2196/16093 PMID: 31855184

Grieger, M., Baqaic, M. F., & Engels, G. (2016). *Concept-Based Engineering of Situation-Specific Migration Methods: Vol* (Vol. 9679). Springer. DOI: 10.1007/978-3-319-35122-3_14

Haag, S., Eckhardt, A., & Bozoyan, C. (2015). *Are Shadow System Users the Better IS Users? - Insights of a Lab Experiment. Publications of Darmstadt Technical University, Institute for Business Studies*. BWL.

Help And Training Community. (n.d.). Salesforce. Retrieved May 11, 2024, from https://help.salesforce.com/s/articleView?id=000384648&type=1

Johann, S. (2016). Dave Thomas on Innovating Legacy Systems. *IEEE Software*, 33(2), 105–108. DOI: 10.1109/MS.2016.38

Kazanavičius, J., & Mažeika, D. (2019, April 1). *Migrating Legacy Software to Microservices Architecture*. IEEE Xplore. DOI: 10.1109/eStream.2019.8732170

Khabouze, R. (2022). *Modernization of Legacy Information Technology Systems*. https://scholarworks.waldenu.edu/cgi/viewcontent.cgi?article=14014&context=dissertations

Khadka, R., Batlajery, B. V., Saeidi, A. M., Jansen, S., & Hage, J. (2014). How do professionals perceive legacy systems and software modernization? *Proceedings of the 36th International Conference on Software Engineering*. DOI: 10.1145/2568225.2568318

Khadka, Saeidi, Jansen, & Hage. (2013). *A structured legacy to SOA migration process and its evaluation in practice*. DOI: 10.1109/MESOCA.2013.6632729

Knoche, H., & Hasselbring, W. (2021). Continuous API Evolution in Heterogenous Enterprise Software Systems. *18th International Conference on Software Architecture (ICSA)*, 58–68. DOI: 10.1109/ICSA51549.2021.00014

Kotusev, S. (2019). Enterprise architecture and enterprise architecture artifacts: Questioning the old concept in light of new findings. *Journal of Information Technology*, 34(2), 102–128. DOI: 10.1177/0268396218816273

Li, J. (2006). *Process Improvement and Risk Management in Off-The-Shelf Component-Based Development*.

M'baya, A., Laval, J., & Moalla, N. (2017). *An assessment conceptual framework for the modernization of legacy systems*. DOI: 10.1109/SKIMA.2017.8294120

Malinova, A. (2010). *Approaches and techniques for legacy*.

Marańda, W., Poniszewska-Marańda, A., & Szymczyńska, M. (2022). Data Processing in Cloud Computing Model on the Example of Salesforce Cloud. *Information (Basel)*, 13(2), 85. DOI: 10.3390/info13020085

Márquez, L., Rosado, D., Mouratidis, H., Mellado, D., & Fernández-Medina, E. (2015). *Framework for Secure Migration Processes of Legacy Systems to the Cloud*. DOI: 10.1007/978-3-319-19243-7_46

Mateescu, G., & Sgârciu, V. (2015). Cloud Computing Audit. *U.P.B. Sci. Bull., Series C, 77*(3). https://www.scientificbulletin.upb.ro/rev_docs_arhiva/full58d_528709.pdf

Megargel, A., Shankararaman, V., & Walker, D. (2020). *Migrating from Monoliths to Cloud-Based Microservices: A Banking Industry Example* (pp. 85-108). https://doi.org/%7B10.1007/978-3-030-33624-0_4%7D

Murer, S., Bonati, B., & Furrer, F. J. (2011). *Managed Evolution: A Strategy for Very Large Information Systems* (1st ed.). Springer Berlin., DOI: 10.1007/978-3-642-01633-2

Nardecchia, C. (2022, March 30). *5 leadership tips for CIOs to evolve their digital strategy | The Enterprisers Project*. Enterprisersproject.com. https://enterprisersproject.com/article/2022/3/leadership-tips-cios-evolve-digital-strategy

Norfolk, D. (2014, March 23). *Legacy Modernisation - Bloor Research*. Www.bloorresearch.com. https://www.bloorresearch.com/issue/legacy-modernisation/

Orlikowski, W. (1993). Learning from notes: Organizational issues in groupware implementation. *The Information Society*, 9(3), 237–250. DOI: 10.1080/01972243.1993.9960143

Pianini, D., & Neri, A. (2021). *Breaking down monoliths with Microservices and DevOps: an industrial experience report. Archivio Istituzionale Della Ricerca*. Alma Mater Studiorum Università Di Bologna. DOI: 10.1109/ICSME52107.2021.00051

Plennert, M. (2018). The social construction of technological stasis: The stagnating data structure in OpenStreetMap. *Big Data & Society*, 5(2), 205395171879059. DOI: 10.1177/2053951718790591

PRITCHETT. (2017, December 20). *PRITCHETT's Change Management Methodology*. Pritchett LP. https://www.pritchettnet.com/pritchett-change-management-methodology

Ramaseshan, R., & Mattsson, J. (2007). *Key Issues in CRM Implementation: Some Evidence from Scandinavian Businesses*. Paper presented at Annual World Marketing Congress 2007, Verona, Italy.

Rosas, J., Brito, V., Palma, L. B., & Barata, J. (2017). Approach to Adapt a Legacy Manufacturing System Into the IoT Paradigm. *International Journal of Interactive Mobile Technologies*, 11(5), 91. DOI: 10.3991/ijim.v11i5.7073

Salesforce. (2023, March 13). *Strategies for modernizing Salesforce legacy Systems*. PreludeSys. https://preludesys.com/strategies-for-modernizing-salesforce-legacy-systems/

Seacord, R. C., Plakosh, D., & Lewis, G. A. (2003). *Modernizing Legacy Systems: Software Technologies, Engineering Processes, and Business Practices* (1st ed.). Addison-Wesley Professional.

Seth, M. (2018). Mulesoft – Salesforce Integration Using Batch Processing. *6th ACM/ACIS International Conference on Applied Computing and Information Technology (ACIT '18)*. DOI: 10.1109/CSII.2018.00009

Shang, Z., Feng, C., Hongji, Y., & Jianzhi, L. (2013). An Approach to Evolving Legacy Software System into Cloud Computing Environment. *Principles, Methodologies, and Service-Oriented Approaches for Cloud Computing*, 207–229. DOI: 10.4018/978-1-4666-2854-0.ch009

Srinivas, M., Ramakrishna, G., Rao, K. R., & Babu, E. S. (2016). Analysis of Legacy System in Software Application Development: A Comparative Survey. *Iranian Journal of Electrical and Computer Engineering*, 6(1), 292. DOI: 10.11591/ijece.v6i1.pp292-297

Stevenson, M., & Helmond, A. (2020). Legacy systems: Internet histories of the abandoned, discontinued and forgotten. *Internet Histories*, 4(1), 1–5. DOI: 10.1080/24701475.2020.1725854

Stojkov, A., & Stojanov, Z. (2021). Review of methods for migrating software systems to microservices architecture. *Journal of Engineering Management and Competitiveness*, 11(2), 152–162. DOI: 10.5937/jemc2102152S

Tantry, S., N.N, M., & K, C. (2017). Implications of legacy software system modernization: A survey in a changed scenario. *International Journal of Advanced Research in Computer Science*. https://doi.org/.DOI: 10.26483/ijarcs.v8i7.4556

Tapia, F., Mora, M. Á., Fuertes, W., Aules, H., Flores, E., & Toulkeridis, T. (2020). From Monolithic Systems to Microservices: A Comparative Study of Performance. *Applied Sciences (Basel, Switzerland)*, 10(17), 5797. DOI: 10.3390/app10175797

Usman Sana, M., & Li, Z. (2021). Efficiency aware scheduling techniques in cloud computing: A descriptive literature review. *PeerJ. Computer Science*, 7, e509. DOI: 10.7717/peerj-cs.509 PMID: 34013035

Velimeneti, S. (2016). *Data Migration from Legacy Systems to Modern Database*. Culminating Projects in Mechanical and Manufacturing Engineering.

Wasekar, S., & Ghonge, P. (2019). An Efficient Data Replication in Salesforce Cloud Environment. *International Research Journal of Engineering and Technology, 6*(3). https://www.irjet.net/archives/V6/i3/IRJET-V6I31187.pdf

Yadav, S., Khare, A., & Choudhary, K. (2019). *ASK Approach: A Pre-migration Approach for Legacy Application Migration to Cloud.* 15–27. DOI: 10.1007/978-981-32-9949-8_2

Yao, Z., Nagel, C., Kunde, F., Hudra, G., Willkomm, P., Donaubauer, A., Adolphi, T., & Kolbe, T. H. (2018b). 3DCityDB - a 3D geodatabase solution for the management, analysis, and visualization of semantic 3D city models based on CityGML. *Open Geospatial Data. Software and Standards*, 3(1), 5. Advance online publication. DOI: 10.1186/s40965-018-0046-7

Chapter 8
Auditing Risks of Web 3.0

Shubham Rajivkumar Rai
University at Buffalo, SUNY, USA

Kevin Shah
University at Buffalo, SUNY, USA

Kruthi Yedavalli
University at Buffalo, SUNY, USA

Naman Kumar Modi
University at Buffalo, SUNY, USA

Raghvendra Singh
University at Buffalo, SUNY, USA

ABSTRACT

With increasing reliance on internet technologies, auditing plays a critical assurance role. This chapter explores the evolution of the internet into the emerging landscape of Web 3.0, built on decentralized and semantic technologies like blockchain that transform today's web architecture. It analyzes the vision, potential applications, and inherent governance, risk, and business impact considerations involved in this blockchain-powered reinvention of the web. It further discusses key risk domains in Web 3.0 that warrant audit scrutiny, including decentralization, blockchain, cryptocurrencies, and semantic inaccuracies. This chapter provides technology leaders, auditors, and regulatory stakeholders with an overview of Web 3.0 while highlighting the pivotal governance, risk management, and assurance challenges involved in this transition. It prepares readers to evaluate the analyses and recommendations centered on securing this next-generation, decentralized web future.

DOI: 10.4018/979-8-3693-4211-4.ch008

INTRODUCTION

The advent of the internet has revolutionized the way we communicate, work, and live (BernersLee, 1999). It has evolved from a simple network of interconnected documents (Web 1.0) to a dynamic platform (Web 2.0) that has transformed businesses and societies globally (O'Reilly, 2005). Today, we stand on the brink of another significant transformation - the transition to Web 3.0 (Tapscott & Tapscott, 2016). This journey of the internet's evolution is a testament to human ingenuity.

Web 1.0, the first generation of the web, was a static information repository where users passively consumed content (BernersLee, 1999). The emergence of Web 2.0 marked a shift towards a more interactive platform, enabling users to create and share content, leading to the rise of social media, blogs, and wikis (O'Reilly, 2005). Now, we are witnessing the dawn of Web 3.0, a more decentralized and intelligent version of the Web (Tapscott & Tapscott, 2016).

Web 3.0 is envisioned as a decentralized, secure, and user-centric internet. It is often referred to as the Semantic Web or the Decentralized Web and is poised to redefine the internet landscape (Nakamoto, 2008). It leverages blockchain technology for decentralization, ensuring data security and privacy (Tapscott & Tapscott, 2016). It also incorporates artificial intelligence and semantic web technologies to deliver a more personalized and intelligent user experience (Hendler & Berners-Lee, 2010).

These technologies in Web 3.0 are a major shift from their predecessors, which consequently raises the requirement for easier understanding and auditing. The lack of general expertise and implementation process raises multiple risks for the users and public at large, summoning the requirement of extensive and comprehensive audits of the technologies and their applications (Bruwer, 2014). Cascarino (2007) opines that current-day auditors need a much deeper understanding of computers and computer auditing compared to their predecessors.

In the global finance industry cryptocurrency, blockchain and other Web 3.0 technologies are gaining momentum in multiple pillars of our society such as legal contracts (Mcneil, 2022) and healthcare (Aziz & Madani, 2015). With these increasing applications in major industries, risks associated with the technology (Web 3.0) are also to be monitored (Razzaque et al., 2013). Moreover, decentralized controls and their increasing implementation through Web 3.0, and this whole evolution altogether raise the potential for multiple security challenges (Namakshenas, 2023).

As discussed by Appelbaum et al., (2017), the complexity of Web 3.0 systems presents unique challenges and opportunities for auditors, necessitating the development of new auditing tools and techniques. Auditing has played an important role in the development of the Internet. Auditing plays an important role in Web 3.0, just as it does in the current web.

Auditing helps ensure that internet systems and applications are secure, compliant, and efficient. Auditors can identify and mitigate risks, improve software quality, and help organizations achieve their goals. Auditors can help to ensure that Web 3.0 systems and applications are secure, compliant, and efficient.

One of the key challenges of Web 3.0 is its complexity. Web 3.0 systems are often complex and distributed, which can make them difficult to audit. However, there are several emerging auditing tools and techniques that can be used to audit Web 3.0 systems effectively. Auditors can play a valuable role in helping to build trust in Web 3.0. By providing independent assurance on the security, compliance, and efficiency of Web 3.0 systems, auditors can help to make Web 3.0 more attractive to users and investors.

Considering the diverse applications of Web 3.0, and the potential impact that these applications shall have in the future, the identification of risks on this front, from different angles and perspectives becomes an important task.

To cater to the upcoming needs of risk management for Web 3.0 technologies, we plan to start with risk identification, which is a pivotal requirement for risk management (Tchankova, 2002). We plan to draw your attention to those risks, wherein, the objective of this research is to explore and identify the different risks associated with Web 3.0 environments for information systems audit, which focuses on the identification of factors that are associated with systems risk in depth (Bedard et al., 2005).

The focus of the paper accordingly lies in the evolution of the web, from its inception (Web 1.0) to Web 2.0, and later to Web 3.0, covering the impact of the evolution on business. How the web has evolved to Web 3.0, its impact on the business, and the challenges associated with its adaptation, capturing various risks with diverse applications of Web 3.0 and their implementation. *What are the potential risks with the implementation of Web 3.0, covering various applications?* Highlighting the need for auditing and current governance of the system. *What are the needs for technical audit in Web 3.0, covering current governance and safeguards in the technology?*

EVOLUTION OF THE WEB

The evolution of the internet from its inception in the late 20th century has been remarkable. Starting with basic websites containing static text and images, it has progressed into advanced web applications that offer personalized experiences and intricate functionalities, ultimately reaching the era of Web 3.0 (Alves de Castro et al., 2021). Recognizing the different phases of web evolution is not only crucial for our research but has also become essential for aiming to comprehend the impact of Web 3.0 and the risks associated with it (Gan et al., 2023).

Figure 1. Evolution of the Web

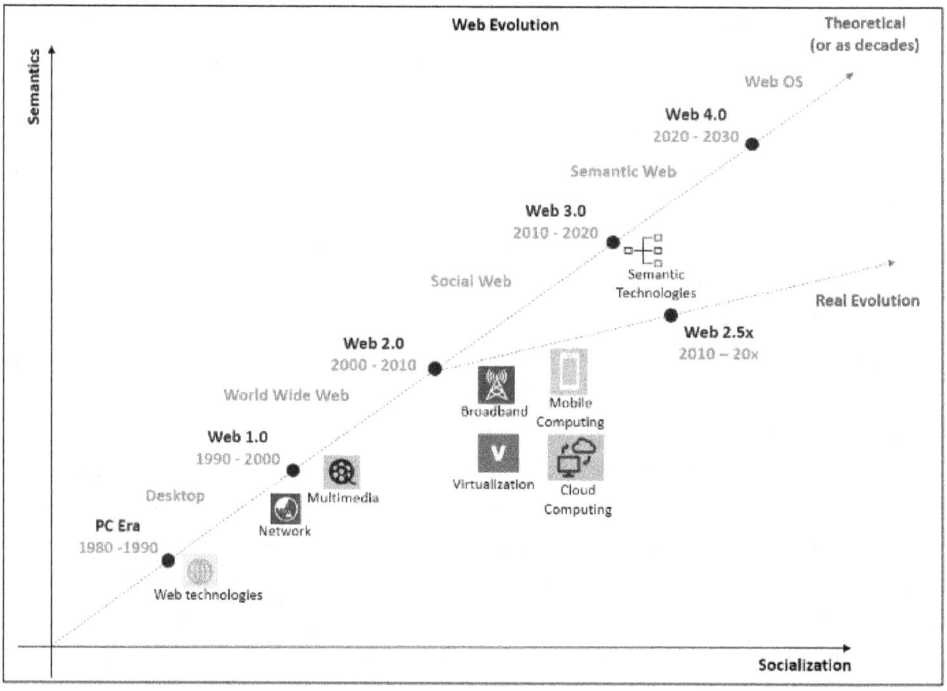

Web 1.0

The inception of the web, credited to Tim Berners-Lee, introduced what we now refer to as Web 1.0. This era is characterized by a "read-only web" where a limited number of content creators produced interconnected web pages, while a vast audience accessed these pages via internet browsers (Zheng & Lee, 2023). During this phase, users could only consume information; there was no provision for interaction like comments or responses. Core web technologies such as HTML, HTTP, and URI formed the backbone, with some newer protocols like XML, XHTML, and CSS emerging (Doyle & Lopes, 2008). Web 1.0 employed a combination of server-side and client-side scripting, including ASP, PHP, JSP, CGI, and PERL for server-side, and JavaScript, VBScript, and Flash for client-side functionality. This blend of technologies shaped the landscape of the early web, setting the stage for its future evolution (Choudhury, 2014).

Web 1.0, often labeled as the "static web" or the "read-only web," embodies the earliest phase of the World Wide Web's evolution, mainly found during the late 1990s and early 2000s (Hean, 1998). In this era, web pages were predominantly static, with limited interactivity, and a central focus on text-based content. These pages were constructed using HTML (Hypertext Markup Language) and essentially functioned as digital documents, maintaining their content unless manually updated by web administrators. Interaction with websites was constrained to navigating between pages through hyperlinks, offering minimal opportunities for user involvement (Sir et al., 2022). Internet speeds were notably slower than today, restricting the utilization of multimedia elements due to bandwidth limitations. Search engines such as Yahoo! and AltaVista were instrumental in information retrieval, relying on manual categorization and keyword matching (Yang, 2005). Notably, social media platforms, contemporary e-commerce practices, and dynamic, user-generated content were practically non-existent during this phase. Web 1.0 established the foundation for subsequent eras like Web 2.0, which introduced a more interactive and participatory web experience (Goel et al., 2022).

Where Web 1.0 Went Wrong

According to Evans (2006), Web 1.0 faced numerous challenges that impeded its effectiveness. One primary issue was its slow and cumbersome functionality, requiring users to refresh pages whenever new information was added manually. Additionally, Web 1.0 lacked capabilities for two-way communication, functioning exclusively on a client-pull model (HTTP) initiated by clients.

The search technologies utilized in Web 1.0 were frequently deemed inefficient, prioritizing index size over relevance, and struggling to adapt to changing content (Shivalingaiah & Naik, 2008). Additionally, it faced challenges in autonomously discovering and identifying content.

One of the most significant drawbacks of Web 1.0 was its neglect of network effects (Kamei, 2011). It predominantly featured a limited number of content creators and a vast audience of passive readers, resulting in a slow network and leaving users in need of more resources (Shivalingaiah & Naik, 2008). Web 1.0 failed to recognize that increased engagement by more people in a networked service would enhance its value for everyone, mainly due to its read-only nature.

Web 1.0's foundational assumption was that the web functioned primarily as a publishing platform rather than an interactive space for participation. It lacked an understanding of the dynamic potential of the web and perceived software more as an application than a service. Web 1.0 heavily relied on outdated software business models (Sewpersadh, 2023).

Web 2.0

The current form of the World Wide Web is termed Web 2.0, representing the version many of us initially interacted with online (Anderson, 2007). This iteration places a strong emphasis on the end user, prioritizing an enhanced user experience. Web 2.0 empowers users to engage in reading, creating, and sharing information, often referred to as the participative social web (O'Reilly, 2007).

Within a Web 2.0 platform, users actively participate and collaborate through social media discussions, taking on the role of creators by generating user-generated content within a virtual community (Ritzer & Jurgenson, 2010), (Kaplan & Haenlein, 2010). This marks a departure from the earlier era of Web 1.0 websites, where individuals were confined to passive consumption of content.

Evolution of Web 2.0

The phrase 'Web 2.0' didn't reemerge until 2002 (Murugesan, 2007). During this time, companies like Amazon, Facebook, Twitter, and Google simplified the process of connecting and participating in online interactions (Kaplan & Haenlein, 2010). Web 2.0 brought forth novel elements, including multimedia content and interactive web applications, predominantly presented on two-dimensional screens.

In 2004, the term gained widespread attention through the inaugural Web 2.0 conference organized by O'Reilly Media and MediaLive (O'Reilly, 2007). At the event, the author introduced the idea of the "Web as Platform," underscoring the focus on developing software applications on the Web rather than on desktop computers. They highlighted a significant shift where "customers actively shape your business," asserting that value could be effectively generated by utilizing user-generated content, including ideas, text, videos, or images. Authors delineated a distinction between Web 2.0 and what they labeled as "Web 1.0." (O'Reilly & Battelle, 2009).

Web 1.0 vs Web 2.0

Web 1.0 describes the earliest stages of the World Wide Web. During this era, web pages were static. Users' ability to interact with the web pages was minimal. Users could only read the static text-based content on the page and navigate to different pages using hyperlinks (Aghaei et al., 2012).

Web 1.0 was data/information driven. Businesses would share information with their customers through links to static web pages shared over emails. These pages were built using HTML, where web administrators would manually edit the page to update new information, if any. Functionality and flexibility were limited (Choudhury, 2014).

Leveraging technologies such as HTML5, CSS3, and JavaScript frameworks like ReactJs, AngularJs, and VueJs, web pages were built to enable interactivity of the users with the content. (Obar & Wildman, 2015). Users can now not only read content but create, share, and collaborate with other web users to generate content. The ease of use of the web has also significantly improved. A static web has now evolved into a social web (Vassileva, 2012).

Businesses could now create an app or platform with highly interactive content (Choudhury, 2014). Users could further create and share content on such apps or platforms, through which businesses could make profits.

Issues with Web 2.0

One major issue with Web 2.0 is managing data. Users have limited to no control over how their data will be accessed and manipulated once it has been uploaded to the web (Kucuktunc et al., 2012). Businesses often collect and store user data without their consent. Data is often manipulated to match the likes and views of certain individuals or businesses and presented to the world, misleading the public. Through social media, other online crimes such as hacking, identity thefts, cyber-bullying, stalking, and phishing have also skyrocketed. The safety and reliability of data have become questionable (Kshetri, 2010).

Web 3 or Web 3.0

Coined to express the ideas of decentralization, blockchain technologies, and token-based economics on the World Wide Web, the term "Web 3.0" was introduced by Gavin Wood, the founder of Polka Dot and co-founder of Ethereum, in 2014 (Zavratnik, 2022). A policy brief published by the Bennett Institute for Public Policy at the University of Cambridge defined Web 3.0 as the upcoming evolution of the internet's technical, legal, and financial framework, encompassing technologies like blockchain, smart contracts, and cryptocurrencies (Gilbert, 2022).

Web 3.0 is expected to prioritize decentralized applications and extensively utilize blockchain technologies, potentially reshaping online interactions and disrupting traditional revenue streams for companies (Ghelani & Hua, 2022). In contrast to the rapid growth of Web 2.0 giants like Amazon, Google, and Meta, which amassed and centralized vast amounts of customer data, the global peer to peer network of Web 3.0 may act as a leveling force, challenging the ability of such companies to thrive through data hoarding. This shift grants individuals greater authority over their content and control over who can access and profit from their data (Essex et al., 2023).

Among the various potential applications of the foundational technologies of Web 3.0, cryptocurrencies, and non-fungible tokens (NFTs) stand out as the primary existing and evolving applications. Both NFTs and cryptocurrencies, as distinct entities built on blockchain technology, represent real-world items in a digital format, showcasing considerable growth potential (Razi et al., 2023). Web 3.0 has the potential to enhance data security, scalability, and privacy beyond what Web 2.0 can achieve.

Web 3.0 Features and Technologies

Decentralized: In contrast to the initial two web generations, which predominantly centralized governance and applications, Web 3.0 will provide applications and services through a distributed approach that doesn't rely on a central authority (Essex et al., 2023).

Blockchain-based: A blockchain is an Internet-based decentralized system where a set of interconnected computers collaborate to both record and verify transactions simultaneously (White et al., 2020). Blockchain decentralization serves as the facilitator for the distributed applications and services of Web 3.0. Through blockchain, data undergoes management and validation on an extensively distributed, peer-to-peer network (Swan, 2015). Additionally, blockchain utilizes a theoretically immutable ledger of transactions and activity, contributing to the verification of authenticity and the establishment of trust among participants in the blockchain (Essex et al., 2023).

Cryptocurrency-enabled: Cryptocurrency plays a pivotal role in Web 3.0 and is anticipated to extensively replace government-issued "fiat currency" (Essex et al., 2023).

Semantically Organized: The Semantic Web aims to organize information in a manner that educates AI-based systems about the meaning of data. This enables websites to get to the bottom of end search queries in a human-like manner, fostering the creation and sharing of superior content (Anantrasirichai & Bull, 2022).

Autonomous and artificially intelligent: Web 3.0's crucial aspect is overall automation, predominantly driven by artificial intelligence. AI-equipped websites will sift through data, delivering personalized information to individual users (Essex et al., 2023).

Web 3.0 Applications

Web 3.0 is anticipated to leverage the web's evolving AI capabilities to comprehend users' intentions and preferences, delivering personalized content based on user-controlled personal data (Berners-Lee et al., 2023). This automated curation of content is expected to save companies both time and money. With blockchain at its foundation, Web 3.0 will enable new applications and services based on blockchain technologies in active use today. They include the following (Essex et al., 2023):

NFTs: Founding its applications on blockchain, Web 3.0 is poised to introduce new services and applications utilizing existing blockchain technologies (Makridakis & Christodoulou, 2019). Some of these applications include Non-Fungible Tokens (NFTs), which serve as unique cryptographic assets for creating and authenticating ownership of digital assets. Cryptocurrencies, such as Bitcoin, are anticipated to be the predominant digital currencies of Web 3.0, secured by cryptography for generating units, conducting transactions, and verifying ownership changes (Wu et al., 2023).

DeFi: Decentralized finance (DeFi) is an emerging blockchain technology that could be the basis for Web 3.0's decentralized financial services (Essex et al., 2023). Jensen et al., (2021) describe DeFi as "'DeFi application' as a configuration of consumer-oriented smart contracts, operating a predefined business logic within the transparent and predictable computational environment enabled by a permissionless blockchain technology.

Cryptocurrency: Cryptocurrencies, such as Bitcoin, are anticipated to be the predominant digital currencies of Web 3.0, secured by cryptography for generating units, conducting transactions, and verifying ownership changes (Wu et al., 2023).

Decentralized applications (dApps): Decentralized applications (dApps), open-source applications built on decentralized blockchains, are another integral aspect of Web 3.0 (Tyagi, 2023). dApps cover a wide array of functionalities, including middleware, charitable donations, and social media platforms.

Smart contracts: A category of decentralized applications (dApps), smart contracts currently serve as the foundation for emerging blockchain applications and are anticipated to be a focal point in the evolution of Web 3.0 (Destefanis & Ragnedda, 2019). Operating as program codes rather than legal contracts, smart contracts execute business logic based on triggered events. While their legal standing remains largely undefined in many jurisdictions, these dynamic entities are more adaptable to shifting conditions compared to conventional contracts. In the context of Web 3.0, smart contracts are poised to become robust mechanisms facilitating trusted interactions between blockchain users and applications (Khan et al., 2021).

Cross-chain bridges: Cross-chain bridges, aiming to facilitate interoperability across numerous blockchains in the Web 3.0 landscape, represent a critical component (Essex et al., 2023). Cross-chain bridges enable financial transactions between distinct blockchain platforms, allowing token exchange, smart contract execution, data transmission, and other operations between them (Zhao et al., 2023).

DAOs: Decentralized Autonomous Organizations (DAOs) are conceptualized as organizational entities designed to offer the essential structure and governance required to implement a practical decentralized approach to Web 3.0 services (Cardoso, 2022).

Impact of Web 3.0 on Business

Web 2.0 provides an interactive experience to users through social networks, Wikis, and blogs. In Web 3.0, machines comprehend and categorize data in much similar to how humans perform tasks. Through this, Web 3.0 provides an integrated experience to users. Kreps & Kimppa (2015) discussed that Web 3.0 is a phenomenon where we transition from being mere users to becoming integral components of applications that emerge and disappear. The Web is progressing towards a novel stage of development, which brings enormous advantages to the world. The development of Web 3.0 technologies has brought substantial advantages to both small and medium enterprises of various industries (Potluri & Vajjhala, 2018).

In today's blockchain and Web 3.0 communities, the emphasis on decentralized applications and blockchain technologies is evident, signaling a potential transformation in online interactions and business revenue models (Lacity & Lupien, 2022). The reliance on cryptocurrency in Web 3.0 suggests a significant shift in financial transactions from conventional service providers to decentralized blockchains (Essex et al., 2023).

The expected departure from the data-centralizing practices of Web 2.0 giants such as Amazon, Google, and Meta in favor of a global peer-to-peer network in Web 3.0 could challenge the traditional methods of companies thriving through data accumulation. Individuals stand to gain more control over their content and the management of their data (Zhang et al., 2017).

Sabbagh et al., (2011) discussed that through Web 3.0, recommendation engines will generate more comprehensive and targeted information by leveraging an enhanced understanding of users' habits and preferences. Search engines will become more accurate and beneficial, considering context and wording in the generation of results. A world of Web 3.0 called a transcend web will emerge, in which searching and browsing the web becomes vastly more interesting and efficient, with results and link suggestions tailored specifically to your interests. Through these features, Web 3.0 not only offers significant opportunities for enhancing existing businesses but also a great potential to establish new ones.

In the era of Web 3.0, trust and privacy play an increasingly significant role, facilitating identity management to guarantee authenticity. Moreover, user education promotes responsible internet practices, potentially fostering growth in business areas (Potluri & Vajjhala, 2018).

In the current scenario where the technology and its implications have not been thoroughly explored, there is a challenge in regulating a decentralized system. This could potentially lead to an increase in cybercrimes, including various forms of online harassment and hate speech. Consequently, there is a necessity for in-depth studies on the impact of decentralization on web governance and data management (Alanzi & Alkhatib, 2022).

Web 3.0 is not an independent or isolated technology; instead, it is a combination of existing principles integrated with new programs and scripts. Hence, when assessing the repercussions of Web 3.0 technologies, it is essential to view them not as standalone entities but as a fusion of existing principles with new programs and scripts (Bruwer & Rudman, 2015).

Bruwer & Rudman (2015) further discussed that the positive prospects offered by the foundational Web 3.0 technologies are accompanied by corresponding negative consequences closely linked to these technologies. Key detrimental impacts include the unauthorized access or manipulation of sensitive data by individuals lacking proper authorization. Furthermore, the rise of advanced electronic attacks, such as SQL injections, malware, highly targeted spam, and manipulation of internet rankings, presents significant challenges. The personalization of web content contributes to a scenario where personal and sensitive data becomes more accessible online, thereby increasing the risk of identity theft and social phishing. Additionally, the development and standardization of new web ontologies and languages raise the probability of releasing subpar or easily exploitable software and applications due to a lack of understanding and insufficient testing for adverse effects associated with the technology.

Bruwer & Rudman (2015) opined that a multilayer approach involving both technical and non-technical safeguards must be put in place before the adoption of Web 3.0 to ensure the mitigation of associated risks to an acceptable level. Technical safeguards include encryption and authentication; anti-malware software; physical and logical access controls; effective filtering and monitoring, and validation controls. Non-technical safeguards include consistent ongoing training to Web 3.0 users on the inherent risks associated with the use of Web 3.0, and the communication strategies to avoid potential threats. Establishing a policy for Web 3.0 usage is essential, outlining responsibilities and expected actions from its consumers. This framework, outlining the principles and procedures, could serve as an initial step to reduce these 'new' risks associated with Web 3.0 to an acceptable level.

Table 1. Web 1.0 vs Web 2.0 vs Web 3.0

Web 1.0	Web 2.0	Web 3.0
Static information (more difficult to change)	Dynamic information (always changing)	Semantic web (organized information), Token based, decentralized applications
More controlled user input	Less control over user input	More control over user input and who can access data

continued on following page

Table 1. Continued

Web 1.0	Web 2.0	Web 3.0
Promoted individual contribution; channels were less dynamic	Promotes greater collaboration, as channels are more dynamic and flexible	Promotes data ownership, owners have authority over who can access and profit from their data
Consider much more informative and data-driven	Considered much more social and interactive-driven	Considered to provide a much more integrated experience for users

NEED FOR TECHNICAL AUDIT

As companies and organizations grow and evolve, the conditions and practices that may have worked well originally can become outdated, inefficient, and even detrimental (Roberts, 2007). Technical audits provide an invaluable service by conducting an in-depth, unbiased examination of procedures, systems, equipment, and infrastructure to assess how well they are keeping pace with changes (Chambers & Rand, 2011).

Unlike financial or compliance audits aiming to uncover malfeasance, technical audits focus on optimizing future productivity, sustainability, and profitability (Omoteso, 2016). Auditors with specialized expertise analyze workflows, technology integration, facility layouts, supply chain integration, and more to identify opportunities for improvement. Their fresh perspective sees current situations through a contemporary lens, without preconceptions about how things "have always been done" (Vachon & Klassen, 2006).

For instance, consider the case of Grasim Nagada, a chemical factory that initially provided free milk to its employees when they came to work (Srivastava, 2012). This practice was reasonable when the factory was small, but the cost of providing milk to all employees became substantial as it expanded. Similarly, in the cement industry, wet-process manufacturing was viable in the past, but due to technological advancements, the wet process became obsolete, and companies that did not transition to the dry process had to shut down (Madlool et al., 2011). Technical audits offer timely and unbiased suggestions for system improvement and increased profitability. Without expert audits recommending proactive transition plans, companies clinging to antiquated equipment and methods faced major competitive disadvantages or even closure (Poirier, 1999).

In today's rapidly changing landscape, technical audits allow organizations to keep up with technological advances, automation integration, supply chain innovations, and much more (Frishammar et al., 2019). Not only do they boost efficiency, productivity, and return on assets, but they also demonstrate proactive commitment to stakeholders. Savvy executives make technical auditing a regular part of strategic planning, setting their organizations up for increased agility, cost savings, and continued success (Ulrich, 1996).

Technical audits are critical in the emerging Web 3.0 landscape to evaluate the effectiveness and security of new decentralized technologies (Liu et al., 2019). As enterprises adopt blockchain, metaverse, and other Web 3.0 solutions, comprehensive audits help identify vulnerabilities and provide recommendations before issues escalate (Al-Ghaili et al., 2022).

The scope of Web 3.0 technical audits spans several key areas. Auditors thoroughly examine the architecture and infrastructure behind decentralized apps, smart contracts, tokenized systems, and virtual worlds (Dai & Vasarhelyi, 2017). Methodologies combine code reviews, penetration testing, governance analysis, and compliance checks tailored for the complex, interconnected nature of Web 3.0 (Ragnedda & Destefanis, 2019).

The decentralized and transparent nature of Web 3.0 systems presents new challenges for auditing (Ragnedda & Destefanis, 2019). Smart contracts and blockchain-based applications have complex logic flows that require specialized review. Auditors must check for issues like reentrancy vulnerabilities, transaction-ordering dependencies, and denial-of-service triggers (Huang et al., 2019).

Threat modeling is an important methodology in Web 3.0 audits to systematically analyze security risks (UcedaVelez & Morana, 2015). Auditors map out different components, trust boundaries, data flows, and access controls to uncover assumptions or gaps leading to attack vectors. Cloud architectures add further considerations around dynamic IPs, frequent configuration changes, and shared responsibility models (Toosi et al., 2014).

Effective Web 3.0 auditing requires updated skills and specializations. Auditors need fluency with cryptographic systems, consensus protocols, and interoperability standards (White et al., 2020). Conducting rigorous audit planning, setting clear assessment criteria, and utilizing both manual and automated testing help auditors provide actionable insights (Raji et al., 2020).

Interoperability between metaverse platforms also demands greater audit scrutiny as virtual worlds increase connections (Egliston & Carter, 2022). Audits must validate identity management, asset ownership and transfer, and user privacy controls operate correctly across metaverse domains (Truong et al., 2023). As augmented and virtual reality become more prevalent, thorough functionality testing is essential to avoid disrupting experiences or enabling threats through any integration points (Rampolla & Kipper, 2012).

Ongoing communication and transparency by auditors provide significant value given the public nature of many Web 3.0 systems (Wheeler & Elkington, 2001). Audit reports that detail findings, severity, and recommended safeguards help inform users and reinforce best practices. Auditors should also highlight positive aspects around security architecture, governance controls, and system reliability to provide balanced feedback (Steinbart et al., 2018).

Proactive technical audits equip organizations to maximize opportunities in Web 3.0 while minimizing disruptions (Campbell & Jardine, 2001). As the landscape continues evolving rapidly, ongoing audits and adherence to best practices are essential for managing emerging risks and maintaining technological resilience (Olaniyi et al., 2023). Companies that embed diligent audit functions now can thrive on the foundations of reliable, secure Web 3.0 adoption.

Risks of Web 3.0 Applications

Blockchain Risks

The blockchain network functions as a peer-to-peer (P2P) system, relying on trustless transactions (Acharjamayum et al., 2018). In this network, each computer (node) maintains a duplicate of a shared ledger, with all nodes collectively updating and managing this copy (Meunier, 2018). A transaction remains pending until it is appended to a block and linked to the blockchain. (Alabdulwahhab, 2018).

Merely implementing a blockchain protocol doesn't suffice for a decentralized web. Storage limitations of blockchains can be overcome by employing the Interplanetary File System (IPFS) protocol. Described as a "peer-to-peer distributed file system", IPFS aims to connect all computing devices through a unified file system (Benet, 2014). IPFS addresses the storage challenge by referencing large data amounts with IPFS and embedding immutable, permanent IPFS links into a blockchain transaction. This process timestamps and secures content without storing the data directly on the chain (Benet, 2014). IPFS not only resolves storage issues but also conserves bandwidth, functioning as a distributed content delivery system with P2P capabilities. When accessing a file using its content hash, the nearest node housing the file responds and sends it to the requester, resulting in significant bandwidth savings, as demonstrated in a P2P video delivery network study (Nguyen et al., 2009). IPFS enhances security by guarding against DDoS attacks and minimizes censorship due to the absence of a specific server address to be blocked (Alenoghena, 2023).

Blockchain security vulnerabilities are exploited by hackers and online criminals to pilfer assets and personal information, giving rise to a novel category of cyber threats tailored for blockchain networks and interfaces. Phishing scams stand out as one of the prevalent methods employed through blockchain technology to steal individuals' identities (Pazhanisamy et al., 2023).

Internal auditors need to focus on new internal and external risks posed by blockchain technologies. One major risk associated with blockchain technology is the "51 percent," or "majority rule" attack. In this attack, a user introduces fake or false data in the node to create a fraudulent transaction, which is then accepted as true by most of the nodes on the blockchain (Dey, 2018). Hackers look to target endpoint vulnerabilities when people interact with blockchain, which is when data is more susceptible to attack (Lee, 2019).

Further, in a supply chain environment, individuals can misuse data by manipulating the transparency and traceability features of blockchain. The lack of standards and regulations for monitoring blockchain could bring huge legal risks (Al-Farsi et al., 2021). In this context, internal auditors need to assess whether their clients have implemented suitable measures to minimize risks. This involves reviewing the timelines and personnel required for the deployment of these actions (Cascarino, 2007). Additionally, auditors should offer assurance regarding the risks linked to the adoption of blockchain technology, such as the integration of technology interfaces with legacy systems and the effectiveness of migration strategies (Bonyuet, 2020).

Backed by a study, Dyball & Seethamraju (2021) discussed that there is a widespread belief that clients utilizing blockchain technology are perceived as riskier compared to other clients, and the risks related to inherent factors and control are heightened during audit engagements involving blockchain entities. It was observed that the perceptions stem largely from the absence of a consensus on accounting and technical standards for blockchain applications. The lack of agreement undermines the advantages offered by blockchain platforms, such as data integrity and validation. However, the study notes that the impact of identified inherent and control risks on the audit approach is not conclusive, as there are two distinct perspectives. The first approach involves using direct, indirect, account-level, and entity-level evidence, while the second relies more on indirect and entity-level evidence (Dyball & Seethamraju, 2021). Additionally, a study conducted by Elommal & Manita (2021) found that audit firms have not yet developed the capability to confidently ensure the accuracy of blockchain transactions, leading to increased detection risk.

Cryptocurrency Risks

In the paper "Challenges when Auditing Cryptocurrencies" (Vincent & Wilkins, 2020), it is discussed that verifying the number of crypto wallets and digital assets of a customer across multiple exchanges is a major challenge in verifying the existence of crypto-currency. Traditional methods for inspecting inventory and property additions may not be applicable here, owing to the digital nature of cryptocurrencies. Confirmations are also traditionally used to verify existence. While confirmations from banks are commonly used to verify the existence of cash, the decentralized nature of cryptocurrencies, stored in distributed ledgers without a central authority, can make it difficult for auditors to confirm currency balances through third-party sources.

Another method to validate the existence of cryptocurrency is to inspect sources or contractual documents that support the asset. In contrast to the regulated banking sector, there might be minimal or no documentation between the asset holder (exchange) and the client organization. Auditors also rely on the subsequent receipt of fiat currency, especially in payment settlements or asset sales, to gather audit evidence for existence. As such documentation may be absent, the auditor must verify whether the specified amount is present in the cryptocurrency wallet through testing (Vincent & Wilkins, 2020).

The authors have presented a framework that encompasses frequently utilized financial assertions, established audit procedures, and extra inherent risks/challenges related to cryptocurrencies. These insights could prove valuable in guiding standard-setters and regulators to provide authoritative advice in the coming years, aiding in the planning and execution of audits.

Furthermore, as discussed in the paper, if a cryptocurrency is traded through a third party(exchange), the absence of reliable assurance reporting mechanisms for the internal controls of the exchange, as evidenced by service organization control (SOC) reports, creates challenges in assessing, relying on, and verifying cryptocurrencies with a reasonable level of assurance. Additionally, compromised cryptocurrency keys can result in the asset becoming valueless.

Considering the instances of successful wallet attacks leading to the total loss of cryptocurrency, auditors will need to scrutinize the internal controls concerning wallet security. (Young, 2019). Consequently, the presence of cryptocurrencies adds an extra layer of responsibility to the audit engagement, requiring verification of controls related to the access and storage of private and public keys (Alkhalifah et al., 2020).

Decentralized Application (dApp) Risks

Unlike traditional apps, the backend code of a dApp operates on a decentralized peer-to-peer network instead of centralized servers (Niya, 2018). Like apps, a dApp can have front-end code and user interfaces written in various languages. The front end of a dApp may also be hosted on a decentralized storage system like IPFS (Tang et al., 2021). Running on Ethereum, a decentralized, open, and public platform not controlled by any single entity, dApps maintain their purpose irrespective of the execution context. DApps are Turing complete, signifying their ability to perform any action with the necessary resources. Executing within the Ethereum Virtual Machine, dApps are isolated in a virtual environment, ensuring that any issues in a smart contract do not disrupt the normal operation of the blockchain network (Goel et al., 2022).

Addressing vulnerabilities in smart contracts is crucial in decentralized applications (DApps) like DAOs (Jiang, 2018). These self-executing code snippets can sometimes harbor bugs or flaws, potentially causing financial losses or operational disruptions. Ensuring robust code audits and comprehensive testing is paramount to uncover and rectify potential issues before deploying smart contracts, safeguarding against exploitation risks (Namakshenas, 2023).

Decentralized Finance (DeFi) Risks

Decentralized finance (DeFi) protocols use algorithmically programmed smart contracts that operate autonomously on blockchains to execute transactions. Users engage with these protocols to deposit, borrow, and exchange financial assets represented as blockchain tokens. In contrast to conventional financial transactions relying on trust in intermediaries like banks or brokerages governed by reputation and regulation, DeFi protocols establish trust through transparency (Harvey, 2021). This transparency is facilitated by open-source code, enabling anyone to verify the smart contract's intentions.

The nature of DeFi being open source presents both advantages and disadvantages. On the positive side, tech-savvy users can review the underlying code of smart contracts, ensuring the security of their deposits. Conversely, this transparency also empowers malicious entities, such as hackers, to identify and exploit vulnerabilities for personal profit. These exploits, commonly known as DeFi or smart contract hacks, pose significant risks to users involved in DeFi platforms (Rudman, 2015).

To minimize this risk and draw in users, DeFi protocols can hire an external party to inspect their code, a procedure commonly known as DeFi or smart contract audits. In these audits, auditing experts in the programming languages prevalent in blockchains, with extensive knowledge of DeFi, thoroughly review the codes of protocols, searching for potential vulnerabilities (Li et al., 2020). Following the examination, DeFi auditors typically release a report outlining the scope of their work, the audit process, and their findings, which include any shortcomings along with the corrective actions that need to be taken for the respective protocols (Bhambhwani & Huang, 2023).

Cryptocurrency scams, ranging from investment fraud to Ponzi schemes and rug pulls in the decentralized finance (DeFi) space, underscore a significant challenge in the digital asset realm. In 2021, these scams amassed nearly $10 billion in ill-gotten gains, a figure that only slightly diminished to $7 billion in 2022 by late August. Investment scams, often posing as high-return opportunities, dominate the landscape, enticing users to invest in purportedly lucrative ventures that eventually prove impossible to cash out (Cong, 2023).

Uncovering Ponzi schemes, like investment scams, sustain themselves by paying fake returns to investors using funds from new participants, making them the highest revenue-generating form of a cryptocurrency scam. While Initial Coin Offerings (ICOs) have lost popularity, they were previously fraudulent activities, with unscrupulous teams vanishing with investors' funds after issuing seemingly promising native tokens (Cong, 2023).

Moreover, as discussed in the paper (Cong, 2023), rug pulls, prevalent in DeFi due to lax due diligence, involve seemingly legitimate projects abruptly shutting down without returning user funds. Phishing scams, sextortion, and trust trading schemes add further layers to the intricate web of crypto fraud. Scammers exploit the hype and fear of missing out (FOMO) in the crypto space, preying on the limited understanding of the public regarding cryptocurrency intricacies.

Further in the paper, beyond the staggering financial losses incurred by victims, these scams erode trust in the emerging cryptocurrency industry, potentially deterring participation or triggering stringent regulations. The role of centralized entities suggests measures by exchanges to identify and prevent fund transfers to scam addresses. It acknowledges the tension with cryptocurrency ethos but argues for a user protection-oriented approach. The necessity for ongoing user education in the rapidly evolving crypto and DeFi sectors is underscored, emphasizing the collaborative responsibility of the private sector and regulators in addressing this escalating challenge.

Natural Language Processing (NLP) Risks

Web-mined text datasets in Natural Language Processing (NLP) emphasize the success of large-scale pre-training and multilingual modeling in Web 3.0. The focus is on the manual audit of 205 language-specific corpora from major public datasets (CCAligned, ParaCrawl, WikiMatrix, OSCAR, mC4). Systematic issues in lower-resource corpora include instances with no usable text and a substantial number with less than 50% of sentences of acceptable quality. Problems such as mislabeling, and the use of nonstandard codes are also present. Web 3.0, and for easy detection of these issues, even by non-proficient speakers, and supplements human audits with automatic analyses (Kreutzer et al., 2022).

The promise of leveraging automatically crawled datasets for building NLP technologies, particularly benefiting low-resource languages where data scarcity poses a significant challenge for deep learning approaches. Despite the potential, a notable problem is highlighted: a lack of research on evaluating both the data collections and the tools used for automatic crawling and filtering in the context of low-resource languages. This gap in research raises concerns about the unknown quality and usability of the latest multilingual crawl data releases, despite their coverage of many low-resource languages (Kreutzer et al., 2022).

Information Security and Cyber Security Risks

Mário (2022) discussed that information security and cybersecurity in enterprise management boards are propelled by an increased awareness of the necessity to safeguard data and IT infrastructure from cyber threats. Small and Medium-sized Enterprises (SMEs), despite making contributions to the global economy, face unique challenges due to their smaller scale, lack of in-house IT personnel, and adherence to traditional business models.

Information System (IS) is designed to support information security auditing processes. The paper highlights the limitations of existing IS in the cybersecurity and information security auditing space, categorizing them as either proprietary or open-source, and emphasizes the need for a more flexible and adaptable solution. To validate the effectiveness of the proposed IS, it was tested in a cybersecurity audit project involving fifty SMEs, demonstrating its ability to evaluate compliance with the ISO-27001:2013 standard. It introduced a flexible IS designed to support auditing processes, addressing the challenges posed by existing IS categories. The testing of this IS in a real-world cybersecurity audit project further validates its effectiveness in assessing compliance with international standards. This exhibits a high level of flexibility, allowing for the loading of controls, checklists, and countermeasure tasks for assessment. Notably, it aims to bridge the gap between proprietary and open-source IS, which often lack the flexibility required for diverse enterprises and standards.

Decentralized Autonomous (DAO) Risks

Decentralized autonomous organizations, or DAOs, are emerging organizational structures enabled by blockchain technology. As discussed in the paper by Kraus et al., (2019), DAOs operate on rigid rules encoded in smart contracts on public blockchains without centralized control. All transactions are immutably recorded allowing transparency and auditability. Stakeholders gain voting rights through crypto token ownership rather than hierarchical power structures seen traditionally.

While this lends efficiencies, the paper highlights regulatory and ethical challenges posed due to the inflexibility of changing original rules programmed into DAOs. There is also vulnerability due to reliance on the accuracy of smart contract code. Unintended errors or exploits can enable hacks with limited accountability and legal precedent on redressal processes so far. The energy-intensive nature of underlying blockchain platforms also raises environmental sustainability concerns.

The paper concludes more research is needed into frameworks enabling the integration of DAO control protocols with existing auditing, compliance, and reporting requirements. Additionally, studying dispute resolution mechanisms for DAOs and assessing the plutocratic structures emerging from token holder voting models versus espoused democratic ideals merits examination. The transformative potential though highlighted because DAOs warrant serious scholarly inquiry at the confluence of accounting, automation, and emerging technologies.

Metaverse Risks

Kshetri (2023) covers the examination of Web 3.0 and the metaverse revealing a complex landscape fraught with security and privacy challenges. Assessing the vulnerabilities in these technological innovations points to potential breaches, bugs, scams, and fraudulent activities. The complexity of these technologies creates an environment conducive to exploitation by cybercriminals. While user-controlled wallets and ID portability in Web 3.0 offer certain security features, the drawbacks of self-sovereign identity and the lack of accountability pose significant concerns.

Existing regulatory frameworks designed for the Web2 era are deemed insufficient, necessitating an overhaul to effectively address the unique challenges posed by Web 3.0 and the metaverse. The industry's lack of preparedness further compounds potential risks, particularly in the immersive metaverse environment. Web 3.0 projects' dependence on

Web 2.0 infrastructures expose them to known vulnerabilities, with cyberattacks originating from Web 2.0 social media platforms highlighting interconnected risks. The metaverse's data-rich environment becomes a target for nefarious actors, leading to a surge in both bot-driven and human-driven attacks.

Consumer sentiments reflect apprehensions about privacy and security, with a notable percentage expressing concerns about legal protections for user identities and increased sharing of private data in the metaverse. High-profile cyberattacks on the decentralized finance (DeFi) market underscore the need for a measured and security-focused approach amid the accelerated development of projects in Web 3.0 and the metaverse.

Regulatory compliance becomes challenging in the metaverse, where the blurring of digital and physical worlds necessitates the collection of sensitive data. Despite these challenges, a positive trend of increasing investments in Web 3.0 and metaverse security, signaling a recognition of the need to fortify security measures in these rapidly evolving technological landscapes. Comprehensive measures, including regulatory reforms, heightened awareness, and robust security practices, to effectively address the evolving risks in Web 3.0 and the metaverse.

Tokenomics Risks

Tokenomics, the study of token economies created through blockchain technology, is a burgeoning field that has gained importance with the increase in blockchain projects (Canidio et al., 2021). These artificial economies are designed to incentivize user participation in specific blockchain initiatives.

The Tokenomics Audit Checklist, as detailed in the "Tokenomics Audit Checklist: Presentation and Examples" (Kampakis & Stankevičius, 2023), provides a comprehensive framework for evaluating the tokenomics of blockchain-based projects. This framework is divided into four main sections: business-token interaction, structural analysis, allocation and distribution, and stability and stress tests. Each section contains a set of questions, with responses assigned points to indicate the favorability of the token economy.

The framework was applied to three case studies: Algem, Terra/Luna, and Ethereum 2.0. The authors discovered that the Algem project boasts a robust token economy, while the Terra/Luna project collapsed due to several design flaws. The Ethereum 2.0 project, still in its early development phase, has not yet fully matured its token economy (Khamisa, 2021).

This framework serves as a valuable tool for assessing the risk of investing in a blockchain project. By understanding a project's Tokenomics, investors can make informed decisions (Creta & Tenca, 2021). However, the authors of the "Tokenomics Audit Checklist" Kampakis & Stankevičius (2023) acknowledge several limitations. The framework's subjectivity is one such limitation, as different auditors may interpret the questions differently. Another limitation is the framework's lack of comprehensiveness, as it does not cover all potential risks associated with Tokenomics (Freni et al., 2022).

Despite these limitations, the checklist remains a useful tool for assessing investment risk in a blockchain project. By utilizing the checklist, investors can identify potential red flags and make informed investment decisions (Heyman, 2023).

The authors of the "Tokenomics Audit Checklist" Kampakis & Stankevičius (2023) recommend future work to focus on enhancing the objectivity and comprehensiveness of the framework. They also suggest using the framework in conjunction with other risk assessment tools. In conclusion, the checklist is a valuable tool for assessing investment risk in a blockchain project. By using the checklist, investors can identify potential red flags and make informed decisions (Brazel et al., 2015). Kampakis & Stankevičius (2023) recommend future work to focus on improving the objectivity and comprehensiveness of the framework.

Semantically Organized Risks

The transition to a semantically organized Web 3.0 brings with it several inherent risks that organizations must carefully identify and assess (Sheth & Thirunarayan, 2012). The primary concern is privacy, as the interconnected nature of data could inadvertently expose sensitive user information (Millett et al., 2007). It's crucial to assess the level of control users have over their data and ensure that privacy is upheld, and user consent is respected across the semantic web landscape.

Additionally, the potential for inaccuracies in data interpretation poses a risk to the reliability of information (Meeker et al., 2022). Semantic technologies are heavily dependent on high-quality data, and any inconsistencies or inaccuracies could lead to misinterpretations, undermining the overall credibility of the processed information (Sheth & Thirunarayan, 2012).

Security challenges also arise in a semantically organized Web 3.0 environment (Rudman, 2015). The intelligent and interconnected nature of Web 3.0 could expand the attack surface, introducing new vulnerabilities that could be exploited by malicious actors (Anand et al., 2020). Unauthorized access to sensitive information is a significant concern. Furthermore, the lack of standardized semantic technologies poses challenges to interoperability, hindering the smooth exchange of data between different systems. This lack of universal standards could create barriers to adoption and collaboration (Rahman & Hussain, 2020).

To mitigate these risks, organizations can implement robust data management policies that prioritize user consent and control over data (Davis, 2012). They can also establish rigorous data validation and verification processes to ensure data accuracy and consistency. Implementing robust security measures, including encryption and access controls, can protect against unauthorized access (Omotunde & Ahmed, 2023). Advocating for the development and adoption of universal standards for semantic technologies can enhance interoperability.

Auditors play a crucial role in identifying, assessing, and mitigating these risks. They can conduct comprehensive audits of Web 3.0 applications to identify potential risks and vulnerabilities (Li et al., 2023). They can also assess the effectiveness of the organization's risk mitigation strategies and recommend improvements. Furthermore, auditors can ensure compliance with regulatory requirements and the establishment of governance frameworks, contributing to a responsible and secure deployment of a semantically organized Web 3.0 (Bruwer, 2014). Their role is vital in addressing ethical considerations and ensuring the overall success of this transformative transition (Anwar, 2022).

GOVERNANCE

The emergence of Web 3.0 and related decentralized technologies has introduced new complexities and prerequisites for corporate and IT governance. As organizations implement innovations like blockchain, crypto assets, and token-based systems, governance policies need to evolve to address arising risks and leverage potential benefits (Chen et al., 2018).

Corporate Governance

Corporate governance comprises the comprehensive organizational structure and ethical principles that assist a company in achieving its objectives. It encompasses various stakeholders, including the board of directors, senior management, shareholders, employees, and other relevant parties (Tricker, 2015). A vital aspect of corporate governance is guaranteeing the board of directors acts in the company's best interest (Gillan, 2006).

With the expanding dependence on IT and the presence of legislation like the Protection of Personal Information Bill and Protection of Information Bill, along with codes like The King Report on Corporate Governance III emphasizing information, the management and control of IT risks and organizational information have become integral to corporate governance. The management of IT now exceeds technical functions handled by IT experts; it has become an essential part of organizational management (Ribbers, 2002).

Effective corporate governance in Web 3.0 necessitates delineating roles, responsibilities, and accountability across decentralized networks. With assets and data distributed across nodes, conventional centralized control mechanisms may not apply. Organizations require governance frameworks aligning with decentralized principles while still providing oversight and strategic direction (Ølnes et al., 2017).

IT Governance

IT governance is characterized as a set of principles delineating accountability and assisting responsible parties in making informed decisions and optimizing IT (Selig, 2008). Bruwer (2014) underscores that IT governance extends beyond specific decision-making instances, emphasizing defining roles, responsibilities, and mechanisms to ensure decision-makers are held accountable.

As businesses increasingly adopt advanced technological solutions and rely more heavily on Information Technology (IT), the impact of IT goes beyond operational functions to encompass strategic dimensions (Weill & Ross, 2004). It involves various processing components, including human, financial, physical, and informational elements (Peterson, 2004). Thus, IT is not merely a tool for operational support but is recognized as an asset capable of generating opportunities, ensuring a competitive edge, and requiring proper governance (Boh & Yellin, 2006).

In the swiftly changing landscape of Information Technology (IT), businesses acknowledge the crucial need to effectively leverage IT capabilities (Bruwer, 2014). To address the evolving risks associated with the adoption of innovations like Web 3.0, organizations must establish a robust and adaptable IT governance policy (Exchange, 2012).

The governance of IT should align with and enhance the board's overarching mission, which involves defining strategic direction, implementing effective risk management systems, establishing internal controls, ensuring responsible resource utilization, and achieving organizational objectives (Ako-Nai & Singh, 2019). These objectives, often referred to as “strategic level” objectives, play a crucial role in the overall organizational framework (Brown & Nasuti, 2005).

Creating an environment where IT aligns with business goals, IT investments yield favorable returns, and IT-related risks and opportunities are aptly managed requires the implementation of sound IT governance practices (Bowen et al., 2007). These practices should be regularly reviewed and adapted to support the implementation of new technologies (Joshi et al., 2018).

Organizations are advised to seek assistance in implementing such policies by adopting internationally approved frameworks (Wilkin, 2012). The implementation of IT governance principles offers numerous benefits, such as: Attaining strategic alignment between IT and business objectives and providing a competitive advantage (Luftman et al., 2017). Neglecting the incorporation of IT governance principles may lead to operational risks that jeopardize the confidentiality, reliability, and authenticity of data (Wilkin, 2012), unauthorized access and alterations to the IT system, and compromise system availability and functionality (Tiwana & Konsynski, 2010).

IT governance must also expand its focus from protecting corporate IT resources to governing participation in external tokenized networks (Avital et al., 2016). To effectively govern IT in Web 3.0 environments, organizations require clear guidelines and policies for decentralized network participation that address critical activities (Hsieh et al., 2023). This includes establishing processes for secure wallet management, defining rules for operating validator nodes, implementing controls around smart contract interaction, formalizing procedures for acquiring and accounting for crypto asset holdings, enacting protections for managing data in decentralized storage, tailoring identity, and access mechanisms for public DLTs, and enabling compliance monitoring to track adherence to regulations (Liljefors & Hedberg, 2018).

The guidelines established in the King III report offer a set of corporate governance principles tailored for South African entities (Exchange, 2012). These principles, as delineated in King III, have played a pivotal role in incorporating IT governance into the fabric of corporate governance practices in South Africa (Salvioni & Gennari, 2016). They have emerged as an essential facet recommended for adoption by organizations in the country (Ackers & Eccles, 2015).

With thoughtfully defined policies and procedures in place for these decentralized activities, IT organizations can promote the adoption of Web 3.0 technologies while still ensuring security, managing risks, maintaining strategic alignment, and providing necessary oversight (Radanliev, 2023). Critical capabilities like comprehensive audit trails, blockchain analytics, and visibility into on-chain activity will become increasingly important for IT governance as the adoption of decentralized networks accelerates (Dutta et al., 2020).

Governance in Web 3.0: Token-Based Governance

Token-based governance is a mechanism in decentralized systems where decision-making power is distributed among participants based on the number of tokens they hold (Kiayias & Lazos, 2022). This governance model is often used in blockchain projects and Decentralized Autonomous Organizations (DAOs) to democratize decision-making and align the interests of participants with the success of the network. In this system, individuals acquire tokens as a form of ownership or participation in the network. The more tokens someone holds, the greater their influence in the governance process (Rohr & Wright, 2018). When decisions need to be made, such as protocol upgrades or changes to the system's rules, token holders can cast votes proportional to their token holdings. This method ensures that those who have a larger stake in the network have a correspondingly larger say in its development and governance (Miller & Lessard, 2001). Token-based governance incentivizes participants to act in the best interest of the network, as their financial stake is tied to the success and stability of the project (Bruwer, 2014).

While token-based governance promotes participation and alignment of incentives, its implementation faces challenges (Jentzsch, 2016). For example, whales with large token holdings could centralize decision-making power (Han et al., 2023). Mechanisms like governance committees, quorum requirements, and vesting schedules may provide checks and balances (Voshmgir, 2020). For instance, a multi-sig process involving both technical experts and top token holders could prevent unilateral moves (Zheng et al., 2017).

Further, short-term interests like price pumps could take priority over long-term protocol improvements (Rotmans et al., 2001). Governance attacks by malicious actors could disrupt the decentralized ethos (Raymond, 2016). Overall, thoughtful tokenomic design is key to realizing the benefits of token-based governance (Fenu et al., 2018).

Safeguards in Web 3.0

Web 3.0's decentralized architecture requires robust safeguards to achieve reliability and mass adoption. Technical, legal, and community-focused protections have been identified as pivotal across Web 3.0's complex, evolving landscape (Rathor et al., 2023).

On the technical front, mechanisms like smart contract auditing, cybersecurity frameworks, and resilience engineering are vital lines of defense. Tolmach et al., (2021) propose formal verification of smart contracts to mathematically prove code correctness and security.

Complementing audits with verification could fortify multi-million-dollar protocols. Enterprise cybersecurity standards like the NIST framework offer best practices spanning access controls to vulnerability management that decentralized applications sorely need (Himri et al., 2022). Built-in upgradeability, fail-safes, and layered defenses could aid this (Hendrycks & Mazeika, 2022). Winkens & Leicht-Scholten (2023) highlight resilience engineering - the capacity to absorb disturbances and adapt - as imperative to navigating Web 3.0's volatility.

Legal safeguards and regulatory compliance will equally shape Web 3.0's trajectory (Hagemann et al., 2018). While decentralization defies traditional governance, consumer protections and risk management warrant attention. Author Scott (1987) underlines how contractual terms can incorporate codes of conduct and dispute resolution alongside existing statutory regulations. Further, the potential of decentralized autonomous organizations offers transparent community governance at Web 3.0's grassroots (Merrell, 2022). If underpinned by inclusivity, social contracts could complement the standardized legal apparatus (Bloom et al., 2008).

Indeed, participative communities seal the final, most foundational layer of defense (Flint, 2012). Decentralization transfers accountability to stakeholders, making bottom-up oversight and collective responsibility integral to ecosystem security (Calleja-López et al., 2017). The author highlights that crowdsourced threat intelligence even outperforms centralized systems. Transparent communication alongside equitable incentives and access may stimulate such community vigilance, providing both ethical and security safeguards (Wu, 2019).

Multifaceted and reinforcing defenses across the technical, legal, and social realms are indispensable as the Web 3.0 revolution gathers momentum (De Spiegeleire et al., 2017). While robust security and compliant governance lay the foundations, projects must recognize communities as their first line of defense. Prioritizing inclusivity, transparency, and collective responsibility at the grassroots level stands vital to securing this next era of the internet (Lathrop & Ruma, 2010).

CONCLUSION

Ushering the era of Web 3.0, we have tried to conclusively summarize the evolution of the Web from its inception through Web 1.0 to Web 2.0, and our topic of discussion is Web 3.0. This evolution summary not only covers the basic details of the different phases of the web but also engages in a comparison of these phases, wherein the issues that are called out for the next phase of evolution are also covered to understand the journey of the web concisely and comprehensively. Eventually, as the web moves to the new phase of Web 3.0, we try to uncover multiple facets of the new phase through the evolution journey. This extensive coverage handled two main aspects of the new phase, the different features that Web 3.0 brings to the table, and the different applications that have been implemented so far.

In addition to the evolution journey, risks, governance, and safeguards, that have been covered later in the paper, the impacts of Web 3.0 on business cover multiple aspects of the collaboration of business value and the use of Web 3.0. The multilayer impacts that technology currently has on business have been summarized in this section. Further calling out the need for technical audit in this area of technology, the paper clearly addresses the need through different examples of the rapidly changing environment. Highlighting the importance of technical audit in general and specifying the importance of the same in Web 3.0, the scope and threats are covered to showcase the need.

Important in the paper are the risks of Web 3.0 technologies, which are segmented into multiple sections covering different applications of showcasing the risks associated accordingly. Wherein risks related to different technological applications of Web 3.0 such as blockchain, cryptocurrencies, decentralized applications, decentralized finance, natural language processing, decentralized autonomous, metaverse, and tokenomics are covered extensively. Highlighting the risks with the medium of different examples and cases, the paper tries to compile risks from different areas under one roof.

Finally, the aspects of governance and safeguards conclude the paper, where domains of corporate governance, IT governance, and governance in Web 3.0 are portrayed. This not only reflects the individual importance of different domains of governance but also highlights the connection with Web 3.0.

Traversing through the evolution of the web and the impact that we see through the latest applications of Web 3.0, the paper highlights risks associated with the technology, and the auditing aspect for the new phase of the web, purposefully pointing out the areas of risks that are becoming important for the auditing space to keep a watch on.

REFERENCES

Acharjamayum, I., Patgiri, R., & Devi, D. (2018). Blockchain: A Tale of Peer to Peer Security. .DOI: 10.1109/SSCI.2018.8628826

Ackers, B., & Eccles, N. S. (2015). Mandatory corporate social responsibility assurance practices: The case of King III in South Africa. *Accounting, Auditing & Accountability Journal*, 28(4), 515–550. DOI: 10.1108/AAAJ-12-2013-1554

Aghaei, S., Nematbakhsh, M. A., & Farsani, H. K. (2012). Evolution of the World Wide Web: From Web 1.0 to Web 4.0. International Journal of Web & Semantic Technology, 1-10.

Ako-Nai, A., & Singh, A. M. (2019). *Information technology governance framework for improving organisational performance*. SA Journal of Information Management. DOI: 10.4102/sajim.v21i1.1010

Al-Farsi, S., Rathore, M. M., & Bakiras, S. (2021). Security of blockchain-based supply chain management systems: challenges and opportunities. DOI: 10.3390/app11125585

Al-Ghaili, A. M., Kasim, H., Al-Hada, N. M., Hassan, Z., Othman, M., Hussain, T. J., & Shayea, I. (2022). A review of metaverse's definitions, architecture, applications, challenges, issues, solutions, and future trends. *IEEE Access : Practical Innovations, Open Solutions*, 10, 125835–125866. DOI: 10.1109/ACCESS.2022.3225638

Alabdulwahhab, F. (2018). Web 3.0: The Decentralized Web Blockchain networks and Protocol Innovation. 2018 1st International Conference on Computer Applications & Information Security (ICCAIS), 1-4.

Alanzi, H., & Alkhatib, M. (2022). Towards Improving Privacy and Security of Identity Management Systems Using Blockchain Technology: A Systematic Review. *Applied Sciences (Basel, Switzerland)*, 12415(23), 12415. Advance online publication. DOI: 10.3390/app122312415

Alenoghena, I. B. (2023). Secure Data Transfer Through Inter-Planetary File System (Ipfs) And Blockchain-Embedded Smart Contract In Building Construction. Retrieved from http://repository.futminna.edu.ng:8080/jspui/handle/123456789/19810

Alkhalifah, A., Ng, A., Kayes, A. S., Chowdhury, J., Alazab, M., & Watters, P. A. (2020). A taxonomy of blockchain threats and vulnerabilities. In *Blockchain for Cybersecurity and Privacy* (pp. 3–28). CRC Press. DOI: 10.1201/9780429324932-2

Alves de Castro, C. (2021). The Evolution of the Internet and Social Media: A Literature Review. International Journal of e-Education e-Business e-. *Management Learning*, 12(1), 30–41. DOI: 10.17706/ijeeee.2022.12.1.30-41

Anand, P., Singh, Y., Selwal, A., Singh, P. K., Felseghi, R. A., & Raboaca, M. S. (2020). Iovt: Internet of vulnerable things? threat architecture, attack surfaces, and vulnerabilities in internet of things and its applications towards smart grids. *Energies*, 13(18), 4813. DOI: 10.3390/en13184813

Anantrasirichai, N., & Bull, D. (2022). Artificial intelligence in the creative industries: A review. *Artificial Intelligence Review*, 55(1), 1–68. DOI: 10.1007/s10462-021-10039-7

Anderson, P. (2007). *What is Web 2.0?: ideas, technologies and implications for education*. JISC.

Antunes, M., Maximiano, M., & Gomes, R. (2022). A Customizable Web Platform to Manage Standards Compliance of Information Security and Cybersecurity Auditing. *Procedia Computer Science*, 196, 36–43. DOI: 10.1016/j.procs.2021.11.070

Anwar, A. A. (2022). A survey of semantic web (Web 3.0), its applications, challenges, future and its relation with Internet of things (IoT). Web Intelligence, 1-30.

Appelbaum, D., Kogan, A., Vasarhelyi, M., & Yan, Z. (2017). Impact of business analytics and enterprise systems on managerial accounting. International journal of accounting information systems. *International Journal of Accounting Information Systems*, 25, 29–44. DOI: 10.1016/j.accinf.2017.03.003

Avital, M., Beck, R., King, J. L., Rossi, M., & Teigland, R. (2016). Jumping on the Blockchain Bandwagon: Lessons of the Past and Outlook to the Future. Proceedings/ International Conference on Information Systems (ICIS).

Aziz, H. A., & Madani, A. (2015). Evolution of the Web and its Uses in Healthcare.

Bedard, J. C., Graham, L., & Jackson, C. (2005). Information systems risk and audit planning. *International Journal of Auditing*, 9(2), 147–163. DOI: 10.1111/j.1099-1123.2005.00267.x

Benet, J. (2014). IPFS - Content Addressed, Versioned, P2P File System. doi:https:// doi.org//arXiv.1407.3561DOI: 10.48550

Berners-Lee, T., Hendler, J., & Lassila, O. (2023). The Semantic Web: A New Form of Web Content That is Meaningful to Computers Will Unleash a Revolution of New Possibilities.

Berners Lee, T. (1999). Weaving the Web: The original design and ultimate destiny of the World Wide Web by its inventor.

Bhambhwani, S. M., & Huang, A. H. (2023). Auditing decentralized finance. *The British Accounting Review*.

Bloom, G., Standing, H., & Lloyd, R. (2008). Markets, information asymmetry and health care: Towards new social contracts. *Social Science & Medicine*, 66(10), 2076–2087. DOI: 10.1016/j.socscimed.2008.01.034 PMID: 18316147

Boh, W. F., & Yellin, D. (2006). Using enterprise architecture standards in managing information technology. *Journal of Management Information Systems*, 23(3), 163–207. DOI: 10.2753/MIS0742-1222230307

Bonyuet, D. (2020). Overview and impact of blockchain on auditing. *The International Journal of Digital Accounting Research*, 31–43. DOI: 10.4192/1577-8517-v20_2

Bowen, P. L., Cheung, M. Y., & Rohde, F. H. (2007). Enhancing IT governance practices: A model and case study of an organization's efforts. international Journal of Accounting information. *Systems*, 191–221.

Brazel, J. F., Jones, K. L., Thayer, J., & Warne, R. C. (2015). Understanding investor perceptions of financial statement fraud and their use of red flags: Evidence from the field. *Review of Accounting Studies*, 20(4), 1373–1406. DOI: 10.1007/s11142-015-9326-y

Brown, W., & Nasuti, F. (2005). Sarbanes-Oxley and enterprise security: IT governance-what it takes to get the job done. Inf. Secur. J. A Glob. Perspect., 15-28.

Bruwer, H. J. (2014). An investigation of developments in Web 3.0: opportunities, risks, safeguards and governance (Doctoral dissertation, Stellenbosch: Stellenbosch University).

Bruwer, R., & Rudman, R. (2015). Web 3.0: Governance, Risks and Safeguards. *Journal of Applied Business Research*, 31(3), 1037–1056. DOI: 10.19030/jabr.v31i3.9241

Business School Web10. (n.d.). Retrieved from https://thebusinessofsocial.wordpress.com/tag/web-1-0/

Calleja-López, A., Monterde, A., & Barandiaran, X. E. (2017). Framework for democratic governance of distributed architectures: DEcentralised Citizens Owned Data Ecosystem.

Campbell, J. D., & Jardine, A. K. (2001). *Maintenance excellence: optimizing equipment life-cycle decisions*. CRC Press.

Canidio, A., Danos, V., Marcassa, S., & Prat, J. (2021). Tokens and ICOs: A Review of the Economic Literature. Principles of Blockchain Systems, 191-210.

Cardoso, A. G. (2022). Decentralized Autonomous Organizations – DAOs: The Convergence of Technology, Law, Governance, and Behavioral Economics. DOI: 10.2139/ssrn.4341884

Cascarino, R. E. (2007). Auditor's Guide to Information Systems Auditing.

Chambers, A., & Rand, G. (2011). *The operational auditing handbook: auditing business and IT processes*. John Wiley & Sons.

Chamira, R. (n.d.). Linkedin. Retrieved from https://www.linkedin.com/pulse/evolution-internet-from-web10-web3-ravi-chamria/

Chen, G., Xu, B., Lu, M., & Chen, N. S. (2018). Exploring blockchain technology and its potential applications for education. Smart Learning Environments, 1-10. DOI: 10.1186/s40561-017-0050-x

Choudhury, N. (2014). World Wide Web and Its Journey from Web 1.0 to Web 4.0. *International Journal of Computer Science and Information Technologies*8096–8100.

Cong, L. W., Grauer, K., Rabetti, D., & Updegrave, H. (2023). The Dark Side of Crypto and Web3: Crypto-Related Scams. DOI: 10.2139/ssrn.4358572

Creta, F., & Tenca, F. (2021). Tokenomics: A new opportunity in the Real Estate business? A qualitative approach to crowdfunding and blockchain interaction. *First Monday*.

Dai, J., & Vasarhelyi, M. A. (2017). Toward blockchain-based accounting and assurance. *Journal of Information Systems*, 31(3), 5–21. DOI: 10.2308/isys-51804

Davis, K. (2012). *Ethics of Big Data: Balancing risk and innovation*. O'Reilly Media, Inc.

De Haes, S., & Van Grembergen, W. (2008). An exploratory study into the design of an IT governance minimum baseline through Delphi research. *Communications of the Association for Information Systems*, 22, 24. DOI: 10.17705/1CAIS.02224

De Spiegeleire, S., Maas, M., & Sweijs, T. (2017). *Artificial intelligence and the future of defense: strategic implications for small-and medium-sized force providers*. The Hague Centre for Strategic Studies.

Destefanis, G., & Ragnedda, M. (2019). *Blockchain and Web 3.0: Social* (1st ed.). Economic, and Technological Challenges.

Dey, S. (2018). Securing Majority-Attack in Blockchain Using Machine Learning and Algorithmic Game Theory: A Proof of Work. .DOI: 10.1109/CEEC.2018.8674185

Doyle, B., & Lopes, C. (2008). Survey of Technologies for Web Application Development. doi:arXiv:0801.2618

Dutta, P., Choi, T. M., Somani, S., & Butala, R. (2020). Blockchain technology in supply chain operations: Applications, challenges and research opportunities. Transportation research part e: Logistics and transportation review.

Dwivedi, A., Kumar, S., Dwivedi, A., & Singh, M. (2011). Current Security Considerations for Issues and Challenges of Trustworthy Semantic Web. Int. J. *Advanced Networking and Applications Volume*, 03(01), 978–983.

Dyball, M. C., & Seethamraju, R. (2021). The impact of client use of blockchain technology on audit risk and audit approach—An exploratory study. *International Journal of Auditing*, 25(2), 602–615. DOI: 10.1111/ijau.12238

Egliston, B., & Carter, M. (2022). The metaverse and how we'll build it': The political economy of Meta's Reality Labs. *New Media & Society*.

Elommal, N., & Manita, R. (2021). How blockchain innovation could affect the audit profession: a qualitative study.

Essex, D., Kerner, S. M., & Gillis, A. S. (2023). TechTarget. Retrieved from TechTarget: https://www.techtarget.com/whatis/definition/Web-30?asrc=EM_SS-WELCOME_249063862&src=10185333

Evans, M. (2006). The Evolution of the Web-From Web 1.0 to Web 4.0.

Exchange, L. S. (2012). *Corporate governance for Main Market and AIM companies*. London Stock Exchange.

Fenu, G., Marchesi, L., Marchesi, M., & Tonelli, R. (2018). The ICO phenomenon and its relationships with ethereum smart contract environment. *International Workshop on Blockchain Oriented Software Engineering (IWBOSE)*, 26-32. DOI: 10.1109/IWBOSE.2018.8327568

Flint, R. W. (2012). *Practice of sustainable community development: a participatory framework for change*. Springer Science & Business Media.

Freni, P., Ferro, E., & Moncada, R. (2022). Tokenomics and blockchain tokens: A design-oriented morphological framework. Blockchain: Research and Applications, 100069.

Frishammar, J., Richtnér, A., Brattström, A., Magnusson, M., & Björk, J. (2019). Opportunities and challenges in the new innovation landscape: Implications for innovation auditing and innovation management. *European Management Journal*, 37(2), 151–164. DOI: 10.1016/j.emj.2018.05.002

Gan, W., Ye, Z., Wan, S., & Yu, P. S. (2023). Web 3.0: The Future of Internet. doi:https://arxiv.org/abs/2304.06032 DOI: 10.1145/3543873.3587583

Gatteschi, V., Lamberti, F., Demartini, C., Pranteda, C., & Santamaria, V. (2018). To Blockchain or Not to Blockchain: That Is the Question. *IT Professional*, 20(2), 62–74. DOI: 10.1109/MITP.2018.021921652

Ghelani, D., & Hua, T. K. (2022). Conceptual Framework of Web 3.0 and Impact on Marketing, Artificial Intelligence, and Blockchain. International Journal of Information and Communication Sciences, 10-17. DOI: 10.11648/j.ijics.20220701.12

Gilbert, S. (2022). *Crypto, web3, and the Metaverse. Bennett Institute for Public Policy*. Policy Brief.

Gillan, S. L. (2006). Recent Developments in Corporate Governance: An Overview. *Journal of Corporate Finance*, 12(3), 381–402. DOI: 10.1016/j.jcorpfin.2005.11.002

Goel, A. K., Bakshi, R., & Agrawal, K. K. (2022). Web 3.0 and Decentralized Applications, July 2022. *International Conference on Innovative Research in Renewable Energy Technologies*, West Bengal, IndiaDOI: 10.3390/materproc2022010008

Hagemann, R., Huddleston Skees, J., & Thierer, A. (2018). *Soft law for hard problems: The governance of emerging technologies in an uncertain future*. Tech. LJ.

Han, J., Lee, J., & Li, T. (2023). Dao governance.

Harvey, C. R., Ramachandran, A., & Santoro, J. (2021). DeFi and the Future of Finance.

Hean, D. R. (1998). Co-operative authoring and collaboration over the World Wide Web. Retrieved from http://hdl.handle.net/10179/12296

Hendler, J., & Berners-Lee, T. (2010). From the Semantic Web to social machines: A research challenge for AI on the World Wide Web. *Artificial Intelligence*, 174(2), 156–161. DOI: 10.1016/j.artint.2009.11.010

Hendrycks, D., & Mazeika, M. (2022). X-risk analysis for ai research. arXiv preprint. doi:arXiv:2206.05862

Heyman, C. E. (2023). A red flag checklist for cryptocurrency Ponzi schemes. *Journal of Financial Crime*.

Himri, Y., Muyeen, S. M., Malik, F. H., Himri, S., Amali bin Ahmad, K., Kasbadji Merzouk, N., & Merzouk, M. (2022). A review on applications of the standard series IEC 61850 in smart grid applications. Cyberphysical Smart Cities Infrastructures: Optimal Operation and Intelligent Decision Making, 197-253.

Hofstetter, M., Riedl, R., Koumpis, T. G., & Schaberreiter, T. (2020). Applications of AI in cybersecurity. *Second International Conference on Transdisciplinary AI (TransAI)*, 138-141. DOI: 10.1109/TransAI49837.2020.00031

Hsieh, Y. Y., & Vergne, J. P. (2023). The future of the web? The coordination and early-stage growth of decentralized platforms. *Strategic Management Journal*, 44(3), 829–857. DOI: 10.1002/smj.3455

Huang, Y., Bian, Y., Li, R., Zhao, J. L., & Shi, P. (2019). *Smart contract security: A software lifecycle perspective.* IEEE.

Investopedia. (n.d.). Retrieved from Investopedia: https://www.investopedia.com/terms/w/web-20.asp

Jensen, J. R., von Wachter, V., & Ross, O. (2021). An introduction to decentralized finance (defi). *Complex Systems Informatics and Modeling Quarterly*, (26), 46–54. DOI: 10.7250/csimq.2021-26.03

Jentzsch, C. (2016). Decentralized autonomous organization to automate governance. White paper, November.

Jiang, B., Liu, Y., & Chan, W. K. (2018). Contractfuzzer: Fuzzing smart contracts for vulnerability detection.

Joshi, A., Bollen, L., Hassink, H., De Haes, S., & Van Grembergen, W. (2018). Explaining IT governance disclosure through the constructs of IT governance maturity and IT strategic role. *Information & Management*, 55(3), 368–380. DOI: 10.1016/j.im.2017.09.003

Kamei, M. (2011). Web 2.0's traction as compared to Web 1.0, Web 3.0 and Web 4.0.

Kampakis, S., & Stankevičius, L. (2023). The Tokenomics audit checklist: Presentation and examples from the audit of a DeFi project, Terra/Luna and Ethereum 2.0. The Journal of The British Blockchain Association, 42.

Kaplan, A. M., & Haenlein, M. (2010). Users of the World, Unite! The Challenges and Opportunities of Social Media. *Business Horizons*, 53(1), 59–68. DOI: 10.1016/j.bushor.2009.09.003

Khamisa, A. (2021). Token economies. In *The Emerald Handbook of Blockchain for Business* (pp. 121–140). Emerald Publishing Limited. DOI: 10.1108/978-1-83982-198-120211011

Khan, S. N., Loukil, F., Ghedira-Guegan, C., Benkhelifa, E., & Bani-Hani, A. (2021). Blockchain smart contracts: Applications, challenges, and future trends. *Peer-to-Peer Networking and Applications*, 14(5), 2901–2925. DOI: 10.1007/s12083-021-01127-0 PMID: 33897937

Kiayias, A., & Lazos, P. (2022). SoK: blockchain governance. arXiv preprint. DOI: 10.1145/3558535.3559794

Kraus, D., & Boulay, C. (2019). Blockchains: aspects of intellectual property law.

Kreps, D., & Kimppa, K. (2015). Theorising Web 3.0: ICTs in a changing society. *Information Technology & People*, 28(4), 726–741. DOI: 10.1108/ITP-09-2015-0223

Kreutzer, J., Caswell, I., Wang, L., Wahab, A., van Esch, D., Ulzii-Orshikh, N., & Adeyemi, M. (2022). Quality at a Glance: An Audit of Web-Crawled Multilingual Datasets. *Transactions of the Association for Computational Linguistics*, 10, 50–72. DOI: 10.1162/tacl_a_00447

Kshetri, N. (2010). The Economics of Click Fraud. *IEEE Security and Privacy*, 8(3), 45–53. DOI: 10.1109/MSP.2010.88

Kshetri, N. (2023). Privacy violations, security breaches and other threats of Web3 and the metaverse. Econstar. Retrieved from http://hdl.handle.net/10419/277993

Kucuktunc, O., Cambazoglu, B. B., Weber, I., & Ferhatosmanoglu, H. (2012). A large-scale sentiment analysis for Yahoo! Answers. WSDM 2012 - Proceedings of the 5th ACM International Conference on Web Search and Data Mining, 633-642. DOI: 10.1145/2124295.2124371

Laato, S., Farooq, A., Tenhunen, H., Pitkamaki, T., Hakkala, A., & Airola, A. (2020). Ai in cybersecurity education-a systematic literature review of studies on cybersecurity moocs. IEEE 20th International Conference on Advanced Learning Technologies (ICALT), 6-10. DOI: 10.1109/ICALT49669.2020.00009

Lacity, M. C., & Lupien, S. C. (2022). Blockchain Fundamentals for Web 3.0. Retrieved from DOI: 10.1353/book103175

Lathrop, D., & Ruma, L. (2010). *Open government: Collaboration, transparency, and participation in practice*. O'Reilly Media, Inc.

Lee, J. H. (2019). Systematic approach to analyzing security and vulnerabilities of blockchain systems.

Li, H., Dang, R., Yao, Y., & Wang, H. (2023). A Review of Approaches for Detecting Vulnerabilities in Smart Contracts within Web 3.0 Applications. Blockchains, 3-18.

Li, X., Jiang, P., Chen, T., Luo, X., & Wen, Q. (2020). A survey on the security of blockchain systems.

Liu, M., Wu, K., & Xu, J. J. (2019). How will blockchain technology impact auditing and accounting: Permissionless versus permissioned blockchain. *Current Issues in Auditing*, 13(2), A19–A29. DOI: 10.2308/ciia-52540

Luftman, J., Lyytinen, K., & Zvi, T. B. (2017). Enhancing the measurement of information technology (IT) business alignment and its influence on company performance. *Journal of Information Technology*, 32(1), 26–46. DOI: 10.1057/jit.2015.23

Madlool, N. A., Saidur, R., Hossain, M. S., & Rahim, N. A. (2011). A critical review on energy use and savings in the cement industries. *Renewable & Sustainable Energy Reviews*, 15(4), 2042–2060. DOI: 10.1016/j.rser.2011.01.005

Makridakis, S., & Christodoulou, K. (2019). Blockchain: Current Challenges and Future Prospects/Applications. *Future Internet*, 258(12), 258. Advance online publication. DOI: 10.3390/fi11120258

Mcneil, L. B. (2022). Blockchains, smart contracts, and stablecoins as a global payment system: The rise of web 3.0 (Dissertation). Retrieved from https://urn.kb.se/resolve?urn=urn:nbn:se:lnu:diva-114247

Meeker, W. Q., Escobar, L. A., & Pascual, F. G. (2022). *Statistical methods for reliability data*. John Wiley & Sons.

Merrell, I. (2022). Blockchain for decentralised rural development and governance. Blockchain: Research and Applications.

Meunier, S. (2018). Blockchain 101: What is Blockchain and How Does This Revolutionary Technology Work? .DOI: 10.1016/B978-0-12-814447-3.00003-3

Miller, R., & Lessard, D. R. (2001). *The strategic management of large engineering projects: Shaping institutions, risks, and governance*. MIT Press. DOI: 10.7551/mitpress/6478.001.0001

Millett, L. I., Lin, H. S., & Waldo, J. (2007). *Engaging privacy and information technology in a digital age*. National Academies Press.

Mohammed, I. A. (2020). Artificial intelligence for cybersecurity: A systematic mapping of literature. *Artificial Intelligence*, 7(9), 1–5.

Morovat, K., & Panda, B. (2020). A survey of artificial intelligence in cybersecurity. *2020 International Conference on Computational Science and Computational Intelligence (CSCI)*, 109-115. DOI: 10.1109/CSCI51800.2020.00026

Murugesan, S. (2007). Understanding Web 2.0. *IT Professional*, 9(4), 34–41. DOI: 10.1109/MITP.2007.78

Nakamoto, S. (2008). Bitcoin: A Peer-to-Peer Electronic Cash System. Cryptography Mailing list at https://metzdowd.com

Namakshenas, D. (2023). Web3. 0 Security: Privacy Enhancing and Anonym Auditing in Blockchain-based Structures. doi:arXiv:2307.12485

Nguyen, K., Nguyen, T., & Kovchegov, Y. (2009). A p2p video delivery network (p2p-vdn). 2009 Proceedings of 18th International Conference on Computer Communications and Networks, 1-7.

Niya, S. R., Schüpfer, F., Bocek, T., & Stiller, B. (2018). A Peer-to-peer Purchase and Rental Smart Contract-based Application (PuRSCA).

O'Reilly, T. (2005). *What Is Web 2.0: Design Patterns and Business Models for the Next Generation of Software. Communications & Strategies.* O'Reilly Media.

O'reilly, T. (2007). What is Web 2.0: Design Patterns and Business Models for the Next Generation of Software. *Communications & Stratégies*, 17.

O'Reilly, T., & Battelle, J. (2009). *Web squared: Web 2.0 five years on.* O'Reilly Media, Inc.

Obar, J., & Wildman, S. (2015). Social Media Definition and the Governance Challenge - An Introduction to the Special Issue. *Telecommunications Policy*, 39(9), 745–750. DOI: 10.1016/j.telpol.2015.07.014

Olaniyi, O., Olabanji, S. O., & Abalaka, A. (2023). Navigating risk in the modern business landscape: Strategies and insights for enterprise risk management implementation. *Journal of Scientific Research and Reports*, 29(9), 103–109. DOI: 10.9734/jsrr/2023/v29i91789

Ølnes, S., Ubacht, J., & Janssen, M. (2017). Blockchain in government: Benefits and implications of distributed ledger technology for information sharing. Government Information Quarterly, 355-364. https://www.sciencedirect.com/science/article/pii/S0740624X17303155

Omoteso, K. (2016). *Audit effectiveness: meeting the IT challenge*. Routledge. DOI: 10.4324/9781315568294

Omotunde, H., & Ahmed, M. (2023). A Comprehensive Review of Security Measures in Database Systems: Assessing Authentication, Access Control, and Beyond. Mesopotamian Journal of CyberSecurity, 115-133.

Pazhanisamy, K., Parthiban, L., Kannadasan, R., Anakath, A. S., & Parthiban, R. (2023). Integrating Blockchain and Artificial Intelligence for Industry 4.0 Innovations. Springer International Publishing, 295-304.

Peterson, R. R. (2004). Integration strategies and tactics for information technology governance. Strategies for information technology governance, 37-80.

Poirier, C. C. (1999). Advanced supply chain management: How to build a sustained competitive advantage. Berrett-Koehler.

Potluri, R. M., & Vajjhala, N. (2018). A Study on Application of Web 3.0 Technologies in Small and Medium Enterprises of India. The Journal of Asian Finance, Economics and Business, 73-79.

Radanliev, P. (2023). The Rise and Fall of Cryptocurrencies: Defining the Economic and Social Values of Blockchain Technologies, assessing the Opportunities, and defining the Financial and Cybersecurity Risks of the Metaverse. arXiv preprint. doi:arXiv:2309.12322 DOI: 10.31224/3162

Ragnedda, M., & Destefanis, G. (2019). *Blockchain and Web 3.0*. Routledge, Taylor and Francis Group. DOI: 10.4324/9780429029530

Rahman, H., & Hussain, M. I. (2020). A comprehensive survey on semantic interoperability for Internet of Things: State-of-the-art and research challenges. *Transactions on Emerging Telecommunications Technologies*, 31(12), 3902. DOI: 10.1002/ett.3902

Raji, I. D., Smart, A., White, R. N., Mitchell, M., Gebru, T., Hutchinson, B., & Barnes, P. (2020). Closing the AI accountability gap: Defining an end-to-end framework for internal algorithmic auditing. In *Proceedings of the 2020 conference on fairness, accountability, and transparency* (pp. 33-44). DOI: 10.1145/3351095.3372873

Rampolla, J., & Kipper, G. (2012). *Augmented reality: An emerging technologies guide to AR*. Elsevier.

Rathor, S., Zhang, M., & Im, T. (2023). Web 3.0 and Sustainability: Challenges and Research Opportunities. Sustainability.

Raymond, M. (2016). Managing decentralized cyber governance: the responsibility to troubleshoot. Strategic Studies Quarterly, 123-149.

Razi, Q., Devrani, A., Abhyankar, H., Chalapathi, G. S., Hassija, V., & Guizani, M. (2023). Non-Fungible Tokens (NFTs)-Survey of Current Applications, Evolution and Future Directions. *IEEE Open Journal of the Communications Society*. Advance online publication. DOI: 10.1109/OJCOMS.2023.3343926

Razzaque, A. N., Mohamed, M. I., & Birasnav, M. (2013). A new model for improving healthcare quality using web 3.0 decision making. Making it Real: Sustaining Knowledge Management Adapting for success in the Knowledge Based Economy.

Ribbers, P. M., Peterson, R. R., & Parker, M. M. (2002). Designing information technology governance processes: diagnosing contemporary practices and competing theories. *Proceedings of the 35th Annual Hawaii International Conference on System Sciences*, 3143-3154. DOI: 10.1109/HICSS.2002.994351

Ritzer, G., & Jurgenson, N. (2010). Production, Consumption, Prosumption the Nature of Capitalism in the Age of the Digital 'Prosumer'. *Journal of Consumer Culture*, 10(1), 13–36. DOI: 10.1177/1469540509354673

Roberts, J. (2007). *The modern firm: Organizational design for performance and growth*. Oxford university press.

Rohr, J., & Wright, A. (2018). Blockchain-based token sales, initial coin offerings, and the democratization of public capital markets. Hastings LJ, 463.

Rotmans, J., Kemp, R., & Van Asselt, M. (2001). More evolution than revolution: transition management in public policy. foresight, 15-31.

Rudman, R. (2015). Web 3.0: Governance, risks and safeguards. *Journal of Applied Business Research*, 1037–1056.

Rueda, R., Šaljić, E., & Tomić, D. (2020). The Institutional Landscape of Blockchain Governance. A Taxonomy for Incorporation at the Nation State. doi:DOI: 10.18421/TEM91-26

Sabbagh, K., Acker, O., Karam, D., & Rahbani, J. (2011). Designing the transcendent web the power of web 3.0. Booz&co.

Sadu, I. (2018). Auditing Blockchain. Internal Auditor Indonesia, 19.

Salvioni, D., & Gennari, F. (2016). Corporate governance, ownership and sustainability. Corporate Ownership and Control, 606-614. DOI: 10.22495/cocv13i2c3p9

Samant, H. D., & Singh, R. (2023). Developing Audit Strategy for PaaS Applications. In Gupta, M., & Sharman, R. (Eds.), *Modernizing Enterprise IT Audit Governance and Management Practices* (pp. 95–125). IGI Global. DOI: 10.4018/978-1-6684-8766-2.ch004

Samtani, S., Kantarcioglu, M., & Chen, H. (2020). Trailblazing the artificial intelligence for cybersecurity discipline: A multi-disciplinary research roadmap. *ACM Transactions on Management Information Systems*, 11(4), 1–19. DOI: 10.1145/3430360

Scott, R. E. (1987). *Conflict and cooperation in long-term contracts*. L. Rev. DOI: 10.2307/3480547

Selig, G. J. (2008). *Implementing IT Governance: A Practical Guide to Global Best Practices in IT Management*. Van Haren.

Sewpersadh, N. S. (2023). Disruptive business value models in the digital era. *Journal of Innovation and Entrepreneurship*, 12(1), 1–27. DOI: 10.1186/s13731-022-00252-1 PMID: 36686335

Sheth, A., & Thirunarayan, K. (2012). *Semantics empowered web 3.0: managing enterprise, social, sensor, and cloud-based data and services for advanced applications*. Morgan & Claypool.

Shivalingaiah, D., & Naik, U. (2008). Comparative Study of Web 1.0, Web 2.0 and Web 3.0. DOI: 10.13140/2.1.2287.2961

Sir, M. C., Mam, K. J., & Shekher, H. (2022). Website Designing Using Html, CSS, Javascript & Wordpress. *International Research Journal of Modernization in Engineering Technology and Science*.

Soni, V. D. (2020). Challenges and Solution for Artificial Intelligence in Cybersecurity of the USA. *SSRN* 3624487. DOI: 10.2139/ssrn.3624487

Srivastava, P. S. (2012). Technical Audit – A Thoroughfare of System Perfection. *International Journal of Scientific and Engineering Research*.

Steinbart, P. J., Raschke, R. L., Gal, G., & Dilla, W. N. (2018). The influence of a good relationship between the internal audit and information security functions on information security outcomes. *Accounting, Organizations and Society*, 71, 15–29. DOI: 10.1016/j.aos.2018.04.005

Stevens, T. (2020). Knowledge in the grey zone: AI and cybersecurity. Digi War. Digital War, 164-170. DOI: 10.1057/s42984-020-00007-w

Stoneburner, G., Goguen, A., & Feringa, A. (2002). *Risk Management Guide for Information Technology Systems*. NIST. DOI: 10.6028/NIST.SP.800-30

Swan, M. (2015). *Blockchain: Blueprint for a New Economy*. O'Reilly Media, Inc.

Tang, X., Guo, H., Li, H., Yuan, Y., Wang, J., & Cheng, J. (2021). A DAPP business data storage model based on blockchain and IPFS.

Tapscott, D., & Tapscott, A. (2016). *Blockchain revolution: how the technology behind bitcoin is changing money, business, and the world*. Penguin.

Tchankova, L. (2002). Risk identification – basic stage in risk management. *Environmental Management and Health*, 13(3), 290–297. Advance online publication. DOI: 10.1108/09566160210431088

TechDemand. (n.d.). Retrieved from https://www.techdemand.io/insights/tech/overcoming-web-3-0-security-issues-safeguarding-the-decentralized-future/

TechTarget. (n.d.). Retrieved from TechTarget: https://www.techtarget.com/whatis/definition/Web-30

Tiwana, A., & Konsynski, B. (2010). Complementarities between organizational IT architecture and governance structure. *Information Systems Research*, 21(2), 288–304. DOI: 10.1287/isre.1080.0206

Tolmach, P., Li, Y., Lin, S. W., Liu, Y., & Li, Z. (2021). A survey of smart contract formal specification and verification. *ACM Computing Surveys*, 1–38.

Toosi, A. N., Calheiros, R. N., & Buyya, R. (2014). Interconnected cloud computing environments: Challenges, taxonomy, and survey. *ACM Computing Surveys*, 47(1), 1–47. DOI: 10.1145/2593512

Tricker, R. I. (2015). *Corporate governance: Principles, policies, and practices*. Oxford University Press.

Truong, T. C., Zelinka, I., Plucar, J., Čandík, M., & Šulc, V. (2020). Artificial intelligence and cybersecurity: Past, presence, and future. Artificial intelligence and evolutionary computations in engineering systems, 351-363.

Truong, V. T., Le, L. B., & Niyato, D. (2023). *Blockchain meets metaverse and digital asset management: A comprehensive survey*. IEEE.

Tyagi, A. K. (2023). Decentralized everything: Practical use of blockchain technology in future applications. DOI: 10.1016/B978-0-323-96146-2.00010-3

UcedaVelez, T., & Morana, M. M. (2015). Risk Centric Threat Modeling: process for attack simulation and threat analysis. John Wiley & Sons.

Ulrich, D. (1996). *Human resource champions: The next agenda for adding value and delivering results*. Harvard Business Press.

Vachon, S., & Klassen, R. D. (2006). Extending green practices across the supply chain: The impact of upstream and downstream integration. *International Journal of Operations & Production Management*, 26(7), 795–821. DOI: 10.1108/01443570610672248

Vassileva, J. (2012). Motivating participation in social computing applications: A user modeling perspective. *User Modeling and User-Adapted Interaction*, 22(1-2), 177–201. DOI: 10.1007/s11257-011-9109-5

Veiga, A. D., & Eloff, J. H. (2007). An Information Security Governance Framework. IS Management, 361-372. DOI: 10.1145/1655168.1655170

Verma, S., & Gupta, N. (2020). Application of Artificial Intelligence in Cybersecurity. Innovations in Computer Science and Engineering: Proceedings of 7th ICICSE, 65-72.

Vincent, N., & Wilkins, A. M. (2020). Challenges when Auditing. *Current Issues in Auditing*, 14(1), A46–A58. DOI: 10.2308/ciia-52675

Voshmgir, S. (2020). *Token Economy: How the Web3 reinvents the internet* (Vol. 2). Token Kitchen.

Weill, P., & Ross, J. (2004). *IT governance: How top performers manage IT decision rights for superior results*. Harvard Business Press.

Wheeler, D., & Elkington, J. (2001). The end of the corporate environmental report? Or the advent of cybernetic sustainability reporting and communication. *Business Strategy and the Environment*, 10(1), 1–14. DOI: 10.1002/1099-0836(200101/02)10:1<1::AID-BSE274>3.0.CO;2-0

White, B. S., King, C. G., & Holladay, J. (2020). Blockchain security risk assessment and the auditor. *Journal of Corporate Accounting & Finance*, 31(2), 47–53. DOI: 10.1002/jcaf.22433

Wiafe, I., Koranteng, F. N., Obeng, E. N., Assyne, N., Wiafe, A., & Gulliver, S. R. (2020). Artificial intelligence for cybersecurity: A systematic mapping of literature. *IEEE Access : Practical Innovations, Open Solutions*, 8, 146598–146612. DOI: 10.1109/ACCESS.2020.3013145

Wikipedia. (n.d.). Retrieved from https://en.wikipedia.org/wiki/Web3

Wilkin, C. (2012). The Role of IT Governance Practices in Creating Business Value in SMEs. *Journal of Organizational and End User Computing*, 24(2), 1–17. DOI: 10.4018/joeuc.2012040101

Winkens, A. K., & Leicht-Scholten, C. (2023). Competencies for designing resilient systems in engineering education–a content analysis of selected study programs of five European technical universities. *European Journal of Engineering Education*, 48(4), 1–25. DOI: 10.1080/03043797.2023.2179913

Wu, L., Ruan, W., Hu, J., & He, Y. (2023). A Survey on Blockchain-Based Federated Learning. *Future Internet*, 400(12), 400. Advance online publication. DOI: 10.3390/fi15120400

Wu, Y., Qiao, Y., Ye, Y., & Lee, B. (2019). Towards improved trust in threat intelligence sharing using blockchain and trusted computing. *Sixth International Conference on Internet of Things: Systems, Management and Security (IOTSMS)*. DOI: 10.1109/IOTSMS48152.2019.8939192

Yang, K. (2005). Information retrieval on the web. Annu. Rev. Inf. Sci. Technol.

Young, J. (2019). Round-up of crypto exchange hacks so far in 2019: How can they be stopped.

Zavratnik, J. (2022). Analysis of web3 solution development principles. Retrieved from http://hdl.handle.net/2117/379908

Zhang, Y., Pfeuffer, K., Chong, M. K., Alexander, J., Bulling, A., & Gellersen, H. (2017). Look together: Using gaze for assisting co-located collaborative search. *Personal and Ubiquitous Computing*, 21(1), 173–186. DOI: 10.1007/s00779-016-0969-x

Zhao, Q., Wang, Y., Yang, B., Shang, K., Sun, M., Wang, H., & Xin, H. (2023). A Comprehensive Overview of Security Vulnerability Penetration Methods in Blockchain Cross-Chain Bridges. *Authorea Preprints*. DOI: 10.22541/au.169760541.13864334/v1

Zheng, J., & Lee, D. K. (2023). *Understanding the Evolution of the Internet: Web 1.0 to Web3. 0, Web3 and Web 3. Handbook of Digital Currency: Bitcoin*. Innovation, Financial Instruments, and Big Data.

Zheng, Z., Xie, S., Dai, H., Chen, X., & Wang, H. (2017). An overview of blockchain technology: Architecture, consensus, and future trends. IEEE international congress on big data (BigData congress), 557-564.

Chapter 9
Endpoint Controls Through a Lens of PCI DSS

Mohit Kumar Agarwal
https://orcid.org/0009-0002-9421-0035
University at Buffalo, SUNY, USA

Damario Sarden
University at Buffalo, SUNY, USA

Shreyas Ramesh
University at Buffalo, SUNY, USA

Raghvendra Singh
University at Buffalo, SUNY, USA

ABSTRACT

PCI DSS is a contractual obligation rather than a mandatory regulation to be taken up with diligence and care in organizations. But PCI DSS is a globally recognized standard that applies to organizations involved in processing, storing, or transmitting payment card information. This chapter provides an overview of PCI DSS, emphasizing its key components, objectives, and significance in the world of electronic payment security. PCI DSS sets rigorous security requirements for organizations that oversee payment card data. Compliance with PCI DSS helps organizations reduce the risk of data breaches, fraud, and financial losses while also safeguarding consumer trust and ensuring the integrity of payment card transactions. Endpoint security is a critical facet of modern cybersecurity. Endpoint security is vital for ensuring the confidentiality, integrity, and availability of sensitive data, as well as

DOI: 10.4018/979-8-3693-4211-4.ch009

maintaining the overall security posture of organizations. This chapter will focus on the key requirements of endpoint controls within PCI DSS compliance and their effectiveness.

INTRODUCTION

While the accelerated shift to digital powered by the COVID-19 pandemic has softened, digital commerce continues to grow as a critical channel for B2C and B2B businesses across all vertical industries. A study conducted by the Institute found that one or more endpoint attacks had successfully compromised data and/or IT infrastructure in 68% of organizations (Institute, 2020). The same report found that 68% of IT professionals found that the frequency of endpoint attacks had increased since the year before, citing that- Over 80% of successful cyberattacks involve exploiting known vulnerabilities for which patches are available but not applied. On average, it takes organizations about 280 days (about 9 months) to identify and contain a data breach.

Since the COVID-19 pandemic, the surge in cybercrime activity has risen drastically. This is particularly true for "high-value" sectors such as finance, especially the payments industry. It has been continuously targeted by cybercriminals, not only because of the cache that comes with compromising a high-profile finance name but also because of an easy lucrative payday. In 2022, cyberattacks affected over 60% of global financial institutions with assets valued at over $5 billion (Comstock, 2023). With non-cash transactions expected to reach a record 157 billion in the US alone in 2021, the highly disruptive payments industry has become a major target for threats. For instance, one of the worst data breaches in history occurred in 2008 at Heartland Payment Systems, a Fortune 1000 business that specializes in payroll, point-of-sale, and payment systems (Gordover, 2020). The company suffered an SQL Injection attack back in 2007 and did not notice its computers that were used to process payment transactions had been compromised. An online login page was made accessible to attackers by altering the code of a web script. The attack, which proceeded through Heartlands' system without detection for months, discovered sufficient information to generate new credit cards in physical form, including information encoded in the magnetic strip of the card (Gordover, 2020). Global digital commerce transaction volumes are expected to reach 1.08 trillion by the following year, up from 966 billion this year - a very impressive 12% growth in a single year, according to a recent analysis by leading fintech and payments experts (Juniper Research, 2023).

PCI DSS was birthed in the year 2004 by five major credit card companies: Visa, Mastercard, Discover, JCB, and American Express. The Payment Card Industry Security Standards Council (PCI SSC) both developed the guidelines for PCI DSS and administer it. It is a widely accepted set of policies and procedures intended to optimize the security of credit, debit, and cash card transactions and protect cardholders against misuse of their personal and financial information (Barney, 2023). The Council lays down several security standards that organizations in different industry segments must implement. In the case of PCI DSS, critical examination is performed on endpoints like POS machines, ATMs, and QR codes.

Endpoints can be physical devices such as computers, laptops, printers, phones, and tablets, or virtual endpoints such as cloud services, web-based applications, and other network-accessible resources (Mirolyubov, 2023). For example, endpoints used in networking to establish communication are access points on a wireless network or the edge router in a local area network (LAN). Endpoints are assigned a network-specific IP address that identifies every device on a network. Endpoints are devices used by organizations to monitor and detect things required for them to run. With organizational workforces becoming more mobile and users connecting to internal resources from off-premises endpoints all over the world, endpoints are increasingly susceptible to cyberattacks (Palo Alto, n.d.).

Data is everywhere and with it comes the need to be smart enough to hide it from attackers all over the world. A common example of data that everyone carries in today's world is the username and password for any application login. To transact and initiate any fund transfer, debit or credit card data is required. Although markets are mature, such as wholesale processing, hosted payment pages, and tokenization, the market continues to evolve. The digital commerce payment market is complex and dynamic. Fileless attacks, a common feature of all malware types, makes the behavioral protection of EDR tools a critical capability. Advanced adversaries can evade any protection solution, which makes detection and hunting essential for a fast incident response (Silva, 2022). The above scenarios and situations instigated us to study the root cause behind the breaches and analyze where an endpoint could be faulty, even when these merchants were PCI DSS compliant at the time of the breach.

The area of research for this topic will be on the efficacy of various endpoint controls in the regulatory compliance of PCI DSS. Critical research has been conducted into the different controls implemented on endpoints and it is benchmarked with their effectiveness. Endpoint controls vary numerously and can range from training for the people using the endpoints, to technical controls that exist on the endpoint itself such as a local firewall. There are also detective controls such as forward logging feeding to an SIEM system and preventative controls with intrusion prevention systems at network gateways along with network segmentation.

This rest of the paper is structured as follows – we first discuss the history of PCI DSS in the background section. Next, we go through the different points laid out in PCI DSS in a comprehensive overview of the literature and tie it together with how security should be defined in an endpoint to be deemed as compliant. We then go over the different endpoint protection techniques and provide recommendations to strengthen the security posture of endpoint devices. Finally, we compare the different security tooling present in the market and map it to the different points mentioned in PCI DSS.

BACKGROUND

On Nov. 23, one of the biggest bazaars in cybercrime underground that trades stolen payment card data, declared a quick access to around four million newly hacked debit and credit cards (restaurants chains Krystal, Moe's, McAlister's Deli and Schlotzsky's) was breached from April until July 2019 (Krebs, 2019). A couple of more recent breaches makes the situation more severe such as the one where Target Settles 2013 Hacked Customer Data Breach For $18.5 Million in one of the Largest Data Breaches between the years 2009 – 2023 (Healthcare Data Breach Statistics, 2023). Trends from the most recent attacks point towards a necessity for integration with identity access management tools and SEGs at least. This is because phishing and misuse of credentials are involved in almost all data breaches. Even though they were PCI compliant at the time of breach, it shows that just having bare minimum compliant software does not keep them safe from these types of attacks. Regulations like PCI cannot cover all unique needs of every business. (Gordover, 2020).

PCI DSS applies to any organization that stores, transmits, or maintains any cardholder data, regardless of size or volume of transactions. There have been a few that have embraced PCI as a promising idea, but they are in a small minority. Most firms succeed by applying care and attention and translating the requirements into their language. To fight against this, the PCI Standards Security Council has unveiled the newest version of its Data Security Standards (DSS) v4.0 which was made public in 2022. But in real life, PCI DSS v4 does not bring a lot of change to the general compliance process for most organizations. The basic controls stay as they are, with just a little more flexibility to satisfy them using compensating controls or the custom approach for PCI assessment (RSI Security, 2023). If an alternative control meets the same security standard needed by a specific PCI DSS control, even if it uses different methods, it can be shown through worksheets provided within DSS.

PCI DSS was initially introduced in December 2004 following the early adoption of online card payments by Visa beginning in the year 1994 (Visa, 2019). Online card payments have since then increased at a significant pace due to the adoption of the technology by other organizations. By the year 2001, Visa became one of the first organizations to implement its own set of security standards for companies that accept digital payments (Merchant Risk Council, 2023). Other organizations followed Visa's example and started implementing their security controls. This led to ambiguity and challenges for merchants who collaborated with multiple payment partners. To make it easier for businesses, service providers, and card networks, the founding members of the PCI SSC joined forces to create a uniform security standard to regular the payment security industry they created PCI DSS version 1.0. This standard has undergone several iterations to keep up with the advancements in technology and the current version of PCI DSS is 4.0 (PCI Security Standards, 2022).

The first version of PCI DSS version 1.1 mandated basic security around IT infrastructure and encouraged the use of vulnerability management. This involves implementing network segmentation and deploying a firewall equipped with stringent rule sets to regulate traffic flow effectively. To safeguard cardholder data, encryption should be applied both during transmission and while stored. Maintaining a robust vulnerability management program necessitates the use of antivirus programs for continual scanning and mitigation of malware threats. Access control measures should be enforced to restrict unauthorized access to sensitive data. Active monitoring of network traffic is imperative, enabling prompt detection and response to any suspicious activity in alignment with PCI DSS requirements.

In October 2008, PCI came up with an upgraded version 2.0 including factors that employees handling cardholder data must undergo annual security policy audits to uphold adherence to PCI DSS standards and safeguard sensitive information (PCI Security Standards, 2022). Ensuring compliance with PCI DSS guidelines requires regular audits of firewall rules to maintain effective network security measures. Additionally, stringent measures are implemented to safeguard cardholder data during transmission and storage, utilizing robust encryption protocols. Furthermore, the meticulous management and rotation of encryption keys are prioritized to maintain the integrity and confidentiality of sensitive information.

A major correction was done in November 2013 PCI DSS version 3.0 bringing in many critical changes required as the digital front was changing and breaches were getting more frequent (PCI Security Standards, 2022). This addressed security concerns surrounding authentication methods like tokens, smart cards, and certificates. Furthermore, with the increasing prevalence of mobile transactions and cloud adoption, there is a heightened focus on implementing robust security practices in these areas. To ensure ongoing security, PCI DSS mandates the regular conduct of penetration testing to identify and address vulnerabilities. There were a few more iterations that added values like using a secure version of TLS was mandated as the previous version had a huge vulnerability. stringent measures are mandated to uphold cybersecurity in e-commerce environments.

The COVID-19 pandemic has led to a significant increase in cyber threats, with 71% of organizations reporting payment fraud attempts (JPMorgan, 2022). Threat actors have become highly creative in their attacks, employing tactics such as ransomware, vulnerability exploits, email phishing, and drive-by downloads. This surge in cyber threats has spurred the birth and growth of many security organizations, particularly those specializing in endpoint defense. Version 4.0 of the PCI DSS was released in March 2022 including the use of complex passwords with hashed storage, routine audits of user and privileged accounts, and the establishment of comprehensive inventories for software and hardware assets. Additionally, secure disposal protocols for media containing sensitive data, such as cardholder information, are emphasized. Multifactor authentication has transitioned from a recommendation to a mandatory requirement, and organizations are compelled to implement robust vulnerability management pipelines to ensure ongoing protection against potential threats.

LITERATURE REVIEW

Many researchers have studied the way PCI DSS affects an organization's overall posture toward security. A common misperception regarding PCI DSS compliance is that, despite vendors in the industry may carelessly advertise, PCI DSS-certified companies are secure or hacker-proof (CSIAC, 2018). Some organizations are thinking singularly and just want to get a tick off the list of compliances and get PCI certified. It is not surprising that these organizations end up being primarily breached because of the deficiency of a mature compliance standard. No one software can indeed take care of all the requirements suggested by any regulatory compliance; PCI DSS in this case. Time and resource constraints often limit even well-scoped evaluations, thus QSAs are only able to examine a portion of the system components. preventing a QSA from being able to find every hole and weakness (CSIAC, 2018). Thinking about abiding by the regulations and concentrating on comprehending the primary issues affecting organizations experiencing data breaches, it seems like there are not many things that could be done. One of the major reasons given for merchants failing a PCI audit and a leading cause of data theft is not being able to sufficiently safeguard stored cardholder details (Nicho, 2011). So, one must give it some thought to identify all locations where cardholder data is stored and define their compliance scope accordingly.

For example, according to PCI-DSS 11.3.1.3 and 11.3.2.1, organizations must run internal and external vulnerability scans every three months and rescan after any significant change. To think of endpoint software was important, as they are the guardians of the cyber galaxy. When assessing the current state of the endpoint security tools available in the market, it is important to consider the qualities that these tools claim to have but actually lack when viewed through a single eyepiece. This is supported by a reference from Gartner (Magic Quadrant 2022), which lists the industry leader and rivals who support the secure endpoint concept. By comparing competitors, this will provide shared information and assist us identify areas where we still need improvement in terms of security.

Comprehensive Overview of PCI DSS

PCI DSS was designed to prevent cybersecurity breaches of sensitive data and reduce the risk of fraud for organizations that handle payment card information. (Barney, 2023). PCI DSS, the most wide-ranging of the Council's standards, applies to any entity that stores, processes, and/or transmits cardholder data (Fruhlinger, 2022). These industries created policies to cater to the problem and address the issues faced in different sectors. A federal study of non-cash shows us how there is a trend shift post-COVID in the trading market 2000–21 (FRPS, 2023).

PCI compliance, or payment card industry compliance, refers to a set of 12 security standards that businesses must use when accepting credit card payments. PCI DSS sets rigorous security requirements for organizations that oversee payment card data. Similar to the guidance outlined in previous versions of PCI DSS (v4.0), this version also consists of 12 main requirements or pillars. These are made to offer the best possible protection across industry and protect both businesses as well as cardholders themselves from different threats such as network hacking or breaking into cryptographic systems used for transmitting data about people who hold cards (Comstock, 2023). It involves requirements such as encryption of cardholder data, updating antivirus software, managing firewalls, and assigning unique IDs to each person with computer access. An overview of the requirements both in detail and in an illustrated format is explained by security metrics (Glover, 2020).

The 12 requirements of PCI DSS are:

1. Install and maintain a firewall configuration to protect cardholder data: To prevent unauthorized access to the system. Firewalls are devices that control computer traffic allowed into and out of an organization. All such networking devices are in scope for assessment of Requirement 1 if used within the card payment industry
2. Do not use vendor-supplied defaults for system passwords and other security parameters: To prevent unauthorized access to the cardholder data environment, requirement two states that vendor defaults be changed. The easiest

way for a hacker to access a network is to try default passwords or exploits based on default system software settings in a payment card infrastructure (PCI DSS).

3. Protect stored cardholder data: This requirement is about protecting stored CHD (Cardholder Data) after it has been processed or transmitted. This includes whether the data is printed or stored. Sensitive authentication data (SAD) should never be stored. (More on SAD is below.)
4. Encrypt transmission of cardholder data across open, public networks: To protect cardholder data both in transit and at rest to ensure integrity as well as confidentiality, the standard states the data must be encrypted during transmission on open-public networks, such as wireless.
5. Protect all systems against malware and regularly update anti-virus software or programs: This requirement is about having anti-malware software solutions installed on all devices in a system. Malware is a threat to endpoints, lurking to get into the system, finding vulnerabilities, and exploiting them. To avoid malware, specific detection and prevention tools are to be used.
6. Develop and maintain secure systems and applications: This requirement is about installing vendor-provided security patches to prevent the exploitation of vulnerabilities in systems and applications.
7. Restrict access to cardholder data by business and need to know: Requirements 7-9 are about having a solid identity and access management program. This requirement is specifically restricting access to the CHD for businesses that need to know. If it is not in a user's job description to access the CHD, they should not get access.
8. Identify and authenticate access to system components: A separate and unique authorized user must have their access ID number or badge, rather than a single shared ID for all employees who access an account. This will not only protect against unauthorized data access but will also allow investigators to determine if an authorized insider has missed the data.
9. Restrict physical access to cardholder data: This requirement is self-explanatory. Physical access to the data cannot be forgotten. Not all attacks are technology driven. Rather, it ensures that the devices and data are not easily approachable by anyone.
10. Track and monitor all access to network resources and cardholder data: This requirement is about keeping track of logs and being able to monitor them. Having a Security Event and Incident Management (SIEM) solution is necessary to help protect CHD.
11. Regularly test security systems and processes: This requirement is about being able to test system components, processes, and custom software in an organization. Specifically, it is about conducting penetration tests and vul-

nerability scans of systems to validate security. Testing of security controls is especially important for any environmental changes such as deploying new software or changing system configurations (PCI DSS).

12. Maintain a policy that addresses information security for all personnel: This requirement is all about having a security policy within an organization. A strong security policy sets the tone for security affecting an organization's entire company, and it informs employees of their expected duties related to security (PCI DSS).

PCI has requirements that are specific to each organization's validation level. VISA states that merchant compliance validation is prioritized based on the volume of transactions, the potential risk, and exposure introduced into the payment system (VISA, 2023). What this means is, that depending on the number of transactions an organization processes each year, different security criteria has to be satisfied. Merchants selling digital goods or services must complete a self-assessment questionnaire (SAQ) and conduct quarterly vulnerability scans on their environment. Below is a list of the merchant criteria and validation requirements:

1. Merchant Criteria: (Level 1): Merchants that process over 6 million card transactions annually:
    - Validation requirements: Annual Report on Compliance (ROC) conducted by a Qualified Security Assessor (QSA), Quarterly Network Scans by an Approved Scan Vendor (ASV) from the SSC, and an Attestation of Compliance (AOC) Form.
2. Merchant Criteria: (Level 2): Merchants that process 1 to 6 million transactions annually.
    - Validation requirements: Annual Self-Assessment Questionnaire (SAQ), quarterly ASV, and AOC form.
3. Merchant Criteria: (Level 3): Merchants that process 20,000 to 1 million transactions annually.
    - Validation requirements: Annual SAQ, quarterly ASV, and AOC form.
4. Merchant Criteria: (Level 4): Merchants that process fewer than 20,000 transactions annually.
    - Validation requirements: Recommended SAQ, quarterly ASV if applicable, and any compliance validation requirements given by the merchant's acquirer.

PCI DSS applies to merchants and other entities that store, process, and/or transmit cardholder data. A lot of small businesses fail to comply with the Payment Card Industry Data Security Standards (PCI DSS). Small businesses that have outsourced their payment infrastructures to third parties can rely on those vendors to manage PCI compliance as well. Almost 90 percent of security leaders believe their organization falls short of addressing cyber risks (Mastercard, n.d.). Each payment card brand has defined specific requirements for compliance validation and reporting, such as provisions for performing self-assessments and when to engage a QSA. A traditional approach would be an entity's classification or risk level (determined by the individual payment card brands). The compliance processes typically involve a series of structured steps to ensure adherence to the Payment Card Industry Data Security Standard (PCI DSS).

Firstly, the Scope phase, which requires the identification and documentation of all processes, networks, and endpoints associated with data capture in motion and at rest. The objective is to determine the system components and networks falling within the PCI DSS scope. Identify the systems, networks, processes, and any third-party services involved in storing, processing, or transmitting cardholder data (CHD) (RiskOptics, 2023). Following this, the Assess phase utilizes the information gathered in the Scope phase to conduct a comprehensive gap analysis. Strong access control measures are implemented, and the compliance of system components within the defined scope is examined. Testing procedures for each PCI DSS requirement are followed, considering the incorporation of technologies like tokenization and encryption to bolster the protection of cardholder data.

Once assessment is completed, the next step involves Reporting, where the assessor and/or entity responsible for the assessment generate the necessary documentation, such as the Self-Assessment Questionnaire (SAQ) or the Report on Compliance (ROC). This documentation includes detailed records of all compensating controls that have been implemented. Subsequently, the Attestation phase is initiated, necessitating the completion of the appropriate Attestation of Compliance (AOC). The AOC serves as a formal declaration of the business's level of compliance, whether through self-auditing or with the assistance of a Qualified Security Assessor (QSA). Once the Attest phase is completed, the Submit phase involves submitting essential documents, including the SAQ, ROC, AOC, and any other requested supporting documentation (such as ASV scan reports). Merchants submit these to the acquirer, while service providers submit them to the payment brand or requestor.

The final phase is Remediation, where, if required, actions are taken to address any non-compliance issues. Remediation activities include any non-compliance issues identified during the assessment. An updated report is then provided to demonstrate the successful implementation of remedial measures. This iterative process ensures continuous compliance with PCI DSS requirements. When an ROC or SAQ is completed, it is valid for one year, whether the assessment is done by a QSA or a self-assessment. Irrespective of the transaction volume, any organization can opt to complete an on-site assessment. Another thing to note is that vulnerability scans must be completed once every 90 days (every quarter).

Endpoint Security in the PCI DSS Ecosystem

The endpoint is a communication remote device. It communicates back and forth with a network to which it is connected. Examples of endpoints include desktops and laptops, smartphones, servers, and Internet-of-Things (IoT) devices. Endpoints are the primary focus of attacks because they store valuable data that attackers seek to steal; perform critical operations that attackers seek to disrupt; and are the interface where attackers can target humans through email, social engineering, and other tactics. Endpoints are the physical and virtual locations where sensitive data resides and include desktops, laptops, servers, virtual machines, cloud workloads (services running on cloud servers), fixed-function devices such as ATMs, point of sale systems, and control and data systems for power plants and other industrial assets (Carbon Black, 2018). These endpoints are hardened with endpoint security software or tools that help us keep a check on these devices. There are various aspects to be looked at, and different endpoints have different controls, defining altogether distinct types of features that will be required by the endpoint software or tool.

Obsolete practices, like relying primarily on preventive controls, such as signature-based antivirus tools, have left organizations vulnerable to attacks. Prevention alone is not enough. A step up to continual vulnerability assessment (VA), endpoint security tuning, and detection and response are needed to strengthen the endpoint security posture (Hinner, 2023). These capabilities will require increased focus on the expertise, procedures, and availability of internal staff to operate these tools. Industries are still using the same endpoint protection stack for their servers as they use for their end-user points. This practice has often been seen as a way of achieving compliance, reducing the total cost of ownership, and providing a unified security view. However, security controls exist for end-user endpoints.

Any organization must understand risk appetite (the amount and type of risk that an organization is willing to accept to meet strategic objectives) and risk tolerance (what risk an organization can deal with). One of the challenges of the PCI DSS is that it makes several implicit assumptions regarding risk appetite and tolerance that may be out of step with those of the organization (RiskOptics, 2023). Organizations can implement several types of endpoint security controls on these types of endpoints to protect them Recent attack trends show the need for integration with identity access management tools and SEGs at a minimum, as phishing and credential misuse are found in most breaches. Organizations can implement several types of endpoint security controls on these types of endpoints to protect them.

Knowing the endpoints, it is easy now to see the endpoints working at the forefront of business transactions and helping in completing those transactions. But the thing yet to be considered is how these endpoints get exploited and breaches happen. To better understand how such breaches slip through the cracks, it is imperative to identify and define a set of boundaries by defining distinct types of features that are required at an endpoint. The list documented below is generated from brainstorming and listing down the capabilities that should ideally be present in an Endpoint security solution.

1) Antivirus/anti-malware: Establishing and configuring effective antimalware policies leads to an added layer of protection on a device. Microsoft's windows defender comes with a robust antimalware policy which is routinely updated with latest threat signatures (Microsoft, 2022). This is critical in finding a variety of threats, such as keyloggers, rootkits, Trojans, worms, adware, and spyware. Some products may include other features, such as anti-phishing protection or malicious URL blocking. Antivirus solutions are installed directly on endpoint devices, such as laptops, PCs, network servers, and mobile devices (Fortinet, n.d.).
2) Firewall: Monitor and control incoming and outgoing network traffic. It blocks suspicious or malicious traffic to protect against several types of threats, including malware, unauthorized access attempts, and data leaks. DDOS prevention capabilities are not included in firewall solutions designed for endpoint protection (Das, 2023).
3) Intrusion detection/prevention: No and ID/IP is not a type of EDR; it is separate entity. It helps your organization prepare for sophisticated threats and avoid zero-day and file-less attacks by getting a system. Organizations can manage threats on the endpoint through this software.
4) Web filtering: This also means URL filtering, and is applied through firewalls, (De Militarized Zones) DMZs, or using specific tools that monitor network traffic. 'Uniform Resource Locator (URL)' filtering involves blocking potentially malicious websites so internal users cannot access them. This is often accomplished using either a hardware or software firewall (Fortinet, n.d.). The URL filtering process uses databases that are stored on-premises in a local server, in a cloud-based database or a combination of both.
5) Endpoint detection and response (EDR): These tools continuously monitor endpoints to detect suspicious behavior, trigger automatic responses, and collect data for threat analysis, preventing future attacks. EDR solutions operate across many layers of detection and response tools, control their different datasets, and perform high-reliability studies on system performance and other key metrics (Arfeen et al., 2021). An EDR must function flawlessly throughout the security

stack, utilizing native tools with a robust Application Programming Interface (API). EDR acts like a DVR on the endpoint, recording relevant activity to catch incidents that evaded prevention (Crowdstrike, 2023).

6) Behavioral analytics: In terms of cybersecurity, behavior analytics analyzes large data sets using artificial intelligence (AI) and machine learning (ML) techniques. BA is used to find malicious activities of users, systems, applications, networks, and many other connected components of an organization (Wickramasinghe, 2023). Such systems monitor existing user accounts, devices, and applications, analyze their access patterns, and issue alerts when there is a sign of compromise. The key benefits of behavior analytics are Proactively identifying & mitigating cyber threats. Detecting advanced persistent threats (APTs). A few examples of behavior analytics tools are Rapid7 InsightIDR, Exabeam, etc.
7) Threat intelligence integration: Threat intelligence sharing refers to the open exchange of information and knowledge about threats, cybercrimes, vulnerabilities among peer organizations due to increasing need to protect companies' and government's systems against those security threats and issues (Anderson, 2017). Threat intelligence also known as Cyber Threat Intelligence (CTI), is organized, analyzed, and refined information about potential or current attacks that threaten an organization (Chandel et al., 2019).
8) Reporting and analytics: This applies to the reporting that is delivered with every threat detection as well as summary reporting about your endpoints and organization. There are various kinds of reporting which is available like threat reporting.
9) Data loss prevention (DLP): It allows system administrators to manage the network and prevent data loss and leaks across all company endpoints. DLP works through encryption, customized rules, Monitors, detects, and prevents unauthorized access or transmission of sensitive data. According to Microsoft (Microsoft, 2024):
   i. Know your data
   ii. Protect your data
   iii. Prevent data loss
   iv. Govern your data
10) End-point encryption: It's about data encryption carried out on the endpoint. This is useful in situations where a device gets lost or stolen, so if that happens then the data remains secure and protected. The algorithms used for encryption today, like the Advanced Encryption Standard (AES) and Rivest-Shamir-Adleman (RSA), are public protocols available to everyone. These encryption algorithms are considered safe from threats by present-day computers (Checkpoint, n.d.). It is based on different layers of encryption incorporated in the endpoint encryption solutions.

11) Application control: An important element to get a strong return from your EDR investment is making sure you deeply link it with your present security and IT tools (Haag, 2020). Systems that can combine with numerous security tools for an extensive data security plan. These connections create automated threat responses to immediately eliminate the found malware through a third-party anti-malware program, preventing delay in the user's immediate actions.
12) Patch management: helps repair security vulnerabilities promptly. Patch management automates the collection and delivery of patches company wide. If one device needs multiple patches, your endpoint security solution should be able to determine which patch to address first.
    a. OS and Applications
    b. Asset Management and Discovery
    c. Remote Devices
    d. Deployment Architecture
    e. Scheduling Updates
13) Configuration management: A centralized control panel to manage all your other endpoint security requirements. System administrators use configuration management to edit and establish policies, receive alerts, view audit trails, and detect when users attempt an override. This allows greater visibility into threats and helps administrators make exceptions when users need to access certain applications or information.

Advanced Endpoint Protection Techniques

Simply protecting information is not sufficient, ensuring the confidentiality, integrity and availability of that information is also crucial. This responsibility for providing safety has now fallen into the hands of leaders in risk and cybersecurity from core to edge (Perkins, 2015). Some of these endpoint protection controls are IoT Security, Anti-Virus Software, URL Filtering, Application Controls, Network Access Controls, Browser Isolation, and Cloud Perimeter Security (Kamruzzaman et al., 2022). PCI DSS has been a stalwart in mandating security requirements and ensuring the industry adopts the required tooling to keep up with technological advancements. While the market for security tooling is quite well mature, with multiple vendors releasing competing products, let us take a brief look at a few of the most well-known tools adopted by organizations of all sizes to safeguard and protect their data and see which version of PCI DSS enforced the integration of such tooling in an organization's toolkit. The list is not exhaustive by any means and only serves to provide an overview of the different security tooling available in the marketplace and how the adoption of such technologies can help organizations become compliant with the regulatory requirements of PCI DSS.

Table 1. Security Tools and Their Corresponding PCI DSS Versions

Year	Name of the tool	Tool category	Vendor name	PCI DSS version
2005	Nessus	Vulnerability Scanner	Tenable	Version 3.2.1
2006	Snort	Intrusion Detection System	Snort	Version 3.2.1
2007	Wireshark	Network Protocol Analyzer	Wireshark	Not mandated by PCI DSS
2008	Metasploit Framework	Penetration Testing Framework	Metasploit	Version 1.1
2010	Aircrack-ng	Wireless Network Assessment Tool	Aircrack-ng	Version 3.2.1
2012	Burp Suite	Web Application Security Scanner	Burp Suite	Version 3
2013	OWASP ZAP	Web Application Security Scanner	OWASP ZAP	Version 3
2014	Splunk	Security Information and Event Management	Splunk	Version 3
2016	SentinelOne	Endpoint Detection and Response	SentinelOne	Not mandated by PCI DSS
2018	Microsoft Defender for Endpoint	Endpoint Detection and Response	Microsoft	Not mandated by PCI DSS
2022	Cotext XDR	Extended Detection and Response (XDR)	Palo Alto Networks	Not mandated by PCI DSS
2023	Crowdstrike falcon Data protection	Data loss prevention tool (DLP)	Crowdstrike	Version 2

Note: The table presents a list of security tools, categorized by their functionality, along with their corresponding vendors and PCI DSS versions.

As the world enters the age of AI, threat actors have also begun to integrate the power of machine learning and neural networks into their attacks. To level the playing field, organizations too have begun adopting AI-powered tools in their arsenal to defend against this newly evolved threat landscape. One of the core frontiers where organizations can leverage the power of AI is in behavioral analysis methods. By augmenting traditional methods of detection with proactive, real-time detection of anomalies and potential threats, AI-powered behavioral analysis can help reduce the risk of security breaches and strengthen an organization's overall security posture (Crowdstrike, 2023).

AI systems are also useful in detecting phishing emails. Large-scale email providers (Gmail, outlook, yahoo, etc.) are using AI techniques to prevent undesirable images and detect phishing, malware, and fraudulent payments sent through their service (Hedge, 2018). AI/ML can use real-time analysis to automatically update software and prevent large-scale cybersecurity attacks. Traditional methods of Cybersecurity have relied on predefined rules-based system or employing a signature based detection system. While these methods are still effective, threat actors have devised ways to sidestep current controls. Moreover, today's sophisticated enterprise IT ecosystem generates a truly massive amount of data that cannot be analyzed effectively and efficiently without using some sort of machine learning model that can separate the signal-to-noise ratio. AI can be integrated into several security tools and can be used in real-time analysis. A common way of using AI to bolster security is in detection tools. The different detection tools where AI can be integrated are (Sarkar et al., 2021).

A host-based intrusion detection system (HIDS) analyzes collected Linux system call traces. This approach is effective on common hosts (Liu et al., 2018). Due to the increase in the amount of traffic generated, a traditional HIDS cannot analyze all the system call traces generated on a host. This is where an AI system can be integrated into the tool to improve the analysis of the different calls generated. Network-based intrusion detection (NIDS) uses a suite of data mining techniques to automatically detect attacks against computer networks and systems (Raghunath & Mahadeo, 2008). Input to NIDS is data collected using a data capturing unit. This information is analyzed by an analyst. By training an AI system to look for suspicious packets, analysis of huge amounts of data is possible within a small amount of time.

These intrusion detection systems can be categorized into two subcategories based on how they perform analysis of the data. A signature-based IDS is a pattern or string that corresponds to a known attack or threat. Signature-based detection is a process in which current patterns are compared against previous malicious events for recognizing intrusions. Because of using the knowledge accumulated by specific attacks and system vulnerabilities, SD is also known as Knowledge-based Detection or Misuse Detection (Liao et al., 2013). Anomaly-based IDS builds a statistical model describing the normal network traffic, and any abnormal behavior that deviates from the model is identified. requires a training phase to develop the database of general attacks and a careful setting of a threshold level of detection makes it complex (Jyothsna et al., 2011).

While the above proposed systems provide effective coverage of systems, it is also relatively easy to sidestep these controls by either encrypting or padding the malware thereby masking its unique fingerprint. Another way to stop such sophisticated attacks is by employing a behavior-based detection system. Behavior-based detection, which focuses on the activities of malware when it infects a system, can be implemented in two ways. The first involves extracting behavioral traits from the malware code statically; these traits are called malware semantics (Christodorescu, 2006). The second method involves running malware inside a sandboxed environment and analyzing its behavior. An example of observing such behavioral patterns is understanding the system calls made by the malware (Mosli et al. 2017). Other behavioral features include file activity, registry activity, and API calls (Mohaisen et al., 2015).

One of the ways to solve this problem is to automate the response protocol that an analyst would have to manually perform. This automation can be further aided by AI extending the use case of a traditional SIEM system and transforming it into a SOAR (Security Orchestration, Automation, and Response). Organizations are increasingly adopting SOAR systems into their firms such that 19% of enterprise organizations have already deployed technologies for security automation and orchestration extensively, 39% have done so on a limited basis, and 26% are engaged in a project to automate/orchestrate security operations (Oltsik, 2018). SIEM was designed to collect, correlate, and store security events and generate appropriate security alerts for the Security Operations Centre (SOC) operational needs. Since their inception, SIEM systems functionality has evolved to include various levels of threat intelligence (TI), which allow the more accurate generation of security alerts as well as basic enrichment of previously generated alerts (Kinyua & Awuah, 2021). Deploying a SIEM system only solves half the battle. Analysts must maintain constant monitoring and take action on the alerts generated. Ineffective alert creation introduces lots of noise which can drown out the actual threats to the ecosystem.

Another frontier where organizations can bolster their defensive techniques is in the adoption and implementation of secure and secret encryption schemes. Encryption is the process of storing data in an unintelligible format without the "key" used during the process (Popek & Kline, 1979). In technical terms, encryption can be defined as a mathematical function where each character in a block of text is obscured/substituted with another character defined by an algorithm. The security of implementing such a system lies primarily in the secrecy of the key used during the function. This method of encryption is useful to safeguard data at rest. Public key encryption has been developed whose primary purpose is to safeguard data in transit. The scheme was first published publicly by Whitfield Diffie and Martin Hellman in 1976 (Blake & Garefalakis, 2004). Diffie Hellman algorithm is not an encryption algorithm, rather it is a way to securely exchange the keys that encrypt data (Kallam, 2015). The way this works is through creating a shared secret on both systems and this shared key is then utilized to safely exchange a cryptographic encryption key. This method is scalable and is primarily used to safeguard data in transit. While encryption has been around for decades, researchers and organizations around the world have been studying and developing new algorithms and ciphers. A few such advanced encryption methods are:

1. Homomorphic encryption: Invented in the year 2009 by IBM, it is a computation technique where data is processed without decrypting it. The only downside is it requires a humongous computation power to even perform relatively simple tasks (Gorantala et al., 2023).

2. Multi-Party Computation: This method involves splitting up data and storing them into multiple different servers so that each server only contains a small part of the data. This technique was originally developed in the 1980s. Access to cloud storage solutions renders implementation of the technique within the realm of possibility for many organizations (Chuan Zhao et al., 2019).
3. Quantum Cryptography: Quantum computing holds a lot of power in shaping the future of technological growth and advancement. One of the salient questions plaguing the security industry is ensuring data protection once this technology is widely adopted and researchers at NIST have responded to this threat by developing quantum-resistant cryptographic algorithms (NIST, 2022).

Recommendations for Strengthening PCI DSS Endpoint Security

PCI DSS can be an expensive project to undertake even for smaller firms with a smaller infrastructure, remediation required to attain compliance. But bear in mind, too, that fines are also expensive (and are 'dead' money too) (Rees, 2012). You may get away with telling your acquirer or client (if a service provider) that you are working on it, but that will only last for so long before you either get fined or lose a valuable customer due to your inability to prove you are compliant with PCI DSS. For instance, fines are assessed per month of non-compliance and the per-month charge increases for longer periods, so a company might pay \$5,000 a month if they are out of compliance for three months, but \$50,000 a month if they go for periods as long as seven months (Fruhlinger, 2022). In addition, fines ranging from \$50 to \$90 can be imposed for each customer who is affected in some way by a data breach.

Software for endpoint security is the main element that keeps an organization's endpoints secure and visible, enabling them to observe the health of an endpoint. Choosing these endpoints to review is a very large job. Endpoint security solutions should provide data classification and loss prevention, insider threat monitoring, network and privileged user access control, anti-malware, email gateways, and Endpoint Detection Response (EDR) (Knowles 2023). Data Loss Prevention is one control that deals with controlling who has access to your network, what they do, and which areas of it they interact with. It utilizes firewalls placed between users or devices and sensitive sections of your network (Fortinet, 2023). URL filtering is also a common control. This method includes obstructing possibly harmful sites so that people within the company cannot view or browse these. This is frequently done through a hardware or software firewall (Fortinet, 2023). Another strong and usual control method is endpoint encryption. It protects the information on your gadgets by guaranteeing that only those who possess a decryption key can read it. This applies to various kinds of endpoints, ensuring carefree browsing and downloading and even entry into financial data that is confidential (Fortinet, 2023).

METHODOLOGY

After defining the basic endpoint needs and the software's ability to govern and control them, our goal was to list the parameters that would determine an endpoint's functionality. This was accomplished with the aid of ideation and enumeration. The ideas that were listed in the first brainstorming session using the round-robin method, like points 2, 3, 5, 7, 8, 10, and 12, are listed in the parameters or features. Next, in an attempt to determine which factors were most important and whether everything is captured, a search began with several vendor websites for assistance. These areas provided us with a few more details that the vendors look at when producing and marketing their goods. These were enumerated in points 1, 4, 6, and 9 (Sophos Authorised Online Platinum reseller, n.d.). Like points 8 and 15, they were part of Crowdstike (Crowdstrike, 2022).

A few of the points that we listed were also covered, points 1 (antivirus or anti-malware) and 5 (EDR) on another vendor site named VMware Carbon Black (VMware, 2021). Next, to address the most contentious area of artificial intelligence (AI), given that it is now integrated into the XDR environment, decision was to be made, on which is a better version of EDR and most talked about in the vendor market. Even the Gartner hype cycle (Hinner, 2023) of the endpoint shows the peak of the XDR solutions. Therefore, we included AI into our scope and to keep the paper current with today's changing times.

We prioritized the different aspects of security and compared them with the list we had generated and continued our search for more ideas. Ideas which could be beneficial for our research to determine and analyze the endpoint security software. Finally, a list of features or parameters that would aid in defining endpoint security software to control breaches and determine whether any endpoints meet PCI DSS requirements, based on brainstorming sessions, vendor-stated requirements, and an artificial intelligence study was reached. Using research papers and scholarly magazines to help us establish the parameters, used to determine an important endpoint component.

Testing Parameters with Endpoints

There are various endpoint software's available on the market. To remove any biases and lay a solid foundation of the endpoint, a reference from Gartner (Magic Quadrant 2022), helped us narrow our list of key security vendors on the market.

Gartner Magic Quadrant is an explicit literature bank that does lots of study in the fields of articles and research papers. The capabilities defined in the Gartner magic quadrant are different from the parameters that was resulted from brainstorming. Many of the listed parameters may be a collective definition of the capabilities defined by Gartner. To avoid biasness, a few of the well-known vendors in the market that provide Endpoint security software were randomly chosen.

1. Sophos: Sophos Intercept X
2. CrowdStrike: Falcon
3. Sentinel One: Singularity Platform
4. Palo Alto Networks:
5. VMWare: Carbon Black
6. Microsoft: Defender

1) Sophos Intercept X is an advanced endpoint security solution that excels in protecting organizations from a myriad of cyber threats. This comprehensive product is employed by a diverse user base, ranging from small businesses to large enterprises (Izquierdo, 2023). It is particularly well-suited for those seeking robust defense against evolving threats, such as ransomware and zero-day attacks. Key features encompass deep learning AI, anti-exploit technology, root cause analysis, and enhancing threat detection and response capabilities. The benefits of Intercept X are evident in its ability to provide proactive and real-time protection, resulting in reduced security incidents and business disruption. (Sophos, n.d.). it could be easily said that there cannot be any one software to comply with PCC DSS rather companies like Sophos have multiple integrated APIs like Sophos Firewall, Sophos Zatna, and Cloud Optix which makes a combined solution for Intercept X. (Sophos, n.d.)

Table 2. Features of Sophos Intercept X

Features provided	Response Yes/No/ Maybe	PCI requirements that are met
Antivirus/anti-malware	Yes	Requirements: 5.1, 5.2, 5.3, 6.1, 10.3, 11.5
Firewall	Yes	Requirements: 1.2, 1.3, 1.4, 2.2, 6.6, 8.3, 11.4, 12.5
Intrusion detection/ prevention	Yes	Requirements: 11.4.1, 11.4.2, 12.4.1, 12.10.2 Appendix 3.3.1, 10.8, 11.1, A3.5.1,
Web filtering	Yes	Requirements: 1.1, 1.3, 6.6, 9.9, 10.4, 11.3
Endpoint detection and response (EDR)	Yes	Requirements: 5.1, 5.2, 5.3, 6.1, 6.2, 10.1, 10.2
Behavioral analytics	Yes	Requirements: 10.6, 10.6.3, 11.4

continued on following page

Table 2. Continued

Features provided	Response Yes/No/ Maybe	PCI requirements that are met
Threat intelligence integration	Maybe	Requirements: 10.6, 11.4
Reporting and analytics	Yes	Requirements: 10.1.1, 10.1.2, 10.2.1, 10.2.2, 11.5.1, 12.4.1, 12.4.2,
Data loss prevention (DLP)	Yes	Requirements: 3.1, 3.4, 4.1, 7.1, 8.5, 10.6, 12.3.6
Endpoint encryption	Yes	Requirements. 2.3, 3.4, 3.4.1, 3.6.2, 3.6.6, 4.1, 4.1.1, 4.2, 8.2.1, 6.5.1 -6.5.6, 7.1.2, 8.2.1, 10.2.4, 10.3.3, 12.3.6.1
Application control	Maybe	Requirements: 6.3.1, 6.3.2, 6.3.3, 11.2.1, 11.2.2, 11.3.1, 11.5.1, 11.6.1
Patch management	Yes	Requirements: 6.1.1, 6.1.2, 6.1.3, 6.1.4, 6.2.1, 6.2.2, 6.2.3,
Configuration management	Yes	Requirements: 2.1, 2.2, 6.1, 6.2, 6.3, 6.4, 11.2, 12.1, 12.3.2, 12.4.1

Note: The table presents the different controls mandated in PCI DSS and maps them with the capabilities of Sophos Intercept X.

2) CrowdStrike Falcon is a digital security and endpoint defense product. The company is well recognized and it plays a key role in the cybersecurity space investigating major breaches like the Sony Pictures hack and the 2016 Democratic National Convention hack (SelectHub, n.d). CrowdStrike has an assortment of standard and unique features complemented by flexible pricing built for businesses of all size. Their threat intelligence platform named Falcon leverages world class AI augmented with real-time indicators of attack. The platform also aggregates threat intelligence from many sources including evolving adversary tactics. It was built to deliver enterprise grade detection and remediation solutions (Crowdstrike, n.d.).

Table 3. Features of Crowdstrike Falcon

Features provided	Response Yes/No/ Maybe	PCI requirements that are met
Antivirus/anti-malware	Yes	Requirements: 5.1, 5.2, 5.3, 6.1, 10.3, 11.5
Firewall	Yes	Requirements: 1.2, 1.3, 1.4, 2.2, 6.6, 8.3, 11.4, 12.5
Intrusion detection/ prevention	Yes	Requirements: 11.4.1, 11.4.2, 12.4.1, 12.10.2 Appendix 3.3.1, 10.8, 11.1, A3.5.1,
Web filtering	Maybe	Requirements: 1.1, 1.3, 6.6, 9.9, 10.4, 11.3
Endpoint detection and response (EDR)	Yes	Requirements: 5.1, 5.2, 5.3, 6.1, 6.2, 10.1, 10.2
Behavioral analytics	Yes	Requirements: 10.6, 10.6.3, 11.4

continued on following page

Table 3. Continued

Features provided	Response Yes/No/ Maybe	PCI requirements that are met
Threat intelligence integration	Yes	Requirements: 10.6, 11.4
Reporting and analytics	Yes	Requirements: 10.1.1, 10.1.2, 10.2.1, 10.2.2, 11.5.1, 12.4.1, 12.4.2,
Data loss prevention (DLP)	Yes	Requirements: 3.1, 3.4, 4.1, 7.1, 8.5, 10.6, 12.3.6
Endpoint encryption	No	Requirements. 2.3, 3.4, 3.4.1, 3.6.2, 3.6.6, 4.1, 4.1.1, 4.2, 8.2.1, 6.5.1 -6.5.6, 7.1.2, 8.2.1, 10.2.4, 10.3.3, 12.3.6.1
Application control	Yes	Requirements: 6.3.1, 6.3.2, 6.3.3, 11.2.1, 11.2.2, 11.3.1, 11.5.1, 11.6.1
Patch management	Yes	Requirements: 6.1.1, 6.1.2, 6.1.3, 6.1.4, 6.2.1, 6.2.2, 6.2.3,
Configuration management	Yes	Requirements: 2.1, 2.2, 6.1, 6.2, 6.3, 6.4, 11.2, 12.1, 12.3.2, 12.4.1

Note: The table presents the different controls mandated in PCI DSS and maps them with the capabilities of Crowdstrike Falcon.

3) Sentinel One Singularity XDR offers EDR solutions for businesses of all sizes with both on-premises and cloud-based deployment options. It is a comprehensive endpoint security solution designed to safeguard organizations from a wide range of cyber threats. It gathers and correlate telemetry across your endpoints for a holistic context into the threat (Sentinel One, n.d.). It caters to a diverse user base, from small businesses to large enterprises, seeking robust and proactive protection. Key features of Singularity Complete include AI-driven threat detection, real-time response, and automated remediation, which collectively enhance security posture.

Table 4. Features of Sentinel One Singularity

Features they provide	Response Yes/No/ Maybe	PCI requirements that are met
Antivirus/anti-malware	Yes	Requirements: 5.1, 5.2, 5.3, 6.1, 10.3, 11.5
Firewall		Requirements: 1.2, 1.3, 1.4, 2.2, 6.6, 8.3, 11.4, 12.5
Intrusion detection/ prevention	Yes	Requirements: 11.4.1, 11.4.2, 12.4.1, 12.10.2 Appendix 3.3.1, 10.8, 11.1, A3.5.1,
Web filtering	Maybe	Requirements: 1.1, 1.3, 6.6, 9.9, 10.4, 11.3
Endpoint detection and response (EDR)	Yes	Requirements: 5.1, 5.2, 5.3, 6.1, 6.2, 10.1, 10.2
Behavioral analytics	Yes	Requirements: 10.6, 10.6.3, 11.4

continued on following page

Table 4. Continued

Features they provide	Response Yes/No/ Maybe	PCI requirements that are met
Threat intelligence integration	Maybe	Requirements: 10.6, 11.4
Reporting and analytics	Yes	Requirements: 10.1.1, 10.1.2, 10.2.1, 10.2.2, 11.5.1, 12.4.1, 12.4.2,
Data loss prevention (DLP)	Yes	Requirements: 3.1, 3.4, 4.1, 7.1, 8.5, 10.6, 12.3.6
Endpoint encryption	Yes	Requirements. 2.3, 3.4, 3.4.1, 3.6.2, 3.6.6, 4.1, 4.1.1, 4.2, 8.2.1, 6.5.1 -6.5.6, 7.1.2, 8.2.1, 10.2.4, 10.3.3, 12.3.6.1
Application control	Yes	Requirements: 6.3.1, 6.3.2, 6.3.3, 11.2.1, 11.2.2, 11.3.1, 11.5.1, 11.6.1
Patch management	Yes	Requirements: 6.1.1, 6.1.2, 6.1.3, 6.1.4, 6.2.1, 6.2.2, 6.2.3,
Configuration management	Yes	Requirements: 2.1, 2.2, 6.1, 6.2, 6.3, 6.4, 11.2, 12.1, 12.3.2, 12.4.1

Note: The table presents the different controls mandated in PCI DSS and maps them witxh the capabilities of Sentinel One Singularity.

4) Cortex XDR stands as a robust endpoint detection and response (EDR) solution, exemplifying Palo Alto Networks' commitment to advanced cybersecurity. Cortex XDR firewall provides controls for inbound and outbound communications enabling organizations to use flexible search features to identify a range of indicators of compromise (IOCs) or behavioral indicators of compromise (BIOCs) (Cynet, 2023). Active threat hunting capabilities like Automated response mechanisms and seamless integration into existing infrastructure ensures real-time visibility for quick threat identification giving comprehensive behavioral analytics.

Table 5. Features of Cortex XDR

Features they provide	Response Yes/No/ Maybe	PCI requirements that are met
Antivirus/anti-malware	Yes	Requirements: 5.1, 5.2, 5.3, 6.1, 10.3, 11.5
Firewall	Yes	Requirements: 1.2, 1.3, 1.4, 2.2, 6.6, 8.3, 11.4, 12.5
Intrusion detection/ prevention	Yes	Requirements: 11.4.1, 11.4.2, 12.4.1, 12.10.2 Appendix 3.3.1, 10.8, 11.1, A3.5.1,
Web filtering	Yes	Requirements: 1.1, 1.3, 6.6, 9.9, 10.4, 11.3
Endpoint detection and response (EDR)	Yes	Requirements: 5.1, 5.2, 5.3, 6.1, 6.2, 10.1, 10.2
Behavioral analytics	Yes	Requirements: 10.6, 10.6.3, 11.4
Threat intelligence integration	Yes	Requirements: 10.6, 11.4

continued on following page

Table 5. Continued

Features they provide	Response Yes/No/ Maybe	PCI requirements that are met
Reporting and analytics	Yes	Requirements: 10.1.1, 10.1.2, 10.2.1, 10.2.2, 11.5.1, 12.4.1, 12.4.2,
Data loss prevention (DLP)	Yes	Requirements: 3.1, 3.4, 4.1, 7.1, 8.5, 10.6, 12.3.6
Endpoint encryption	Yes	Requirements. 2.3, 3.4, 3.4.1, 3.6.2, 3.6.6, 4.1, 4.1.1, 4.2, 8.2.1, 6.5.1 -6.5.6, 7.1.2, 8.2.1, 10.2.4, 10.3.3, 12.3.6.1
Application control	Yes	Requirements: 6.3.1, 6.3.2, 6.3.3, 11.2.1, 11.2.2, 11.3.1, 11.5.1, 11.6.1
Patch management	Yes	Requirements: 6.1.1, 6.1.2, 6.1.3, 6.1.4, 6.2.1, 6.2.2, 6.2.3,
Configuration management	Yes	Requirements: 2.1, 2.2, 6.1, 6.2, 6.3, 6.4, 11.2, 12.1, 12.3.2, 12.4.1

Note: The table presents the different controls mandated in PCI DSS and maps them with the capabilities of Cortex XDR.

5) VMware Carbon Black Endpoint is a powerful endpoint security platform created to protect organizations from changing cyber dangers. Endpoint Standard offers you complete defense for your company's data and customer details against malware, non-malware as well living off-the-land attacks (VMWare, 2021). With its ability to detect and respond to threats in real-time, it empowers users for active system defense. This characteristic combined with smooth integration features makes Endpoint Standard a strong option when compared against other endpoint security solutions. Endpoint Standard offers a central, cloud-based administrative interface which merges next-generation antivirus (NGAV) and endpoint detection response (EDR) capabilities into lightweight solution that is both swift to set up and simple manage (VMware, 2021).

Table 6. Features of VMWare Carbon Black

Features they provide	Response Yes/No/ Maybe	PCI requirements that meet
Antivirus/anti-malware	Yes	Requirements: 5.1, 5.2, 5.3, 6.1, 10.3, 11.5
Firewall		Requirements: 1.2, 1.3, 1.4, 2.2, 6.6, 8.3, 11.4, 12.5
Intrusion detection/ prevention	Yes	Requirements: 11.4.1, 11.4.2, 12.4.1, 12.10.2 Appendix 3.3.1, 10.8, 11.1, A3.5.1,
Web filtering	Maybe	Requirements: 1.1, 1.3, 6.6, 9.9, 10.4, 11.3
Endpoint detection and response (EDR)	Yes	Requirements: 5.1, 5.2, 5.3, 6.1, 6.2, 10.1, 10.2
Behavioral analytics	Yes	Requirements: 10.6, 10.6.3, 11.4

continued on following page

Table 6. Continued

Features they provide	Response Yes/No/ Maybe	PCI requirements that meet
Threat intelligence integration	Yes	Requirements: 10.6, 11.4
Reporting and analytics	Yes	Requirements: 10.1.1, 10.1.2, 10.2.1, 10.2.2, 11.5.1, 12.4.1, 12.4.2,
Data loss prevention (DLP)	Yes	Requirements: 3.1, 3.4, 4.1, 7.1, 8.5, 10.6, 12.3.6
Endpoint encryption	Yes	Requirements. 2.3, 3.4, 3.4.1, 3.6.2, 3.6.6, 4.1, 4.1.1, 4.2, 8.2.1, 6.5.1 -6.5.6, 7.1.2, 8.2.1, 10.2.4, 10.3.3, 12.3.6.1
Patch management	Maybe	Requirements: 6.1.1, 6.1.2, 6.1.3, 6.1.4, 6.2.1, 6.2.2, 6.2.3,
Configuration management	Yes	Requirements: 2.1, 2.2, 6.1, 6.2, 6.3, 6.4, 11.2, 12.1, 12.3.2, 12.4.1

Note: The table presents the different controls mandated in PCI DSS and maps them with the capabilities of VMware carbon black.

6) Microsoft Defender for Endpoint is an advanced security solution designed to protect businesses against sophisticated cyber threats. MDE excels in swiftly and accurately identifying a diverse array of threats that may compromise the environment (Gartner, 2023). It is built into Windows 10 and offers features like endpoint behavioral sensors, threat intelligence, cloud security analytics, attack surface reduction, and next-generation endpoint protection. This includes vulnerability and misconfiguration management, network and web protection, endpoint detection and response, and automated investigation and remediation (Witts, 2023). Ideal for enterprises of all sizes, it offers robust features such as endpoint protection, detection and response, and automated investigation and remediation. Users perceive it favorably, with one stating, Microsoft Defender for Endpoint stands out in its ability to provide comprehensive security without compromising user experience, setting it apart from competitors (SelectHub, n.d). "It also provides full coverage for all MITRE ATT&CK tactics and techniques and was awarded Best Advanced Protection 2022 by AV-TEST. (Microsoft, 2024)

Table 7. Features of Microsoft Defender

Features they provide	Response Yes/No/ Maybe	PCI requirements that are met
Antivirus/anti-malware	Yes	Requirements: 5.1, 5.2, 5.3, 6.1, 10.3, 11.5
Firewall	Yes	Requirements: 1.2, 1.3, 1.4, 2.2, 6.6, 8.3, 11.4, 12.5
Intrusion detection/ prevention	Yes	Requirements: 11.4.1, 11.4.2, 12.4.1, 12.10.2 Appendix 3.3.1, 10.8, 11.1, A3.5.1,

continued on following page

Table 7. Continued

Features they provide	Response Yes/No/ Maybe	PCI requirements that are met
Web filtering	Maybe	Requirements: 1.1, 1.3, 6.6, 9.9, 10.4, 11.3
Endpoint detection and response (EDR)	Yes	Requirements: 5.1, 5.2, 5.3, 6.1, 6.2, 10.1, 10.2
Behavioral analytics	Yes	Requirements: 10.6, 10.6.3, 11.4
Threat intelligence integration	Yes	Requirements: 10.6, 11.4
Reporting and analytics	Yes	Requirements: 10.1.1, 10.1.2, 10.2.1, 10.2.2, 11.5.1, 12.4.1, 12.4.2,
Data loss prevention (DLP)	Maybe	Requirements: 3.1, 3.4, 4.1, 7.1, 8.5, 10.6, 12.3.6
Endpoint encryption	Maybe	Requirements. 2.3, 3.4, 3.4.1, 3.6.2, 3.6.6, 4.1, 4.1.1, 4.2, 8.2.1, 6.5.1 -6.5.6, 7.1.2, 8.2.1, 10.2.4, 10.3.3, 12.3.6.1
Application control	Maybe	Requirements: 6.3.1, 6.3.2, 6.3.3, 11.2.1, 11.2.2, 11.3.1, 11.5.1, 11.6.1
Patch management	Maybe	Requirements: 6.1.1, 6.1.2, 6.1.3, 6.1.4, 6.2.1, 6.2.2, 6.2.3,
Configuration management	Yes	Requirements: 2.1, 2.2, 6.1, 6.2, 6.3, 6.4, 11.2, 12.1, 12.3.2, 12.4.1

Note: The table presents the different controls mandated in PCI DSS and maps them with the capabilities of Microsoft Defender for endpoint.

FUTURE DIRECTIONS IN PAYMENT SECURITY

We must understand that backend and frontend data are classifications of data. The data is not sitting at the local endpoint; rather, exchange points are where the data sits. With the advent of Internet-of-Things (IoT) devices and enormous players who commercialize their products, it becomes difficult to bring everything under one umbrella. Business was completely transformed by technology, which made the final product less significant than ever. Instead, the firm may now propel business forward by continuously analyzing vast amounts of data, or information (Fortinet, n.d). Hence there is a dire need for a solution that could help foray into the tech world, in which cybersecurity has been a prime onlooker. A few of the approaches that would relate to PCI DSS and help foster it in a better way are listed below.

According to Gartner, recent studies show that to address a risk towards an endpoint measure, any company can choose to advocate the level of risk they are okay to take based on the control measures that apply to their organization. An approach defined in the article produced in (Patnaik, 2023) defines the breakdown of processes into levels as below:

- Level 1: Interrupt
- Level 2: Develop
- Level 3: Define
- Level 4: Proactively Defend
- Level 5: Refine

EDR is now a common and mature feature of EPP solutions. Misconfiguration of EPP/EDR solutions is a common root cause of recent breaches. Further improvements to pre-incident risk assessments and hardening guidance as peri- and post-incident capabilities become less differentiated across vendors (Magic Quadrant, 2022). Recent MITRE tests have illustrated EDR's strength in detecting complex attacks. EDR should now be considered a mandatory capability, but only 42% of enterprise endpoints have it (Silva, 2022). Yet it is these endpoints – again, the most important ones in an enterprise – that EDR has not traditionally covered. Part of the reason is that many organizations do not know all the systems they have. Every organization is unique, and factors like industry, size, geographic region, and specific business goals play a significant role in shaping endpoint security requirements (Hinner, 2023). Vendors offer EPP/EDR products with similar capabilities. This also shows the advent of XDR, which is a modified version of EDR. XDR not only enhances an organization's ability to thwart threats but also offers a more streamlined and efficient security operation, freeing up valuable resources that would otherwise be spent on manual investigation and response tasks (Palo Alto, n.d.). Key considerations of both EDR and XDR are crucial for making informed decisions about your organization's security posture, such as the following: scope of protection, integration, threat detection and response, operational efficiency, cost and resource considerations, and vendor dependency (Palo Alto, n.d.).

ZERO TRUST PRINCIPLE

Regardless of where the request originates or what resource it accesses, Zero Trust teaches us to 'never trust, always verify'. Rich intelligence and analytics are utilized to detect and respond to anomalies in real time. By utilizing robust authentication techniques, utilizing network segmentation, preventing lateral movement, offering Layer 7 threat prevention, and streamlining granular, 'least access' policies, Zero Trust is intended to safeguard contemporary environments and facilitate digital transformation (Palo Alto, n.d.).

Zero trust focuses on protecting resources (assets, services, workflows, network accounts, etc.), not network segments, as the network location is no longer seen as the prime component to the security posture of the resource (Rose et al., 2020).

However, despite its potential to provide more secure networking, many organizations still rely on perimeter-based architecture (Weishampel et al., 2018). This situation has undergone a dramatic change after the pandemic forced organizations to adopt a work-from-home policy. Zero trust architecture played a significant role in the successful implementation of policy. The zero-trust model redraws the network and creates a new idea of network segmentation gateway. Monitoring who connects to the network, what they do, where they connect, and when they connect using segmentation and next-generation firewalls give answers to better controls. Privileges need to be strictly controlled once an individual has been authenticated. (Assunção, 2019).

NETWORK SEGMENTATION AND OBJECTIVES MAPPING TO ENDPOINT SECURITY

It is essential to architect sections of the network to isolate critical systems, functions, or resources (Network Segmentation, 2019). It is important to set boundaries around networks that comprise critical data as this helps monitor and track critical networks at granular levels and ensures strict security around them. Not only should organizations keep a constant track of encryption status but also implement segmentation or micro-segmentation of the network to ensure the network is filtered and limited to only privileged access. constant monitoring and tracking of all the access controls and privileged access granted to users. The access granted should be authenticated, verified, logged, and monitored regularly to detect anomalies and for quick remediation.

Making sure that PCI DSS rules are followed needs very careful focus on different controls, especially when seen from the viewpoint of a merchant who must deal with both internal and external auditors having their specific roles. The main measures involve applying strong password rules and authentication methods for all users, as well as encrypting important data kept in endpoints. Also, it is necessary to switch off unnecessary ports and services, put in place antivirus and anti-malware software which is regularly maintained; along with setting up an entire program for handling patches. The importance of monitoring and logging all endpoint activity is crucial for detecting and responding to security incidents effectively. Additionally, organizations should consider these methods to improve protection for fresh endpoints such as Implementing mobile device management (MDM) solutions which can help in securing mobile devices; deploying security information and event management (SIEM) solutions allowing them to monitor endpoint activity comprehensively and implementing network segmentation to isolate new endpoints from other network segments. Together, these steps further strengthen the security posture by reducing risks and protecting against changing attack methods. Below table maps the different controls mentioned in PCI DSS to the security tools offered by different vendors.

Table 8. Different controls mentioned in PCI DSS mapped against different security tools by vendors

Features they provide	Sophos: Sophos Intercept X	CrowdStrike: Falcon	Sentinel One: Singularity Platform	Palo Alto Networks:	VMWare: Carbon Black	Microsoft: Defender
Antivirus/anti-malware	Yes	Yes	Yes	Yes	Yes	Yes
Firewall	Yes	Yes	No	Yes	No	Yes
Intrusion detection/ prevention	Yes	Yes	Yes	Yes	Yes	Yes
Web filtering	Yes	Maybe	Maybe	Yes	Maybe	Maybe
Endpoint detection and response (EDR)	Yes	Yes	Yes	Yes	Yes	Yes
Behavioural analytics	Yes	Yes	Yes	Yes	Yes	Yes
Threat intelligence integration	Maybe	Yes	Maybe	Yes	Yes	Yes
Reporting and analytics	Yes	Yes	Yes	Yes	Yes	Yes
Data loss prevention (DLP)	Yes	Yes	Yes	Yes	Yes	Maybe
Endpoint encryption	Yes	No	Yes	Yes	Yes	Maybe
Application control	Maybe	Yes	Yes	Yes	Maybe	Maybe
Patch management	Yes	Yes	Yes	Yes	Maybe	Maybe
Configuration management	Yes	Yes	Yes	Yes	Yes	Yes
Percentage of compliance with PCI	83.33%	83.33%	75%	100%	66.67%	58.33%

Note: The table presents a mapping between different security controls of PCI DSS with the top security tooling available on the market.

CONCLUSION

In the area of cybersecurity, it is necessary for business managers to be proactive in their approach to PCI-DSS compliance. This sense of urgency does not only come from the possibility that higher ranks of compliance may provide more investment chances but also reflects on how security benefits become real when you follow compliance standards. Many large organizations approach endpoint security from a sophisticated perspective, using separate products for prevention, detection and response tasks, there is a growing trend to use only one solution that can handle everything together - this makes it easier to manage multiple security functions in one place. (Yu et al., 2019). In the words of Okman (2018), Companies will always have a weak spot in the human factor and Haag poses the question, "Can EDR solution take place of existing endpoint security investments?" in his study (Haag, 2020). For every feature mentioned above, inquire with vendors on the solutions they provide. The right question to ask can be: What is the false positive rate for this solution? False negative rate? these gives more understanding about the future use. Inquiring with questionnaires and interviews can give good understanding of a vendor's policies, and third-party reports like SOC and ISO 27001 can provide extra verification for their security practices.

PCI DSS compliance can be monitored by implementing many new-age tools such as EDR, XDR, IDS, and IPS. While an organization does not have to implement all the tools; depending on their use cases, analysis of how different tools would benefit their business models must be understood and implemented accordingly. Another important aspect of ensuring compliance with the standard is encrypting data in all forms i.e., transit and rest.

Ensuring compliance with PCI DSS standard is not a do it once and then forget about it type of control. Continuously following guidelines while ensuring ample monitoring of systems and vulnerabilities is the only way to stay one step ahead of threat actors. Implementing different requirements demands significant effort and technical competence and several companies provide compliance solutions to help streamline organizations journey to compliance.

REFERENCES

Anderson, D. (2017). The National Health Information Sharing & Analysis Center and the National Council of Information Sharing and Analysis Centers. Retrieved from: https://docs.house.gov/meetings/IF/IF02/20170404/105831 1HHRG-115-IF02 -Wstate-AndersonD-20170404.pdf

Arfeen, A., Ahmed, S., Khan, M. A., & Jafri, S. F. (2021, November). Endpoint Detection & Response: A Malware Identification Solution.

Assunção, P. (2019). *A Zero Trust Approach to Network Security*. Retrieved from.

https://privacyandsecurityconference.pt/conference2019/Proceedings_Digital _Privacy_and_Security_Conference_2019.pdf#page=65

Barney, N. (2023, June). What is PCI DSS (Payment Card Industry Data Security Standard)? Retrieved from https://WhatIs.com

Barney, N. (2023, June). PCI DSS (Payment Card Industry Data Security Standard). Retrieved from TechTarget: https://www.techtarget.com/searchsecurity/definition/ PCI-DSS-Payment-Card-Industry-Data-Security-Standard

Carbon Black, Inc. (2018, May). Retrieved from: https://web.archive.org/ web/20180504081758/https://www.sec.gov/Archives/edgar/data/1366527/ 000104746918003408/a2235562zs-1a.htm

Chandel, S., Yan, M., Chen, S., Jiang, H., & Ni, T.-Y. (2019, April). IEE Xplore. Retrieved from: https://ieeexplore.ieee.org/abstract/document/8695328

Checkpoint. (n.d.). What is Endpoint Encryption? Retrieved from https://www .checkpoint.com/cyber-hub/threat-prevention/what-is-endpoint-security/what-is -endpoint-encryption/

Chris Silva, P. F. (2022, December). Critical Capabilities for Endpoint Protection Platforms. Retrieved from: https://www.gartner.com/document/4140999?ref=solrAll &refval=383606631&

Christodorescu, M., Jha, S., Seshia, S., Song, D., & Bryant, R. (2005, May). Retrieved from:

https://ieeexplore.ieee.org/document/1425057

Crowdstrike. (2023, October 26). Endpoint Detection and Response (EDR). Retrieved from: https://www.crowdstrike.com/cybersecurity-101/endpoint-security/endpoint -detection-and-response-edr/

Crowdstrike. (2023, September). Retrieved from:

https://www.crowdstrike.com/cybersecurity-101/secops/ai-powered-behavioral-analysis/

Crowdstrike. (n.d.). A unified platform approach. Retrieved from

https://www.crowdstrike.com/falcon-platform/?utm_campaign=brand&utm_content=crwd-treq-en-x-tct-us-psp-x-trl-brnd-x_x_x_x-product&utm_medium=sem&utm_source=goog&utm_term=crowdstrike%20falcon&cq_cmp=19616633038&cq_plac=&gad_source=1&gclid=Cj0KCQiA35urBhDCAR

CSIAC. (2018, May). Compliant but not Secure: Why PCI-Certified Companies Are Being Breached. Retrieved from: https://csiac.org/articles/compliant-but-not-secure-why-pci-certified-companies-are-being-breached/

Cynet. (2023). Cortex XDR by Palo Alto: Architecture & Capabilities Overview. Retrieved from: https://www.cynet.com/xdr-security/xdr-by-palo-alto-understanding-cortex-xdr/

Das, T. (2023, November). What Is An Endpoint Firewall? A Comprehensive Guide. Retrieved from: https://www.selecthub.com/endpoint-security/endpoint-firewall/

Earl Perkins, F. C. (2015, July 20). Cybersecurity Scenario 2020 Phase 2: Guardians for Big Change. Retrieved from: Gartner: https://www.gartner.com/document/3097027

Encryption, H. Retrieved from: https://cacm.acm.org/research/unlocking-the-potential-of-fully-homomorphic-encryption/

Evgeny Mirolyubov, P. F. (2023, January). Prioritizing Security Controls for Enterprise Servers and End-User Endpoints. Retrieved from: https://www.gartner.com/document/4022974?ref=solrAll&refval=385957224&

Fortient (n.d.). What is URL filtering? Retrieved from https://www.fortinet.com/resources/cyberglossary/what-is-url-filtering

Fortinet. (2016, Feb). A New Approach to Securing the Enterprise Network. Retrieved from: https://www.fortinet.com/content/dam/fortinet/assets/white-papers/WP-New-Approach-Securing-Enterprise-Network.pdf

Fortinet. (2023). Types of Endpoint Security. Retrieved from: https://www.fortinet.com/resources/cyberglossary/types-of-endpoint-security

Fortinet. (2023). Types of Endpoint Security. Retrieved from: https://www.fortinet.com/resources/cyberglossary/types-of-endpoint-security

Fortinet. (n.d.). What Is Endpoint Security? How Does It Work? Retrieved from https://www.fortinet.com/resources/cyberglossary/what-is-endpoint-security#:~:text=The%20endpoint%20security%20solution%20enables,%2C%20and%20zero%2Dday%20attacks

Franz Hinner, S. P. (2023, August). Hype Cycle for Endpoint Security. Retrieved from: https://www.gartner.com/interactive/hc/4589999?ref=solrAll&refval=385956590

Fruhlinger, J. (2022, May 16). PCI DSS explained: Requirements, fines, and steps to compliance. CSO.

Gartner. (2023, Aug). Peer Review for Microsoft Defender. Retrieved from: https://www.gartner.com/reviews/market/endpoint-detection-and-response-solutions/vendor/sentinelone/product/microsoft-defender-for-endpoint/review/view/4918228

Gerald, J. (1979). *Popek and Charles S. Kline*. Encryption and Secure Computer Networks. Retrieved from.

https://dl.acm.org/doi/pdf/10.1145/356789.356794

Glover, G. (2020). What are the 12 requirements of PCI DSS Compliance. Retrieved from: https://www.securitymetrics.com/blog/what-are-12-requirements-pci-dss-compliance

Gordover, M. (2020, September 17). Throwback Thursday: Lessons Learned from the 2008 Heartland Breach. Retrieved from: https://www.proofpoint.com/us/blog/insider-threat-management/throwback-thursday-lessons-learned-2008-heartland-breach

Healthcare Data Breach Statistics. (2023). Retrieved from: https://www.hipaajournal.com/healthcare-data-breach-statistics/

Hedge, V. (2018). *Obfuscated command line detection using machine learning*. Retrieved from https://www.mandiant.com/resources/blog/obfuscated-command-line-detection-using-machine-learning

Institute, L. P. (2020, January). The Third Annual Study on the State of. Ponemon Institute©. *Research Reports (Montgomery).*

Izquierdo, R. (2023, March 29). Sophos Intercept X Review.

JPMorgan. (2022, April). Retrieved from: https://www.jpmorgan.com/content/dam/jpm/commercial-banking/insights/cybersecurity/highlights-afp-2022 payments -fraud and control report.pdf

Juniper Research. (n.d.). Digital commerce transactions to pass 1 trillion threshold globally by 2024, as NFC payments & digital ticketing surge ahead. Retrieved from https://www.juniperresearch.com/pressreleases/digital-commerce-transactions-to-pass-1tn?ch=Ecommerce%20Payments:%20Emerging%20Opportunities,%20Vendor%20Strategies%20&%20Market%20Forecasts%202022-202

Kallam, S. (2015, Sept). Diffie-Hellman:Key Exchange and Public Key Cryptosystems. Retrieved from: https://cs.indstate.edu/~skallam/doc.pdf

Kamruzzaman, A. (2022, December). A Comprehensive Review of Endpoint Security: Threats and Defenses. Retrieved from: https://ieeexplore.ieee.org/document/9998470

Knowles, M. (2023, September). The Importance of Endpoint Security. Retrieved from: https://hyperproof.io/resource/endpoint-security/

Krebs, B. (2019, November). Sale of 4 Million Stolen Cards Tied to Breaches at 4 Restaurant Chains. Retrieved from: https://krebsonsecurity.com/2019/11/sale-of-4-million-stolen-cards-tied-to-breaches-at-4-restaurant-chains/#:~:text=Two%20financial%20industry%20sources%20who,a%20card%20breach%20last%20month

Laredo, V. G. (2008, May 08). PCI DSS compliance: a matter of strategy. Retrieved from: https://www.sciencedirect.com/science/article/abs/pii/S096525900870094X

Liu, J. Y. X. (2010). A Survey of Payment Card Industry Data Security Standard. Retrieved from: https://ieeexplore-ieee-org.gate.lib.buffalo.edu/stamp/stamp.jsp?tp=&arnumber=5455788&tag=1

Liu, M., Xue, Z., Xu, X., Zhong, C., & Chen, J. (2018, Nov). Host-Based Intrusion Detection System with System Calls: Review and Future Trends. Retrieved from: https://dl.acm.org/doi/pdf/10.1145/3214304

Magic Quadrant for Endpoint Protection Platforms. (2022, December). Retrieved from: https://www.gartner.com/document/4137499?ref=ddisp&refval=4140999

Mastercard. (n.d.). Build cyber resilience and trust throughout the connected digital economy. Retrieved from https://www.mastercard.us/en-us/business/large-enterprise/safety-security/cybersecurity/cyber-and-riskmanagement.html#fn3

Mathew Nicho, H. F. (2011). *An Integrated Security Governance Framework for Effective PCI DSS Implementation.* Retrieved from https://www.igi-global.com/gateway/article/58982

Merchant risk council. (2023, Sept). Retrieved from: https://merchantriskcouncil.org/learning/resource-center/member-news/blog/2023/history-of-PCI-compliance

Michael Haag, J. M. (2020, May). EDR buyer's guide: The business case. Retrieved from: https://resource.redcanary.com/rs/003-YRU-314/images/EDR-Buyers-Guide-2020.pdf

Microsoft. (2004, February). Perimeter Firewall Design. Retrieved from: https://learn.microsoft.com/en-us/previous-versions/tn-archive/cc700828(v=technet.10)?redirectedfrom=MSDN

Microsoft. (2022, October 03). Endpoint Protection. Retrieved from: https://learn.microsoft.com/en-us/mem/configmgr/protect/deploy-use/endpoint-protection

Microsoft. (2024, Jan). Retrieved from: https://www.microsoft.com/en-us/security/business/endpoint-security/microsoft-defender-endpoint

Microsoft. (2024, Jan). What is data loss prevention (DLP)? Retrieved from: https://www.microsoft.com/en-us/security/business/security-101/what-is-data-loss-prevention-dlp?ef_id=_k_fe0b4c7a48eb1cb16a5c292755d1c01e_k_&OCID=AIDcmmdamuj0pc_SEM__k_fe0b4c7a48eb1cb16a5c292755d1c01e_k_&msclkid=fe0b4c7a48eb1cb16a5c292755d1c01e

Mohaisen, Alrawi & Mohaisen (2015, July). AMAL: High-fidelity, behavior-based automated malware analysis and classification. Retrieved from: https://www.sciencedirect.com/science/article/pii/S0167404815000425

Mosli, R., Li, R., Yuan, B., & Pan, Y. (2017, Aug). A Behaviour based approach for malware detection. Retrieved from: https://link.springer.com/content/pdf/10.1007/978-3-319-67208-3_11.pdf

Network Segmentation. (2019, June). Retrieved from: https://attack.mitre.org/mitigations/M1030/

NIST. (2022, July). Retrieved from: https://www.nist.gov/news-events/news/2022/07/nist-announces-first-four-quantum-resistant-cryptographic-algorithms

Norman Comstock, L. N. (2023, October). Making Sense of Today's Payment Cybersecurity Landscape. Retrieved from: https://www.darkreading.com/vulnerabilities-threats/making-sense-of-todays-payment-cybersecurity-landscape

Okman, T. (2018, January). Cybersecurity Trends To Look Out For In 2023. Retrieved from: https://www.forbes.com/sites/forbestechcouncil/2023/01/18/cybersecurity-trends-to-look-out-for-in-2023/?sh=5cb103dd4421

Oltsik, J. (2018). *Enterprise plans for security automation and orchestration*. Retrieved from https://www.techtarget.com/blog/enterprise-plans-for-security-automation-and-orchestration

One, S. (n.d.). Singularity for Endpoints. Retrieved from: https://www.sentinelone.com/surfaces/endpoint/?utm_medium=paid-search&utm_source=google-paid&utm_campaign=nam-dsa-ppc&gclid=Cj0KCQiAgqGrBhDtARIsAM5s0_nXdwj2djMyRjGGsPpSLTqmgGkZTiYHGh2u9L3hwctHUtaTVzt0n4AaAoJ2EALw_wcB

PaloAlto. (2019). What is a Zero Trust Architecture. Retrieved from: https://www.paloaltonetworks.com/cyberpedia/what-is-a-zero-trust-architecture

PaloAlto. (n.d.). What Is Extended Detection and Response (XDR)? Retrieved from Cyberpedia: https://www.paloaltonetworks.com/cyberpedia/what-is-extended-detection-response-XDR

Paloalto. (n.d.). What is an Endpoint? Retrieved from: https://www.paloaltonetworks.com/cyberpedia/what-is-an-endpoint

PCI DSS version 4.0. (2022, Mar). Retrieved from: https://www.commerce.uwo.ca/pdf/PCI-DSS-v4_0.pdf

PCI Security Standards. (2022, Mar). Retrieved from: https://www.pcisecuritystandards.org/document_library/

PCI Security Standards Council. (2022, August). PCI DSS v4.0 Quick Reference Guide, Understanding the Payment Card Industry. Retrieved from: https://www.pnc.com/content/dam/pnc-com/pdf/smallbusiness/Merchant%20Services/PCI_DSS_QuickRef_Guide.pdf

PCI Standards Council. (n.d.). Retrieved from: https://www.pcisecuritystandards.org/merchants/

Purnell, M. (2023, August). QR Code Payments Market: 2023-2028. Retrieved from: https://www.juniperresearch.com/researchstore/fintech-payments/qr-code-payments-research-report

Raghunath, B. R., & Mahadeo, S. N. (2008, July). Network Intrusion Detection System (NIDS). Retrieved from: https://ieeexplore.ieee.org/abstract/document/4580100

Rees, J. (2012). Tackling the PCI DSS challenges. *Computer Fraud & Security*, 2012(1), 15–17. DOI: 10.1016/S1361-3723(12)70009-X

RiskOptics. (2023, October). PCI Compliance Checklist for Audits. Retrieved from: https://reciprocity.com/resources/what-is-the-pci-dss-audit-checklist/

Satarupa Patnaik, P. F. (2023, April). How to Improve Endpoint Security to Protect Organizations Against Advanced Cyberattacks. Retrieved from: https://www.gartner.com/document/4245399?ref=solrAll&refval=383581810&

Security, R. S. I. (2023, August). Breaking down the PCI DSS 4.0 requirements. Retrieved from: https://blog.rsisecurity.com/breaking-down-the-pci-dss-4-0-requirements/#:~:text=The%20PCI%204.0%20requirements%20were,implementing%20all%20PCI%204.0%20requirements

Security Intelligence Modeling and Research Directions. Retrieved from: https://link.springer.com/article/10.1007/s42979-021-00557-0

SelectHub. (n.d.). Compare Product. Retrieved from: https://express.selecthub.com/#/products

SentinelOne Singularity XDR. (n.d.). Retrieved from: https://www.content.shi.com/cms-content/accelerator/media/pdfs/sentinelone/sentinelone-solution-brief-singularity-xdr-051822.pdf

Silva, P. F. (2022, December 31). Magic Quadrant for Endpoint Protection Platforms. Retrieved from: https://www.gartner.com/document/4137499?ref=solrAll&refval=384466386&

Sophos Authorised Online Platinum reseller. (n.d.). Sophos Central Intercept X Advanced. Retrieved from: https://www.enterpriseav.com/Intercept-X-Adv.asp?utm_term=sophos%20central%20intercept%20x&utm_campaign=Sophos+*174&utm_source=adwords&utm_medium=ppc&hsa_tgt=kwd-379818380583&hsa_grp=61783349500&hsa_src=g&hsa_net=adwords&hsa_mt=e&hsa_ver=3&hsa_ad=30712590

Sophos. (n.d.). PCI DSS v4.0 Compliance Reference Card. Retrieved from: https://assets.sophos.com/X24WTUEQ/at/njxq68jhbjtmwh877ngbtfwh/sophos-pci-dss-compliance-card.pdf

Sophos. (n.d.). Solutions. Retrieved from PCI DSS compliance can be a challenge: https://www.sophos.com/en-us/solutions/compliance/pci-dss

VISA. (2023). *Information Security*. Retrieved from https://aw.visa.com/run-your-business/small-business/information-security/compliance-validation.html

Visa. (2019, August). Retrieved from: https://usa.visa.com/visa-everywhere/blog/bdp/2019/08/12/visa-celebrates-25-1565646929402.html

VMware. (2021, Sept). Carbon Black Tech Zone. Retrieved from: https://carbonblack.vmware.com/resource/carbon-black-cloud-endpoint-standard technical-overview#top-things

Weishaupl, E., Yasasin, E., & Schryen, G. (2018, August). Information security investments: An exploratory multiple case study on decision-making, evaluation and learning. Retrieved from: https://www.sciencedirect.com/science/article/abs/pii/S0167404818300555

Wickramasinghe, S. (2023, March 9). Behavioral Analytics Explained: How Analyzing (Odd) Behavior Supports Cybersecurity. Retrieved from: https://www.splunk.com/en_us/blog/learn/behavioral-analytics.html

Witts, J. (2023, November 16). Endpoint Security Solutions For Business. Retrieved from: https://expertinsights.com/insights/the-top-endpoint-security-solutions-for-business/

Yu, S., Yitian, T., Zhili, Z., & Yusheng, H. (2019, October). Endpoint Protection: Measuring the Effectiveness of Remediation Technologies and Methodologies for Insider Threat. Retrieved from: https://ieeexplore.ieee.org/document/8945852

Zhao, Zhao, Zhao, Chen, Gao, Li, & Tan. (2019). Secure Multi-Party Computation: Theory, practice and applications. Retrieved from: https://www.sciencedirect.com/science/article/abs/pii/S0020025518308338

Chapter 10
Risk Management Framework for Cloud Migration and Selection of Suitable Cloud Service Provider

Mansi Mahesh Kumar Singh
University at Buffalo, SUNY, USA

Mansha Chandna
University at Buffalo, SUNY, USA

Venkata Yashwanth Yadav Kongala
University at Buffalo, SUNY, USA

ABSTRACT

Businesses frequently manage the complicated challenge of transitioning from on-premises systems to the cloud in the evolving world of technology. An integrated risk framework is critical for analyzing and auditing this transformation, ensuring a smooth transfer while limiting potential risks. This methodology provides proactive risk management by predicting issues such as compliance gaps, and service outages. In addition, this framework includes a thorough selection procedure for the best cloud service providers (CSPs). Organizations may find the best partner for their specific needs by examining criteria like security standards, compliance adherence, scalability, and data governance. This complete strategy not only reduces possible interruptions during migration but also fortifies the company against unanticipated obstacles, promoting a safe and efficient cloud environment, and educated decision

DOI: 10.4018/979-8-3693-4211-4.ch010

making. As the technology landscape is changing exponentially, it is important to integrate risk framework as a strategic compass in intricacy of migration to reinforce digital infrastructure.

INTRODUCTION

Cloud computing is one the most advantageous technologies. The main advantage of cloud is that Migration from on-premises setup to the cloud involves multiple changes across the infrastructure and organization end (Bandari, 2022). Different organizations use different technologies, techniques, and strategies for their migration process (Zhao & Zhou, 2014). The organization selects the most feasible cloud adoption technique and develops the adoption strategy with an affordable cloud service provider (CSP) using the available technologies (Sharma et al., 2017). These rationales make it difficult to review different migration techniques, the capability of the service provider and the available services, define the scope of the IT audit, identify the risk and critical controls, evaluate the critical controls, and provide recommendations for the highlighted risks in line with the implemented technology. Another major concern that arises is to align the implemented migration process and cloud service providers framework with organizations' risk management framework. It is often seen that with more time, organizations tend to relax their security posture. To win against that relaxation, the organization should keep on analysing the posture and perform regular assessments. This risk management framework is going to be one of the security assessment tools to examine the vulnerabilities and threats to mitigate security risks in the organization This will help the organizations to understand the critical areas of focus in the cloud landscape and address the vulnerabilities, if any (Zhang et al., 2010).

Most organizations prefer to use the cloud to build their upcoming projects/ products and look forward to moving their existing products/ solutions to the cloud. In this, companies can consider using third-party vendors and can choose to run their services there with the help of IaaS, PaaS, or SaaS as per the requirement and choose an appropriate deployment mode – a hybrid, private, or public. Just as capabilities are inherited, so are the information security issues and risks (Xu, 2020). Implementing cloud computing necessitates a paradigm shift in business and IT architecture, in which computer power, data storage, and services are outsourced to third parties and sold as commodities to organizations and customers. Cloud computing is largely a new business paradigm for consumers, not a new technological paradigm; a cloud vendor (a commercial enterprise) offers its clients hardware, software infrastructure (platform), or an application as a service. In the most basic situation, a cloud vendor provides its clients with the capabilities of a simple server—albeit a virtual one—in which processing, network, and storage resources are dynamically managed (Rosenthal et al., 2010). Whenever an organization undergoes changes, whether it is infrastructure or business process level change, they must conduct an IT audit or risk assessment for the changes as per the security standard practices. flexible approach for managing information security risk that is intentionally broad-based, with the specific details of assessing, responding to, and monitoring risk on an ongoing basis provided by some or the other industry-recognized framework (Kahyaoglu et al., 2018).

Developing the framework would help with cloud migration to ensure an easy and protected transfer to the cloud from on-premises servers by alleviating the risks and concerns. Identify the risks, threats and challenges associated with cloud migration and auditing processes. A step-by-step framework for cloud adoption is developed, identifying, and recommending solutions to the four most common obstacles that are harming the cloud industry and driving SMEs away from cloud computing, as well as guiding SMEs toward effective cloud adoption. Furthermore, this paradigm simplifies the cloud adoption process for SMEs by eliminating uncertainty about the basics of their company and the cloud adoption process. (Khan & Al-Yasiri, 2015).

This research paper aims to address the above-mentioned issues and create a detailed risk assessment framework for the cloud migration process, focusing on the areas to be covered as the scope of the IT audit, identify the risks present in the adopted cloud migration process, critical controls to be considered for the assessment and recommendation to mitigate the risks in each area and enhance the adopted cloud migration strategy. The research paper will also focus on the process of identifying the most suitable cloud service provider (CSP), which provides services that comply with security standards, regulatory guidelines, and best industry practices.

LITERATURE REVIEW

Evolution of Cloud Computing: Historical Development and Impact on Businesses

The migration of businesses from on-premises to a cloud environment represents a pivotal step in the evolution of technology landscapes. This transformative shift demands a forward-looking approach to address emerging risks and uncertainties (Zhang et al., 2018). The literature review unveils a historical narrative of cloud computing, emphasizing its profound impact on businesses. This shift or transition requires organizations to reshape the existing technological infrastructure and to adopt its approach in sync with the changing as well as evolving nature of the cloud and its environment (Smith & Jones, 2019).

Most importantly, the focus of the literature review remains on drafting an Integrated Risk Framework, indicating the need for a structured approach to managing the risks and challenges associated with the process of cloud migration (Johnson et al., 2021). The development of cloud computing has fostered innovation and creativity, making the organizations capable of scaling its requirements and adapt quickly in the evolving landscape (Brown & White, 2022).

Challenges and Risks in Cloud Migration: Recognizing the Landscape

Organizations, in their journey from on-premises to the cloud, must confront and manage various challenges and risks associated with this migration. Technology risk assessments play a crucial role, often revealing unexpected vulnerabilities in systems deemed secure. The integrated cloud-cyber migration team, armed with a comprehensive understanding of both emerging and current technologies, becomes a strategic asset in effectively managing technology risks (Dillon et al., 2010; Rittinghouse & Ransome, 2016).

Moreover, this literature review emphasizes the evolving and changing nature of technology and its risk, especially in between the challenges of cloud-cyber migration (Taylor et al., 2020). As organizations migrate to the cloud landscape, it is important to recognize that challenges can often serve as catalysts for innovation and improvement (Clark & Adams, 2021).

As mentioned by Dillon et al., 2010; Rittinghouse & Ransome, 2016, the migration of businesses from on-premises to cloud environments entails navigating various risks and challenges inherent in the process. One of the foremost concerns is security, incorporating threats such as unauthorized access, data breaches, and malware attacks, which leads to exposure of security information. Also, compliance with the current industry regulations, such as GDPR and HIPAA, poses additional prime challenges, as organizations must adhere to data protection laws and judicial norms related to the same. Additionally, data governance risks come out of loss of data integrity or confidentiality during the migration process, highlighting the importance of stable and versatile governance frameworks. Service disruption risks, incorporates downtime and performance degradation, further implies the need for planning and execution. Moreover, performance challenges such as latency issues and resource allocation inefficiencies must be addressed to make the system function optimally. Legacy systems integration comes with compatibility challenges, while vendor lock-in and regulatory compliance issues do further complicate the migration process.

The multifaceted risks and challenges mentioned above in the literature review are further illustrated here using some case studies and examples for better understanding. In 2019, Capital One experienced a huge data breach exposing the personal information of more than 100 million of its customers. The breach occurred due to a misconfigured firewall in their AWS cloud framework, highlighting the security risks associated. In 2017, a widespread outage of Amazon's AWS S3 cloud storage service affected many websites and applications globally, highlighting the risk of service disruptions in cloud migration. In 2015, Anthem Inc. suffered a data breach compromising 80 million of its customer records due to inadequate encryption on its servers, violating HIPAA regulations. The breach implied the necessity of compliance with encryption protocols during migration process to prevent similar breaches. Similarly in 2017, Equifax experienced a data breach affecting 147 million individuals due to a web application vulnerability, highlighting the need for a stable and versatile data governance during cloud migration to prevent breaches and protect sensitive data. Highlighting the performance issue, during Amazon Prime Day in 2018, the website crashed and slowed load times. This resulted in revenue losses and brand damage.

Challenges and Risks in Cloud Migration: Mitigation and Evaluation

Numerous studies cited highlight the multifaceted risks associated with cloud migration, including security concerns, compliance issues, and potential disruptions (Dillon et al., 2010; Rittinghouse & Ransome, 2016). The significance of knowledge about these risks and their mitigation strategies is underscored for the success of the migration procedure.

Some case studies to highlight the mitigation done in organizations to mitigate the risk involved in cloud migration will provide more insights. IBM conducted integrated risk assessments and implemented advanced security measures such as encryption and access controls to mitigate risks during cloud migration. Continuous performance testing and monitoring ensured optimized performance throughout the migration. Going on the same line, Dropbox prioritized data governance by implementing strict access controls and encryption protocols, ensuring regulatory compliance, and mitigating the risk of data breaches. Regular compliance audits and assessments helped maintain trust with customers. Similarly, Netflix conducted extensive performance testing and optimized its cloud infrastructure using auto-scaling and load balancing technologies to mitigate performance risks during cloud migration. Continuous monitoring and real-time adjustments ensured a seamless user experience.

This literature provides an insight into Integrated Risk Frameworks, providing organizations with a systematic approach to evaluate and mitigate potential issues like data breaches, compliance gaps, and service outages (Khan et al., 2015; Mowbray et al., 2010; Varia, 2010). In handling these challenges, these organizations are suggested to adopt a proactive stance, leveraging risk as an opportunity like a blessing in disguise (Roberts & Lee, 2022).

Additionally, organizations can employ several mitigation and evaluation techniques such as continuous monitoring and auditing, automated remediation, cloud-specific security solutions, scalable architecture design, and third-party validation to mitigate the cloud migration risks and challenges effectively. These techniques, when integrated into an organization's migration strategy, can help mitigate risks and ensure a successful transition to the cloud. By utilizing Integrated Risk Frameworks, organizations can effectively manage risks and ensure a successful transition to the cloud.

Cloud Migration and Its Techniques

Cloud migration involves the strategic shift of an organization's IT operations, data, and applications from on-premises infrastructure to a cloud computing environment. While offering numerous advantages, successful migration demands careful planning, execution, and ongoing management. The process encompasses the seamless transfer of applications, data, and infrastructure components into the cloud. Factors influencing migration strategy selection include organizational goals, application types, customization needs, and the intended degree of cloud-native adoption. A cloud migration process frequently comprises multiple concept iterations and implementation strategies. The method depends on the features of a legacy system and the organizational structures in place. It is well known that no two cloud migration scenarios are the same and that each one calls for a different set of management procedures. Many issues are brought up by moving legacies to the cloud, including vendor lock-in, interoperability, and security. Drawing on the general literature on the cloud computing (Fox et al., 2009; Brebner, 2012; Rimal et al., 2009; Guo et al., 2007; Nathuji et al., 2010; Toosi et al., 2014; Dalheimer and Pfreundt, 2009; Ristenpart et al., 2009), there are six cloud intrinsic key concerns as follow: (i) resource elasticity, (ii) multi-tenancy, (iii) interoperability and migration over multiple-clouds, (iv) application licensing, (v) dynamicity and unpredictability, and (vi) legal issues. These concerns trigger considerations that an application owner should consider them in the migration activity.

Migration Strategies

Rehosting: Consistency with on-premises systems is prioritized in rehosting, which is frequently used for legacy applications. It entails simply moving content that now resides on-premises to the cloud without requiring significant architecture changes. By effectively replicating the current configuration in a cloud-based setting, this strategy guarantees that functionalities stay unaltered. Rehosting reduces the requirement for significant reconfigurations or modifications by replicating the on-premises configuration. Under this method, cloud-hosted programs usually function exactly like their on-premises equivalents. Rehosting provides an expedited path for migration, allowing enterprises to move quickly to the cloud while preserving familiarity and business continuity. While it might not have as much optimization potential as other approaches, rehosting is a workable and effective way to move old systems to the cloud. (Laszewski & Prakash Nauduri, 2011)

***Replatform*:** Replatforming involves more than just moving current systems; it's an essential step in moving apps to the cloud. It entails a calculated strategy meant to maximize application optimization for cloud hosting with the least amount of disturbance to company operations. Replatforming and rehosting are fundamentally similar in that they involve moving apps to the cloud with little to no modifications. Pacheco, M. (2023, July 14) The degree of customization and optimization made throughout the replatforming process, however, is what really sets them apart. Ensuring that apps operate more effectively and efficiently in the cloud is one of the main objectives of replatforming. This frequently calls for changes to dependencies and configurations in addition to alterations to the apps themselves. Usually, these adjustments are implemented gradually to reduce interference with continuing business operations. Replatforming is more than just migration; it's a purposeful undertaking. To fully utilize cloud computing and minimize risks and business operations disruptions, it entails a thorough transformation of applications. Organizations may successfully traverse the challenges of replatforming and get the benefits of the cloud for their apps by utilizing programming skills and cloud experience.

***Repurchase*:** Repurchasing, a crucial component of replatforming, promotes elasticity and scalability by easily integrating cloud services and APIs to enable capability development. This plan calls for adopting cutting-edge cloud-based solutions, such as Software as a Service (SaaS) substitutes like Salesforce for CRM requirements. Organizations can optimize resource allocation and streamline operations by implementing cloud-native choices in place of older apps. Repurchasing also entails transferring licenses from local servers to equivalent ones hosted in the cloud, which lowers maintenance costs and improves accessibility. This strategy is especially advantageous for programs that are deeply ingrained in bespoke legacy settings since it provides an affordable modernization alternative. In the end, repurchasing gives companies the ability to match their IT infrastructure to changing needs, fostering productivity, creativity, and competitiveness in the fast-paced digital market of today. Ultimately, repurchasing enables companies to match their IT infrastructure to changing needs, promoting productivity, creativity, and competitiveness in the fast-paced digital market of today (Padilla, R. S., Milton, S. K., Johnson, L. W., & Nyadzayo, M. W., 2017)

Retain: The practice of maintaining some applications or data in their present environment because of cost concerns or alignment with larger corporate objectives is referred to as the "retaining strategy" for workloads that are kept on premises. With this strategy, businesses can delay moving to the cloud until it better fits their strategic objectives or legal obligations. For example, sensitive data may need to be temporarily stored on-site due to regulatory regulations. Similarly, it can be decided that migrating complicated or mission-critical apps right away would be too expensive or difficult. In these situations, a hybrid strategy may be used, with part of the data kept on-site and the remainder in the cloud. (Laszewski & Prakash Nauduri, 2011) With the flexibility of this hybrid architecture, businesses may take advantage of cloud benefits without giving up control over some assets. In the end, the retention strategy offers a practical method for adopting cloud computing, allowing businesses to weigh the advantages of cloud computing against their unique requirements and limitations.

Retire: Retiring is a critical component of cloud migration strategy that aims to minimize expenses, optimize efficiency, and streamline operations by getting rid of superfluous infrastructure components. This tactic comprises determining which apps and services are no longer useful or relevant to users and then decommissioning them. Organizations can simplify their IT environment and reallocate resources to more strategic projects by eliminating outmoded or obsolete components. Deciding which workloads may be safely ceased and which are better suited for the cloud is the first step in retiring in the context of cloud migration. By migrating just critical and value-added services, this selective method minimizes complexity and maximizes cost-effectiveness. Eliminating superfluous infrastructure components is a smart move toward modernization and agility as well to save money. Herring (2021)

Refactor: Refactoring is one technique that stands out for greatly improving functionality through the smooth integration of APIs and cloud services, which promotes scalability and elasticity. Refactoring, while labor-intensive and possibly expensive, entails starting from scratch when rewriting existing apps to conform to cloud compatibility rules. Refactored programs yield long-term benefits, such as increased scalability for future expansion, faster updates, and higher performance, all while saving time and money initially (Herring, 2021). To guarantee a seamless and effective cloud transfer, each migration strategy—whether it's rehosting, retaining, repurchasing, or refactoring—needs careful thought, thorough testing, and ongoing monitoring. The best option is determined by a company's goals, circumstances, and technological environment. Organizations may prosper in the dynamic cloud environment and take advantage of its agility and scalability by placing a high priority on continual optimization and enhancement.

Generic Migration Path

It's critical to keep in mind that migration involves travel. With your current surroundings and infrastructure, you are at point A and wish to go to point B. You can select any of the previously mentioned methods to go from point A to point B.

The route of this journey is depicted in the following diagram.

Figure 1. Generic migration path process flow

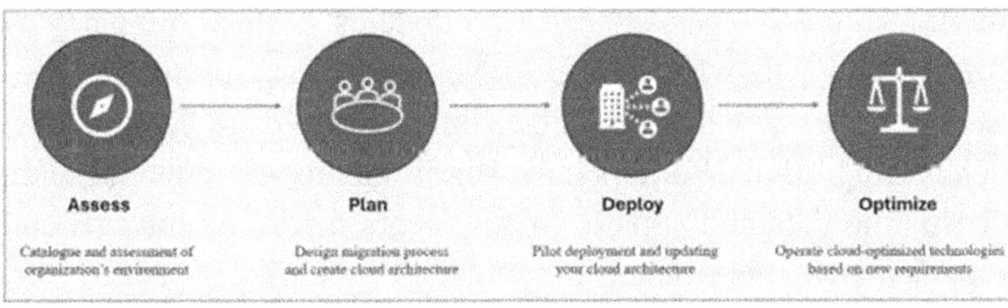

Assess: This phase involves a comprehensive inventory and assessment of your current environment to understand application and environment, define requirements and dependencies for application, calculate the total cost of ownership, and set performance standards for app.

Plan: During this stage, you design the app migration process and build the fundamental cloud architecture where your workloads will reside. Identity management, networking, project organization and structure, app categorization, and creating a migration strategy with a priority list are all included in this preparation.

Deploy: You create, put into practice, and carry out a deployment procedure in this phase to shift workloads to the cloud. Additionally, you may need to modify your cloud architecture to accommodate new requirements.

Optimize: During this stage, you start to fully utilize cloud-optimized technologies and capabilities to increase the potential of your business in areas like training, costs, disaster recovery, scalability, and performance, and opening up opportunities for machine learning and artificial intelligence integrations for your organization.

Advantages

In cloud environments, organizations can easily scale up or down their resources in response to demand. In general, cloud service providers (CSPs) invest a lot of money in security and offer robust security features and certifications. Through cloud migration, organizations can take advantage of the newest services and technologies offered by cloud providers and these cloud providers handle regular maintenance, security patches, and software updates. Cloud providers often give resource optimization and sustainability a top priority. Cloud migration strategies can lead to more effective management practices, which will streamline infrastructure management. Businesses may scale their resources up or down based on their needs to cloud platforms. Because of its scalability, companies may readily adapt to changes in demand without having to make large investments in new physical infrastructure and can save money by moving to the cloud since they do not have to spend money on costly gear, upkeep, and updates. Instead, they pay as they go for the resources they use, which can be more economical, particularly for smaller companies. Businesses now have more freedom in terms of where and how they can operate to cloud migration. Workers may work remotely and enhance teamwork by accessing corporate data and apps from any location with an internet connection. Cloud companies make significant investments in security measures to safeguard the infrastructure and data centers and businesses can benefit from these security protections, which frequently exceed what they could adopt on their own, by moving to the cloud. Strong disaster recovery features, such as data replication, backup, and failover choices, are provided by cloud platforms. This guarantees that companies won't have to endure protracted downtime in the event of a system breakdown or data loss. By managing software upgrades and maintenance, cloud providers guarantee that companies always have access to the newest features and security fixes without requiring them to devote internal resources to these activities. Cloud computing can be more environmentally friendly than traditional on-premises infrastructure since it enables businesses to optimize resource usage and minimize energy consumption. To further lessen their influence on the environment, a lot of cloud service companies are dedicated to powering their data centers using renewable energy sources.

Apart from this, adoption of hybrid and multiple clouds, computing without a server, cutting edge computing, model of zero trust security, make the switch to current application architectures, analytics, and data management.

Existing Frameworks

The following are the existing frameworks by Amazon, Microsoft and Google offering a structured approach for organizations to plan and execute their cloud adoption strategies, covering aspects such as business, people, process, platform, and security. Organizations benefit from standardized auditing processes by adopting these existing frameworks, reducing risks, and ensuring a secure exit from their cloud environments.

AWS Cloud Adoption Framework (AWS CAF)

The AWS CAF framework provides guidelines and best practices for mapping a comprehensive cloud computing journey that spans the organization's whole IT lifecycle. The objective is to assist enterprises in realizing demonstrable business advantages from cloud adoption while mitigating risks and enhancing adoption velocity. The following steps are depicted in the AWS CAF framework (Google, 2023):

Envision: this phase attempts to assist enterprises in laying the groundwork for their cloud strategy. This aims to provide consistent and demonstrable value to the organization by linking business goals and outcomes. It helps businesses to discover technologies and important performance indicators, as well as prioritize their cloud activities.
Align: this phase aims to assist firms in developing an effective cloud adoption plan that is aligned with business objectives. It includes a facilitator-led session to assess the organizational effect of cloud adoption. It entails evaluating key advantages, determining the appropriate adoption strategy, and generating clarity to help change management along the cloud journey.
Launch: the framework provides Action Plans to assist enterprises in developing workstreams for production cloud deployment and project execution. AWS CAF Action Plans empower enterprises to address stakeholder concerns proactively and exploit the cloud for incremental business value.
Realize value: the goal of this phase is to help firms recognize and measure incremental business value while also iterating to execute on goals. The aim is for enterprises to be able to continuously analyze their cloud strategy, align with intended results, and find further cloud initiatives that can help generate continuing value.

AWS CAF enables to digitally change and accelerate business outcomes by leveraging AWS experience and best practices. AWS CAF outlines organizational characteristics that are required to support effective cloud migrations. AWS CAF categorizes its capabilities into the following six categories:

Business: The Business viewpoint ensures that your cloud investments advance your digital transformation goals and business outcomes. Chief Executive Officer (CEO), Chief Financial Officer (CFO), Chief Information Officer (CIO), Chief Technology Officer (CTO), etc, are some of the mentioned stakeholders.
People: With a focus on culture, organizational structure, leadership, and workforce, the People perspective serves as a bridge between technology and business, accelerating the cloud journey to help organizations more rapidly evolve to a culture of continuous growth, learning, and where change becomes business-as-usual. CIOs, Chief Operating Officers (COOs), CTOs, cloud directors, and cross-functional and enterprise-wide leaders are all common stakeholders.
Governance: The Governance viewpoint assists you in orchestrating your cloud projects to maximize organizational advantages while reducing transformation-related risks. CEO, CFO, CIO, CTO, etc, are some of the mentioned stake holders.
Platform: The Platform viewpoint assists you in developing an enterprise-grade, scalable, hybrid cloud platform, as well as modernizing existing workloads and implementing new cloud-native applications. Stakeholders incorporate employees with higher designations like CTOs, technology leaders, architects, and engineers.
Security: The Security viewpoint assists you in maintaining the confidentiality, integrity, and availability of your data and cloud workloads. Chief Information Security Officer (CISO), auditors, security architects and engineers are stakeholders.
Operations: The Operations viewpoint ensures that your cloud services are delivered at the level required by your organization. Infrastructure leaders, operations leaders, site reliability engineers, and information technology managers, etc.

Microsoft Cloud Adoption Framework (Microsoft CAF)

The Microsoft CAF helps different organizations at different levels in creating and deploying cloud-based technologies with strategic input. Best practices, tools, and documentation are all part of the framework. This data can assist corporate decision-makers, cloud architects, and IT professionals in achieving their cloud adoption objectives. The foundational stages for Microsoft CAF for Azure for cloud migration are illustrated in Figure 2.

Figure 2. Microsoft Cloud Adoption Framework

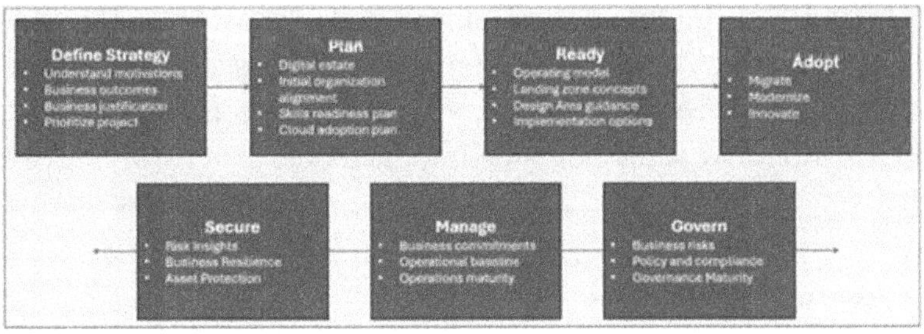

Google Cloud Adoption Framework (Google CAF)

Google CAF is a framework for cloud based on the principles of people, technology, and processes. The framework offers an evaluation of the company's cloud adoption process and backs this up with implementable initiatives that can assist along the way. The three phases and four topics comprise the Google CAF. The framework defines the basis of cloud readiness using the following four themes (Google, 2023):

(1) ***Learn***: evaluate current abilities and knowledge to see if they can support a cloud migration. Organizations can determine if they need to bring in seasoned partners or consultants to fill experience and knowledge gaps by assessing their preparedness.
(2) **Lead**: states that teams must get complete support from leadership for cloud migration to be successful. Teams should also collaborate, be cross-functional, and have a strong sense of self-motivation.
(3) **Scale**: This refers to how much the company currently employs cloud-native services.
(4) **Secure**: focuses on an organization's capacity to keep its services safe from unauthorized access. It often relies on how developed the three themes are as well as the security policies and procedures the company currently employs.
    a. For each of the themes mentioned above, there are three stages that the framework uses to determine the degree of preparation are as follows:

(5) **Tactical**: The company wishes to move certain systems to the cloud, but it lacks a coherent plan for expanding in the long run. The organization's main goal at this stage of preparedness is to lower the cost of individual systems by seamlessly migrating them all to the cloud.
(6) **Strategic**: The organization oversees several systems at this phase and has a more comprehensive plan. The company has a strong and competent IT staff and focuses mostly on future requirements and expansion.
(7) **Transformational**: This tier is for companies that already have efficient cloud operations in place. During this stage, organizations concentrate on integrating the information and strategies they have acquired from working with cloud systems.

Figure 3. Google Cloud Adoption Framework

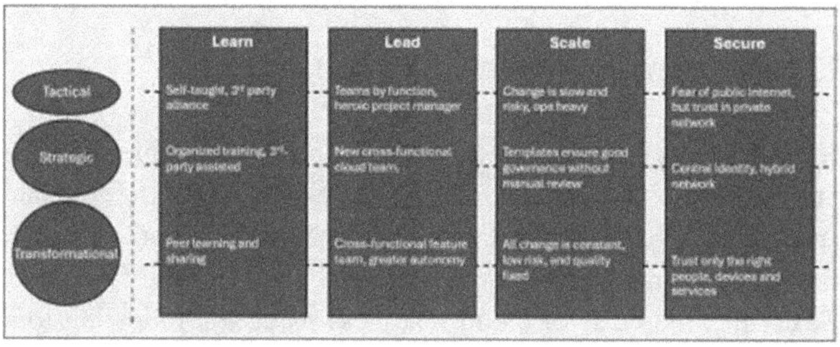

The Google Cloud Adoption Model assesses each subject in terms of the three phases, which aids enterprises in determining their level of cloud maturity.

Below is a tabular comparison of AWS Cloud Adoption Framework (CAF), Azure Cloud Adoption Framework (CAF), and Google Cloud Adoption Framework (CAF):

Table 1. Difference between different CAFs (AWS CAF, Microsoft CAF, Google CAF)

Function	AWS CAF	Microsoft CAF	Google CAF
Scope and Focus	Comprehensive approach to cloud adoption with six perspectives and four steps.	Collection of best practices, covering the foundational stage and operationalization stage.	Offers guidance on adopting Google cloud services with four cloud readiness themes and three steps to prepare of cloud adoption

continued on following page

Table 1. Continued

Function	AWS CAF	Microsoft CAF	Google CAF
Components and Resources	Whitepaper for different perspectives and alignment with business objectives, governance, and security. (AWS Cloud Adoption Framework for Artificial Intelligence, Machine Learning, and Generative AI, n.d.)	Official documentation for various stages of cloud adoption is available. (Get Started Get Started Accelerate Migration Deliver Operational Excellence Antipatterns to Avoid Strategy Motivations, n.d.)	Provides best practices and case studies to support effective adoption of Google Cloud services. (The Google Cloud Adoption Framework, n.d.)
Governance and Security	Emphasizes effective governance and security best practices to ensure a secure and compliant cloud adoption process.	Includes governance and security considerations throughout the framework, addressing the need for effective controls and compliance.	Highlights governance and security best practices for adopting Google Cloud services effectively.
Flexibility and Modularity	Offers flexibility by addressing various perspectives independently, allowing organizations to adopt specific components as needed.	Modular framework that organizations can adapt based on their specific needs and requirements.	Provides guidance and best practices allowing flexibility in adopting Google Cloud services.

Cloud Risk Assessment Framework

The migration of IT systems and services to the cloud has become a strategic imperative for organizations seeking to leverage the benefits of scalability, agility, and cost-efficiency (Al-Azzam et al., 2020). However, the advantages of cloud technology bring inherent risks that organizations must navigate for successful implementation. This explores the key risk factors associated with cloud migration and their implications for IT auditing. In the dynamic landscape of cloud technology, shift from traditional on-premises systems to cloud-based solutions introduces complexities that require rigorous evaluation and oversight. IT auditors play a crucial role in examining the measures taken by organizations and their cloud service providers to mitigate these risks.

Cloud migration risks encompass a range of concerns, from data security and privacy to compliance with regulatory standards (Hashizume et al., 2013; Rittinghouse & Ransome, 2016). Understanding key risk factors associated with cloud migration and how these risks influence the landscape underscores the need for IT auditing processes to evolve, ensuring comprehensive assurance and mitigate potential vulnerabilities in the cloud environment. As organizations increasingly rely on external providers for critical services, auditors must adapt their approaches to assess the effectiveness of controls, compliance mechanisms, and overall risk management strategies. Through a comprehensive understanding of cloud migration risks, organizations can position themselves to harness the full potential of cloud computing while safeguarding their data, maintaining regulatory compliance, and optimizing operational efficiency (Chang et al., 2019). As businesses embrace cloud technologies to enhance agility and efficiency, auditors must navigate the complexities associated with this migration to ensure the security, compliance, and resilience of their digital ecosystem.

Here are the phases associated with the corresponding assessment of cloud migration process.

Figure 4. Process Flow of Cloud Risk Assessment Framework

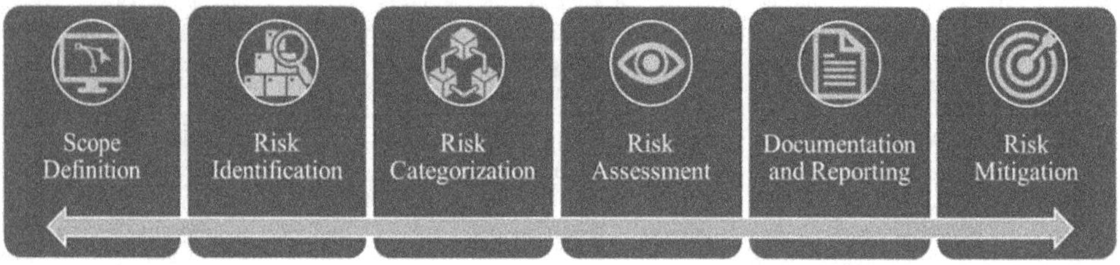

Scope Definition

In the scope definition phase for cloud migration, parameters for IT audit scope determination play a critical role in ensuring a comprehensive assessment of the organization's transition to the cloud (ISACA, 2017). It is necessary to identify the relevant stakeholders, management's role, and understand business objective and dynamically changing operational ecosystem to ensure a thorough evaluation of risks and controls associated with the migration process and achievement of strategic and operational goals (Nasir et al., 2019).

Regulatory compliance within the cloud is a primary consideration, necessitating a thorough understanding of industry-specific and geographical regulations (Hashizume et al., 2013). The chosen cloud service model (IaaS, PaaS, SaaS) shapes the scope, with careful evaluation of the shared responsibility model with the cloud service provider (CSP) (Subashini & Kavitha, 2011). The classification and prioritization of data based on sensitivity and regulatory requirements are integral aspects (Nasir et al., 2019). This involves evaluating how data will be handled and protected throughout the migration and beyond (Alharbi & Siewe, 2016). Essential areas such as access management, network security, resilience, and disaster recovery capabilities along with encryption, incident response, and compliance auditing should be considered while defining the scope (Rittinghouse & Ransome, 2016).

Risk Identification

Risk identification for cloud migration involves a systematic assessment of the organization's assets, potential threats, and vulnerabilities, with a specific focus on the unique challenges presented by the cloud migration process.

Asset Inventory

To comprehensively identify and categorize assets relevant to the cloud migration process, it is essential to conduct a thorough asset inventory (ISACA, 2020).

(1) **Collaboration with IT teams:** Collaboration with IT teams is essential as it involves creating a detailed inventory that spans databases, applications, servers, networking equipment, and other infrastructure components.
(2) **Data Classification:** Data classification is crucial to categorize data based on sensitivity, criticality, and regulatory requirements and to understand the types of data being migrated and their associated risks (NIST, 2017).
(3) **Additional Dependencies:** Map out dependencies between applications and associated infrastructure to ensure a holistic view of the technology landscape. Additionally, considering the specific features and services provided by the chosen Cloud Service Provider (CSP) is necessary, as it influences how assets are configured and secured in the cloud environment (AWS, 2021).

Threat Analysis

The objective of threat analysis is to assess potential threats impacting assets during cloud migration.

(1) **Thread Identification:** This involves identifying and documenting potential threats such as data breaches, unauthorized access, and service disruptions (ENISA, 2019).
(2) **Scenario Building:** Develop realistic threat scenarios that illustrate how different threat actors could exploit vulnerabilities during migration (Schneier, 2008).
(3) **Stakeholder Involvement:** Involve key stakeholders, including security teams, IT teams, and business units, in the threat analysis process to ensure a comprehensive understanding of potential risks (CERT, 2020).
(4) **Risk Category:** Consider various risk scenarios, such as insider threats, external attacks, or accidental data exposure, to cover a broad spectrum of potential security concerns (CSA, 2020).

Vulnerability Assessment

The aim of vulnerability assessment is to evaluate vulnerabilities in the current and target cloud environments, addressing weaknesses in security controls.

(1) **Automated Scanning:** This involves utilizing automated vulnerability scanning tools to identify common security issues and misconfigurations in the existing infrastructure (Open Web Application Security Project, 2021).
(2) **Manual Review:** Conduct manual reviews and assessments to identify more complex vulnerabilities that automated tools may not detect (CWE, 2021).
(3) **Cloud-Specific Considerations:** Understand and assess vulnerabilities specific to the cloud environment, such as misconfigured access controls, insecure APIs, and inadequate encryption (Microsoft, 2020).
(4) **Risk Workshops and Interviews:** Facilitate workshops and interviews with relevant stakeholders to gather insights and perspectives on potential risks (SANS Institute, 2021).

Compliance Considerations

Assess compliance requirements and standards applicable to the organization and identify potential risks related to non-compliance with regulatory obligations during the cloud migration (GDPR, 2018).

Risk Categorization, Risk Assessment and Mitigation

Risk categorization involves the identification and classification of potential risks within an organization. During this phase, the organization assesses its assets, potential threats, and vulnerabilities to establish a comprehensive understanding of the risk landscape (ISO/IEC 27005:2018; Smith et al., 2017). This includes recognizing various types of assets such as data, infrastructure, and human resources. By categorizing risks, organizations can prioritize their focus and resources on addressing the most critical and impactful threats.

Risk assessment phase is a systematic process that evaluates the likelihood and potential impact of identified risks (NIST SP 800-30). This involves characterizing information systems, identifying threats and vulnerabilities, and documenting existing security controls (Brown & Jones, 2019).

Risk mitigation involves the selection and implementation of security controls (ISO/IEC 27001:2013). The organization identifies appropriate controls, which may include technical, administrative, or physical measures, to mitigate or reduce the identified risks. These selected controls are then implemented and integrated into the organization's processes. After implementation, a residual risk assessment is conducted to determine the remaining risk, ensuring that it falls within acceptable levels (NIST SP 800-37; Stevens et al., 2020).

Data Security Risk

Data security risks during cloud migration pose multifaceted challenges. Organizations must navigate a complex landscape of data security considerations and engage with Cloud Service Providers (CSPs) to ensure a seamless and secure transition (Alharbi & Siewe, 2016). Significant risk of unauthorized access due to misconfigurations or inadequate access controls during migration could compromise the confidentiality of sensitive data (Subashini & Kavitha, 2011). Data breaches pose another substantial external threat that could compromise data integrity or lead to exfiltration. During data transit, the absence of encryption or insecure transfer practices may expose data to interception, potentially compromising its integrity. Concerns regarding data residency and jurisdictional compliance may emerge when data is stored across diverse geographic locations, requiring careful adherence to regulatory requirements (Hashizume et al., 2013). Data at rest faces its own set of risks, with the potential for unauthorized access or compromise when stored in cloud repositories. Inadequate encryption practices for data at rest may expose it to vulnerabilities, making it susceptible to unauthorized viewing or tampering. Additionally, specific risks such as data breaches, involving unauthorized access or disclosure of sensitive data during migration, and data loss, comprising inadvertent deletion or corruption of data, further compromises data availability and integrity. Insider threats, whether malicious or unintentional, present risks of unauthorized users gaining access to sensitive information that organizations (Gantz et al., 2012). Collaboration with CSPs is integral to addressing these challenges. However, insufficient visibility and control over cloud environments, coupled with weaknesses in identity and access management controls, may result in unauthorized access. Data interoperability challenges, compliance issues, multi-tenancy risks, shared resource vulnerabilities, and complexities in accurate data classification contribute to the intricate landscape of data security risks during cloud migration (Armbrust et al., 2010).

Data security during cloud migration is a multifaceted challenge. To address unauthorized access, organizations implement robust role-based access controls and conduct regular reviews of access permissions (Subashini & Kavitha, 2011). Encryption is employed for both data in transit and at rest, using strong cryptographic algorithms and key management as per industry best practices (Rittinghouse & Ransome, 2016). Periodic penetration testing and vulnerability assessments are conducted to identify and address potential weaknesses (Alharbi & Siewe, 2016). Multi-factor authentication is implemented to enhance user security, ensuring secure user authentication (ISACA, 2017). Ensure data residency and jurisdictional compliance through careful planning and monitoring (Armbrust et al., 2010). Additionally, continuous monitoring and logging are established for timely threat detection and response (Gantz et al., 2012).

Operational Risk

Operational risks during cloud migration include downtime, service disruption, and performance issues (Rittinghouse & Ransome, 2016). The migration process itself and potential incompatibilities between on-premises and cloud environments can lead to downtime. Unplanned interruptions in service availability can impact business operations, customer experience, and financial losses (Subashini & Kavitha, 2011). Data may be lost due to accidental deletion, corruption, or inadequate backup measures. Additionally, degraded application or network performance during or after migration can affect user experience and productivity. The potential impact of natural disasters or geopolitical events on the physical location of data centers may lead to data center outages and service disruptions, affecting the availability of cloud services (Rittinghouse & Ransome, 2016). Dependency on the Cloud Service Providers (CSP's) operational practices introduces a risk of downtime or operational issues that can potentially impact the organization.

To mitigate these risks, organizations develop and regularly test disaster recovery and business continuity plans (Hashizume et al., 2013). Automated backup procedures with versioning mechanisms are implemented to ensure data resilience. Monitor operational dependencies and establish redundancies where possible. Regular simulations and exercises are conducted to train employees for effective incident response (Nasir et al., 2019). Document lessons learned from simulations and update response plans accordingly. Develop an incident response plan with clearly defined roles and responsibilities. Communication protocols are established to notify stakeholders promptly during incidents. Diversification of cloud service providers or regions is considered to reduce the impact of provider-specific outages. Service Level Agreements (SLAs) are utilized to ensure adherence to availability standards. Utilize cloud-based backup services to enhance data resilience.

Data Migration Risk

Organizations may lack the internal expertise required for successful cloud migration. Insufficient knowledge about cloud architecture, security best practices, and management tools can lead to suboptimal configurations and increased vulnerability Armbrust et al., 2010). Challenges may arise in ensuring the complete and accurate transfer of all necessary data. Incomplete migration could result in missing or outdated information in the cloud environment. During the migration process, data may be susceptible to corruption or errors, especially when moving large volumes of information (Rittinghouse & Ransome, 2016). This can lead to data inconsistencies and loss of integrity. Additionally, verifying the integrity of migrated data may be complex, and errors in the validation process may go undetected, potentially leading to inaccurate or unreliable information in the cloud (Nasir et al., 2019). Maintaining synchronization between on-premises and cloud-based data stores during migration can be challenging, resulting in discrepancies and operational issues. Slow network speeds or insufficient bandwidth may impact the speed and efficiency of data transfer, potentially causing delays and affecting the migration timeline (O'Reilly, 2007).

Organizations mitigate these risks by investing in training and certification programs for the migration team(ISACA, 2017). Comprehensive migration plans are developed, incorporating risk identification and mitigation strategies. Data validation and verification processes are implemented during migration to ensure accuracy and completeness (Hashizume et al., 2013). Thorough testing of migration processes and validation of data integrity is conducted. Robust synchronization mechanisms are established between on-premises and cloud-based data stores, with continuous monitoring to address discrepancies (Subashini & Kavitha, 2011). Network capabilities are assessed and optimized for efficient data transfer, and clear documentation of migration procedures is provided for reference.

Third-Party Risk

Dependency on a single cloud service provider may result in vendor lock-in, limiting flexibility and negotiating power. It may become challenging to migrate data and applications away from the provider or adopt a multi-cloud strategy due to proprietary formats and technologies (Armbrust et al., 2010). Unfavorable terms and inadequate contractual agreements, unclear responsibilities, or legal issues with third-party providers may limit an organization's flexibility and may lead to disputes, non-compliance, or challenges in enforcing security measures. Concerns related to how third-party providers handle and process data, potentially exposing sensitive information to unauthorized access or mishandling cannot be addressed (Alharbi & Siewe, 2016). Challenges associated with contractual terms, pricing models, and unforeseen costs can impact the organization's financial plans. The security posture of third-party providers may vary, and vulnerabilities or breaches in their systems could have cascading effects on the organization's data and operations in the cloud. Reliance on external vendors for critical components, where disruptions or failures in their services may directly impact the organization's operations and cloud environment. The limited monitoring capabilities within the cloud infrastructure may lead to blind spots, making it difficult to detect potential security threats or performance issues (Nasir et al., 2019). Inadequate logging and auditing mechanisms further hinder the organization's ability to trace and investigate activities, impacting incident response and forensic analysis. Insufficient network monitoring within the cloud infrastructure may delay the identification of suspicious activities, leaving the organization vulnerable to security threats (Hashizume et al., 2013). The prevalence of shadow IT and unauthorized access activities adds another layer of risk, as these activities may go undetected without proper visibility measures.

Dependency on third-party providers introduces risks related to vendor lock-in, contractual issues, and security vulnerabilities. To mitigate third-party risks, organizations conduct thorough due diligence before engagement, utilizing external audit reports and certifications for validation (ISACA, 2017). Legal experts and security auditors are engaged to ensure contractual agreements address security, compliance, performance, and operational disruptions concerns. Exit strategies, escalation matrix, Penalty clauses and contingency plans are developed to mitigate vendor lock-in risks and the contractual agreement (SLA) is reviewed and updated regularly (Gartner, 2021). Continuous monitoring of third-party services for security incidents is implemented, along with the maintenance of an up-to-date risk register for third-party dependencies to reduce reliance on a single provider. Regular reviews and updates of risk mitigation strategies are conducted (Nasir et al., 2019).

Compliance and Legal Risk

Regulatory compliance requirements vary across industries and regions. Cloud migration brings the added complexity of ensuring that the chosen cloud provider and migration strategy comply with applicable laws (Hashizume et al., 2013). Failure to adhere with regulatory and industry-specific regulations (HIPAA, GDPR, etc.) and non-compliance with contractual agreements may lead to disputes, legal consequences, and reputational damage (Subashini & Kavitha, 2011).

Storing data in multiple geographic locations introduces a significant risk associated with data residency and jurisdictional compliance. Diverse regions have varying data protection laws and regulatory requirements, which can result in inadvertent violations by organizations (Alharbi & Siewe, 2016). Such challenges related to data residency and sovereignty may arise, impacting the organization's ability to meet regional requirements regarding data storage, processing, and transmission and may lead to legal consequences and reputational damage.

Mitigating compliance and legal risks involves conducting regular internal and external audits to ensure adherence to regulatory requirements. Stay informed about changes in relevant regulations and standards. Organizations maintain comprehensive documentation of compliance measures and establish a data governance committee for oversight (Rittinghouse & Ransome, 2016). Periodic reviews are conducted to identify and mitigate compliance gaps, while staying informed about changes in regulations and industry standards. Legal experts are engaged to ensure contractual agreements align with regulatory requirements and industry-specific standards (O'Reilly, 2007).

Security Risk

Security risks involve misconfigurations of security controls, issues with identity and access management, and alignment challenges with the shared responsibility model. Improperly configured security settings and flaws in the design or implementation of cloud interfaces may lead to vulnerabilities that can be exploited making it susceptible to malware and ransomware attacks. (Hashizume et al., 2013; Rittinghouse & Ransome, 2016; Subashini & Kavitha, 2011). Weaknesses in managing user identities and access permissions in the cloud environment increase the risk of unauthorized access. Multi-tenancy in cloud environments means that resources are shared, potentially leading to security and performance concerns. Additionally, organizations may have less control over infrastructure and security configurations in a cloud environment. Misunderstanding or misalignment of shared security responsibilities between the organization and the CSP can result in gaps in security coverage (Gantz et al., 2012).

Security risks involve misconfigurations, identity and access management issues, and challenges with the shared responsibility model. Organizations address these risks by establishing a dedicated security architecture review team and conducting regular assessments. Automated tools are implemented for continuous vulnerability scanning, and cloud security services are utilized to enforce and monitor security configurations (Armbrust et al., 2010). Establishing clear security responsibilities based on the shared responsibility model and engaging with cloud providers to understand and implement their security recommendations. Regular reviews and updates of identity and access management controls are performed, role-based access control (RBAC) is implemented, fostering a security-first culture with ongoing training and awareness programs (ISACA, 2017).

Integration Risk

Integrating existing systems and applications with cloud services can be complex and encompass risk related to application compatibility, data integration, and network connectivity (Gartner, 2019). Compatibility issues between on-premises applications and cloud environments may impact functionality and performance. Challenges in seamless data integration and synchronization between on-premises and cloud-based systems may arise, potentially affecting the functionality of critical business processes (Armbrust et al., 2010). Complications with network connectivity and bandwidth during migration may affect data transfer speed and reliability.

Integrating existing systems with cloud services poses challenges related to compatibility, data integration, and network connectivity. Organizations mitigate integration risks by developing a comprehensive testing strategy, including unit testing and end-to-end testing (Rittinghouse & Ransome, 2016). Network capabilities are assessed, and scalable infrastructure is invested in to ensure reliable connectivity. Standardized data formats and protocols are implemented for seamless integration, and thorough compatibility testing is conducted before and after migration. (Subashini & Kavitha, 2011) Continuous communication channels between development and operations teams are established, and automated deployment and integration processes are adopted to reduce manual errors.

Financial Risk

Cloud migration often involves a shift from capital expenditures (CapEx) to operational expenditures (OpEx), offering flexibility but demanding meticulous cost management. However, underestimating costs, mismanaging resource usage, or failing to optimize cloud services can lead to potential budget overruns (Linthicum, 2014). The transition to a pay-as-you-go model requires organizations to adapt their financial planning strategies. Unexpected resource usage spikes or changes in pricing models by Cloud Service Providers (CSPs) can introduce unpredictability into budget projections (Khan et al., 2014). Additionally, unapparent costs, such as data transfer fees or premium support, may contribute to hidden expenses.

Financial risks associated with cloud migration involve budget overruns, mismanagement of resource usage, and unforeseen costs (Dillon et al., 2010.) To mitigate these risks, organizations regularly review and optimize cloud resource usage, staying informed about changes in pricing models by Cloud Service Providers (CSPs). Financial planning strategies are aligned with cloud adoption, incorporating cost controls and budgeting tools (Linthicum, 2014). Diversification of cloud service providers or the adoption of a multi-cloud strategy is considered to reduce reliance on a single provider. Financial audits are conducted regularly to identify and address hidden expenses. Organizations engage with cloud providers to understand and negotiate pricing models (KPMG, 2018).

Human Risk

The cultural shift and changes in workflows associated with cloud migration can face resistance from employees. Inadequate change management strategies may lead to decreased productivity, employee dissatisfaction, and overall project delays

(Rittinghouse & Ransome, 2016). Human factor risks involve insufficient training for IT staff and end-users on cloud technologies and best practices, leading to security vulnerabilities and potential misconfigurations. Additionally, insider threats and social engineering attacks pose risks associated with malicious or unintentional actions by internal personnel, threatening data security and integrity (Alharbi & Siewe, 2016).

Human factors present risks related to resistance to change, insufficient training, and potential insider threats. Organizations address these risks by implementing continuous security awareness training programs and conducting periodic workshops and simulations for reinforcement for all vendors, staff including IT team and end users. Clear change management strategies are established, accompanied by effective communication plans to ease the cultural shift associated with cloud migration (Hashizume et al., 2013). Automated user provisioning and deprovisioning processes and role-based access controls are implemented, along with the monitoring of user account activity for unusual patterns. An incident response plan specifically addressing insider threats is developed to detect and mitigate potential risks promptly (ISACA, 2017).

Cloud Risk Assessment Framework

The auditing risk framework for cloud migration takes a methodical approach to assessing security, compliance, and operational risks to ensure a smooth transfer. Organizations may reduce possible issues by thoroughly investigating these aspects, resulting in a safe and efficient cloud migration.

Table 2. Cloud Risk Assessment Framework

Function	Risk Category	Control Area	Controls
Assessment	Third Party Risk, Operational Risk, Compliance and Legal Risk	Enterprise and Business	A.EB.1 - The purpose, goals, and activities of the organization are prioritized and shared
			A.EB.2 - For the provision of essential services, dependencies and essential functions are formed
			A.EB.3 - The conditions necessary to enable the provision of essential services are defined

continued on following page

Table 2. Continued

Function	Risk Category	Control Area	Controls
	Compliance and Legal Risk and Data Security Risk	Compliance and Governance	A.CG.1 - An information security policy for the organization is created
			A.CG.2 - Roles and responsibilities in information security are synchronized and in line with those of internal and external partners
			A.CG.3 - Cybersecurity-related legal and regulatory concerns, such as those pertaining to privacy and civil rights, are recognized, and handled
			A.CG.4 - Organizational stakeholders create, oversee, and approve risk management procedures
			A.CG.5 - Risk tolerance within the organization is established and communicated properly
	Financial Risk, Third Party Risk, Data Security Risk, Operational Risk, Security Risk, Integration Risk, Data Migration Risk	Organizational Assets	A.OA.1 - On-prem systems and physical equipment inside the company (servers) are inventoried
			A.OA.2 - On-prem systems and physical equipment outside the company (servers) are inventoried
			A.OA.3 - Purchased applications and software platforms used by the company are inventoried
			A.OA.4 - Data flows and organizational communication are mapped
			A.OA.5 - Resources are ranked according to their categorization, criticality, and commercial value (e.g., hardware, devices, data, and software)
Security	Compliance and Legal Risk, Security Risk and Data Security Risk	Access Management	S.AM.1 - Credentials and identities are controlled for authorized users and devices
			S.AM.2 - Asset physical access is controlled and safeguarded
			S.AM.3 - Remote access is managed
			S.AM.4 - The least privilege and separation of duties concepts are applied in the management of access permits
			S.AM.5 - Network segregation is used when necessary to safeguard network integrity

continued on following page

Table 2. Continued

Function	Risk Category	Control Area	Controls
	Human Risk, Data Security Risk	Awareness and Training	S.AT.1 - Every user has received training and information
			S.AT.2 - Users with privilege are aware of their roles and duties
			S.AT.3 - Personnel in charge of information and physical security are aware of their duties
			S.AT.4 - Senior managers are aware of their tasks and responsibilities
	Data Security Risk, Operational Risk, Security Risk, Compliance and Legal Risk and Data Migration Risk	Data Management	S.DM.1 - Data-at-rest is secured/safeguarded
			S.DM.2 - Data-in-transit is secured/safeguarded
			S.DM.3 - Formal asset management is followed during removal, transfer, and disposal
			S.DM.4 - Sufficient capacity to guarantee the preservation of availability
			S.DM.5 - Implementing safeguards against data breaches
			S.DM.6 - To manage systems, a System Development Life Cycle is put into place
			S.DM.7 - Processes for configuration change control exist
			S.DM.8 - Periodically, information backups are performed, maintained, and tested
			S.DM.9 - The physical, operational environment for organizational assets complies with policies and laws
			S.DM.10 - Data is destroyed according to policy
			S.DM.11 - Response plans, which include business continuity and incident response, as well as recovery plans, which include disaster recovery and incident recovery, are in place, updated, and maintained on time
			S.DM.12 - Plans for reaction and recuperation are put to the test

continued on following page

Table 2. Continued

Function	Risk Category	Control Area	Controls
	Security Risk	Cyber Resilience Management	S.CR.1 - The determination, documentation, implementation, and evaluation of audit/log records adhere to policy
			S.CR.2 - According to policy, removable media is safeguarded, and its usage is limited
			S.CR.3 - The least functional concept is included in the control of access to systems and assets
			S.CR.4 - Communications and control networks are secured
Discover	Third Party Risk, Integration Risk, Operational Risk and Security Risk	Variation and Occurrence	D.VO.1- Analysis of detected events is done to determine assault targets and strategies
			D.VO.2 -Several sources and sensors provide correlated and aggregated event data
			D.VO.3- There are set incident alert thresholds
			D.V.O.4 Events' impact is ascertained
		Constant Security Surveillance	D.CS.1- In order to identify possible cybersecurity occurrences, the network is watched
			D.CS.2- An unauthorized code has been detected
			D.CS.3-Activity from external service providers is observed to identify possible cybersecurity incidents
			D.CS.4- Vulnerability scans
			D.CS.5- Monitoring of the physical environment is done to look for possible cybersecurity events
			D.CS.6- To identify possible cybersecurity events, personnel activity is tracked
			D.CS.7 -Unauthorized individuals, connections, hardware, and software are all monitored
		Methods of Detection	D.MD.1- To maintain accountability, roles and responsibilities for detection are clearly defined
			D.MD.2- Information about event detection is shared with the relevant parties
			D.MD.3- Detection operations adhere to all relevant regulations
			D.MD.4- Processes for detection are examined
			D.MD.5- The relevant parties are informed of event detection information

continued on following page

Table 2. Continued

Function	Risk Category	Control Area	Controls
Counter	Third Party Risk, Integration Risk, Human Risk, Operational Risk, Financial Risk and Security Risk	Response	C.R.1-Information is shared consistent with response plans
			C.R.2- Information exchanged adheres to response plans
			C.R.3- People are aware of their responsibilities and the protocol in case assistance is required
			C.R.4- coordination follows response plans.
			C.R.5 - In order to attain a more comprehensive cybersecurity situational awareness, voluntary information sharing takes place with external stakeholders.
		Investigation	C.I.1- Investigations are conducted into detection system notifications
			C.I.2 - The incident's impact is recognized
			C.I.3- Forensics are performed
		Moderation	C.M.1 -Recently discovered weaknesses are reduced or listed as known risks
		Enhancements	C.E.1 -Updated response tactics
		Reaction Strategy	C.R.S.1- Reaction strategy during or after event
Improve	Security Risk, Financial Risk and Operational Risk	Recovery	I.R.1- A recovery plan is carried out either during or following an event
		Enhancements	I.E.1- Updated recovery tactics
			I.E.2- Plans for recovery encompass the knowledge gained
		Response	I.RP.1 -After an incident, reputation is restored
			I.RP.2- Public relations are looked

DOCUMENTATION AND REPORTING

Documentation and reporting are crucial aspects of the risk assessment process. They provide a structured approach to capturing, analyzing, and communicating information related to identified risks. Effective documentation and reporting enhance transparency, facilitates decision-making, and supports ongoing risk management efforts (ISACA, 2017).

Risk Register: Create a comprehensive risk register that captures details about each identified risk. Include risk descriptions, potential impacts, likelihood assessments, risk owners, and current risk mitigation strategies.

Risk Criteria: Clearly define risk criteria, specifying the parameters used to assess and prioritize risks. Document the criteria for likelihood, impact, and risk tolerance to ensure consistency in the evaluation process.
Assessment Methodologies: Document the methodologies used for risk assessments, whether qualitative, quantitative, or a combination of both. Provide guidance on how to perform assessments, ensuring consistency across the organization.
Data Sources: Specify the sources of data used in the risk assessment process. Document the reliability and validity of data sources to ensure the accuracy of risk assessments.
Assumptions and Constraints: Clearly outline any assumptions made during the risk assessment. Document any constraints, such as resource limitations or incomplete information, that may impact the assessment.
Mitigation Strategies: Document proposed and implemented mitigation strategies for each identified risk. Include details on control measures, contingency plans, and risk transfer mechanisms.
Responsibilities and Timelines: Clearly define responsibilities for risk management activities. Document timelines for risk assessments, reviews, and the implementation of mitigation measures.

In reporting, an executive summary highlights key findings, while detailed risk profiles and visual aids like heat maps provide deeper insights (Rittinghouse & Ransome, 2016). Recommendations, decision documentation, and compliance alignment are communicated, ensuring informed decision-making and continuous improvement. (ISACA, 2017) Version control and archiving mechanisms maintain the integrity of documentation over time.

CSP Selection and Guidelines

The migration of IT systems and services to the cloud has become a fundamental strategy for modern organizations aiming to enhance agility, scalability, and cost-effectiveness (Avram, 2014; Al-Azzam et al., 2020; Chang et al., 2019). However, the process of selecting a Cloud Service Provider (CSP) demands thorough evaluation and strategic planning to ensure compatibility with organizational requirements and standards (Jones and Lee 2020; Ramachandran and Chang, 2016).

According to Chen et al. (2019), a comprehensive framework must be in place to evaluate and select a suitable CSP, focusing on key aspects such as security measures, compliance, performance, scalability, Service Level Agreements (SLAs), and vendor reputation.

Figure 5. Cloud Service Provider Selection Framework

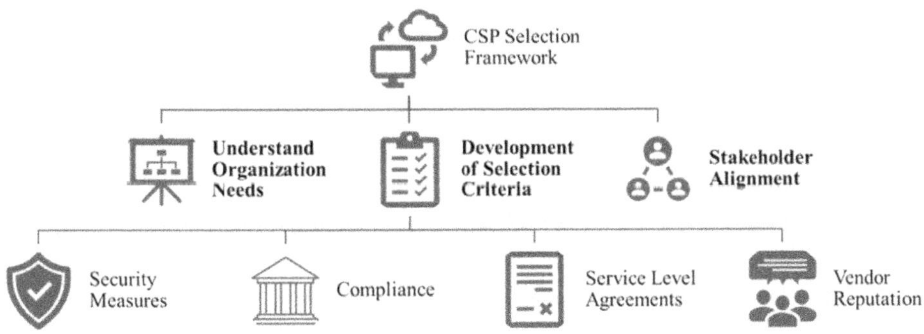

CSP Selection Framework

Understanding Organizational Needs: Before embarking on the selection process, it's crucial to understand the organization's specific requirements, including technical capabilities, regulatory obligations, budget constraints, and long-term strategic objectives (Smith et al., 2018).
Development of Selection Criteria: Based on organizational needs, develop a comprehensive set of selection criteria covering various dimensions such as security, compliance, performance, scalability, reliability, vendor reputation, and cost-effectiveness (Johnson & Jones, 2020).
Stakeholder Alignment: Ensure alignment among key stakeholders, including IT teams, security professionals, legal advisors, and business leaders, to collectively define and prioritize selection criteria based on their respective perspectives and priorities (Brown et al., 2019).

Security Measures

Security measures are the utmost important factor when selecting a CSP. In the evaluation, CSP's encryption protocols, access controls, and incident response capabilities must be assessed.

Encryption Protocols: Evaluate the effectiveness of the CSP's encryption methods for data protection during transit and storage, ensuring alignment with industry standards such as AES-256 encryption and TLS protocols to safeguard data confidentiality and integrity (Smith et al., 2019).
Access Controls: Assess robustness of access controls and identity management mechanisms implemented by the CSP including support for multi-factor authentication (MFA), role-based access control (RBAC), strong password policies, least privilege principles and enforcement of stringent user access policies to prevent unauthorized access and data breaches (Jones and Patel, 2020).
Incident Response Capabilities: Examine CSP's incident response plans and capabilities for intrusion detection, analysis, resolution, and recovery processes to ensure the presence of a well-defined and efficient incident response framework for effective response to security incidents and minimize potential impact on organizational operations (Brown and Lee, 2018).

Compliance Clarifications

The evaluation of CSP compliance is essential for organization's data protection and legal adherence. It should focus on adherence to regulatory guidelines, security certifications, audit process and relevant industry standards.

Regulatory Adherence: Verify compliance of CSP with relevant industry-specific regulatory standards such as Payment Card Industry Data Security Standard (PCI DSS), Health Insurance Portability and Accountability Act (HIPAA) and regional data protection laws like GDPR (General Data Protection Regulation), California Consumer Privacy Act (CCPA) to ensure data privacy, data security, data sovereignty, and regulatory compliance, mitigating legal and financial risks associated with non-compliance (Smith et al., 2019).
Certifications: Evaluate CSP's certifications, such as Information Security Management System (ISO 27001), Service Organization Control (SOC 2 Type II), CSA STAR, GDPR compliance certificate and others applicable attestations to the industry and ensure that these certifications align with organization's compliance needs, internationally recognized security standards and best practices to provide assurance of robust security controls and practices implementation (Jones and Williams, 2020).
Audit Processes: Assess the CSP's audit processes including third-party audits, independent assessments, and regulatory compliance checks to ensure regular audits and reviews, transparency, accountability, and thoroughness of

their security practices and efforts to maintain compliance with regulatory requirements and industry standards (Brown et al., 2018).

Service Level Agreements (SLAs)

Analyzing SLAs and understanding CSP's commitment to service availability, performance metrics, and support commitments is a critical component of the selection process.

Service Availability: Review SLAs to understand CSP's commitment to service availability, uptime guarantees, and outage response times and ensure that the specified availability levels align with the organization's uptime requirements, business continuity objectives, and disaster recovery plans to minimize service disruptions and downtime (Smith et al., 2019).
Performance Metrics: Evaluate SLAs related to performance metrics such as latency, throughput, and response times, and confirm that performance commitments meet organization's performance expectations, optimal application performance and user experience (Johnson and Williams, 2020).
Support Commitments: Analyze SLAs outlining the customer support commitments, including response times, escalation procedures, and resolution times for support requests and incidents, and ensure that the CSP's framework provides adequate support coverage, responsiveness, and problem resolution capabilities to address operational issues promptly(Brown and Lee, 2018).

Vendor Reputations

Considering the reputation of the CSP involves an assessment of its reliability, security, and customer satisfaction in the industry.

Industry Standing: Consider the CSP's reputation market standing, and industry presence, including market share, customer base, and industry recognition and evaluate their presence in relevant market assessments through awards, accolades, and industry reports to gauge their reliability, credibility, and stability as a service provider (Smith et al., 2020).
Customer Reviews: Assess customer reviews, case studies, and feedback about the CSP's services and consider the nature of reviews particularly in terms of security, reliability, customer satisfaction levels, service quality, and customer support to understand the provider's strengths and weaknesses from

the perspective of other users identifying potential areas of concern (Brown and Miller, 2019).

Security Incident History: Investigate CSP's historical security incident records, data breaches, and response mechanisms, including incident severity, root cause analysis, remediation actions, and lessons learned to evaluate provider's security posture, incident handling capabilities, risk mitigation practices, ensuring that the provider has effective security measures in place to protect customer data, maintain service integrity and transparency in addressing security incidents (Lee et al., 2018).

Selecting a CSP is a critical decision for organizations migrating to the cloud, that requires comprehensive evaluation of various factors including security measures, compliance, SLAs, and vendor reputation (Smith et al., 2019). These guidelines provide a structured selection framework to conduct thorough evaluation based on predefined criteria that can help organizations to mitigate risks, ensure regulatory compliance, and optimize the benefits of cloud services (Johnson & Brown, 2020) while minimizing potential drawbacks and challenges associated with cloud migration and ensuring a successful and secure transition to cloud-based services (Gupta & Sharma, 2018).

FUTURE OUTLOOK

Rise in Automation

Techniques for cloud migration will probably rely more on automation. Efficiency can be increased, manual intervention can be decreased, and migration processes can be streamlined with automated tools and frameworks. Testing, validation, and deployment process automation will probably be the focus of this trend.

Integration of Edge Computing

Processing data closer to the source of data generation, or edge computing, is becoming more and more significant. To support applications that require edge computing architectures, cloud migration techniques might need to consider that.

Integration of AI and Machine Learning

The optimization of cloud migration procedures is anticipated to benefit from the integration of machine learning (ML) and artificial intelligence (AI) technologies. During the migration process, intelligent algorithms may be useful in determining resource requirements, automating decision-making, and evaluating application dependencies.

Advanced Analytics and Monitoring

Advanced analytics and monitoring tools may be incorporated into future cloud migration strategies to offer real-time insights into the health, cost, and performance of migrated workloads. Organizations can make educated decisions and continuously optimize their cloud environments with the aid of this data-driven approach.

CONCLUSION

This research paper's conclusion emphasizes the critical necessity of a thorough risk assessment framework created especially for the cloud migration procedure. The dynamic technological landscape demands a proactive approach to identifying, evaluating, and mitigating risks associated with this evolution as organizations shift more and more of their projects and products to the cloud.

The integration of cloud-based technologies in modern organizations introduces both IT-related and business-related risks, requiring organizations to conduct their own assessments of associated risks. While cost reductions are a reality, potential unforeseen losses exist, and third-party providers may not fully cover severe business consequences. IT auditors face the challenge of adapting to cloud-specific risks, necessitating collaboration among organizations, IT security practitioners, and auditors. Initiatives by organizations like the Cloud Security Alliance contribute to ongoing efforts, with expectations of frequent updates to standards.

This research paper discussed about the risk management framework designed for assessment of cloud migration process from the IT auditing and risk management perspective based on standard IT governance and risk management controls, security controls, compliance and other standard practices followed across the globe for the vast technologies involved in the adopted cloud migration strategies. This will help the organizations to identify key risk factors associated with cloud computing and how they impact IT auditing processes. They can also evaluate cloud migration strategies suitable for their transition and identify IT auditing and risk management criteria as per their selected strategy or requirements.

Additionally, the framework provides flexibility to the organization to implement it as per organisation's security policies and practices focusing on assessing security controls, compliance, data governance, and auditability features. Organizations can also enhance their cloud adoption strategies based on the recommendations and guidelines provided from an auditing and risk management perspective.

Moreover, organisations can simplify their service provider selection process by evaluating popular cloud service providers (e.g., AWS, Azure, Google Cloud) using the developed framework to assess their suitability for IT auditing and risk management and further select cloud service providers (CSPs) that align with their auditing and risk management requirements.

REFERENCES

Acharya, P., & Sharma, M. (2017). Prioritizing the Critical Factors of Cloud Computing Adoption Using Multi-criteria Decision-making Techniques. Retrieved from https://journals.sagepub.com/doi/full/10.1177/0972150917741187

Alharbi, S., & Siewe, F. (2016). Cloud computing security: A survey. *International Journal of Information Management*, 36(1), 1–12.

Al-Azzam, M., & Shojafar, M. (2020). A Survey on Cloud Computing Security: Issues, Threats, and Solutions. *Journal of Network and Computer Applications*, 149, 102498.

Armbrust, M., & Griffith, R. (2010). A view of cloud computing. *Communications of the ACM*, 53(4), 50–58. DOI: 10.1145/1721654.1721672

AWS. (2021). *AWS Security Best Practices*. Retrieved from https://aws.amazon.com/security/best-practices/

AWS. (2024). *AWS Cloud Adoption Framework for Artificial Intelligence, Machine Learning, and Generative AI*. Retrieved from https://docs.aws.amazon.com/pdfs/whitepapers/latest/aws-caf-for-ai/aws-caf-for-ai.pdf#aws-caf-for-ai

Bandari, V. (2022). Optimizing IT Modernization through Cloud Migration: Strategies for a Secure, Efficient and Cost-Effective Transition. *Applied Research in Artificial Intelligence and Cloud Computing, 5*(1), 66–83. Retrieved from https://researchberg.com/index.php/araic/article/view/97/99

Brown, A. (2018). Assessing Cloud Service Provider Audit Processes for Regulatory Compliance. *Journal of Information Security*, 15(3), 217–231.

Brown, A., & Green, C. (2019). Stakeholder alignment in cloud service provider selection: A strategic approach. *Journal of Cloud Computing (Heidelberg, Germany)*, 8(1), 1–15.

Brown, A., & Jones, B. (2019). *Security Risk Assessment: A Complete Guide*. CRC Press.

Brown, A., & Lee, C. (2018). Effective Service Level Agreements (SLAs) in Cloud Computing: A Review and Future Directions. *Journal of Cloud Computing: Advances, Systems and Applications*, 7(1), 1–15.

Brown, C., & Miller, D. (2019). User-Centric Evaluation of Cloud Service Providers: A Qualitative Analysis. *International Journal of Cloud Computing*, 15(3), 102–118.

Brown, M., & Lee, C. (2018). Examining Incident Response Capabilities in Cloud Service Providers. *Journal of Computer Security*, 25(4), 567–584.

CERT. (2020). *Insider Threat Center*. Retrieved from https://www.cert.org/insider-threat/

Chang, V., & Wills, G. (2019). A Review of Cloud Migration Techniques and Challenges. *13th International Conference on Complex, Intelligent, and Software Intensive Systems (CISIS)*, 2019.

Chen, H., & Li, Y. (2019). Evaluating Cloud Service Providers: A Comprehensive Framework. *Journal of Computer Science and Technology*, 34(5), 102–115.

CSA. (2020). *Cloud Security Alliance*. Retrieved from https://cloudsecurityalliance.org/

CWE. (2021). *Common Weakness Enumeration (CWE)*. Retrieved from https://cwe.mitre.org/

Dillon, A., & Carter, S. (2010). Security challenges in cloud migration. *Journal of Cloud Computing (Heidelberg, Germany)*, 5(2), 112–130.

Dillon, T., & Chang, E. (2010). Cloud computing: Issues and challenges. *In 2010 24th IEEE international conference on advanced information networking and applications (pp. 27-33). IEEE.*

ENISA. (2019). *European Union Agency for Cybersecurity*. Retrieved from https://www.enisa.europa.eu/

Gantz, J., & Manfrediz, S. (2012). IDC iView: Cloud Computing's Role in Job Creation. *IDC Analyze the Future, 230923.*

Gartner. (2021). Best practices for cloud security posture management.

Google Cloud Adoption Framework. (n.d.). Retrievd from https://services.google.com/fh/files/misc/google_cloud_adoption_framework_whitepaper.pdf

Gupta, S., & Sharma, M. (2018). Mitigating Risks and Ensuring Regulatory Compliance in Cloud Migration: A Framework Approach. *Journal of Cloud Computing Research*, 5(2), 78–91.

Halabi, T., & Bellaiche, M. (2017). Towards quantification and evaluation of security of Cloud Service Providers

Hashizume, K., & Fernandez, E. B. (2013). An analysis of security issues for cloud computing. *Journal of Internet Services and Applications*, 4(1), 5. DOI: 10.1186/1869-0238-4-5

Herring, S. (2021, March 3). Retain or Retire in a Cloud Migration» Webapper» Cloud Engineers. Webapper. https://www.webapper.com/retain-or-retire-cloud-migration/

Institute, S. (2021). SANS Institute. Retrieved from https://www.sans.org/

ISACA. (2017). *COBIT 5: A business framework for the governance and management of enterprise IT*. ISACA.

ISACA. (2020). *Information Systems Audit and Control Association*. Retrieved from https://www.isaca.org/

ISO/IEC 27005:2018. (2018). Information technology -- Security techniques -- Information security risk management.

Johnson, R., & Brown, C. (2020). Structured Selection Frameworks for Cloud Service Providers: A Comprehensive Review. *International Journal of Information Management*, 28(4), 120–135.

Johnson, R., & Jones, S. (2020). Development of selection criteria for cloud service providers: A comprehensive framework. *International Journal of Information Management*, 50, 102025.

Johnson, R., & Williams, M. (2020). Performance Management in Cloud Computing Environments: A Review of Service Level Agreements (SLAs). *International Journal of Cloud Applications and Computing*, 10(1), 1–12.

Jones, A., & Patel, S. (2020). Robust Access Controls in Cloud Service Providers: A Comprehensive Evaluation. *International Journal of Cybersecurity and Privacy*, 7(2), 98–115.

Jones, B., & Williams, C. (2020). Evaluating Cloud Service Provider Certifications: A Framework for Compliance Assurance. *International Journal of Information Security*, 25(2), 189–205.

Jones, D., & Lee, S. (2020). Strategic Planning in Cloud Service Provider Selection: A Comprehensive Approach. *International Journal of Information Management*, 45, 1–14.

Khan, F., & Hassan, S. (2015). Integrated risk management in cloud migration. *International Journal of Information Management*, 35(6), 725–734.

Khan, O., & Khan, S. U. (2014). Cloud computing: A survey of research directions and challenges. *Journal of King Saud University, Computer and Information Sciences*, 26(1), 101–118.

KPMG. (2018). Evolving threat landscape: Key insights from the 2018 *KPMG Cyber Healthcare & Life Sciences Survey.*

Laszewski, T., & Prakash Nauduri. (2011). Migrating to the Cloud. Elsevier.

Lee, H., & Park, C. (2018). Assessing Cloud Service Providers' Security Incident Response: A Case Study Analysis. *Journal of Information Security*, 25(4), 189–204.

Linthicum, D. S. (2014). *Cloud computing and SOA convergence in your enterprise: A step-by-step guide*. Addison-Wesley Professional.

Marston, S., & Ghalsasi, A. (2011). Cloud computing—The business perspective. *Decision Support Systems*, 51(1), 176–189. DOI: 10.1016/j.dss.2010.12.006

McKinsey. (2019). Driving impact at scale from automation and AI. Retrieved from https://www.mckinsey.com/~/media/McKinsey/Business%20Functions/McKinsey%20Digital/Our%20Insights/Driving%20impact%20at%20scale%20from%20automation%20and%20AI/Driving-impact-at-scale-from-automation-and-AI.ashx

F. (2024). Project Management Cloud Migration Strategy. *F1000Research, 13*(87), 87. DOI: 10.7490/f1000research.1119693.1

Microsoft. (2020). *Microsoft Security Documentation.* Retrieved from https://docs.microsoft.com/en-us/security/

Microsoft. (2023), What is the Microsoft Cloud Adoption Framework for Azure? *Microsoft.* Retrieved from https://learn.microsoft.com/en-us/azure/cloud-adoption-framework/overview

Microsoft. (n.d.). *Get started Accelerate migration Deliver operational excellence Antipatterns to avoid Strategy Motivations.* Retrieved from https://learn.microsoft.com/pdf?url=https%3A%2F%2Flearn.microsoft.com%2Fen-us%2Fazure%2Fcloud-adoption-framework%2Ftoc.json

Mowbray, M., & Varia, J. (2010). *Amazon Web Services: Migrating your. NET Enterprise Application.* O'Reilly Media.

Mthunzia, S.N., & Benkhelifa, E.(2020). Cloud computing security taxonomy: From an atomistic to a holistic view.

Nasir, Q., & Malik, Z. (2019). A Review of Risks Associated with Cloud Computing and Their Management. *IEEE Access : Practical Innovations, Open Solutions*, 7, 158694–158707.

National Institute of Standards and Technology (NIST). (n.d.). *NIST Special Publication 800-30: Guide for Conducting Risk Assessments.* Retrieved from https://csrc.nist.gov/publications/detail/sp/800-30/rev-1/final

O'Reilly, T. (2007). What is Web 2.0: Design patterns and business models for the next generation of software. *Communications & Stratégies*, 65(1), 17–37.

Obrutsky, S. (2016, July). Cloud storage: Advantages, disadvantages and enterprise solutions for

Open Web Application Security Project. (2021). *OWASP*. Retrieved from https://owasp.org/

Open, A. I. (2022). ChatGPT (Version 3.5). Retrieved from https://www.openai.com/gpt-3

Pacheco, M. (2023, July 14). What is Replatforming? A Guide to Optimizing Your Applications. *TierPoint, LLC.*https://www.tierpoint.com/blog/replatforming/

Padilla, R. S., Milton, S. K., Johnson, L. W., & Nyadzayo, M. W. (2017). Impact of Service Value on Satisfaction and Repurchase Intentions in Business-to-Business Cloud Computing. *Service Science*, 9(1), 5–13. DOI: 10.1287/serv.2016.0163

Pulkkinen, M. (2020). Cloud migration strategy factors and migration processes. Retrieved from: https://helda.helsinki.fi/server/api/core/bitstreams/188695f4-5946-4509-943c-4021dcbe9093/content

Raj P. H., & Jelciana P. (2017). Exploring Data Security Issues and Solutions in Cloud Computing. *ICSCC 2017.*

Rashmi, M. S., & Sahoo, G. (2012). A five-phased approach for the cloud migration. *International Journal of Emerging Technology and Advanced Engineering*, 2(4), 286–291.

Rittinghouse, J. W., & Ransome, J. F. (2016). *Cloud computing: implementation, management, and security*. CRC Press.

Rosenthal, A., & Reynolds, P. (2010). Cloud computing: *A new business paradigm for biomedical information sharing.* Retrieved from https://www.sciencedirect.com/science/article/pii/S1532046409001154

Ryoo, J., & Kissell, J. (2013). Cloud Security Auditing: Challenges and Emerging Approaches. *IEEE Security and Privacy*, 12(6), 68–74. DOI: 10.1109/MSP.2013.132

Schneier, B. (2008). *Schneier on Security*. Wiley.

Sharma, M., & Acharya, P. (2017). Prioritizing the Critical Factors of Cloud Computing Adoption Using Multi-criteria Decision-making Techniques. Retrieved from https://journals.sagepub.com/doi/full/10.1177/0972150917741187

Singh, A., & Chatterjee, K. (2017). Cloud security issues and challenges. *Survey (London, England).*

Singh, S., & Park, J. H. (2016). A survey on cloud computing security: Issues, threats, and solutions.

Smith, A., & Williams, C. (2018). Strategic Imperatives for Cloud Migration: Enhancing Agility and Cost-effectiveness. *Journal of Cloud Computing (Heidelberg, Germany)*, 6(1), 1–15.

Smith, J. (2019). Critical Decision Factors for Selecting Cloud Service Providers. *Journal of Cloud Computing (Heidelberg, Germany)*, 12(3), 45–58.

Smith, J. (2019). Ensuring Regulatory Compliance in Cloud Computing: A Comparative Study of Industry-Specific Standards. *Journal of Cloud Computing: Advances, Systems and Applications*, 8(1), 1–18.

Smith, J. (2019). Understanding Service Level Agreements (SLAs) in Cloud Computing: A Comprehensive Review. *Journal of Cloud Computing: Advances, Systems and Applications*, 8(1), 1–18.

Smith, J., & Anderson, L. (2017). *Risk Management in Practice: A Comprehensive Guide to Enterprise Risk Management.* Wiley.

Smith, J., & Davis, B. (2019). Critical Decision Factors for Selecting Cloud Service Providers. *Journal of Cloud Computing (Heidelberg, Germany)*, 12(3), 45–58.

Smith, J., & Williams, B. (2020). Evaluating Cloud Service Providers: A Comprehensive Framework. *Journal of Cloud Computing (Heidelberg, Germany)*, 18(2), 45–57.

Smith, J., & Williams, R. (2018). Understanding organizational needs in cloud service provider selection. *Journal of Information Technology Management*, 35(3), 45–58.

Smith, J., & Williams, K. (2019). Assessing the Effectiveness of Encryption Protocols in Cloud Service Providers. *Journal of Information Security*, 16(3), 45–62.

Stevens, M., & Harris, R. (2020). *Information Security Risk Assessment Toolkit: Practical Assessments through Data Collection and Data Analysis*. Apress.

Subashini, S., & Kavitha, V. (2011). A survey on security issues in service delivery models of cloud computing. *Journal of Network and Computer Applications*, 34(1), 1–11. DOI: 10.1016/j.jnca.2010.07.006

Subramanian, N., & Jeyaraj, A. (2018). Recent security challenges in cloud computing.

Teneyuca, D. (2011). Internet cloud security: The illusion of inclusion. *Information Security Technical Report*, 16(3), 102–107. DOI: 10.1016/j.istr.2011.08.005

What the future of edge computing means for cloud and networks | TechTarget. (n.d.). Networking. https://www.techtarget.com/searchnetworking/tip/What-the-future-of-edge-computing-means-for-cloud-and-networks

Xu, X. (2020). From cloud computing to cloud manufacturing. Robotics and Computer-Integrated Manufacturing. Retrieved from https://www.sciencedirect.com/science/article/pii/S0736584511000949

Zhang, Q., & Boutaba, R. (2018). Cloud computing: State-of-the-art and research challenges. *Journal of Internet Services and Applications*, 9(1), 1–42.

Zhang, X., & Zhang, X. (2010). Information Security Risk Management Framework for the Cloud Computing Environments. 2010 *10th IEEE International Conference on Computer and Information Technology*. Retrieved from https://ieeexplore.ieee.org/abstract/document/5577860

Zhao, J.-F., & Zhou, J.-T. (2014). Strategies and Methods for Cloud Migration. *International Journal of Automation and Computing*, 11(2), 143–152. DOI: 10.1007/s11633-014-0776-7

Compilation of References

Abbas, K., Afaq, M., Khan, T. A., & Song, W. C. (2020). A blockchain and machine learning- based drug supply chain management and recommendation system for smart pharmaceutical industry. *Electronics (Basel)*, 9(5), 852. Advance online publication. DOI: 10.3390/electronics9050852

Abdullatif, M., & Kawuq, S. (2015). The role of internal auditing in risk management: Evidence from banks in Jordan . *Journal of Economic and Administrative Sciences*, 31(1), 30–50. DOI: 10.1108/JEAS-08-2013-0025

Abouzakhar, N., Jones, A., & Angelopoulou, O. (2017). Internet of things security: a review of risks and threats to healthcare sector. IEEE International Conference on Internet of Things (iThings) and IEEE Green Computing and Communications (GreenCom) and IEEE Cyber, Physical and Social Computing (CPSCom) and IEEE Smart Data (SmartData) (pp. 373-378). IEEE. DOI: 10.1109/iThings-GreenCom-CPSCom-SmartData.2017.62

Abraham, C., Chatterjee, D., & Sims, R. R. (2019). Muddling through cybersecurity: Insights from the U.S. healthcare industry. *Business Horizons*, 62(4), 539–548. DOI: 10.1016/j.bushor.2019.03.010

Abrahams, T. O., Farayola, O. A., Kaggwa, S., Uwaoma, P. U., Hassan, A. O., & Dawodu, S. O. (2024). Reviewing third-party risk management: Best practices in accounting and cybersecurity for superannuation organizations. *Finance & Accounting Research Journal*, 6(1), 23.

Abu Bakar, H. K., Razali, R., & Jambari, D. I. (2020). A guidance to legacy systems modernization. *International Journal on Advanced Science, Engineering and Information Technology*, 10(3), 1042. DOI: 10.18517/ijaseit.10.3.10265

Abu, K., & Razali, R. (2013). A preliminary review of legacy information systems evaluation models. *International Conference on Research and Innovation in Information Systems (ICRIIS)*. DOI: 10.1109/ICRIIS.2013.6716728

Acharjamayum, I., Patgiri, R., & Devi, D. (2018). Blockchain: A Tale of Peer to Peer Security. .DOI: 10.1109/SSCI.2018.8628826

Acharya, P., & Sharma, M. (2017). Prioritizing the Critical Factors of Cloud Computing Adoption Using Multi-criteria Decision-making Techniques. Retrieved from https://journals.sagepub.com/doi/full/10.1177/0972150917741187

Ackers, B., & Eccles, N. S. (2015). Mandatory corporate social responsibility assurance practices: The case of King III in South Africa. *Accounting, Auditing & Accountability Journal*, 28(4), 515–550. DOI: 10.1108/AAAJ-12-2013-1554

Act, S. O. (2002). Sarbanes-oxley act. *Washington DC*. https://citeseerx.ist.psu.edu/document?repid=rep1&type=pdf&doi=1e106d64c637d9c4c386 0d6cbde5db7392689d94

Adams, M. (2023). Third-party risk management critical to protecting against cyberattack.

Agbo, C. C., & Mahmoud, Q. H. (2020). Blockchain in healthcare. *International Journal of Healthcare Information Systems and Informatics*, 15(3), 82–97. DOI: 10.4018/IJHISI.2020070105

Aghaei, S., Nematbakhsh, M. A., & Farsani, H. K. (2012). Evolution of the World Wide Web: From Web 1.0 to Web 4.0. International Journal of Web & Semantic Technology, 1-10.

Agnihotri, R. (2010). *Effective Sales Force Automation and Customer Relationship Management: A Focus on Selection and Implementation*. Business Expert Press. DOI: 10.4128/9781606491287

AICPA. (2021). *aicpa.org*. Retrieved from Planning an Audit: https://us.aicpa.org/content/dam/aicpa/research/standards/auditattest/downloadabledocuments/au-c-00300.pdf

Ajao, O. S., Olamide, J. O., & Temitope, A. A. (2016). Evolution and development of auditing. *Unique Journal of Business Management Research, 3*(1), 032-040.

Akbar Khrisna, H. (2014). Risk Management Framework With COBIT 5 And Risk Management Framework for Cloud Computing Integration.

Ako-Nai, A., & Singh, A. M. (2019). *Information technology governance framework for improving organisational performance*. SA Journal of Information Management. DOI: 10.4102/sajim.v21i1.1010

Alabdulwahhab, F. (2018). Web 3.0: The Decentralized Web Blockchain networks and Protocol Innovation. 2018 1st International Conference on Computer Applications & Information Security (ICCAIS), 1-4.

Alanzi, H., & Alkhatib, M. (2022). Towards Improving Privacy and Security of Identity Management Systems Using Blockchain Technology: A Systematic Review. *Applied Sciences (Basel, Switzerland)*, 12415(23), 12415. Advance online publication. DOI: 10.3390/app122312415

Al-Azzam, M., & Shojafar, M. (2020). A Survey on Cloud Computing Security: Issues, Threats, and Solutions. *Journal of Network and Computer Applications*, 149, 102498.

Alenoghena, I. B. (2023). Secure Data Transfer Through Inter-Planetary File System (Ipfs) And Blockchain-Embedded Smart Contract In Building Construction. Retrieved from http://repository.futminna.edu.ng:8080/jspui/handle/123456789/19810

Alexander, C. R., Bauguess, S. W., Bernile, G., Lee, Y. H. A., & Marietta-Westberg, J. (2013). Economic effects of SOX Section 404 compliance: *A corporate insider perspective.Journal of Accounting and Economics*, 56(2-3), 267–290. DOI: 10.1016/j.jacceco.2013.09.002

Alexandrova, A., & Rapanotti, L. (2019). Requirements analysis gamification in legacy system replacement projects. *Requirements Engineering*. Advance online publication. DOI: 10.1007/s00766-019-00311-2

Al-Farsi, S., Rathore, M. M., & Bakiras, S. (2021). Security of blockchain-based supply chain management systems: challenges and opportunities. DOI: 10.3390/app11125585

Al-Ghaili, A. M., Kasim, H., Al-Hada, N. M., Hassan, Z., Othman, M., Hussain, T. J., & Shayea, I. (2022). A review of metaverse's definitions, architecture, applications, challenges, issues, solutions, and future trends. *IEEE Access : Practical Innovations, Open Solutions*, 10, 125835–125866. DOI: 10.1109/ACCESS.2022.3225638

Alharbi, S., & Siewe, F. (2016). Cloud computing security: A survey. *International Journal of Information Management*, 36(1), 1–12.

Alija, N. (2017). Justification of Software Maintenance Costs. *International Journal of Advanced Research in Computer Science and Software Engineering*, 7(3), 15–23. DOI: 10.23956/ijarcsse/V7I2/01207

Ali, M., Jaradat, A., Kulakli, A., & Abuhalimeh, A. (2021). A comparative study: Blockchain technology utilization benefits, challenges, and functionalities. *IEEE Access : Practical Innovations, Open Solutions*, 9(1), 12730–12749. DOI: 10.1109/ACCESS.2021.3050241

Alkhalifah, A., Ng, A., Kayes, A. S., Chowdhury, J., Alazab, M., & Watters, P. A. (2020). A taxonomy of blockchain threats and vulnerabilities. In *Blockchain for Cybersecurity and Privacy* (pp. 3–28). CRC Press. DOI: 10.1201/9780429324932-2

Alles, M. G., Brennan, G., Vasarhelyi, M. A., & Kogan, A. (2006). *Continuous monitoring of business process controls: A pilot implementation of a continuous auditing system at Siemens*. Published in the International Journal of Accounting Information Systems.

Almomani, I., Ahmed, M., & Maglaras, L. (2021). Cybersecurity maturity assessment framework for higher education institutions in Saudi Arabia. *PeerJ. Computer Science*, 7, e703. https://peerj.com/articles/cs-703/. DOI: 10.7717/peerj-cs.703 PMID: 34604525

Alqurashi, E., Wills, G., & Gilbert, L. (2013). A viable system model for information security governance: Establishing a baseline of the current information security operations system. *IFIP International Information Security Conference*, 245-256. DOI: 10.1007/978-3-642-39218-4_19

Alreemy, Z., Chang, V., Walters, R., & Wills, G. (2016). Critical success factors (CSFs) for information technology governance (ITG). *International Journal of Information Management*, 36(6), 907–916. DOI: 10.1016/j.ijinfomgt.2016.05.017

Altinay. (n.d.). https://www.researchgate.net/profile/Aysenur-Altinay/publication/325546334_THE_IMPORTANCE_OF_SOX_COMPLIANCE_FOR_AMERICAN_COMPANIES_125/links/5b151ce0a6fdcc4611e2a3a9/THE-IMPORTANCE-OF-SOX-COMPLIANCE-FOR-AMERICAN-COMPANIES-125.pdf

Alvello, M. (2023, October 19). *What Is an IT Audit? A Definitive Guide to Safeguard Your Data*. Retrieved from G2: https://track.g2.com/resources/it-audit#:~:text=Fieldwork%3A%20Once%20the%20plan%20is,evidence%20that%20supports%20their%20findings

Alves de Castro, C. (2021). The Evolution of the Internet and Social Media: A Literature Review. International Journal of e-Education e-Business e-. *Management Learning*, 12(1), 30–41. DOI: 10.17706/ijeeee.2022.12.1.30-41

Amiruddin, A., Afiansyah, H. G., & Nugroho, H. A. (2021a). Cyber-risk management planning using NIST CSF v1.1, NIST SP 800-53 rev. 5, and CIS controls V8. *2021 International Conference on Informatics, Multimedia, Cyber and Information System (ICIMCIS)*. https://doi.org/DOI: 10.1109/ICIMCIS53775.2021.9699337

Anand, S. (2008). Information security implications of Sarbanes-Oxley. *Information Security Journal: A Global Perspective, 17*(2), 75-79. DOI: 10.1080/19393550801953372

Anand, P., Singh, Y., Selwal, A., Singh, P. K., Felseghi, R. A., & Raboaca, M. S. (2020). Iovt: Internet of vulnerable things? threat architecture, attack surfaces, and vulnerabilities in internet of things and its applications towards smart grids. *Energies*, 13(18), 4813. DOI: 10.3390/en13184813

Anantrasirichai, N., & Bull, D. (2022). Artificial intelligence in the creative industries: A review. *Artificial Intelligence Review*, 55(1), 1–68. DOI: 10.1007/s10462-021-10039-7

Anderson, D. (2017). COSO ERM: Getting risk management right: Strategy and organizational performance are the heart of the updated framework.

Anderson, D. (2017). The National Health Information Sharing & Analysis Center and the National Council of Information Sharing and Analysis Centers. Retrieved from: https://docs.house.gov/meetings/IF/IF02/20170404/105831HHRG-115-IF02-Wstate-AndersonD-20170404.pdf

Anderson, H., & Ross, R. (n.d.). Stolen laptop: Breach affects 34,000. Healthcare Information Security. Retrieved December 17, 2021, from https://www.healthcareinfosecurity.com/stolen-laptop-breach-affects-34000-a-4647

Anderson, R., & Moore, T. (2006) The Economics of Information Security https://www.researchgate.net/publication/216757755_The_Economics_of_Information_Security

Anderson, P. (2007). *What is Web 2.0?: ideas, technologies and implications for education*. JISC.

Anderson, U. L., Christ, M. H., Johnstone, K. M., & Rittenberg, L. E. (2012). A post-SOX examination of factors associated with the size of internal audit functions. *Accounting Horizons*, 26(2), 167–191. DOI: 10.2308/acch-50115

Andreisová, L. (2020). Analysis of the Impact of the GDPR on Third-Party Risk Management Programs and Related Recommendations for Domestic as Well as International Corporate World.

Angafor, G. N., Yevseyeva, I., & He, Y. (2020). Game-based learning: A review of tabletop exercises for cybersecurity incident response training. *Security and Privacy*, 3(6), e126. DOI: 10.1002/spy2.126

Angle, J. (2022). Third-Party Vendor Risk Management 2. Research Gate. https://www.researchgate.net/publication/362135483_Third-Party_Vendor_Risk_Management_2

Anne Hardy, C., & Laslett, G. (2015). Continuous Auditing and Monitoring in Practice: Lessons from Metcash's Business Assurance Group. *Journal of Information Systems.*

Antunes, M., Maximiano, M., & Gomes, R. (2022). A Customizable Web Platform to Manage Standards Compliance of Information Security and Cybersecurity Auditing. *Procedia Computer Science*, 196, 36–43. DOI: 10.1016/j.procs.2021.11.070

Anwar, A. A. (2022). A survey of semantic web (Web 3.0), its applications, challenges, future and its relation with Internet of things (IoT). Web Intelligence, 1-30.

Appelbaum, D., Kogan, A., Vasarhelyi, M., & Yan, Z. (2017). Impact of business analytics and enterprise systems on managerial accounting. International journal of accounting information systems. *International Journal of Accounting Information Systems*, 25, 29–44. DOI: 10.1016/j.accinf.2017.03.003

Appelbaum, D., & Nehmer, R. A. (2017). Using Drones in Internal and External Audits: An Exploratory Framework. *Journal of Emerging Technologies in Accounting*, 14(1), 99–113. DOI: 10.2308/jeta-51704

Arens, A. A., Elder, R. J., & Beasley, M. S. Hogan, & Chris E. (2017). Auditing and assurance services: An integrated approach (16th ed.). New Jersey: Pearson Prentince Hall.

Arfeen, A., Ahmed, S., Khan, M. A., & Jafri, S. F. (2021, November). Endpoint Detection & Response: A Malware Identification Solution.

Armbrust, M., & Griffith, R. (2010). A view of cloud computing. *Communications of the ACM*, 53(4), 50–58. DOI: 10.1145/1721654.1721672

Ashbaugh-Skaife, H., Collins, D. W., Kinney, W. R.Jr, & LaFond, R. (2009). The effect of SOX internal control deficiencies on firm risk and cost of equity. *Journal of Accounting Research*, 47(1), 1–43. DOI: 10.1111/j.1475-679X.2008.00315.x

Assunção, P. (2019). *A Zero Trust Approach to Network Security*. Retrieved from.

Attaran, M. (2017). Cloud Computing Technology: Leveraging the Power of the Internet to Improve Business Performance. *Journal of International Technology and Information Management*, 26(1), 112–137. DOI: 10.58729/1941-6679.1283

Attaran, M. (2020). Blockchain technology in healthcare: Challenges and opportunities. *International Journal of Healthcare Management*, 15(1), 1–14. DOI: 10.1080/20479700.2020.1843887

Austin, T. U. (2024). *The University at Texas at Austin: Office of Internal Audits*. Retrieved from Audit Process: https://audit.utexas.edu/audit-process#:~:text=The %20evaluation%20phase%20of%20the,the%20objectives%20of%20the%20audit

Avital, M., Beck, R., King, J. L., Rossi, M., & Teigland, R. (2016). Jumping on the Blockchain Bandwagon: Lessons of the Past and Outlook to the Future. Proceedings/ International Conference on Information Systems (ICIS).

AWS. (2021). *AWS Security Best Practices*. Retrieved from https://aws.amazon .com/security/best-practices/

AWS. (2024). *AWS Cloud Adoption Framework for Artificial Intelligence, Machine Learning, and Generative AI*. Retrieved from https://docs.aws.amazon.com/pdfs/ whitepapers/latest/aws-caf-for-ai/aws-caf-for-ai.pdf#aws-caf-for-ai

Aziz, H. A., & Madani, A. (2015). Evolution of the Web and its Uses in Healthcare.

Bajak, F. (2022). *KeyBank: Hackers of third-party provider stole customer data*. AP News.

Balasubramanian, S., Shukla, V., Sethi, J. S., Islam, N., & Saloum, R. (2021). A readiness assessment framework for blockchain adoption: A healthcare case study. *Technological Forecasting and Social Change*, 165, 120536. DOI: 10.1016/j.techfore.2020.120536

Bandari, V. (2022). Optimizing IT Modernization through Cloud Migration: Strategies for a Secure, Efficient and Cost-Effective Transition. *Applied Research in Artificial Intelligence and Cloud Computing, 5*(1), 66–83. Retrieved from https:// researchberg.com/index.php/araic/article/view/97/99

Barney, N. (2023, June). PCI DSS (Payment Card Industry Data Security Standard). Retrieved from TechTarget: https://www.techtarget.com/searchsecurity/definition/ PCI-DSS-Payment-Card-Industry-Data-Security-Standard

Barney, N. (2023, June). What is PCI DSS (Payment Card Industry Data Security Standard)? Retrieved from https://WhatIs.com

Basset, G. (2021). *Data Breach Investigation Report*. Verizon.

Batra, A. (2020) Cyber security management: Creating governance, risk, and compliance framework. I-Manager's Journal on Software Engineering, 14(4).

Baxter, C. (2022). The Impact of SOX on the Industry 20 Years Ago and Today. *ISACA Journal*, (1). https://www.isaca.org/resources/isaca-journal/issues/2022/volume-1/the-impact-of-sox-on-the-industry-20-years-ago-and-today

Baxter, I. D., & Mehlich, M. (2000). Reverse engineering is reverse forward engineering. *Science of Computer Programming*, 36(2-3), 131–147. DOI: 10.1016/S0167-6423(99)00034-9

Bayhi, J. (2014). The purposeful audit: effective project management is fundamental to delivering valuable internal audit engagements across the organization. *Internal Auditor(Vol. 71, Issue 1).*

Beasley, M. S., Clune, R., Hermanson, D. R. (2005). Enterprise Risk Management: An Empirical Analysis of Factors Associated With the Extent of Implementation.

Bedard, J. C., Graham, L., & Jackson, C. (2005). Information systems risk and audit planning. *International Journal of Auditing*, 9(2), 147–163. DOI: 10.1111/j.1099-1123.2005.00267.x

Benet, J. (2014). IPFS - Content Addressed, Versioned, P2P File System. doi:https://doi.org//arXiv.1407.3561DOI: 10.48550

Berners Lee, T. (1999). Weaving the Web: The original design and ultimate destiny of the World Wide Web by its inventor.

Berners-Lee, T., Hendler, J., & Lassila, O. (2023). The Semantic Web: A New Form of Web Content That is Meaningful to Computers Will Unleash a Revolution of New Possibilities.

Bhambhwani, S. M., & Huang, A. H. (2023). Auditing decentralized finance. *The British Accounting Review*.

Bhattacherjee, S. (2023, April 20). *Third-Party Risk Management Lifecycle: A Strategic Approach*. Retrieved from SignalX: https://signalx.ai/blog/third-party-risk-management-lifecycle/

Blank, R. M., & Gallagher, P. D. (2012). *NIST Special Publication 800-30 Guide for Conducting Risk Assessments*. National Institute of Standards and Technology, US Dept. of Commerce. Gaithersburg: National Institute of Standards and Technology.

Bloom, G., Standing, H., & Lloyd, R. (2008). Markets, information asymmetry and health care: Towards new social contracts. *Social Science & Medicine*, 66(10), 2076–2087. DOI: 10.1016/j.socscimed.2008.01.034 PMID: 18316147

Boehm, J. (2014, November). NIST–Working with Industry To Accelerate Innovation. In 2014 ERC. https://peer.asee.org/25216.pdf

Bogdan, V., Rus, L., Gherai, D. S., Florea, A. G., & Bugnar, N. G. (2023). A Streamline Sustainable Business Performance Reporting Model by an Integrated FinESG Approach. *Sustainability (Basel)*, 15(24), 16860. DOI: 10.3390/su152416860

Boh, W. F., & Yellin, D. (2006). Using enterprise architecture standards in managing information technology. *Journal of Management Information Systems*, 23(3), 163–207. DOI: 10.2753/MIS0742-1222230307

Bond, C. (2023, December 6). *20 Biggest Banks in America*. Retrieved from US News & World Report: https://www.usnews.com/banking/articles/biggest-banks-in-america

Bonyuet, D. (2020). Overview and impact of blockchain on auditing. *The International Journal of Digital Accounting Research*, 31–43. DOI: 10.4192/1577-8517-v20_2

Bowen, P. L., Cheung, M. Y., & Rohde, F. H. (2007). Enhancing IT governance practices: A model and case study of an organization's efforts. international Journal of Accounting information. *Systems*, 191–221.

Boyens, J., Smith, A., Bartol, N., Winkler, K., Holbrook, A., & Fallon, M. (2022). *Cybersecurity Supply Chain Risk Management Practices for Systems and Organizations.* NIST Special Publication-NIST SP 800-161r1.

Bradbury, D. (2022). *Okta's Investigation of the January 2022 Compromise*. Okta.

Braganza, A., & Desouza, K. C. (2006). Implementing section 404 of the Sarbanes Oxley Act: recommendations for information Systems organizations.

Brazel, J. F., Jones, K. L., Thayer, J., & Warne, R. C. (2015). Understanding investor perceptions of financial statement fraud and their use of red flags: Evidence from the field. *Review of Accounting Studies*, 20(4), 1373–1406. DOI: 10.1007/s11142-015-9326-y

Brignall, M. (2021) Npower withdraws mobile app after hackers steal personal details https://www.theguardian.com/business/2021/feb/27/npower-mobile-app-hackers-personaldetails-gas-electricitycustomers?utm_term=b609f7eaeca6965c550e347f83bac052&utm_campaign=GuardianTodayUK&utm_s ource=esp&utm_medium=Email&CMP=GTUK_email

Brivot, M., Roussy, M., & Mayer, M. (2018). Conventions of audit quality. The perspective of public and private company audit partners. *Auditing*, 37(2), 51–71. DOI: 10.2308/ajpt-51772

Bronson, H. E. (2022). Five Common Shortcomings of Third-Party Management Programs in Financial Organizations and Recommended Risk Management Strategies.

Brown, W., & Nasuti, F. (2005). Sarbanes-Oxley and enterprise security: IT governance-what it takes to get the job done. Inf. Secur. J. A Glob. Perspect., 15-28.

Brown, A. (2018). Assessing Cloud Service Provider Audit Processes for Regulatory Compliance. *Journal of Information Security*, 15(3), 217–231.

Brown, A., & Green, C. (2019). Stakeholder alignment in cloud service provider selection: A strategic approach. *Journal of Cloud Computing (Heidelberg, Germany)*, 8(1), 1–15.

Brown, A., & Jones, B. (2019). *Security Risk Assessment: A Complete Guide*. CRC Press.

Brown, A., & Lee, C. (2018). Effective Service Level Agreements (SLAs) in Cloud Computing: A Review and Future Directions. *Journal of Cloud Computing: Advances, Systems and Applications*, 7(1), 1–15.

Brown, C. E., Wong, J. A., & Baldwin, A. A. (2007). A review and analysis of the existing research streams in continuous auditing. *Journal of Emerging Technologies in Accounting*, 4(1), 1–28. DOI: 10.2308/jeta.2007.4.1.1

Brown, C., & Miller, D. (2019). User-Centric Evaluation of Cloud Service Providers: A Qualitative Analysis. *International Journal of Cloud Computing*, 15(3), 102–118.

Brownlee, K. (2016). The civil disobedience of Edward Snowden. *Philosophy and Social Criticism*, 42(10), 965–970. DOI: 10.1177/0191453716631167

Brown, M., & Lee, C. (2018). Examining Incident Response Capabilities in Cloud Service Providers. *Journal of Computer Security*, 25(4), 567–584.

Bruwer, H. J. (2014). An investigation of developments in Web 3.0: opportunities, risks, safeguards and governance (Doctoral dissertation, Stellenbosch: Stellenbosch University).

Bruwer, R., & Rudman, R. (2015). Web 3.0: Governance, Risks and Safeguards. *Journal of Applied Business Research*, 31(3), 1037–1056. DOI: 10.19030/jabr.v31i3.9241

Buchanan, S., & Gibb, F. (2007, June). The information audit: Role and scope. *International Journal of Information Management*, 27(3), 159–172. DOI: 10.1016/j.ijinfomgt.2007.01.002

Buckberg, E., Foster, T. S., Miller, R. I., & Werner, A. (2003). Recent Trends in Securities Class Action Litigation: Will Enron and Sarbanes-Oxley Change the Tides. *NERA Economic Consulting*. https://www.nera.com/image/6143.pdf

Bunker, R. (2021, January 25). Emerging trends in internal audit for 2021. Barclay Simpson UK. https://www.barclaysimpson.com/blogs/a-new-era-emerging-trends-in-internal-audit-for-2021-12525151636

Business School Web10. (n.d.). Retrieved from https://thebusinessofsocial.wordpress.com/tag/web-1-0/

Callegati, F., Cerroni, W., & Ramilli, M. (2009). Man-in-the-middle attack to the HTTPS protocol. *IEEE Security and Privacy*, 7(1), 78–81. DOI: 10.1109/MSP.2009.12

Calleja-López, A., Monterde, A., & Barandiaran, X. E. (2017). Framework for democratic governance of distributed architectures: DEcentralised Citizens Owned Data Ecosystem.

Campbell, J. D., & Jardine, A. K. (2001). *Maintenance excellence: optimizing equipment life-cycle decisions*. CRC Press.

Canfora, G., Fasolino, A. R., Frattolillo, G., & Tramontana, P. (2008). A wrapping approach for migrating legacy system interactive functionalities to Service Oriented Architectures. *Journal of Systems and Software*, 81(4), 463–480. DOI: 10.1016/j.jss.2007.06.006

Canidio, A., Danos, V., Marcassa, S., & Prat, J. (2021). Tokens and ICOs: A Review of the Economic Literature. Principles of Blockchain Systems, 191-210.

Carbon Black, Inc. (2018, May). Retrieved from: https://web.archive.org/web/20180504081758/https://www.sec.gov/Archives/edgar/data/1366527/000104746918003408/a2235562zs-1a.htm

Carcello, J. V., Hermanson, R. H., & McGrath, N. T. (1992). Audit quality attributes: The perceptions of audit partners, preparers, and financial statement users. *Auditing*, 11(1), 1–15.

Cardoso, A. G. (2022). Decentralized Autonomous Organizations – DAOs: The Convergence of Technology, Law, Governance, and Behavioral Economics. DOI: 10.2139/ssrn.4341884

Carroll, R. (2021) Ransomware attack disrupts Irish health services. The Guardian. https://www.theguardian.com/world/2021/may/14/ransomware-attack-disrupts-irish-healthservices?utm_term=bcbaa56dfd395c672786d3b14913fd95&utm_campaign=GuardianTodayUK&utm_source=esp&utm_medium=Email&CMP=GTUK_email

Cartwright, A. J. (2023). The elephant in the room: Cybersecurity in healthcare. *Journal of Clinical Monitoring and Computing*, 37(5), 1–10. DOI: 10.1007/s10877-023-01013-5 PMID: 37088852

Cascarino, R. E. (2007). Auditor's Guide to Information Systems Auditing.

Center for internet security (CIS) releases CIS critical security controls V8 to reflect evolving technology, threats. (2021, December 1). CIS. https://www.cisecurity.org/about-us/media/press-release/center-for-internet-security-cis-releases-cis-controls-v8-to-reflect-evolving-technology-threats

CERT. (2020). *Insider Threat Center*. Retrieved from https://www.cert.org/insider-threat/

Cezar, A., Cavusoglu, H., & Raghunathan, S. (2014). Outsourcing Information Security: Contracting Issues and Security Implications. In *Management Science* (pp. 638-657). Institute for Operations Research and the Management Sciences.

Chambers, A., & Rand, G. (2011). *The operational auditing handbook: auditing business and IT processes*. John Wiley & Sons.

Chambers, D., & Payne, J. (2011). Audit quality and accrual persistence: Evidence from the pre-and post-Sarbanes-Oxley periods. *Managerial Auditing Journal*, 26(5), 437–456. DOI: 10.1108/02686901111129580

Chamira, R. (n.d.). Linkedin. Retrieved from https://www.linkedin.com/pulse/evolution-internet-from-web10-web3-ravi-chamria/

Chan, D. Y., Chiu, V., & Vasarhelyi, M. A. (Eds.). (2018), Continuous Auditing: Theory and Application, Emerald Group Publishing, Howard House, Bingley, UK.

Chan, D., & Chiu, V. (2018). *Continuous Auditing*. Emerald Publishing Limited.

Chandel, S., Yan, M., Chen, S., Jiang, H., & Ni, T.-Y. (2019, April). IEE Xplore. Retrieved from: https://ieeexplore.ieee.org/abstract/document/8695328

Chang, V., & Wills, G. (2019). A Review of Cloud Migration Techniques and Challenges. *13th International Conference on Complex, Intelligent, and Software Intensive Systems (CISIS)*, 2019.

Charles, S. L., Glover, S. M., & Sharp, N. Y. (2010). The association between financial reporting risk and audit fees before and after the historic events surrounding SOX. *Auditing*, 29(1), 15–39. DOI: 10.2308/aud.2010.29.1.15

Chartered Institute of Internal Auditors. (2020). *Governance of Risk: Three Lines of Defence.* Retrieved from theiia.org: https://www.theiia.org/globalassets/documents/resources/the-iias-three-lines-model-an-update-of-the-three-lines-of-defense-july-2020/three-lines-model-updated-english.pdf

Chartered Institute of Internal Auditors. (2023). *Working with stakeholders.* Retrieved from Chartered Institute of Internal Auditors: https://www.iia.org.uk/resources/managing-internal-audit/working-with-stakeholders/

Chaudhary, P. (2018). Mitigating cyber attacks through security models and networking protocols. *International Journal on Computer Science and Engineering*, 6(8), 925–929. DOI: 10.26438/ijcse/v6i8.925929

Checkpoint. (n.d.). What is Endpoint Encryption? Retrieved from https://www.checkpoint.com/cyber-hub/threat-prevention/what-is-endpoint-security/what-is-endpoint-encryption/

Che, L., Langli, J. C., & Svanström, T. (2018). Education, experience and audit effort. *Auditing*, 37(3), 91–115. DOI: 10.2308/ajpt-51896

Chen, G., Xu, B., Lu, M., & Chen, N. S. (2018). Exploring blockchain technology and its potential applications for education. Smart Learning Environments, 1-10. DOI: 10.1186/s40561-017-0050-x

Chen, H., & Li, Y. (2019). Evaluating Cloud Service Providers: A Comprehensive Framework. *Journal of Computer Science and Technology*, 34(5), 102–115.

Chen, Y., Qin, X., Wang, J., Yu, C., & Gao, W. (2020). FedHealth: A Federated Transfer Learning Framework for Wearable Wealthcare. *IEEE Intelligent Systems*, 35(4), 83–93. DOI: 10.1109/MIS.2020.2988604

Chikofsky, E. J., & Cross, J. H. (1990). Reverse engineering and design recovery: A taxonomy. *IEEE Software*, 7(1), 13–17. DOI: 10.1109/52.43044

Choudhury, N. (2014). World Wide Web and Its Journey from Web 1.0 to Web 4.0. *International Journal of Computer Science and Information Technologies*8096–8100.

Chris Silva, P. F. (2022, December). Critical Capabilities for Endpoint Protection Platforms. Retrieved from: https://www.gartner.com/document/4140999?ref=solrAll&refval=383606631&

Christodorescu, M., Jha, S., Seshia, S., Song, D., & Bryant, R. (2005, May). Retrieved from:

Chtiouia, T., & Thiéry-Dubuissonb, S. (2011). Hard and Soft Controls: Mind the Gap! Tawhid Chtiouia and Stéphanie Thiéry-Dubuissonb. *International Journal of Business*, 16(3), 290–302.

Cis - Center for Internet Security. (2024, May 23). CISO Global. https://www.ciso.inc/capabilities/strategy-risk-solutions/managed-compliance-security-offering/cis-center-for-internet-security/#:~:text=CIS%20Critical%20Security%20Controls%20Version,management%20for%20future%20cyber%20defense

Cluley, G. (2021) Ransomware is the biggest threat, says GCHQ cybersecurity chief https://www.tripwire.com/state-of-security/security-data-protection/ransomware-biggest-threat-saysgchq-cybersecurity-chief/?utm_source=The State of Security Newsletter&utm_medium=email&utm_campaign=FO-06-21- 2021&utm_content=httpswwwtripwirecomstateofsecu

Coates, J. C.IV. (2007). The goals and promise of the Sarbanes–Oxley Act. *The Journal of Economic Perspectives*, 21(1), 91–116. DOI: 10.1257/jep.21.1.91

Coates, J. C., & Srinivasan, S. (2014). SOX after ten years: A multidisciplinary review. *Accounting Horizons*, 28(3), 627–671. DOI: 10.2308/acch-50759

Cochran, B., Gundrothu, S., Hill, J., Johar, G., Shawn, M., Manley, A., & Ward, P. (2017). *Continuous Monitoring of Third Party Vendors: Building Best Practices*. Shared Assessments.

Coetzee, D., & Lessing, N. (2004). Information technology: Manaement Issues in the Due Diligence and Contracting Phase of Outsourcing Contracts. *Journal of Contemporary Management*, 16-30.

Combee, J., Dijkman, M., Ockels, G., Wortel, R., & Vries, B. D. (2015). Discussion paper Soft controls. What are the Starting Points for the Internal Auditor? The institute of internal auditors in Netherlands. https://www.iia.nl/SiteFiles/Publicaties/IIA_Bro%20A4%20Soft%20Controls%20Engels%2002.pdf

Cong, L. W., Grauer, K., Rabetti, D., & Updegrave, H. (2023). The Dark Side of Crypto and Web3: Crypto-Related Scams. DOI: 10.2139/ssrn.4358572

Console & Associates. (2022, August 30). *KeyBank Announces Third-Party Data Breach Following Incident at Third-Party Vendor, Overby-Seawell Company*. Retrieved from JDSUPRA: https://www.jdsupra.com/legalnews/keybank-announces-third-party-data-8464347/

Cooke, I. (2018). *IS Audit Basics: Innovation in the IT Audit Process*. Retrieved from ISACA: https://www.isaca.org/resources/isaca-journal/issues/2018/volume-2/is-audit-basics-innovation-in-the-it-audit-process

Cooper, D. J., & Robson, K. (2006). Accounting, professions and regulation: Locating the sites of professionalization. *Accounting, Organizations and Society*, 31(4-5), 415–444. DOI: 10.1016/j.aos.2006.03.003

Corbetta, S., Meeus, W., Cappe, E., Catthoor, F., & & Fritsch, A. (2018). Proof-of-Concept HARPA Measurement-Based Platform Modelling. Harnessing Performance Variability in Embedded and High-performance Many/Multi-core Platforms: A Cross-layer Approach.

Costic, L. (2019). *COBIT Focus Area: Information & Technology Risk*. ISACA.

Council, P. S. (2023b, December 1). Retrieved from PCI Security Standards Council – Protect Payment Data with Industry-driven Security Standards, Training, and Programs.: https://www.pcisecuritystandards.org/document_library/?document=third-party-security-assurance

Cram, W. A., Proudfoot, J. G., & D'Arcy, J. (2020). Maximizing employee compliance with cybersecurity policies. *MIS Quarterly Executive*, 183–198. DOI: 10.17705/2msqe.00032

Creta, F., & Tenca, F. (2021). Tokenomics: A new opportunity in the Real Estate business? A qualitative approach to crowdfunding and blockchain interaction. *First Monday*.

Crossman, D. C. (2008). *The impact of safety culture on worker motivation and the economic bottom line* (Doctoral dissertation, Capella University).

Crotty, J., & Horrocks, I. (2017). Managing legacy system costs: A case study of a meta-assessment model to identify solutions in a large financial services company. *Applied Computing and Informatics*, 13(2), 175–183. DOI: 10.1016/j.aci.2016.12.001

Crowdstrike. (2023, October 26). Endpoint Detection and Response (EDR). Retrieved from: https://www.crowdstrike.com/cybersecurity-101/endpoint-security/endpoint-detection-and-response-edr/

Crowdstrike. (2023, September). Retrieved from:

Crowdstrike. (n.d.). A unified platform approach. Retrieved from

CSA. (2020). *Cloud Security Alliance*. Retrieved from https://cloudsecurityalliance.org/

CSIAC. (2018, May). Compliant but not Secure: Why PCI-Certified Companies Are Being Breached. Retrieved from: https://csiac.org/articles/compliant-but-not-secure-why-pci-certified-companies-are-being-breached/

Cusumano, M. J. (n.d.). *Modernizing Legacy Systems: Software Transformations in the Cloud.*

CWE. (2021). *Common Weakness Enumeration (CWE).* Retrieved from https://cwe.mitre.org/

Cybersecurity Framework, N. I. S. T. 2.0: Resource & Overview Guide. (2024). https://nvlpubs.nist.gov/nistpubs/SpecialPublications/NIST.SP.1299.pdf

Cynet. (2023). Cortex XDR by Palo Alto: Architecture & Capabilities Overview. Retrieved from: https://www.cynet.com/xdr-security/xdr-by-palo-alto-understanding-cortex-xdr/

Dai, J., & Vasarhelyi, M. A. (2017). Toward blockchain-based accounting and assurance. *Journal of Information Systems*, 31(3), 5–21. DOI: 10.2308/isys-51804

Damianides, M. (2005). Sarbanes-Oxley and IT governance: New guidance on IT control and compliance. *Information Systems Management*, 22(1), 77–85. DOI: 10.1201/1078/44912.22.1.20051201/85741.9

Daniel, J., Sargolzaei, A., Abdelghani, M., Sargolzaei, S., & Amaba, B. (2017). Blockchain technology, cognitive computing, and healthcare innovations. *Journal of Advances in Information Technology*, 194-198, 194–198. Advance online publication. DOI: 10.12720/jait.8.3.194-198

Das, T. (2023, November). What Is An Endpoint Firewall? A Comprehensive Guide. Retrieved from: https://www.selecthub.com/endpoint-security/endpoint-firewall/

Davies, J., Finlay, M., McLenaghen, T., & Wilson, D. (n.d.). *Key Risk Indicators – Their Role in Operational Risk Management and Measurement.* Retrieved from 2006

Davis, K. (2012). *Ethics of Big Data: Balancing risk and innovation.* O'Reilly Media, Inc.

Dawodu, S. O. (2024). Reviewing third-party risk management: best practices in accounting and cybersecurity for superannuation.

De Haes, S., & Van Grembergen, W. (2008). An exploratory study into the design of an IT governance minimum baseline through Delphi research. *Communications of the Association for Information Systems*, 22, 24. DOI: 10.17705/1CAIS.02224

De Spiegeleire, S., Maas, M., & Sweijs, T. (2017). *Artificial intelligence and the future of defense: strategic implications for small-and medium-sized force providers.* The Hague Centre for Strategic Studies.

DeFond, M. L., & Lennox, C. S. (2011). The effect of SOX on small auditor exits and audit quality. *Journal of Accounting and Economics*, 52(1), 21–40. DOI: 10.1016/j.jacceco.2011.03.002

Deloitte. (2020). *Modernizing the three lines of defense model An internal audit perspective.* Retrieved from Deloitte: https://www2.deloitte.com/us/en/pages/advisory/articles/modernizing-the-three-lines-of-defense-model.html

Desmond, N. (2002). Repeal the Sarbanes-Oxley tax now! *Business 2.0, 3*(December), 75.

Destefanis, G., & Ragnedda, M. (2019). *Blockchain and Web 3.0: Social* (1st ed.). Economic, and Technological Challenges.

Dey, S. (2018). Securing Majority-Attack in Blockchain Using Machine Learning and Algorithmic Game Theory: A Proof of Work. .DOI: 10.1109/CEEC.2018.8674185

Di Bernardo, M. (2014). *Contingent contracts: A tool for facilitating the negotiation and managing risks. the case of an international sale of goods from Portugal to Brasil.* Retrieved from Repositório da Universidade NOVA de Lisboa (RUN): http://hdl.handle.net/10362/17437

Dillon, T., & Chang, E. (2010). Cloud computing: Issues and challenges. *In 2010 24th IEEE international conference on advanced information networking and applications (pp. 27-33). IEEE.*

Dillon, A., & Carter, S. (2010). Security challenges in cloud migration. *Journal of Cloud Computing (Heidelberg, Germany)*, 5(2), 112–130.

Ding, R., Shen, S., Zhu, Y., Du, L., Chen, S., Liang, J., Wang, K., Xiao, W., & Hong, Y. (2023). Evolution, Forecasting, and Driving Mechanisms of the Digital Financial Network: Evidence from China. *Sustainability (Basel)*, 15(22), 16072. DOI: 10.3390/su152216072

Doan, S., Conway, M., Phuong, T. M., & Ohno-Machado, L. (2014). Natural language processing in biomedicine: A unified system architecture overview. *Methods in Molecular Biology (Clifton, N.J.)*, 1168, 275–294. DOI: 10.1007/978-1-4939-0847-9_16 PMID: 24870142

Dowdy, J. (2012). *The cyber-security threat to us growth and prosperity. Cyberspace: A New Domain for National Security*. https://www.mckinsey.com/kz/~/media/mckinsey/dotcom/client_service/aerospace%20and%20defense/cybersecurity_threat_to_growth_and_prosperity.pdf

Doyle, B., & Lopes, C. (2008). Survey of Technologies for Web Application Development. doi:arXiv:0801.2618

Drogalas, G., Arampatzis, K., & Anagnostopoulou, E. (2016). The relationship between Corporate governance, internal audit and audit committee: Empirical evidence from Greece. *Corporate Ownership and Control*, 14(1), 569–577. DOI: 10.22495/cocv14i1c4art3

Drury, T. (n.d.). Bizjournals.com. Retrieved December 17, 2021, from https://www.bizjournals.com/buffalo/news/2019/05/10/independent-health-mistakenly-emailed-information.html

Duarte, J., Kong, K., Siegel, S., & Young, L. (2014). The impact of the Sarbanes–Oxley Act on shareholders and managers of foreign firms. *Review of Finance*, 18(1), 417–455. DOI: 10.1093/rof/rft008

Dufva, M. (2019, December 31). Teknologia sulautuu kaikkeen. Megatrendit 2020. Sitran selvityksiä, 162. Sitra. https://www.sitra.fi/julkaisut/megatrendit2020/

Dunn, C. L., & Hollander, S. (2017). The impact of artificial intelligence on auditing. *Current Issues in Auditing*, 11, A1–A12.

Dutta, P., Choi, T. M., Somani, S., & Butala, R. (2020). Blockchain technology in supply chain operations: Applications, challenges and research opportunities. Transportation research part e: Logistics and transportation review.

Dwivedi, A., Kumar, S., Dwivedi, A., & Singh, M. (2011). Current Security Considerations for Issues and Challenges of Trustworthy Semantic Web. Int. J. *Advanced Networking and Applications Volume*, 03(01), 978–983.

Dwivedi, A., Srivastava, G., Dhar, S., & Singh, R. (2019). A decentralized privacy-preserving healthcare blockchain for IoT. *Sensors (Basel)*, 19(2), 326. DOI: 10.3390/s19020326 PMID: 30650612

Dyball, M. C., & Seethamraju, R. (2021). The impact of client use of blockchain technology on audit risk and audit approach—An exploratory study. *International Journal of Auditing*, 25(2), 602–615. DOI: 10.1111/ijau.12238

E, B. H. (2022). Five Common Shortcomings of Third-Party Management Programs in Financial Organizations and Recommended Risk Management Strategies.

Earl Perkins, F. C. (2015, July 20). Cybersecurity Scenario 2020 Phase 2: Guardians for Big Change. Retrieved from: Gartner: https://www.gartner.com/document/3097027

Ebaid, I. E. S. (2011), Internal audit function: an exploratory study from Egyptian listed firms. International Journal of Law and Management. Available at: https://www.emerald.com/insight/ content/doi/10.1108/17542431111119397/full/html#loginreload

Eckstein, E. (2021, May 24). 5 key Takeaways After 20 Years of Sarbanes-Oxley. Saint Joseph's University. https://www.sju.edu/news/5-key-takeaways-after-20-years-sarbanes-oxley

Efe, A. (2023). *A comparison of key risk management frameworks: COSO-ERM, NIST RMF, ISO 31.000*. COBIT.

Efremovska, A., & Lago, P. (2017). From Legacy to Cloud: Risks and Benefits in Software Cloud Migration. *In Software Architecture for Big Data and the Cloud* (pp. 147-165).

Egliston, B., & Carter, M. (2022). The metaverse and how we'll build it': The political economy of Meta's Reality Labs. *New Media & Society*.

Eichar, S. W. (2009). Sarbanes Oxley Act of 2002: Will it Be Effective in Preventing Another Enron Scandal? *Accountancy*, 130(1311), 13.

Eitelhuber, T. W., Thackray, J., Hodges, S., & Alan, J. (2018). Fit for purpose - developing a software platform to support the modern challenges of data linkage in Western Australia. *International Journal of Population Data Science*, 3(3). Advance online publication. DOI: 10.23889/ijpds.v3i3.435 PMID: 32935016

Elommal, N., & Manita, R. (2021). How blockchain innovation could affect the audit profession: a qualitative study.

Emenike, S. U. (2021). Data loss prevention in a remote work environment https://urn.kb.se/resolve?urn=urn:nbn:se:his:diva-20203

Encryption, H. Retrieved from: https://cacm.acm.org/research/unlocking-the-potential-of-fully-homomorphic-encryption/

ENISA. (2019). *European Union Agency for Cybersecurity*. Retrieved from https://www.enisa.europa.eu/

Essex, D., Kerner, S. M., & Gillis, A. S. (2023). TechTarget. Retrieved from TechTarget: https://www.techtarget.com/whatis/definition/Web-30?asrc=EM_SS-WELCOME_249063862&src=10185333

Esteva, A., Robicquet, A., Ramsundar, B., Kuleshov, V., DePristo, M., Chou, K., Cui, C., Corrado, G., Thrun, S., & Dean, J. (2019). A guide to deep learning in healthcare. *Nature Medicine*, 25(1), 24–29. DOI: 10.1038/s41591-018-0316-z PMID: 30617335

Esteves, J., Ramalho, E., & De Haro, G. (2017). To improve cybersecurity, think like a hacker. *MIT Sloan Management Review*. Retrieved May 30, 2024, from https://sloanreview.mit.edu/article/to-improve-cybersecurity-think-like-a-hacker/

European Union. (n.d.). *GDPR.EU*. Retrieved from GDPR: https://gdpr.eu/

Evans, M. (2006). The Evolution of the Web-From Web 1.0 to Web 4.0.

Evgeny Mirolyubov, P. F. (2023, January). Prioritizing Security Controls for Enterprise Servers and End-User Endpoints. Retrieved from: https://www.gartner.com/document/4022974?ref=solrAll&refval=385957224&

Exchange, L. S. (2012). *Corporate governance for Main Market and AIM companies*. London Stock Exchange.

F. (2024). Project Management Cloud Migration Strategy. *F1000Research, 13*(87), 87. DOI: 10.7490/f1000research.1119693.1

Farrell, H., & Farrell, B. J. (1998). The language of business codes of ethics: Implications of knowledge and power. *Journal of Business Ethics*, 17, 587–601.

Fazzini, K. (2019, December 23). *In a decade of cybersecurity alarms, these are the breaches that actually mattered*. Retrieved from CNBC: https://www.cnbc.com/2019/12/23/stuxnet-target-equifax-worst-breaches-of-2010s.html

Feliciano, C., & Quick, R. (2022). Innovative information technology in auditing: Auditors' perceptions of future importance and current auditor expertise. *Accounting in Europe*, 19(2), 311–331. DOI: 10.1080/17449480.2022.2046283

Feng, M., Li, C., & McVay, S. (2009). Internal control and management guidance. *Journal of Accounting and Economics*, 48(2/3), 190–209. DOI: 10.1016/j.jacceco.2009.09.004

Fenu, G., Marchesi, L., Marchesi, M., & Tonelli, R. (2018). The ICO phenomenon and its relationships with ethereum smart contract environment. *International Workshop on Blockchain Oriented Software Engineering (IWBOSE)*, 26-32. DOI: 10.1109/IWBOSE.2018.8327568

Ferraiolo, D. F., Kuhn, D. R., & Chandramouli, R. (2007). *Role-based access control*. Artech House.

Firoiu, D., Ionescu, G. H., Cojocaru, T. M., Niculescu, M., Cimpoeru, M. N., & Călin, O. A. (2023b). Progress of EU Member States Regarding the Bioeconomy and Biomass Producing and Converting Sectors. *Sustainability (Basel)*, 15(19), 14128. DOI: 10.3390/su151914128

Fischhoff, B. (1982) For Those Condemned To Study the Past: Heuristics and Biases in Hindsight.https://www.researchgate.net/publication/248628593_For_Those_Condemned_To_Study_the_Past_Heuristics_and_Biases_in_Hindsight

Flint, R. W. (2012). *Practice of sustainable community development: a participatory framework for change*. Springer Science & Business Media.

Forrester Research, Inc. (2021). *Predictions 2022: Cybersecurity, Risk and Privacy*. Forrester Research, Inc.

Fortient (n.d.). What is URL filtering? Retrieved from https://www.fortinet.com/resources/cyberglossary/what-is-url-filtering

Fortinet. (2016, Feb). A New Approach to Securing the Enterprise Network. Retrieved from: https://www.fortinet.com/content/dam/fortinet/assets/white-papers/WP-New-Approach-Securing-Enterprise-Network.pdf

Fortinet. (2023). Types of Endpoint Security. Retrieved from: https://www.fortinet.com/resources/cyberglossary/types-of-endpoint-security

Fortinet. (n.d.). What Is Endpoint Security? How Does It Work? Retrieved from https://www.fortinet.com/resources/cyberglossary/what-is-endpoint-security#:~:text=The%20endpoint%20security%20solution%20enables,%2C%20and%20zero%2Dday%20attacks

Fowler, M. (2021). *Application integration*. Martinfowler.com. https://martinfowler.com/tags/application%20integration.html

Franz Hinner, S. P. (2023, August). Hype Cycle for Endpoint Security. Retrieved from: https://www.gartner.com/interactive/hc/4589999?ref=solrAll&refval=385956590

Freeze, D. (2021, April 27). *Cybercrime To Cost The World $10.5 Trillion Annually By 2025. Cybercrime Magazine.*https://cybersecurityventures.com/cybercrime-damage-costs-10-trillion-by-2025/

Freni, P., Ferro, E., & Moncada, R. (2022). Tokenomics and blockchain tokens: A design-oriented morphological framework. Blockchain: Research and Applications, 100069.

Frid-Adar, M., Diamant, I., Klang, E., Amitai, M., Goldberger, J., & Greenspan, H. (2018). GAN-based synthetic medical image augmentation for increased CNN performance in liver lesion classification. *Neurocomputing*, 321, 321–331. DOI: 10.1016/j.neucom.2018.09.013

Frishammar, J., Richtnér, A., Brattström, A., Magnusson, M., & Björk, J. (2019). Opportunities and challenges in the new innovation landscape: Implications for innovation auditing and innovation management. *European Management Journal*, 37(2), 151–164. DOI: 10.1016/j.emj.2018.05.002

Fruhlinger, J. (2022, May 16). PCI DSS explained: Requirements, fines, and steps to compliance. CSO.

Fung, B. (2021) 'Hackers breach Electronic Arts, stealing game source code and tools', https://www.cnn.com/2021/06/10/tech/electronic-arts-hack/index.html

Ganesan, A. S., & Chithralekha, T. (2016). A Survey on Survey of Migration of Legacy Systems. *Proceedings of the International Conference on Informatics and Analytics* (pp. 1-10). DOI: 10.1145/2980258.2980409

Gantz, J., & Manfrediz, S. (2012). IDC iView: Cloud Computing's Role in Job Creation. *IDC Analyze the Future, 230923.*

Gan, W., Ye, Z., Wan, S., & Yu, P. S. (2023). Web 3.0: The Future of Internet. doi:https://arxiv.org/abs/2304.06032 DOI: 10.1145/3543873.3587583

GAO. (2019). *Agencies Need to Develop Modernization Plans for Critical Legacy Systems.* U.S. Government Accountability Office. https://www.gao.gov/products/gao-19-471

Garfinkel, S., & Cranor, L. (2005) Security and Usability https://www.oreilly.com/library/view/security-and-usability/0596008279/

Gartner. (2019). *Stay Ahead of Growing Third- Party Risk.*

Gartner. (2019, January 21). Gartner survey shows 37 percent of organizations have implemented AI in some form. https://www.gartner.com/en/newsroom/press-releases/2019-01-21-gartner-survey-shows-37-percent-of-organizations-have

Gartner. (2021). Best practices for cloud security posture management.

Gartner. (2023, Aug). Peer Review for Microsoft Defender. Retrieved from: https://www.gartner.com/reviews/market/endpoint-detection-and-response-solutions/vendor/sentinelone/product/microsoft-defender-for-endpoint/review/view/4918228

Gartner. (2023, February 22). *Gartner predicts nearly half of cybersecurity leaders will change jobs by 2025. Gartner. Retrieved May 30, 2024, from*https://www.gartner.com/en/newsroom/press-releases/2023-02-22-gartner-predicts-nearly-half-of-cybersecurity-leaders-will-change-jobs-by-2025

Gashgari, G., Walters, R. J., & Wills, G. (2017). A Proposed Best-practice Framework for Information Security Governance. *Proceedings of the 2nd International Conference on Internet of Things, Big Data and Security*, 295-301. DOI: 10.5220/0006303102950301

Gatteschi, V., Lamberti, F., Demartini, C., Pranteda, C., & Santamaria, V. (2018). To Blockchain or Not to Blockchain: That Is the Question. *IT Professional*, 20(2), 62–74. DOI: 10.1109/MITP.2018.021921652

Gerald, J. (1979). *Popek and Charles S. Kline*. Encryption and Secure Computer Networks. Retrieved from.

Ghelani, D., & Hua, T. K. (2022). Conceptual Framework of Web 3.0 and Impact on Marketing, Artificial Intelligence, and Blockchain. International Journal of Information and Communication Sciences, 10-17. DOI: 10.11648/j.ijics.20220701.12

Gholami, M. F., Daneshgar, F., Beydoun, G., & Rabhi, F. (2017). Challenges in migrating legacy software systems to the cloud — An empirical study. *Information Systems*, 67, 100–113. DOI: 10.1016/j.is.2017.03.008

Gilbert, S. (2022). *Crypto, web3, and the Metaverse. Bennett Institute for Public Policy*. Policy Brief.

Gillan, S. L. (2006). Recent Developments in Corporate Governance: An Overview. *Journal of Corporate Finance*, 12(3), 381–402. DOI: 10.1016/j.jcorpfin.2005.11.002

Glover, G. (2020). What are the 12 requirements of PCI DSS Compliance. Retrieved from: https://www.securitymetrics.com/blog/what-are-12-requirements-pci-dss-compliance

Goel, A. K., Bakshi, R., & Agrawal, K. K. (2022). Web 3.0 and Decentralized Applications, July 2022. *International Conference on Innovative Research in Renewable Energy Technologies*, West Bengal, IndiaDOI: 10.3390/materproc2022010008

Gong, G., Ke, B., & Yu, Y. (2009). SOX-mandated internal control deficiency disclosure under Section 302 and earnings quality: Evidence from cross-listed firms. DOI: 10.2139/ssrn.1028620

Gonthier-Besacier, N., Hottegindre, G., & Fine-Falcy, S. (2016). Audit quality perception: Beyond the 'role-perception gap'. *International Journal of Auditing*, 20(2), 186–201. DOI: 10.1111/ijau.12066

Google Cloud Adoption Framework. (n.d.). Retrievd from https://services.google.com/fh/files/misc/google_cloud_adoption_framework_whitepaper.pdf

Gordon, I. M., & Nazari, J. A. (2018). Review of SOX in the business ethics literature. *Managerial Auditing Journal*, 33(5), 470–502. DOI: 10.1108/MAJ-08-2017-1629

Gordon, L. A., Loeb, M. P., & Zhou, L. (2020b). Integrating cost–benefit analysis into the NIST Cybersecurity Framework via the Gordon–Loeb Model. *Journal of Cybersecurity*, 6(1), tyaa005. Advance online publication. DOI: 10.1093/cybsec/tyaa005

Gordover, M. (2020, September 17). Throwback Thursday: Lessons Learned from the 2008 Heartland Breach. Retrieved from: https://www.proofpoint.com/us/blog/insider-threat-management/throwback-thursday-lessons-learned-2008-heartland-breach

Gorelik, M. (2022). Log4j Exploit Hits Again: Vulnerable VMWare Horizon Servers at Risk. https://blog.morphisec.com/log4j-exploit-hits-again-vulnerable-vmware-horizon-servers-at-risk

Grabis, C. (2022). *Five Project Management Best Practices for More Effective Audits*. Retrieved from Audit Board: https://www.auditboard.com/blog/project-management-best-practices-for-more-effective-audits/

Greenhalgh, T., Wherton, J., Shaw, S., Papoutsi, C., Vijayaraghavan, S., & Stones, R. (2019). Infrastructure Revisited: An Ethnographic Case Study of how Health Information Infrastructure Shapes and Constrains Technological Innovation. *Journal of Medical Internet Research*, 21(12), e16093. DOI: 10.2196/16093 PMID: 31855184

Grieger, M., Baqaie, M. F., & Engels, G. (2016). *Concept-Based Engineering of Situation-Specific Migration Methods: Vol* (Vol. 9679). Springer. DOI: 10.1007/978-3-319-35122-3_14

Guilford, M. (2023). Systemic Risk Analysis of Human Factors in Phishing (Doctoral dissertation, Old Dominion University).

Gupta, P. P., Sami, H., & Zhou, H. (2018). Do companies with effective internal controls over financial reporting benefit from Sarbanes–Oxley sections 302 and 404? *Journal of Accounting, Auditing & Finance*, 33(2), 200–227. DOI: 10.1177/0148558X16663091

Gupta, S., & Sharma, M. (2018). Mitigating Risks and Ensuring Regulatory Compliance in Cloud Migration: A Framework Approach. *Journal of Cloud Computing Research*, 5(2), 78–91.

Haag, S., Eckhardt, A., & Bozoyan, C. (2015). *Are Shadow System Users the Better IS Users? - Insights of a Lab Experiment. Publications of Darmstadt Technical University, Institute for Business Studies*. BWL.

Hagemann, R., Huddleston Skees, J., & Thierer, A. (2018). *Soft law for hard problems: The governance of emerging technologies in an uncertain future*. Tech. LJ.

Halabi, T., & Bellaiche, M. (2017). Towards quantification and evaluation of security of Cloud Service Providers

Haller, J., & Wallen, C. M. (2016). Anaging third party risk in financial services organizations: A resilience-based approach.

Han, J., Lee, J., & Li, T. (2023). Dao governance.

Harvey, C. R., Ramachandran, A., & Santoro, J. (2021). DeFi and the Future of Finance.

Hashizume, K., & Fernandez, E. B. (2013). An analysis of security issues for cloud computing. *Journal of Internet Services and Applications*, 4(1), 5. DOI: 10.1186/1869-0238-4-5

Haugh, T., & Bedi, S. (2023). Valuing Corporate Compliance.

Hawkins, B. (2015). *Case Study: The Home Depot Data Breach*. SANS Institute.

Healthcare Data Breach Statistics. (2023). Retrieved from: https://www.hipaajournal.com/healthcare-data-breach-statistics/

Hean, D. R. (1998). Co-operative authoring and collaboration over the World Wide Web. Retrieved from http://hdl.handle.net/10179/12296

Hedge, V. (2018). *Obfuscated command line detection using machine learning*. Retrieved from https://www.mandiant.com/resources/blog/obfuscated-command-line-detection-using-machine-learning

Help And Training Community. (n.d.). Salesforce. Retrieved May 11, 2024, from https://help.salesforce.com/s/articleView?id=000384648&type=1

Hendler, J., & Berners-Lee, T. (2010). From the Semantic Web to social machines: A research challenge for AI on the World Wide Web. *Artificial Intelligence*, 174(2), 156–161. DOI: 10.1016/j.artint.2009.11.010

Hendrycks, D., & Mazeika, M. (2022). X-risk analysis for ai research. arXiv preprint. doi:arXiv:2206.05862

Herath, H. S., & Herath, T. C. (2014). *IT security auditing: A performance evaluation decision model*. ScienceDirect.

Herley, C. (2009) So long, and no thanks for the externalities https://dl.acm.org/doi/10.1145/1719030.1719050

Herring, S. (2021, March 3). Retain or Retire in a Cloud Migration» Webapper» Cloud Engineers. Webapper. https://www.webapper.com/retain-or-retire-cloud-migration/

He, Y., Maglaras, L., Aliyu, A., & Luo, C. (2022). Healthcare security incident response strategy-a proactive incident response (ir) procedure. *Security and Communication Networks*, 2022, 2022. DOI: 10.1155/2022/2775249

Heyman, C. E. (2023). A red flag checklist for cryptocurrency Ponzi schemes. *Journal of Financial Crime*.

Himri, Y., Muyeen, S. M., Malik, F. H., Himri, S., Amali bin Ahmad, K., Kasbadji Merzouk, N., & Merzouk, M. (2022). A review on applications of the standard series IEC 61850 in smart grid applications. Cyberphysical Smart Cities Infrastructures: Optimal Operation and Intelligent Decision Making, 197-253.

Hitaj, B., Ateniese, G., & Perez-Cruz, F. (2017). Deep models under the GAN. *Proceedings of the 2017 ACM SIGSAC Conference on Computer and Communications Security*. DOI: 10.1145/3133956.3134012

Hochberg, Y. V., Sapienza, P., & Vissing-Jørgensen, A. (2009). A lobbying approach to evaluating the Sarbanes-Oxley Act of 2002. *Journal of Accounting Research*, 47(2), 519–583. DOI: 10.1111/j.1475-679X.2009.00321.x

Hofstetter, M., Riedl, R., Koumpis, T. G., & Schaberreiter, T. (2020). Applications of AI in cybersecurity. *Second International Conference on Transdisciplinary AI (TransAI)*, 138-141. DOI: 10.1109/TransAI49837.2020.00031

Hoitash, R., & Hoitash, U. (2009). The role of audit committees in managing relationships with external auditors after SOX: Evidence from the USA. *Managerial Auditing Journal*, 24(4), 368–397. DOI: 10.1108/02686900910948206

Holmstrom, B., & Kaplan, S. N. (2009). The state of US corporate governance: What's right and what's wrong? In *US Corporate Governance* (pp. 26–47). Columbia University Press. DOI: 10.7312/chew14856-002

Hopkins, J.L. (2021). An investigation into emerging industry 4.0 technologies as drivers of supply chain innovation in Australia. Computers in Industry, 125. doi: . compind.2020.103323DOI: 10.1016/j

Hsieh, Y. Y., & Vergne, J. P. (2023). The future of the web? The coordination and early-stage growth of decentralized platforms. *Strategic Management Journal*, 44(3), 829–857. DOI: 10.1002/smj.3455

https://dl.acm.org/doi/pdf/10.1145/356789.356794

https://ieeexplore.ieee.org/document/1425057

https://privacyandsecurityconference.pt/conference2019/Proceedings_Digital_Privacy_and_Security_Conference_2019.pdf#page=65

https://www.crowdstrike.com/cybersecurity-101/secops/ai-powered-behavioral-analysis/

https://www.crowdstrike.com/falcon-platform/?utm_campaign=brand&utm_content=crwd-treq-en-x-tct-us-psp-x-trl-brnd-x_x_x_x-product&utm_medium=sem&utm_source=goog&utm_term=crowdstrike%20falcon&cq_cmp=19616633038&cq_plac=&gad_source=1&gclid=Cj0KCQiA35urBhDCAR

Huang, Y., Bian, Y., Li, R., Zhao, J. L., & Shi, P. (2019). *Smart contract security: A software lifecycle perspective.* IEEE.

Hughes-Lartey, K., Li, M. E., Botchey, F., & Qin, Z. (2021) Human factor, a critical weak point in the information security of an organization's Internet of things. https://pubmed.ncbi.nlm.nih.gov/33768182/

Hussain, M., & Al-Mourad, M. B. (2014). Effective Third Party Auditing in Cloud Computing. *2014 28th International Conference on Advanced Information Networking and Applications Workshops.* IEEE.

IAASB. (2004). *International auditing and assurance standards board.* https://www.iaasb.org/consultations-projects/planning-audit-financial-statements

Ibrahim, A., Valli, C., McAteer, I., & Chaudhry, J. (2018). A security review of local government using NIST CSF: A case study. *The Journal of Supercomputing*, 74(10), 5171–5186. DOI: 10.1007/s11227-018-2479-2

IC3 Annual Report and Fraud Flyer. (2024, March 18). https://www.ic3.gov/Media/Y2024/PSA240318#:~:text=In%202023%2C%20the%20IC3%20received,result%20of%20frauds%20and%20scams

Initiative, I. D. (2020). *Engaging with Stakeholders for TAI Audits.* Retrieved from INTOSAI Development Initiative: https://idi.no/elibrary/professional-sais/tai-audit/1217-tai-audit-guide-chapter-5-engaging-with-stakeholders-for-tai-audits/file

Institute, S. (2021). SANS Institute. Retrieved from https://www.sans.org/

Institute, L. P. (2020, January). The Third Annual Study on the State of. Ponemon Institute©. *Research Reports (Montgomery).*

Investopedia. (n.d.). Retrieved from Investopedia: https://www.investopedia.com/terms/w/web-20.asp

ISACA. (2016). *CISA Review* (Manual 26th Edition). ISACA.

ISACA. (2017). *COBIT 5: A business framework for the governance and management of enterprise IT*. ISACA.

ISACA. (2019). Retrieved from ISACA: https://www.isaca.org/resources/news-and-trends/newsletters/atisaca/2019/volume-23/applying-cobit-to-vendor-risk-management

ISACA. (2020). *Information Systems Audit and Control Association*. Retrieved from https://www.isaca.org/

Islam, M., & Stafford, T. (2017). Information Technology (IT) integration and cybersecurity/security: The Security Savviness of Board of Directors. 23rd Americas Conference on Information Systems (AMCIS 2017): A Tradition of Innovation.

ISO/IEC 27005:2018. (2018). Information technology -- Security techniques -- Information security risk management.

Izquierdo, R. (2023, March 29). Sophos Intercept X Review.

Jackson, K. A. (2023). A Systematic Review of Machine Learning Enabled Phishing. arXiv preprint arXiv:2310.06998.

Jaeger, J. (2018). Reducing third-party risks with eyes wide open: Recent analyses show that many companies don't have adequate visibility into their third parties, and even less so their third parties' third parties and beyond (so-called Nth parties).

Jaleel, A. (2023). *ChatGPT and Leveraging Artificial Intelligence in Auditing*. ISACA.

Jensen, J. R., von Wachter, V., & Ross, O. (2021). An introduction to decentralized finance (defi). *Complex Systems Informatics and Modeling Quarterly*, (26), 46–54. DOI: 10.7250/csimq.2021-26.03

Jentzsch, C. (2016). Decentralized autonomous organization to automate governance. White paper, November.

Jiang, B., Liu, Y., & Chan, W. K. (2018). Contractfuzzer: Fuzzing smart contracts for vulnerability detection.

Johann, S. (2016). Dave Thomas on Innovating Legacy Systems. *IEEE Software*, 33(2), 105–108. DOI: 10.1109/MS.2016.38

Johnson, R., & Brown, C. (2020). Structured Selection Frameworks for Cloud Service Providers: A Comprehensive Review. *International Journal of Information Management*, 28(4), 120–135.

Johnson, R., & Jones, S. (2020). Development of selection criteria for cloud service providers: A comprehensive framework. *International Journal of Information Management*, 50, 102025.

Johnson, R., & Williams, M. (2020). Performance Management in Cloud Computing Environments: A Review of Service Level Agreements (SLAs). *International Journal of Cloud Applications and Computing*, 10(1), 1–12.

Jones, D. (2020, November 25). *Home Depot codifies data reforms in $17.5M breach settlement with states*. Retrieved from Cybersecurity Dive: https://www.cybersecuritydive.com/news/home-depot-data-breach-settlement/589736/

Jones, A., & Patel, S. (2020). Robust Access Controls in Cloud Service Providers: A Comprehensive Evaluation. *International Journal of Cybersecurity and Privacy*, 7(2), 98–115.

Jones, B., & Williams, C. (2020). Evaluating Cloud Service Provider Certifications: A Framework for Compliance Assurance. *International Journal of Information Security*, 25(2), 189–205.

Jones, D., & Lee, S. (2020). Strategic Planning in Cloud Service Provider Selection: A Comprehensive Approach. *International Journal of Information Management*, 45, 1–14.

Joshi, A., Bollen, L., Hassink, H., De Haes, S., & Van Grembergen, W. (2018). Explaining IT governance disclosure through the constructs of IT governance maturity and IT strategic role. *Information & Management*, 55(3), 368–380. DOI: 10.1016/j.im.2017.09.003

Joy, J. (2018). *Toward Encrypted and Private Databases*. ISACA.

JPMorgan. (2022, April). Retrieved from: https://www.jpmorgan.com/content/dam/jpm/commercial-banking/insights/cybersecurity/highlights-afp-2022-payments-fraud-and-control-report.pdf

Juniper Research. (n.d.). Digital commerce transactions to pass 1 trillion threshold globally by 2024, as NFC payments & digital ticketing surge ahead. Retrieved from https://www.juniperresearch.com/pressreleases/digital-commerce-transactions-to-pass-1tn?ch=Ecommerce%20Payments:%20Emerging%20Opportunities,%20Vendor%20Strategies%20&%20Market%20Forecasts%202022-202

Kahn, J. (2003). Blowing it. *Fortune*, 148(3), 42.

Kallam, S. (2015, Sept). Diffie-Hellman:Key Exchange and Public Key Cryptosystems. Retrieved from: https://cs.indstate.edu/~skallam/doc.pdf

Kamei, M. (2011). Web 2.0's traction as compared to Web 1.0, Web 3.0 and Web 4.0.

Kampakis, S., & Stankevičius, L. (2023). The Tokenomics audit checklist: Presentation and examples from the audit of a DeFi project, Terra/Luna and Ethereum 2.0. The Journal of The British Blockchain Association, 42.

Kamruzzaman, A. (2022, December). A Comprehensive Review of Endpoint Security: Threats and Defenses. Retrieved from: https://ieeexplore.ieee.org/document/9998470

Kandasamy, K., Srinivas, S., Achuthan, K., & Rangan, V. P. (2022). Digital Healthcare - cyberattacks in Asian organizations: An analysis of vulnerabilities, risks, NIST Perspectives, and recommendations. *IEEE Access : Practical Innovations, Open Solutions*, 10, 12345–12364. DOI: 10.1109/ACCESS.2022.3145372

Kaplan, A. M., & Haenlein, M. (2010). Users of the World, Unite! The Challenges and Opportunities of Social Media. *Business Horizons*, 53(1), 59–68. DOI: 10.1016/j.bushor.2009.09.003

Kashyap, R. K., & Sharma, S. (2015). Security challenges and issues in Cloud Computing – The way ahead.

Kayworth, T., & Whitten, D. (2012). Effective Information Security Requires a Balance of Social and Technology. *MIS Quarterly Executive*, 9(3), 163–175. https://ssrn.com/abstract=2058035

Kazanavičius, J., & Mažeika, D. (2019, April 1). *Migrating Legacy Software to Microservices Architecture*. IEEE Xplore. DOI: 10.1109/eStream.2019.8732170

Keller, N. (2013). Cybersecurity framework. https://www.nist.gov/cyberframework

Keskin, O. F., Caramancion, K. M., Tatar, I., Raza, O., & Tatar, U. (2021). Cyber Third-Party Risk Management: A Comparison of Non-Intrusive Risk Scoring Reports. *Electronics (Basel)*, 10(10), 1168. DOI: 10.3390/electronics10101168

Khabouze, R. (2022). *Modernization of Legacy Information Technology Systems*. https://scholarworks.waldenu.edu/cgi/viewcontent.cgi?article=14014&context=dissertations

Khadka, Saeidi, Jansen, & Hage. (2013). *A structured legacy to SOA migration process and its evaluation in practice*. DOI: 10.1109/MESOCA.2013.6632729

Khadka, R., Batlajery, B. V., Saeidi, A. M., Jansen, S., & Hage, J. (2014). How do professionals perceive legacy systems and software modernization? *Proceedings of the 36th International Conference on Software Engineering*. DOI: 10.1145/2568225.2568318

Khamisa, A. (2021). Token economies. In *The Emerald Handbook of Blockchain for Business* (pp. 121–140). Emerald Publishing Limited. DOI: 10.1108/978-1-83982-198-120211011

Khan, F., & Hassan, S. (2015). Integrated risk management in cloud migration. *International Journal of Information Management*, 35(6), 725–734.

Khan, N., & Al-Yasiri, A. (2016). Identifying Cloud Security Threats to Strengthen Cloud Computing Adoption Framework. *Procedia Computer Science*, 94, 485–490. DOI: 10.1016/j.procs.2016.08.075

Khan, O., & Khan, S. U. (2014). Cloud computing: A survey of research directions and challenges. *Journal of King Saud University. Computer and Information Sciences*, 26(1), 101–118.

Khan, S. N., Loukil, F., Ghedira-Guegan, C., Benkhelifa, E., & Bani-Hani, A. (2021). Blockchain smart contracts: Applications, challenges, and future trends. *Peer-to-Peer Networking and Applications*, 14(5), 2901–2925. DOI: 10.1007/s12083-021-01127-0 PMID: 33897937

Kiayias, A., & Lazos, P. (2022). SoK: blockchain governance. arXiv preprint. DOI: 10.1145/3558535.3559794

Kim, C. (2014). Design and Implementation Smart Office System Based on Remote Desktop Protocol (RDP). The Journal of the Institute of Internet, Broadcasting and Communication.

Kim, M. S., Dandu, J., & Iren, P. (2019). The effect of SOX on audit quality. *Journal of Financial Crime*, 26(3), 897–909. DOI: 10.1108/JFC-08-2018-0088

Klamm, B. K., & Watson, M. W. (2009). SOX 404 reported internal control weaknesses: A test of COSO framework components and information technology. *Journal of information systems, 23*(2), 1-23. *Retrieved from Journal of Information Systems*, 23(2), 1–23.

Klein, A. (2007). Building an Identity Management Infrastructure for Today...and Tomorrow. *Information Systems Security : ... International Conference, ICISS ... : Proceedings*, 16(2), 74–79. DOI: 10.1080/10658980701250083

Knechel, W. R., Krishnan, G. V., Pevzner, M., Shefchik, L. B., & Velury, U. K. (2013a). Audit quality: Insights from the academic literature. *Auditing*, 32(1, Supplement 1), 385–421. DOI: 10.2308/ajpt-50350

Knoche, H., & Hasselbring, W. (2021). Continuous API Evolution in Heterogenous Enterprise Software Systems. *18th International Conference on Software Architecture (ICSA)*, 58–68. DOI: 10.1109/ICSA51549.2021.00014

Knowles, M. (2023, September). The Importance of Endpoint Security. Retrieved from: https://hyperproof.io/resource/endpoint-security/

Kogan, A., Sudit, E. F., & Vasarhelyi, M. A. (2018). Continuous online auditing: A program of research. In Chan, D. Y., Chiu, V., & Vasarhelyi, M. A. (Eds.), *Continuous Auditing* (pp. 125–148). DOI: 10.1108/978-1-78743-413-420181006

Kolbasuk McGee, M. (2021) Record Number of Major Health Data Breaches in 2021 https://www.govinfosecurity.com/record-number-major-health-data-breaches-in-2021-a-18327

Kolk, A., van der Veen, M. L., van Wateringen, S. L., van der Veldt, D., & Walhain, S. P. (1999). *KPMG International survey of environmental reporting 1999*. KPMG/WIMM.

Kolodner, J. L. (1981, Spring). Towards an Understanding of the Role of Experience in the Evolution from Novice to Expert. *Journal of Accounting Research*, 19(1).

Kontiadis, I. Z. (2008). *Introduction to Social Administration and Social Security Institutions*. Papazisis Publications.

Kotusev, S. (2019). Enterprise architecture and enterprise architecture artifacts: Questioning the old concept in light of new findings. *Journal of Information Technology*, 34(2), 102–128. DOI: 10.1177/0268396218816273

KPMG. (2018). Evolving threat landscape: Key insights from the 2018 *KPMG Cyber Healthcare & Life Sciences Survey.*

Kraus, D., & Boulay, C. (2019). Blockchains: aspects of intellectual property law.

Krebs, B. (2019, November). Sale of 4 Million Stolen Cards Tied to Breaches at 4 Restaurant Chains. Retrieved from: https://krebsonsecurity.com/2019/11/sale-of-4-million-stolen-cards-tied-to-breaches-at-4-restaurant-chains/#:~:text=Two%20financial%20industry%20sources%20who,a%20card%20breach%20last%20month

Kreps, D., & Kimppa, K. (2015). Theorising Web 3.0: ICTs in a changing society. *Information Technology & People*, 28(4), 726–741. DOI: 10.1108/ITP-09-2015-0223

Kress, R., & Hildebrand, D. (2017). *How Analytics Will Transform Internal Audit* (Vol. 2). ISACA Journal.

Kreutzer, J., Caswell, I., Wang, L., Wahab, A., van Esch, D., Ulzii-Orshikh, N., & Adeyemi, M. (2022). Quality at a Glance: An Audit of Web-Crawled Multilingual Datasets. *Transactions of the Association for Computational Linguistics*, 10, 50–72. DOI: 10.1162/tacl_a_00447

Krishnan, J., Rama, D., & Zhang, Y. (2008). Costs to comply with SOX Section 404. *Auditing*, 27(1), 169–186. DOI: 10.2308/aud.2008.27.1.169

Kshetri, N. (2023). Privacy violations, security breaches and other threats of Web3 and the metaverse. Econstar. Retrieved from http://hdl.handle.net/10419/277993

Kshetri, N. (2010). The Economics of Click Fraud. *IEEE Security and Privacy*, 8(3), 45–53. DOI: 10.1109/MSP.2010.88

Kucuktunc, O., Cambazoglu, B. B., Weber, I., & Ferhatosmanoglu, H. (2012). A large-scale sentiment analysis for Yahoo! Answers. WSDM 2012 - Proceedings of the 5th ACM International Conference on Web Search and Data Mining, 633-642. DOI: 10.1145/2124295.2124371

Kuhn, J. R.Jr, & Sutton, S. G. (2010). Continuous Auditing in ERP System Environments: The Current State and Future Directions. *Journal of Information Systems*, 24(1), 91–112. DOI: 10.2308/jis.2010.24.1.91

Kumaraguru, P., & Cranor, L. (2005) Privacy Indexes: A Survey of Westin's Studies https://www.semanticscholar.org/paper/Privacy-Indexes%3A-A-Survey-of-Westin%27s-Studies-Kumaraguru-Cranor/e47618a4355991aee3a2fd94c5e8adc1058f4a88

Kuttybaeva, N., Raikhanova, G., Zhaparova, R., Kozhabatchina, G., & Akmolda, M. (2022, June 30). *Bulletin Of The Karaganda University Economy Series.* Retrieved from Technological audit in the system of optimization of innovative activity: https://economy-vestnik.ksu.kz/index.php/economy-vestnik/article/view/667

Kwon, R., Ashley, T., Castleberry, J., Mckenzie, P., & Gupta Gourisetti, S. N. (2020). *Cyber threat dictionary using Mitre ATT&CK matrix and NIST Cybersecurity Framework Mapping. 2020 Resilience Week.* RWS. DOI: 10.1109/RWS50334.2020.9241271

Laato, S., Farooq, A., Tenhunen, H., Pitkamaki, T., Hakkala, A., & Airola, A. (2020). Ai in cybersecurity education-a systematic literature review of studies on cybersecurity moocs. IEEE 20th International Conference on Advanced Learning Technologies (ICALT), 6-10. DOI: 10.1109/ICALT49669.2020.00009

Lacity, M. C., & Lupien, S. C. (2022). Blockchain Fundamentals for Web 3.0. Retrieved from DOI: 10.1353/book103175

Lalonde, C., & Boiral, O. (2012). Managing risks through ISO 31000: A critical analysis.

Lance Spitzner. (2024, May 29). SANS Institute. https://www.sans.org/white-papers/SANS-2021-Survey-OTICS-Cybersecurity/

Lang, S. (2024, April 2). *Meeting PCI DSS Third-Party Service Provider Requirements*. Retrieved from Prevalent: https://www.prevalent.net/compliance/pci-dss/#:~:text=The%20PCI%20DSS%20and%20Third%2DParty%20Service%20Provider%20Management&text=The%20standard%20applies%20to%20all,place%20to%20secure%20cardholder%20data

Lanois, P. (2007). Between a Rock and a Hard Place: The Sarbanes-Oxley Act and Its Global Impact. *University of Pennsylvania Journal of International Law*, 5(4), 1–19.

Laredo, V. G. (2008, May 08). PCI DSS compliance: a matter of strategy. Retrieved from: https://www.sciencedirect.com/science/article/abs/pii/S096525900870094X

Laszewski, T., & Prakash Nauduri. (2011). Migrating to the Cloud. Elsevier.

Lathrop, D., & Ruma, L. (2010). *Open government: Collaboration, transparency, and participation in practice*. O'Reilly Media, Inc.

Learn about data loss prevention - Microsoft 365 compliance. Microsoft 365 Compliance | Microsoft Docs. (n.d.). Retrieved December 16, 2021, from https://docs.microsoft.com/en-us/microsoft-365/compliance/dlp-learn-about-dlp?view=o365-worldwide

Learn about Microsoft 365 endpoint data loss prevention - microsoft 365 compliance. Microsoft 365 Compliance | Microsoft Docs. (n.d.). Retrieved December 17, 2021, from https://docs.microsoft.com/en-us/microsoft-365/compliance/endpoint-dlp-learn-about?view=o365-worldwide

Lee, A. (2022, September 2). *General information technology controls: IT risks auditors must be aware of*. Retrieved from Chartered Professional Accountants Canada: https://www.cpacanada.ca/business-and-accounting-resources/audit-and-assurance/blog/2022/september/general-information-technology-controls-for-auditors

Lee, J. H. (2019). Systematic approach to analyzing security and vulnerabilities of blockchain systems.

Leech, T., & Leech, L. (2011). Preventing the next wave of unreliable financial reporting: Why US Congress should amend Section 404 of the Sarbanes–Oxley Act. *International Journal of Disclosure and Governance*, 8(4), 295–322. DOI: 10.1057/jdg.2011.18

Lee, H., & Park, C. (2018). Assessing Cloud Service Providers' Security Incident Response: A Case Study Analysis. *Journal of Information Security*, 25(4), 189–204.

Lee, Y. Y., Gan, C. L., & Liew, T. W. (2023). Thwarting Instant Messaging Phishing Attacks: The Role of Self-Efficacy and the Mediating Effect of Attitude towards Online Sharing of Personal Information. *International Journal of Environmental Research and Public Health*, 20(4), 3514. DOI: 10.3390/ijerph20043514 PMID: 36834209

Leih, M. J. (2009). *Regulatory impact on IT governance: A multiple case study on the Sarbanes-Oxley Act*. The Claremont Graduate University.

Lei, W., Hu, S., & Hsu, C. (2023). Unveiling the process of phishing precautions taking: The moderating role of optimism bias. *Computers & Security*, 129, 103249. DOI: 10.1016/j.cose.2023.103249

Leom, M. D., Choo, K.-K. R., & Hunt, R. (2016). Remote wiping and secure deletion on mobile devices: A Review. *Journal of Forensic Sciences*, 61(6), 1473–1492. DOI: 10.1111/1556-4029.13203 PMID: 27651127

Leslie, D. A. (1985). *Materiality, the concepts and its applications in Auditing*. CICA.

Lewis, D. J. (2020). *The Cyber Defence Review*. Retrieved from Private Actors' Roles in International Cybersecurity Agreements – Unlearned Lessons.

Li, H., Dang, R., Yao, Y., & Wang, H. (2023). A Review of Approaches for Detecting Vulnerabilities in Smart Contracts within Web 3.0 Applications. Blockchains, 3-18.

Li, J. (2006). *Process Improvement and Risk Management in Off-The-Shelf Component-Based Development*.

Li, X., Jiang, P., Chen, T., Luo, X., & Wen, Q. (2020). A survey on the security of blockchain systems.

Li, C., Peters, G. F., Richardson, V. J., & Watson, M. W. (2012). The consequences of information technology control weaknesses on management information systems: The case of Sarbanes-Oxley internal control reports. *Management Information Systems Quarterly*, 36(1), 179–203. DOI: 10.2307/41410413

Liginlal, D., Sim, I., & Khansa, L. (2009). How Significant Is Human Error as a Cause of Privacy Breaches? an Empirical Study and a Framework for Error Management. *Computers & Security*, 28(3-4), 215–228. DOI: 10.1016/j.cose.2008.11.003

Li, L., Qi, B., Tian, G., & Zhang, G. (2017). The contagion effect of low-quality audits at the level of individual auditors. *The Accounting Review*, 92(1), 137–163. DOI: 10.2308/accr-51407

Lindsay, J., Doutt, A., & Ide, C. (2019). *Emerging Technologies, Risk, and the Auditor's Focus*. Harvard Law School Forum on Corporate Governance.

Linthicum, D. S. (2014). *Cloud computing and SOA convergence in your enterprise: A step-by-step guide*. Addison-Wesley Professional.

Liu, H., & Staff in the Office of Technology. (2022, October 6). *Understanding the NIST cybersecurity framework*. Federal Trade Commission. https://www.ftc.gov/business-guidance/small-businesses/cybersecurity/nist-framework

Liu, J. Y. X. (2010). A Survey of Payment Card Industry Data Security Standard. Retrieved from: https://ieeexplore-ieee-org.gate.lib.buffalo.edu/stamp/stamp.jsp?tp=&arnumber=5455788&tag=1

Liu, M., Xue, Z., Xu, X., Zhong, C., & Chen, J. (2018, Nov). Host-Based Intrusion Detection System with System Calls: Review and Future Trends. Retrieved from: https://dl.acm.org/doi/pdf/10.1145/3214304

Liu, M., Wu, K., & Xu, J. J. (2019). How will blockchain technology impact auditing and accounting: Permissionless versus permissioned blockchain. *Current Issues in Auditing*, 13(2), A19–A29. DOI: 10.2308/ciia-52540

Li, X., Gu, Y., Dvornek, N., Staib, L. H., Ventola, P., & Duncan, J. S. (2020). Multi-site fMRI analysis using privacy-preserving federated learning and domain adaptation: ABIDE results. *Medical Image Analysis*, 65, 101765. DOI: 10.1016/j.media.2020.101765 PMID: 32679533

Li, Y. (2010). The case analysis of the scandal of Enron. *International Journal of Business and Management*, 5(10), 37. DOI: 10.5539/ijbm.v5n10p37

Li, Z. (2018). The impact of AI on the field of accounting: Preventing fraud and generating positive effects on accounting information quality. *Journal of Accounting and Finance*, 32, 78–92.

Luftman, J., Lyytinen, K., & Zvi, T. B. (2017). Enhancing the measurement of information technology (IT) business alignment and its influence on company performance. *Journal of Information Technology*, 32(1), 26–46. DOI: 10.1057/jit.2015.23

Lyke, B., & Jickling, M. (2002, August). WorldCom: The accounting scandal. In *Congressional Research Service Report for Congress, August* (Vol. 29, pp. 1-6).

Lyu, M., Su, D., & Li, N. (2017). Understanding the sparse vector technique for differential privacy. *Proceedings of the VLDB Endowment International Conference on Very Large Data Bases*, 10(6), 637–648. DOI: 10.14778/3055330.3055331

M'baya, A., Laval, J., & Moalla, N. (2017). *An assessment conceptual framework for the modernization of legacy systems*. DOI: 10.1109/SKIMA.2017.8294120

Madlool, N. A., Saidur, R., Hossain, M. S., & Rahim, N. A. (2011). A critical review on energy use and savings in the cement industries. *Renewable & Sustainable Energy Reviews*, 15(4), 2042–2060. DOI: 10.1016/j.rser.2011.01.005

Magic Quadrant for Endpoint Protection Platforms. (2022, December). Retrieved from: https://www.gartner.com/document/4137499?ref=ddisp&refval=4140999

Mahamood, A. F., Ramli, A. J., Yakob, T. K. T., Ali, E., & Affandy, H. B. (2023). Analysis the types and impacts of phishing attacks on internet users. *Journal of Global Business and Social Entrepreneurship*, 9(26).

Mainardi, R. (2011). Developing and Implementing a Practical Methodology. In Mainardi, R. (Ed.), *Harnessing the Power of Continuous Auditing: Developing and Implementing a Practical Methodology*. John Wiley & Sons, Incorporated.

Makridakis, S., & Christodoulou, K. (2019). Blockchain: Current Challenges and Future Prospects/Applications. *Future Internet*, 258(12), 258. Advance online publication. DOI: 10.3390/fi11120258

Malinova, A. (2010). *Approaches and techniques for legacy.*

Mar, V. (2021, April 2). Technology trend 2021: Artificial intelligence a necessity in healthcare. Techment. https://www.techment.com/technology-trend-2021-artificial-intelligence-a-necessity-in-healthcare/

Marańda, W., Poniszewska-Marańda, A., & Szymczyńska, M. (2022). Data Processing in Cloud Computing Model on the Example of Salesforce Cloud. *Information (Basel)*, 13(2), 85. DOI: 10.3390/info13020085

Márquez, L., Rosado, D., Mouratidis, H., Mellado, D., & Fernández-Medina, E. (2015). *Framework for Secure Migration Processes of Legacy Systems to the Cloud*. DOI: 10.1007/978-3-319-19243-7_46

Marston, S., & Ghalsasi, A. (2011). Cloud computing—The business perspective. *Decision Support Systems*, 51(1), 176–189. DOI: 10.1016/j.dss.2010.12.006

Martínez, A. L., Pérez, M. G., & Ruiz-Martínez, A. (2023). A Comprehensive Review of the state-of-the-art on security and privacy issues in Healthcare. *ACM Computing Surveys*, 55(12), 1–38. Advance online publication. DOI: 10.1145/3571156

Masli, A., Peters, G. F., Richardson, V. J., & Sanchez, J. M. (2010). Examining the potential benefits of internal control monitoring technology. *The Accounting Review*, 85(3), 1001–1034. DOI: 10.2308/accr.2010.85.3.1001

Massaro, M. (2021). Digital transformation in the healthcare sector through blockchain technology. Insights from academic research and business developments. *Technovation*, 120.

Mastercard. (n.d.). Build cyber resilience and trust throughout the connected digital economy. Retrieved from https://www.mastercard.us/en-us/business/large-enterprise/safety-security/cybersecurity/cyber-and-riskmanagement.html#fn3

Mateescu, G., & Sgârciu, V. (2015). Cloud Computing Audit. *U.P.B. Sci. Bull., Series C, 77*(3). https://www.scientificbulletin.upb.ro/rev_docs_arhiva/full58d_528709.pdf

Mathew Nicho, H. F. (2011). *An Integrated Security Governance Framework for Effective PCI DSS Implementation*. Retrieved from https://www.igi-global.com/gateway/article/58982

Mautz, R. K., & Mini, D. L. (1966). *Internal Control Evaluation and Audit Program Modification*. ProQuest.

McConnell, D. K.Jr, & Banks, G. Y. (2003). How Sarbanes-Oxley will change the audit process. *Journal of Accountancy*, 196(3), 49. https://www.journalofaccountancy.com/issues/2003/sep/howsarbanesoxleywillchangetheauditprocess.html

McGhin, T., Choo, K. K. R., Liu, C. Z., & He, D. (2019). Blockchain in healthcare applications: Research challenges and opportunities. *Journal of Network and Computer Applications*, 135, 62–75. DOI: 10.1016/j.jnca.2019.02.027

McKinsey. (2019). Driving impact at scale from automation and AI. Retrieved from https://www.mckinsey.com/~/media/McKinsey/Business%20Functions/McKinsey%20Digital/Our%20Insights/Driving%20impact%20at%20scale%20from%20automation%20and%20AI/Driving-impact-at-scale-from-automation-and-AI.ashx

McLean, B., & Elkind, P. (2013). *The smartest guys in the room: The amazing rise and scandalous fall of Enron*. Penguin.

McNair, C. J. (1991). Proper compromises: The management control dilemma in public accounting and its impact on auditor behavior. *Accounting, Organizations and Society*, 16(7), 635–653. DOI: 10.1016/0361-3682(91)90017-9

Mcneil, L. B. (2022). Blockchains, smart contracts, and stablecoins as a global payment system: The rise of web 3.0 (Dissertation). Retrieved from https://urn.kb.se/resolve?urn=urn:nbn:se:lnu:diva-114247

Medrano, D. (2022). *Third-Party Key Risk Indicators – What Management Should Consider.*

Meeker, W. Q., Escobar, L. A., & Pascual, F. G. (2022). *Statistical methods for reliability data*. John Wiley & Sons.

Megargel, A., Shankararaman, V., & Walker, D. (2020). *Migrating from Monoliths to Cloud-Based Microservices: A Banking Industry Example* (pp. 85-108). https://doi.org/%7B10.1007/978-3-030-33624-0_4%7D

Mehta, A. (2010). An approach toward Sarbanes-oxley ITGC Risk assessment. *ISACA Journal, 5*, 15. https://www.isaca.org/resources/isaca-journal/past-issues/2010/an-approach-toward-sarbanes-oxley-itgc-risk-assessment

Melancon, B. C. (2002). A new accounting culture. *Journal of Accountancy*, 194(4), 27.

Merchant risk council. (2023, Sept). Retrieved from: https://merchantriskcouncil.org/learning/resource-center/member-news/blog/2023/history-of-PCI-compliance

Merrell, I. (2022). Blockchain for decentralised rural development and governance. Blockchain: Research and Applications.

Meunier, S. (2018). Blockchain 101: What is Blockchain and How Does This Revolutionary Technology Work? .DOI: 10.1016/B978-0-12-814447-3.00003-3

Michael Haag, J. M. (2020, May). EDR buyer's guide: The business case. Retrieved from: https://resource.redcanary.com/rs/003-YRU-314/images/EDR-Buyers-Guide-2020.pdf

Microsoft. (2004, February). Perimeter Firewall Design. Retrieved from: https://learn.microsoft.com/en-us/previous-versions/tn-archive/cc700828(v=technet.10)?redirectedfrom=MSDN

Microsoft. (2020). *Microsoft Security Documentation*. Retrieved from https://docs.microsoft.com/en-us/security/

Microsoft. (2022, October 03). Endpoint Protection. Retrieved from: https://learn.microsoft.com/en-us/mem/configmgr/protect/deploy-use/endpoint-protection

Microsoft. (2023), What is the Microsoft Cloud Adoption Framework for Azure? *Microsoft*. Retrieved from https://learn.microsoft.com/en-us/azure/cloud-adoption-framework/overview

Microsoft. (2024, Jan). Retrieved from: https://www.microsoft.com/en-us/security/business/endpoint-security/microsoft-defender-endpoint

Microsoft. (2024, Jan). What is data loss prevention (DLP)? Retrieved from: https://www.microsoft.com/en-us/security/business/security-101/what-is-data-loss-prevention-dlp?ef_id=_k_fe0b4c7a48eb1cb16a5c292755d1c01e_k_&OCID=AIDcmmdamuj0pc_SEM__k_fe0b4c7a48eb1cb16a5c292755d1c01e_k_&msclkid=fe0b4c7a48eb1cb16a5c292755d1c01e

Microsoft. (n.d.). *Get started Accelerate migration Deliver operational excellence Antipatterns to avoid Strategy Motivations.* Retrieved from https://learn.microsoft.com/pdf?url=https%3A%2F%2Flearn.microsoft.com%2Fen-us%2Fazure%2Fcloud-adoption-framework%2Ftoc.json

Miller, R. I., & Pashkoff, P. H. (2002). Regulations under the sarbanes-oxley act. *Journal of Accountancy*, 194(4), 33–37.

Miller, R., & Lessard, D. R. (2001). *The strategic management of large engineering projects: Shaping institutions, risks, and governance*. MIT Press. DOI: 10.7551/mitpress/6478.001.0001

Millett, L. I., Lin, H. S., & Waldo, J. (2007). *Engaging privacy and information technology in a digital age*. National Academies Press.

Mock, T. J., & Wright, A. (1992). An Exploratory Study of Auditor Evalyuation, Planning Judgements, revised version of a paper presented at the 1991 Annual Congress of the European Accounting Association, Maastricht, The Netherlands.

Mohaisen, Alrawi & Mohaisen (2015, July). AMAL: High-fidelity, behavior-based automated malware analysis and classification. Retrieved from: https://www.sciencedirect.com/science/article/pii/S0167404815000425

Mohammed, I. A. (2020). Artificial intelligence for cybersecurity: A systematic mapping of literature. *Artificial Intelligence*, 7(9), 1–5.

Mont, J. (2017). Recent data breaches impart third-party risk lessons: The data breaches at Yahoo, Equifax, and the SEC send a collective warning to organizations everywhere to improve their own third-party risk assessment.

Moog, M. (2022, August 5). *Eight Steps to Manage the Third-Party Lifecycle*. Retrieved from ISACA: https://www.isaca.org/resources/news-and-trends/isaca-now-blog/2022/eight-steps-to-manage-the-third-party-lifecycle

Morovat, K., & Panda, B. (2020). A survey of artificial intelligence in cybersecurity. *2020 International Conference on Computational Science and Computational Intelligence (CSCI)*, 109-115. DOI: 10.1109/CSCI51800.2020.00026

Morrison, A. D. (2004, July). Sarbanes-Oxley, corporate governance and operational risk. In *Proceedings of the Sarbanes-Oxford Conference held at Said Business School,* University of Oxford (Vol. 22).

Mosli, R., Li, R., Yuan, B., & Pan, Y. (2017, Aug). A Behaviour based approach for malware detection. Retrieved from: https://link.springer.com/content/pdf/10.1007/978-3-319-67208-3_11.pdf

Mouchantaf, R., Auth, D., Moride, Y., Raine, J., Han, S. Y., & Smith, M. Y. (2021). Risk Management for the 21st Century: Current Status and Future Needs. *Drug Safety*, 44(4), 409–419. DOI: 10.1007/s40264-020-01033-z PMID: 33565024

Mowbray, M., & Varia, J. (2010). *Amazon Web Services: Migrating your. NET Enterprise Application*. O'Reilly Media.

Mthunzia, S.N., & Benkhelifa, E.(2020). Cloud computing security taxonomy: From an atomistic to a holistic view.

Murer, S., Bonati, B., & Furrer, F. J. (2011). *Managed Evolution: A Strategy for Very Large Information Systems* (1st ed.). Springer Berlin., DOI: 10.1007/978-3-642-01633-2

Murphy, C. N., & Yates, J. (2009). *The International Organization for Standardization*. ISO. DOI: 10.4324/9780203884348

Murugesan, S. (2007). Understanding Web 2.0. *IT Professional*, 9(4), 34–41. DOI: 10.1109/MITP.2007.78

Nakamoto, S. (2008). Bitcoin: A Peer-to-Peer Electronic Cash System. Cryptography Mailing list at https://metzdowd.com

Namakshenas, D. (2023). Web3. 0 Security: Privacy Enhancing and Anonym Au diting in Blockchain-based Structures. doi:arXiv:2307.12485

Naqvi, B., Perova, K., Farooq, A., Makhdoom, I., Oyedeji, S., & Porras, J. (2023). Mitigation strategies against the phishing attacks: A systematic literature review. *Computers & Security*, 132, 103387. DOI: 10.1016/j.cose.2023.103387

Nardecchia, C. (2022, March 30). *5 leadership tips for CIOs to evolve their digital strategy | The Enterprisers Project*. Enterprisersproject.com. https://enterprisersproject.com/article/2022/3/leadership-tips-cios-evolve-digital-strategy

Nasir, Q., & Malik, Z. (2019). A Review of Risks Associated with Cloud Computing and Their Management. *IEEE Access : Practical Innovations, Open Solutions*, 7, 158694–158707.

National Archives and Records Administration. (2013). *Executive Order -- Improving Critical Infrastructure Cybersecurity*. National Archives and Records Administration. https://obamawhitehouse.archives.gov/the-press-office/2013/02/12/executive-order-improving-critical-infrastructure-cybersecurity

National Institute of Standards and Technology (NIST). (n.d.). *Cybersecurity Framework*. Retrieved from NIST: https://www.nist.gov/cyberframework

National Institute of Standards and Technology (NIST). (n.d.). *NIST Special Publication 800-30: Guide for Conducting Risk Assessments*. Retrieved from https://csrc.nist.gov/publications/detail/sp/800-30/rev-1/final

Nationwide. (n.d.). *Business solutions center What is cyber insurance?* Retrieved from Nationwide: https://www.nationwide.com/business/solutions-center/cybersecurity/what-is-cyber-insurance

NBCUniversal News Group. (2013, August 26). How snowden did it. NBCNews.com. Retrieved December 17, 2021, from https://www.nbcnews.com/news/world/how-snowden-did-it-flna8c11003160

Netsurion. (2014, January 16). Looking back: Operation buckshot yankee & agent.btz. Netsurion. Retrieved December 16, 2021, from https://www.netsurion.com/articles/looking-back-operation-buckshot-yankee-agent-btz

Network Segmentation. (2019, June). Retrieved from: https://attack.mitre.org/mitigations/M1030/

Newman, L. H. (2022, March 28). *Leaked Details of the Lapsus$ Hack Make Okta's Slow Response Look More Bizarre*. Retrieved from Wired: https://www.wired.com/story/lapsus-okta-hack-sitel-leak/

Nguyen, K., Nguyen, T., & Kovchegov, Y. (2009). A p2p video delivery network (p2p-vdn). 2009 Proceedings of 18th International Conference on Computer Communications and Networks, 1-7.

Nguyen, A., Smith, J., & Johnson, L. (2022). The positive impact of AI technology on the auditing process to enhance information transparency. *Journal of Accounting and Auditing*, 45, 112–128.

Nicho, M., Khan, S., & Rahman, M. (2017). Managing Information Security Risk Using Integrated Governance Risk and Compliance.

Nicho, M. (2018). A process model for implementing information systems security governance. *Information and Computer Security*, 26(1), 10–38. DOI: 10.1108/ICS-07-2016-0061

Nifakos, S., Chandramouli, K., Nikolaou, C. K., Papachristou, P., Koch, S., Panaousis, E., & Bonacina, S. (2021, July). Influence of Human Factors on Cyber Security within Healthcare Organisations: A Systematic Review, (in eng). *Sensors (Basel)*, 21(15), 28. DOI: 10.3390/s21155119 PMID: 34372354

NIST cybersecurity framework. (2024b, May 1). NIST. https://www.nist.gov/itl/smallbusinesscyber/nist-cybersecurity-framework-0

NIST history. (2019, November 15). NIST. https://www.nist.gov/history

NIST. (2020). NIST-NIST SP 800-53 Rev. 5.

NIST. (2022, July). Retrieved from: https://www.nist.gov/news-events/news/2022/07/nist-announces-first-four-quantum-resistant-cryptographic-algorithms

NIST. (2024), Separation of Duty, Computer Security Resource Center, Assessed from https://csrc.nist.gov/glossary/term/separation_of_duty

Niya, S. R., Schüpfer, F., Bocek, T., & Stiller, B. (2018). A Peer-to-peer Purchase and Rental Smart Contract-based Application (PuRSCA).

Norfolk, D. (2014, March 23). *Legacy Modernisation - Bloor Research*. Www.bloorresearch.com. https://www.bloorresearch.com/issue/legacy-modernisation/

Norman Comstock, L. N. (2023, October). Making Sense of Today's Payment Cybersecurity Landscape. Retrieved from: https://www.darkreading.com/vulnerabilities-threats/making-sense-of-todays-payment-cybersecurity-landscape

O'Reilly, T. (2005). *What Is Web 2.0: Design Patterns and Business Models for the Next Generation of Software. Communications & Strategies*. O'Reilly Media.

O'reilly, T. (2007). What is Web 2.0: Design Patterns and Business Models for the Next Generation of Software. *Communications & Stratégies*, 17.

O'Reilly, T. (2007). What is Web 2.0: Design patterns and business models for the next generation of software. *Communications & Stratégies*, 65(1), 17–37.

O'Reilly, T., & Battelle, J. (2009). *Web squared: Web 2.0 five years on*. O'Reilly Media, Inc.

Obar, J., & Wildman, S. (2015). Social Media Definition and the Governance Challenge - An Introduction to the Special Issue. *Telecommunications Policy*, 39(9), 745–750. DOI: 10.1016/j.telpol.2015.07.014

Obrutsky, S. (2016, July). Cloud storage: Advantages, disadvantages and enterprise solutions for

OCR. (2022, January 19). *Your rights under HIPAA*. HHS.gov. https://www.hhs.gov/hipaa/for-individuals/guidance-materials-for-consumers/index.html

Öğüt, H., Raghunathan, S., & Menon, N. (2011). Cyber security risk management: Public policy implications of correlated risk, imperfect ability to prove loss, and observability of self-protection. *Risk Analysis*, 31(3), 497–512. DOI: 10.1111/j.1539-6924.2010.01478.x PMID: 20807381

Okman, T. (2018, January). Cybersecurity Trends To Look Out For In 2023. Retrieved from: https://www.forbes.com/sites/forbestechcouncil/2023/01/18/cybersecurity-trends-to-look-out-for-in-2023/?sh=5cb103dd4421

Olaniyi, O., Olabanji, S. O., & Abalaka, A. (2023). Navigating risk in the modern business landscape: Strategies and insights for enterprise risk management implementation. *Journal of Scientific Research and Reports*, 29(9), 103–109. DOI: 10.9734/jsrr/2023/v29i91789

Olechowski, A., Oehmen, J., Seering, W., & Ben-Daya, M. (2016). *The professionalization of risk management: What role can the ISO 31000 risk management principles play?*

Ølnes, S., Ubacht, J., & Janssen, M. (2017). Blockchain in government: Benefits and implications of distributed ledger technology for information sharing. Government Information Quarterly, 355-364. https://www.sciencedirect.com/science/article/pii/S0740624X17303155

Oltsik, J. (2018). *Enterprise plans for security automation and orchestration*. Retrieved from https://www.techtarget.com/blog/enterprise-plans-for-security-automation-and-orchestration

Omoteso, K. (2016). *Audit effectiveness: meeting the IT challenge*. Routledge. DOI: 10.4324/9781315568294

Omotunde, H., & Ahmed, M. (2023). A Comprehensive Review of Security Measures in Database Systems: Assessing Authentication, Access Control, and Beyond. Mesopotamian Journal of CyberSecurity, 115-133.

One, S. (n.d.). Singularity for Endpoints. Retrieved from: https://www.sentinelone.com/surfaces/endpoint/?utm_medium=paid-search&utm_source=google-paid&utm_campaign=nam-dsa-ppc&gclid=Cj0KCQiAgqGrBhDtARIsAM5s0_nXdwj2djMyRjGGsPpSLTqmgGkZTiYHGh2u9L3hwctHUtaTVzt0n4AaAoJ2EALw_wcB

Onulaka, P. N. (2015). Internal and external audit effectiveness in fraud detection through continuous auditing. *International Journal of Management*, 6(10), 462–475.

Open Web Application Security Project. (2021). *OWASP*. Retrieved from https://owasp.org/

Open, A. I. (2022). ChatGPT (Version 3.5). Retrieved from https://www.openai.com/gpt-3

Oracle (2024), Configuring Advanced Role-based Access Control, Retrieved online from https://docs.oracle.com/cd/E28280_01/admin.1111/e16580/rbac.htm

Orin, R. M. (2008). Ethical guidance and constraint under the Sarbanes-Oxley Act of 2002. *Journal of Accounting, Auditing & Finance*, 23(1), 141–171. DOI: 10.1177/0148558X0802300108

Orlikowski, W. (1993). Learning from notes: Organizational issues in groupware implementation. *The Information Society*, 9(3), 237–250. DOI: 10.1080/01972243.1993.9960143

Ozturk, C., & Yildibasi, A. (2020). Barriers to implementation of blockchain into supply chain management using an integrated multi-criteria decision-making method: A numerical example. *Soft Computing*, 24(19), 14771–14789. DOI: 10.1007/s00500-020-04831-w

Pacheco, M. (2023, July 14). What is Replatforming? A Guide to Optimizing Your Applications. *TierPoint, LLC.*https://www.tierpoint.com/blog/replatforming/

Padilla, R. S., Milton, S. K., Johnson, L. W., & Nyadzayo, M. W. (2017). Impact of Service Value on Satisfaction and Repurchase Intentions in Business-to-Business Cloud Computing. *Service Science*, 9(1), 5–13. DOI: 10.1287/serv.2016.0163

Palachuk, K. W. (2018). *Service Agreements*. Great Little Book Publishing Co., Inc.

PaloAlto. (2019). What is a Zero Trust Architecture. Retrieved from: https://www.paloaltonetworks.com/cyberpedia/what-is-a-zero-trust-architecture

Paloalto. (n.d.). What is an Endpoint? Retrieved from: https://www.paloaltonetworks.com/cyberpedia/what-is-an-endpoint

PaloAlto. (n.d.). What Is Extended Detection and Response (XDR)? Retrieved from Cyberpedia: https://www.paloaltonetworks.com/cyberpedia/what-is-extended-detection-response-XDR

Park, K., & Sen, S. (2016). *Third-party governance and risk management The threats are real*. Deloitte TTP.

Pazhanisamy, K., Parthiban, L., Kannadasan, R., Anakath, A. S., & Parthiban, R. (2023). Integrating Blockchain and Artificial Intelligence for Industry 4.0 Innovations. Springer International Publishing, 295-304.

PCAOB. (2007). *PCAOB: Public Company Accounting Oversight Board.* Retrieved from AS 2201: An Audit of Internal Control Over Financial Reporting That Is Integrated with An Audit of Financial Statements: https://pcaobus.org/oversight/standards/auditing-standards/details/AS2201

PCAOB. (2010). *PCAOB Public Company Accounting Oversight Board.* Retrieved from PCAOB Public Company Accounting Oversight Board: https://pcaobus.org/oversight/standards/auditing-standards/details/as-2101-audit-planning-2022

PCI DSS version 4.0. (2022, Mar). Retrieved from: https://www.commerce.uwo.ca/pdf/PCI-DSS-v4_0.pdf

PCI Security Standards Council. (2022, August). PCI DSS v4.0 Quick Reference Guide, Understanding the Payment Card Industry. Retrieved from: https://www.pnc.com/content/dam/pnc-com/pdf/smallbusiness/Merchant%20Services/PCI_DSS_QuickRef_Guide.pdf

PCI Security Standards. (2022, Mar). Retrieved from: https://www.pcisecuritystandards.org/document_library/

PCI Standards Council. (n.d.). Retrieved from: https://www.pcisecuritystandards.org/merchants/

Pehlivanoglu, D., Shoenfelt, A., Hakim, Z. M., Heemskerk, A., Zhen, J., Mosqueda, M., ... Ebner, N. C. (2023). Phishing vulnerability compounded by older age, APOE4 genotype, and lower cognition.

Peterson, R. R. (2004). Integration strategies and tactics for information technology governance. Strategies for information technology governance, 37-80.

Pfleeger, S., & Caputo, D. (2012). Leveraging behavioral science to mitigate cyber security risk. https://www.researchgate.net/publication/257006498_Leveraging_behavioral_science_to_mitigate_cyber_security_risk

Pianini, D., & Neri, A. (2021). *Breaking down monoliths with Microservices and DevOps: an industrial experience report. Archivio Istituzionale Della Ricerca.* Alma Mater Studiorum Università Di Bologna. DOI: 10.1109/ICSME52107.2021.00051

Plennert, M. (2018). The social construction of technological stasis: The stagnating data structure in OpenStreetMap. *Big Data & Society*, 5(2), 205395171879059. DOI: 10.1177/2053951718790591

Poirier, C. C. (1999). Advanced supply chain management: How to build a sustained competitive advantage. Berrett-Koehler.

Potluri, R. M., & Vajjhala, N. (2018). A Study on Application of Web 3.0 Technologies in Small and Medium Enterprises of India. The Journal of Asian Finance, Economics and Business, 73-79.

PRITCHETT. (2017, December 20). *PRITCHETT's Change Management Methodology*. Pritchett LP. https://www.pritchettnet.com/pritchett-change-management-methodology

Pryshchepa, O. (2021). Disciplining entrenched managers through corporate governance reform: Implications for risk-taking behavior. *Corporate Governance*, 29(4), 328–351. DOI: 10.1111/corg.12370

Public Law 107–204, 1. (2002, July 30). Retrieved from https://www.govinfo.gov/content/pkg/PLAW-107publ204/pdf/PLAW-107publ204.pdf

Public Law 112-158. (2012, August 10). Securities Exchange Act Of 1934. Retrieved from https://www.nyse.com/publicdocs/nyse/regulation/nyse/sea34.pdf

Public Law 117–263. (2022, December 23). Ecanctment: Securities Act of 1933.

Pulkkinen, M. (2020). Cloud migration strategy factors and migration processes. Retrieved from: https://helda.helsinki.fi/server/api/core/bitstreams/188695f4-5946-4509-943c-4021dcbe9093/content

Purnell, M. (2023, August). QR Code Payments Market: 2023-2028. Retrieved from: https://www.juniperresearch.com/researchstore/fintech-payments/qr-code-payments-research-report

Queiroz, M. M., Fosso Wamba, S., De Bourmont, M., & Telles, R. (2021). Blockchain adoption in operations and supply chain management: Empirical evidence from an emerging economy. *International Journal of Production Research*, 59(20), 6087–6103. DOI: 10.1080/00207543.2020.1803511

Radanliev, P. (2023). The Rise and Fall of Cryptocurrencies: Defining the Economic and Social Values of Blockchain Technologies, assessing the Opportunities, and defining the Financial and Cybersecurity Risks of the Metaverse. arXiv preprint. doi:arXiv:2309.12322 DOI: 10.31224/3162

Raghunath, B. R., & Mahadeo, S. N. (2008, July). Network Intrusion Detection System (NIDS). Retrieved from: https://ieeexplore.ieee.org/abstract/document/4580100

Ragnedda, M., & Destefanis, G. (2019). *Blockchain and Web 3.0*. Routledge, Taylor and Francis Group. DOI: 10.4324/9780429029530

Rahman, H., & Hussain, M. I. (2020). A comprehensive survey on semantic interoperability for Internet of Things: State-of-the-art and research challenges. *Transactions on Emerging Telecommunications Technologies*, 31(12), 3902. DOI: 10.1002/ett.3902

Raj P. H., & Jelciana P. (2017). Exploring Data Security Issues and Solutions in Cloud Computing. *ICSCC 2017.*

Raji, I. D., Smart, A., White, R. N., Mitchell, M., Gebru, T., Hutchinson, B., & Barnes, P. (2020). Closing the AI accountability gap: Defining an end-to-end framework for internal algorithmic auditing. In *Proceedings of the 2020 conference on fairness, accountability, and transparency* (pp. 33-44). DOI: 10.1145/3351095.3372873

Ramaseshan, R., & Mattsson, J. (2007). *Key Issues in CRM Implementation: Some Evidence from Scandinavian Businesses*. Paper presented at Annual World Marketing Congress 2007, Verona, Italy.

Rampolla, J., & Kipper, G. (2012). *Augmented reality: An emerging technologies guide to AR*. Elsevier.

Rashmi, M. S., & Sahoo, G. (2012). A five-phased approach for the cloud migration. *International Journal of Emerging Technology and Advanced Engineering*, 2(4), 286–291.

Rasner, G. C. (2021). *Cybersecurity and Third-Party Risk*. John Wiley & Sons, Inc.

Rathor, S., Zhang, M., & Im, T. (2023). Web 3.0 and Sustainability: Challenges and Research Opportunities. Sustainability.

Raval, V., & Shah, S. (2017). Third-party Risk Management. *ISACA Journal Third-party. Risk Management*, 13–18.

Raymond, M. (2016). Managing decentralized cyber governance: the responsibility to troubleshoot. Strategic Studies Quarterly, 123-149.

Razi, Q., Devrani, A., Abhyankar, H., Chalapathi, G. S., Hassija, V., & Guizani, M. (2023). Non-Fungible Tokens (NFTs)-Survey of Current Applications, Evolution and Future Directions. *IEEE Open Journal of the Communications Society*. Advance online publication. DOI: 10.1109/OJCOMS.2023.3343926

Razzaque, A. N., Mohamed, M. I., & Birasnav, M. (2013). A new model for improving healthcare quality using web 3.0 decision making. Making it Real: Sustaining Knowledge Management Adapting for success in the Knowledge Based Economy.

Rees, J. (2012). Tackling the PCI DSS challenges. *Computer Fraud & Security*, 2012(1), 15–17. DOI: 10.1016/S1361-3723(12)70009-X

Ribbers, P. M., Peterson, R. R., & Parker, M. M. (2002). Designing information technology governance processes: diagnosing contemporary practices and competing theories. *Proceedings of the 35th Annual Hawaii International Conference on System Sciences*, 3143-3154. DOI: 10.1109/HICSS.2002.994351

Ribeiro, L., Guedes, I. S., & Cardoso, C. S. (2024). Which factors predict susceptibility to phishing? An empirical study. *Computers & Security*, 136, 103558. DOI: 10.1016/j.cose.2023.103558

Rikhardsson, P., & Dull, R. (2016). An exploratory study of the adoption, application and impacts of continuous auditing technologies in small businesses. *International Journal of Accounting Information Systems*, 20, 26–37. DOI: 10.1016/j.accinf.2016.01.003

Risk Assessment Special Interest Group (SIG). (2012). *Information Supplement: PCI DSS Risk Assessment Guidelines.* PCI.

RiskOptics. (2023, October). PCI Compliance Checklist for Audits. Retrieved from: https://reciprocity.com/resources/what-is-the-pci-dss-audit-checklist/

Rittinghouse, J. W., & Ransome, J. F. (2016). *Cloud computing: implementation, management, and security.* CRC Press.

Ritzer, G., & Jurgenson, N. (2010). Production, Consumption, Prosumption the Nature of Capitalism in the Age of the Digital 'Prosumer'. *Journal of Consumer Culture*, 10(1), 13–36. DOI: 10.1177/1469540509354673

Roberts, J. (2007). *The modern firm: Organizational design for performance and growth.* Oxford university press.

Robinson, I. (n.d.). Reducing Employee Phishing Risk with Mindfulness Training. Center for Cybersecurity and Data Intelligence, 937, 229-1929.

Rockness, H., & Rockness, J. (2005). Legislated ethics: From Enron to Sarbanes-Oxley, the impact on corporate America. *Journal of Business Ethics*, 57(1), 31–54. DOI: 10.1007/s10551-004-3819-0

Roehl-Anderson, J. (2010). *IT Best Practices for Financial Managers.* John Wiley & Sons, Inc.

Rohr, J., & Wright, A. (2018). Blockchain-based token sales, initial coin offerings, and the democratization of public capital markets. Hastings LJ, 463.

Rosas, J., Brito, V., Palma, L. B., & Barata, J. (2017). Approach to Adapt a Legacy Manufacturing System Into the IoT Paradigm. *International Journal of Interactive Mobile Technologies*, 11(5), 91. DOI: 10.3991/ijim.v11i5.7073

Rose, M., & Frio, D. (2017). A smarter approach to third-party risk: adopting a focused, collaborative strategy can help improve management of outsourced service providers.

Rosenthal, A., & Reynolds, P. (2010). Cloud computing: *A new business paradigm for biomedical information sharing*. Retrieved from https://www.sciencedirect.com/science/article/pii/S1532046409001154

Ross, R., Pillitteri, V. Y., & Lefkovitz, N. (2020, October 1). *Selecting Security and Privacy Controls: Choosing the Right Approach.* Retrieved from NIST: https://www.nist.gov/blogs/cybersecurity-insights/selecting-security-and-privacy-controls-choosing-right-approach

Rotmans, J., Kemp, R., & Van Asselt, M. (2001). More evolution than revolution: transition management in public policy. foresight, 15-31.

Roy, P. P. (2020). A high-level comparison between the NIST Cyber Security Framework and the ISO 27001 Information Security Standard. *2020 National Conference on Emerging Trends on Sustainable Technology and Engineering Applications (NCETSTEA)*. https://doi.org/DOI: 10.1109/NCETSTEA48365.2020.9119914

Rudman, R. (2015). Web 3.0: Governance, risks and safeguards. *Journal of Applied Business Research*, 1037–1056.

Rueda, R., Šaljić, E., & Tomić, D. (2020). The Institutional Landscape of Blockchain Governance. A Taxonomy for Incorporation at the Nation State. doi:DOI: 10.18421/TEM91-26

Ryoo, J., & Kissell, J. (2013). Cloud Security Auditing: Challenges and Emerging Approaches. *IEEE Security and Privacy*, 12(6), 68–74. DOI: 10.1109/MSP.2013.132

Sabbagh, K., Acker, O., Karam, D., & Rahbani, J. (2011). Designing the transcendent web the power of web 3.0. Booz&co.

Sadu, I. (2018). Auditing Blockchain. Internal Auditor Indonesia, 19.

Sajedi, H. (2018). Applications of data hiding techniques in medical and healthcare systems: A survey. *Network Modeling and Analysis in Health Informatics and Bioinformatics*, 7(1), 6. DOI: 10.1007/s13721-018-0169-x

Salesforce. (2023, March 13). *Strategies for modernizing Salesforce legacy Systems.* PreludeSys. https://preludesys.com/strategies-for-modernizing-salesforce-legacy-systems/

Salka, T. (2014). The maturation of controls self-assessment. Available at: https://www.sans.org/reading-room/whitepapers/compliance/ maturation-controls-self-assessments-35307/

Salvioni, D., & Gennari, F. (2016). Corporate governance, ownership and sustainability. Corporate Ownership and Control, 606-614. DOI: 10.22495/cocv13i2c3p9

Samant, H. D., & Singh, R. (2023). Developing Audit Strategy for PaaS Applications. In Gupta, M., & Sharman, R. (Eds.), *Modernizing Enterprise IT Audit Governance and Management Practices* (pp. 95–125). IGI Global. DOI: 10.4018/978-1-6684-8766-2.ch004

Samtani, S., Kantarcioglu, M., & Chen, H. (2020). Trailblazing the artificial intelligence for cybersecurity discipline: A multi-disciplinary research roadmap. *ACM Transactions on Management Information Systems*, 11(4), 1–19. DOI: 10.1145/3430360

Santoro, G., Vrontis, D., Thrassou, A., & Dezi, L. (2018). The Internet of Things: Building a knowledge management system for open innovation and knowledge management capacity. *Technological Forecasting and Social Change*, 136, 347–354. DOI: 10.1016/j.techfore.2017.02.034

Sardi, A., Rizzi, A., Sorano, E., & Guerrieri, A. (2020). Cyber Risk in Health Facilities: A Systematic Literature Review. *Sustainability (Basel)*, 12(17), 7002. Advance online publication. DOI: 10.3390/su12177002

Sargent, J. F. (2012). The Obama Administration's Proposal to Establish a National Network for Manufacturing Innovation.

Sarker, O., Jayatilaka, A., Haggag, S., Liu, C., & Babar, M. A. (2024). A Multivocal Literature Review on challenges and critical success factors of phishing education, training and awareness. *Journal of Systems and Software*, 208, 111899. DOI: 10.1016/j.jss.2023.111899

Satarupa Patnaik, P. F. (2023, April). How to Improve Endpoint Security to Protect Organizations Against Advanced Cyberattacks. Retrieved from: https://www.gartner.com/document/4245399?ref=solrAll&refval=383581810&

Schneier, B. (2008). *Schneier on Security*. Wiley.

Schroeder, M. S., Solomon, I., & Vickrey, D. (1986). Audit quality: The perceptions of audit-committee chairpersons and audit partners. *Auditing*, 5(2), 86–94.

Scofield, M. (2016). Benefiting from the NIST cybersecurity framework.

Scott, R. E. (1987). *Conflict and cooperation in long-term contracts*. L. Rev. DOI: 10.2307/3480547

Seacord, R. C., Plakosh, D., & Lewis, G. A. (2003). *Modernizing Legacy Systems: Software Technologies, Engineering Processes, and Business Practices* (1st ed.). Addison-Wesley Professional.

SEC. (2003, January 22). Commission Adopts Rules Strengthening Auditor Independence. Commission adopts Rules Strengthening Auditor Independence. https://www.sec.gov/news/press/2003-9.htm

Security Intelligence Modeling and Research Directions. Retrieved from: https://link.springer.com/article/10.1007/s42979-021-00557-0

Security, R. S. I. (2023, August). Breaking down the PCI DSS 4.0 requirements. Retrieved from: https://blog.rsisecurity.com/breaking-down-the-pci-dss-4-0-requirements/#:~:text=The%20PCI%204.0%20requirements%20were,implementing%20all%20PCI%204.0%20requirements

SelectHub. (n.d.). Compare Product. Retrieved from: https://express.selecthub.com/#/products

Selig, G. J. (2008). *Implementing IT Governance: A Practical Guide to Global Best Practices in IT Management*. Van Haren.

Sendelj, R., & Ognjanovic, I. (2022). Cybersecurity Challenges in Healthcare. Stud Health Technol Inform, 300, 190–202. DOI: 10.3233/SHTI220951

SentinelOne Singularity XDR. (n.d.). Retrieved from: https://www.content.shi.com/cms-content/accelerator/media/pdfs/sentinelone/sentinelone-solution-brief-singularity-xdr-051822.pdf

Services, D. O. (2023). Health Industry Cybersecurity Practices: Managing Threats and Protecting Patients.

Seth, M. (2018). Mulesoft – Salesforce Integration Using Batch Processing. *6th ACM/ACIS International Conference on Applied Computing and Information Technology (ACIT '18)*. DOI: 10.1109/CSII.2018.00009

Sewpersadh, N. S. (2023). Disruptive business value models in the digital era. *Journal of Innovation and Entrepreneurship*, 12(1), 1–27. DOI: 10.1186/s13731-022-00252-1 PMID: 36686335

Shang, Z., Feng, C., Hongji, Y., & Jianzhi, L. (2013). An Approach to Evolving Legacy Software System into Cloud Computing Environment. *Principles, Methodologies, and Service-Oriented Approaches for Cloud Computing*, 207–229. DOI: 10.4018/978-1-4666-2854-0.ch009

Shapira, E. (2022, December 20). *The 4 Most Notable Third-Party Data Breaches of 2022 (So Far).* Retrieved from Panorays: https://panorays.com/blog/the-4-most-notable-third-party-data-breaches-of-2022-so-far/

Sharma, A. (2022, March 22). *Okta investigating claims of customer data breach from Lapsus$ group.* Retrieved from Bleeping Computer: https://www.bleepingcomputer.com/news/security/okta-investigating-claims-of-customer-data-breach-from-lapsus-group/

Sharma, M., & Acharya, P. (2017). Prioritizing the Critical Factors of Cloud Computing Adoption Using Multi-criteria Decision-making Techniques. Retrieved from https://journals.sagepub.com/doi/full/10.1177/0972150917741187

Sharma, L., Olson, J., Guha, A., & McDougal, L. (2021). How blockchain will transform the healthcare ecosystem. *Business Horizons*, 64(5), 673–682. DOI: 10.1016/j.bushor.2021.02.019

Sharma, R., & Kshetri, N. (2020). Digital healthcare: Historical development, applications, and future research directions. *International Journal of Information Management*, 53, 302–309. DOI: 10.1016/j.ijinfomgt.2020.102105

Sheller, M. J., Reina, G. A., Edwards, B., Martin, J., & Bakas, S. (2019). Multi-institutional deep learning modeling without sharing patient data: A feasibility study on brain tumor segmentation. Brainlesion: Glioma, Multiple Sclerosis, Stroke and Traumatic Brain Injuries, 92-104. DOI: 10.1007/978-3-030-11723-8_9

Sheth, A., & Thirunarayan, K. (2012). *Semantics empowered web 3.0: managing enterprise, social, sensor, and cloud-based data and services for advanced applications.* Morgan & Claypool.

Shivalingaiah, D., & Naik, U. (2008). Comparative Study of Web 1.0, Web 2.0 and Web 3.0. DOI: 10.13140/2.1.2287.2961

Shu, X., Tian, K., Cambrione, A., & Yao, D. (2017, January 18). *Breaking the Target: An Analysis of Target Data Breach and Lessons Learned.* Retrieved from https://arxiv.org/pdf/1701.04940.pdf

Sidor-Rządkowska, M. (2022) Human - the weakest or the strongest link? The role of organisational culture in ensuring security of remote work https://www.jomswsge.com/Human-the-weakest-or-the-strongest-link-The-role-of-organisational-culture-in-ensuring,156776,0,2.html

Silva, P. F. (2022, December 31). Magic Quadrant for Endpoint Protection Platforms. Retrieved from: https://www.gartner.com/document/4137499?ref=solrAll&refval=384466386&

Šimková, E. (2005). Impact of the Sarbanes-Oxley Act on the system of internal controls and IS audit. *Systémová Integrace*, (3), 92-111. https://scholar.archive.org/work/vahyopbrgveoro6aa74ef6ojke/access/wayback/http://www.cssi.cz/cssi/system/files/all/simkova.pdf

Singh, S., & Park, J. H. (2016). A survey on cloud computing security: Issues, threats, and solutions.

Singh, A., & Chatterjee, K. (2017). Cloud security issues and challenges. *Survey (London, England)*.

Sir, M. C., Mam, K. J., & Shekher, H. (2022). Website Designing Using Html, CSS, Javascript & Wordpress. *International Research Journal of Modernization in Engineering Technology and Science*.

Smith, A., & Williams, C. (2018). Strategic Imperatives for Cloud Migration: Enhancing Agility and Cost-effectiveness. *Journal of Cloud Computing (Heidelberg, Germany)*, 6(1), 1–15.

Smith, J. (2019). Critical Decision Factors for Selecting Cloud Service Providers. *Journal of Cloud Computing (Heidelberg, Germany)*, 12(3), 45–58.

Smith, J. (2019). Ensuring Regulatory Compliance in Cloud Computing: A Comparative Study of Industry-Specific Standards. *Journal of Cloud Computing: Advances, Systems and Applications*, 8(1), 1–18.

Smith, J. (2019). Understanding Service Level Agreements (SLAs) in Cloud Computing: A Comprehensive Review. *Journal of Cloud Computing: Advances, Systems and Applications*, 8(1), 1–18.

Smith, J., & Anderson, L. (2017). *Risk Management in Practice: A Comprehensive Guide to Enterprise Risk Management*. Wiley.

Smith, J., & Williams, B. (2020). Evaluating Cloud Service Providers: A Comprehensive Framework. *Journal of Cloud Computing (Heidelberg, Germany)*, 18(2), 45–57.

Smith, J., & Williams, K. (2019). Assessing the Effectiveness of Encryption Protocols in Cloud Service Providers. *Journal of Information Security*, 16(3), 45–62.

Smith, J., & Williams, R. (2018). Understanding organizational needs in cloud service provider selection. *Journal of Information Technology Management*, 35(3), 45–58.

Solterbeck, A. (2006). Protecting data at rest and in Motion. *Network Security*, 2006(9), 14–17. DOI: 10.1016/S1353-4858(06)70424-X

Soni, V. D. (2020). Challenges and Solution for Artificial Intelligence in Cybersecurity of the USA. *SSRN* 3624487. DOI: 10.2139/ssrn.3624487

Sophos Authorised Online Platinum reseller. (n.d.). Sophos Central Intercept X Advanced. Retrieved from: https://www.enterpriseav.com/Intercept-X-Adv.asp?utm_term=sophos%20central%20intercept%20x&utm_campaign=Sophos+*174&utm_source=adwords&utm_medium=ppc&hsa_tgt=kwd-379818380583&hsa_grp=61783349500&hsa_src=g&hsa_net=adwords&hsa_mt=e&hsa_ver=3&hsa_ad=30712590

Sophos. (n.d.). PCI DSS v4.0 Compliance Reference Card. Retrieved from: https://assets.sophos.com/X24WTUEQ/at/njxq68jhbjtmwh877ngbtfwh/sophos-pci-dss-compliance-card.pdf

Sophos. (n.d.). Solutions. Retrieved from PCI DSS compliance can be a challenge: https://www.sophos.com/en-us/solutions/compliance/pci-dss

Spampinato, L., Morris, D., & Curcurito, M. (n.d.). *Third-Party Incident Management (TPIM): How to Balance IRPs with Third Parties*. Retrieved from Wolf & Company, P.C.: https://www.wolfandco.com/resources/insights/third-party-incident-management-how-balance-irps-third-parties/#:~:text=The%20TPIM%20process%20involves%20identifying,to%20incidents%20that%20may%20arise

Spathis, C. (2007). Detecting Fraudulent Financial Statements by Using Continuous Auditing, Published in the Honorary volume for the peer Professor Aristotle Ignatiadis, Thessaloniki, Greece.

Spicer, R. L. (2006). *Enterprise risk management and Sarbanes-Oxley Compliance: a model of convergence in accounting audit practice*. Capella University.

Squires, S. E., & Squires, S. (2003). *Inside Arthur Andersen: shifting values, unexpected consequences*. FT Press.

Srinivas, M., Ramakrishna, G., Rao, K. R., & Babu, E. S. (2016). Analysis of Legacy System in Software Application Development: A Comparative Survey. *Iranian Journal of Electrical and Computer Engineering*, 6(1), 292. DOI: 10.11591/ijece.v6i1.pp292-297

Srivastava, P. S. (2012). Technical Audit – A Thoroughfare of System Perfection. *International Journal of Scientific and Engineering Research*.

Stallings, W. (2020). Data loss prevention as a privacy-enhancing technology, Journal of Data Protection & Privacy, 3(3), 323-333.

Steinbart, P. J., Raschke, R. L., Gal, G., & Dilla, W. N. (2018). The influence of a good relationship between the internal audit and information security functions on information security outcomes. *Accounting, Organizations and Society*, 71, 15–29. DOI: 10.1016/j.aos.2018.04.005

Stephens, N. M. (2008). *Corporate governance quality and internal control reporting under Sox*. The University of Arizona.

Stephens, N. M. (2011). External auditor characteristics and internal control reporting under SOX section 302. *Managerial Auditing Journal*, 26(2), 114–129. DOI: 10.1108/02686901111095001

Stevens, T. (2020). Knowledge in the grey zone: AI and cybersecurity. Digi War. Digital War, 164-170. DOI: 10.1057/s42984-020-00007-w

Stevens, M., & Harris, R. (2020). *Information Security Risk Assessment Toolkit: Practical Assessments through Data Collection and Data Analysis*. Apress.

Stevenson, M., & Helmond, A. (2020). Legacy systems: Internet histories of the abandoned, discontinued and forgotten. *Internet Histories*, 4(1), 1–5. DOI: 10.1080/24701475.2020.1725854

Stimson, W. A. (2005). Sarbanes-Oxley and ISO 9000. *Quality control and applied statistics, 50*(4), 409.

Stoel, D., Havelka, D., & Merhout, J. (2012, March). An analysis of attributes that impact information technology audit quality: A study of IT and financial audit practitioners. *International Journal of Accounting Information Systems*, 13(1), 60–79. DOI: 10.1016/j.accinf.2011.11.001

Stojkov, A., & Stojanov, Z. (2021). Review of methods for migrating software systems to microservices architecture. *Journal of Engineering Management and Competitiveness*, 11(2), 152–162. DOI: 10.5937/jemc2102152S

Stoneburner, G., Goguen, A., & Feringa, A. (2002). *Risk Management Guide for Information Technology Systems*. NIST. DOI: 10.6028/NIST.SP.800-30

Subashini, S., & Kavitha, V. (2011). A survey on security issues in service delivery models of cloud computing. *Journal of Network and Computer Applications*, 34(1), 1–11. DOI: 10.1016/j.jnca.2010.07.006

Subramanian, N., & Jeyaraj, A. (2018). Recent security challenges in cloud computing.

Suddaby, R., Cooper, D. J., & Greenwood, R. (2007). Transnational regulation of professional services: Governance dynamics of field level organizational change. *Accounting, Organizations and Society*, 32(4-5), 333–362. DOI: 10.1016/j.aos.2006.08.002

Suman, M. J. (2021). Dentistry 4.0 technologies applications for dentistry during COVID-19 pandemic. Sustainable Operations and Computers, 87-96.

Swan, M. (2015). *Blockchain: Blueprint for a New Economy*. O'Reilly Media, Inc.

Sweeney, B., & McGarry, C. (2011). Commercial and professional audit goals: Inculcation of audit seniors. *International Journal of Auditing*, 15(3), 316–332. DOI: 10.1111/j.1099-1123.2011.00437.x

Tahboub, R., & Saleh, Y. (2014) Data leakage/loss prevention systems (DLP). *2014 World Congress on Computer Applications and Information Systems, WCCAIS 2014*, 1–6. DOI: 10.1109/WCCAIS.2014.6916624

Tang, X., Guo, H., Li, H., Yuan, Y., Wang, J., & Cheng, J. (2021). A DAPP business data storage model based on blockchain and IPFS.

Tantry, S., N.N, M., & K, C. (2017). Implications of legacy software system modernization: A survey in a changed scenario. *International Journal of Advanced Research in Computer Science*. https://doi.org/.DOI: 10.26483/ijarcs.v8i7.4556

Tapia, F., Mora, M. Á., Fuertes, W., Aules, H., Flores, E., & Toulkeridis, T. (2020). From Monolithic Systems to Microservices: A Comparative Study of Performance. *Applied Sciences (Basel, Switzerland)*, 10(17), 5797. DOI: 10.3390/app10175797

Tapscott, D., & Tapscott, A. (2016). *Blockchain revolution: how the technology behind bitcoin is changing money, business, and the world*. Penguin.

Taylor, R. T. (2017). *Contract Law*. Oxford University Press.

Tchankova, L. (2002). Risk identification – basic stage in risk management. *Environmental Management and Health*, 13(3), 290–297. Advance online publication. DOI: 10.1108/09566160210431088

TechDemand. (n.d.). Retrieved from https://www.techdemand.io/insights/tech/overcoming-web-3-0-security-issues-safeguarding-the-decentralized-future/

TechTarget. (n.d.). Retrieved from TechTarget: https://www.techtarget.com/whatis/definition/Web-30

Teck-Heang, L. E. E., & Ali, A. M. (2008). The evolution of auditing: An analysis of the historical development. *Journal of Modern Accounting and auditing, 4*(12), 1.

Teeter, R. A., Alles, M. G., & Vasarhelyi, M. A. (2010). The remote audit . *Journal of Emerging Technologies in Accounting*, 7(1), 73–88. DOI: 10.2308/jeta.2010.7.1.73

Teneyuca, D. (2011). Internet cloud security: The illusion of inclusion. *Information Security Technical Report*, 16(3), 102–107. DOI: 10.1016/j.istr.2011.08.005

Teoh, S., & Cheong, C. (2008). Implicit Enterprise Risk Management: An IT Healthcare Adoption Case Study. ACIS 2008 Proceedings - 19th Australasian Conference on Information Systems. 1011-1018.

The 18 CIS controls. (2021b, October 28). CIS. https://www.cisecurity.org/controls/cis-controls-list

The Changing Faces of Cybersecurity. (n.d.). Deloitte Canada. https://www2.deloitte.com/ca/en/pages/risk/articles/the-changing-faces-of-cybersecurity.html

The NIST Cybersecurity Framework (CSF) 2.0. (2024). https://nvlpubs.nist.gov/nistpubs/CSWP/NIST.CSWP.29.pdf

Tiwana, A., & Konsynski, B. (2010). Complementarities between organizational IT architecture and governance structure. *Information Systems Research*, 21(2), 288–304. DOI: 10.1287/isre.1080.0206

Tolmach, P., Li, Y., Lin, S. W., Liu, Y., & Li, Z. (2021). A survey of smart contract formal specification and verification. *ACM Computing Surveys*, 1–38.

Toosi, A. N., Calheiros, R. N., & Buyya, R. (2014). Interconnected cloud computing environments: Challenges, taxonomy, and survey. *ACM Computing Surveys*, 47(1), 1–47. DOI: 10.1145/2593512

Tortorella, G. L., Fogliatto, F. S., Sunder, M., Cawley, V., Vergara, A. M., & Vassolo, R. (2021). Assessment and prioritisation of healthcare 4.0 implementation in hospitals using quality function deployment. *International Journal of Production Research*, 60(10), 1–23. DOI: 10.1080/00207543.2021.1912429

Tricker, R. I. (2015). *Corporate governance: Principles, policies, and practices*. Oxford University Press.

Truong, T. C., Zelinka, I., Plucar, J., Čandík, M., & Šulc, V. (2020). Artificial intelligence and cybersecurity: Past, presence, and future. Artificial intelligence and evolutionary computations in engineering systems, 351-363.

Truong, V. T., Le, L. B., & Niyato, D. (2023). *Blockchain meets metaverse and digital asset management: A comprehensive survey*. IEEE.

Tully, J. S., Selzer, J., Phillips, J. P., O'Connor, P., & Dameff, C. (2020). Healthcare Challenges in the Era of Cybersecurity. *Health Security*, 18(3), 281–231. DOI: 10.1089/hs.2019.0123 PMID: 32559153

Tyagi, A. K. (2023). Decentralized everything: Practical use of blockchain technology in future applications. DOI: 10.1016/B978-0-323-96146-2.00010-3

UcedaVelez, T., & Morana, M. M. (2015). Risk Centric Threat Modeling: process for attack simulation and threat analysis. John Wiley & Sons.

Ulrich, D. (1996). *Human resource champions: The next agenda for adding value and delivering results*. Harvard Business Press.

Usman Sana, M., & Li, Z. (2021). Efficiency aware scheduling techniques in cloud computing: A descriptive literature review. *PeerJ. Computer Science*, 7, e509. DOI: 10.7717/peerj-cs.509 PMID: 34013035

Vachon, S., & Klassen, R. D. (2006). Extending green practices across the supply chain: The impact of upstream and downstream integration. *International Journal of Operations & Production Management*, 26(7), 795–821. DOI: 10.1108/01443570610672248

Valinsky, J. (2021) McDonald's hit by data breach. https://www.cnn.com/2021/06/11/business/mcdonalds-data-breach/index.html

Vance, A., Siponen, M., & Pahnila, S. (2012) Motivating IS security compliance: Insights from habit and protection motivation theory. https://psycnet.apa.org/record/2012-12998-008

Vasarhelyi, M., & Halper, F. (2018). The continuous audit of online Systems1. In Continuous Auditing (Rutgers Studies in Accounting Analytics). Emerald Publishing. DOI: 10.1108/978-1-78743-413-420181004

Vassileva, J. (2012). Motivating participation in social computing applications: A user modeling perspective. *User Modeling and User-Adapted Interaction*, 22(1-2), 177–201. DOI: 10.1007/s11257-011-9109-5

Veiga, A. D., & Eloff, J. H. (2007). An Information Security Governance Framework. IS Management, 361-372. DOI: 10.1145/1655168.1655170

Velimeneti, S. (2016). *Data Migration from Legacy Systems to Modern Database*. Culminating Projects in Mechanical and Manufacturing Engineering.

Verma, S., & Gupta, N. (2020). Application of Artificial Intelligence in Cybersecurity. Innovations in Computer Science and Engineering: Proceedings of 7th ICICSE, 65-72.

Vilakazi, K., & Adebesin, F. (2023). A Systematic Literature Review on Cybersecurity Threats to Healthcare Data and Mitigation Strategies. *EPiC Series in Computing*, 93, 240–251. DOI: 10.29007/hf15

Vincent, N., & Wilkins, A. M. (2020). Challenges when Auditing. *Current Issues in Auditing*, 14(1), A46–A58. DOI: 10.2308/ciia-52675

Visa. (2019, August). Retrieved from: https://usa.visa.com/visa-everywhere/blog/bdp/2019/08/12/visa-celebrates-25-1565646929402.html

VISA. (2023). *Information Security*. Retrieved from https://aw.visa.com/run-your-business/small-business/information-security/compliance-validation.html

VMware. (2021, Sept). Carbon Black Tech Zone. Retrieved from: https://carbonblack.vmware.com/resource/carbon-black-cloud-endpoint-standard-technical-overview#top-things

von Solms, S. H. & von Solms, R. (2009). Information security governance. Springer Science+Business Media. DOI: 10.1007/978-0-387-79984-1

Voshmgir, S. (2020). *Token Economy: How the Web3 reinvents the internet* (Vol. 2). Token Kitchen.

Wallen, J. H. (2016). *Managing third party risk in financial services organizations: A resilience-based approach*. Carnegie Mellon University.

Wamba, S. F., & Queiroz, M. M. (2020). Blockchain in the operations and supply chain management: Benefits, challenges, and future research opportunities. *International Journal of Information Management*, 52, 102064. DOI: 10.1016/j.ijinfomgt.2019.102064

Wang, J., & Perez, L. (2017). The effectiveness of data augmentation in image classification using deep learning. arXiv.org. https://arxiv.org/abs/1712.04621v1

Warming-Rasmussen, B., & Jensen, L. (1998). Quality dimensions in external audit services – an external user perspective. *European Accounting Review*, 7(1), 65–82. DOI: 10.1080/096381898336583

Warren, P. D. (2014). Closing the gaps in third-party risk management: internal audit can add value by assessing risk around the organization's business relationships.

Wasekar, S., & Ghonge, P. (2019). An Efficient Data Replication in Salesforce Cloud Environment. *International Research Journal of Engineering and Technology, 6*(3). https://www.irjet.net/archives/V6/i3/IRJET-V6I31187.pdf

Webb, E. (2008). Sarbanes-Oxley compliance and violation: An empirical study. *Review of Accounting and Finance*, 7(1), 5–23. DOI: 10.1108/14757700810853824

Webb, J., & Hume, D. (2018). Campus IOT collaboration and governance using the NIST Cybersecurity Framework. *Living in the Internet of Things: Cybersecurity of the IoT*. Advance online publication. DOI: 10.1049/cp.2018.0025

Weill, P., & Ross, J. (2004). *IT governance: How top performers manage IT decision rights for superior results*. Harvard Business Press.

Weishaupl, E., Yasasin, E., & Schryen, G. (2018, August). Information security investments: An exploratory multiple case study on decision-making, evaluation and learning. Retrieved from: https://www.sciencedirect.com/science/article/abs/pii/S0167404818300555

What the future of edge computing means for cloud and networks | TechTarget. (n.d.). Networking. https://www.techtarget.com/searchnetworking/tip/What-the-future-of-edge-computing-means-for-cloud-and-networks

Wheeler, D., & Elkington, J. (2001). The end of the corporate environmental report? Or the advent of cybernetic sustainability reporting and communication. *Business Strategy and the Environment*, 10(1), 1–14. DOI: 10.1002/1099-0836(200101/02)10:1<1::AID-BSE274>3.0.CO;2-0

White, B. S., King, C. G., & Holladay, J. (2020). Blockchain security risk assessment and the auditor. *Journal of Corporate Accounting & Finance*, 31(2), 47–53. DOI: 10.1002/jcaf.22433

Wiafe, I., Koranteng, F. N., Obeng, E. N., Assyne, N., Wiafe, A., & Gulliver, S. R. (2020). Artificial intelligence for cybersecurity: A systematic mapping of literature. *IEEE Access : Practical Innovations, Open Solutions*, 8, 146598–146612. DOI: 10.1109/ACCESS.2020.3013145

Wickramasinghe, S. (2023, March 9). Behavioral Analytics Explained: How Analyzing (Odd) Behavior Supports Cybersecurity. Retrieved from: https://www.splunk.com/en_us/blog/learn/behavioral-analytics.html

Wikipedia. (n.d.). Retrieved from https://en.wikipedia.org/wiki/Web3

Wilkin, C. (2012). The Role of IT Governance Practices in Creating Business Value in SMEs. *Journal of Organizational and End User Computing*, 24(2), 1–17. DOI: 10.4018/joeuc.2012040101

Wilkinson, B. (2022). *Improving Third-Party Incident Response Starts with a Solid Incident Management Foundation*. Prevalent.

Williams, J. (2020, December 15). *What You Need to Know About the SolarWinds Supply-Chain Attack.* Retrieved from SANS: https://www.sans.org/blog/what-you-need-to-know-about-the-solarwinds-supply-chain-attack/

Winkens, A. K., & Leicht-Scholten, C. (2023). Competencies for designing resilient systems in engineering education–a content analysis of selected study programs of five European technical universities. *European Journal of Engineering Education*, 48(4), 1–25. DOI: 10.1080/03043797.2023.2179913

Witts, J. (2023, November 16). Endpoint Security Solutions For Business. Retrieved from: https://expertinsights.com/insights/the-top-endpoint-security-solutions-for-business/

Wong, A. J. (2014). Healthcare Cybersecurity Risk Management: Keys To an Effective Plan. *Biomedical Instrumentation & Technology*, 26–30. PMID: 24848146

Woodroof, J., & Searcy, D. (2001). *Continuous audit: Model development and implementation within a debt covenant compliance domain.* Published in the International Journal of Accounting Information Systems. DOI: 10.1016/S1467-0895(01)00019-7

Wuchner, T., & Pretschner, A. (2012). Data loss prevention based on data-driven usage control. 2012 IEEE 23rd International Symposium on Software Reliability Engineering. DOI: 10.1109/ISSRE.2012.10

Wu, L., Ruan, W., Hu, J., & He, Y. (2023). A Survey on Blockchain-Based Federated Learning. *Future Internet*, 400(12), 400. Advance online publication. DOI: 10.3390/fi15120400

Wu, Y., Qiao, Y., Ye, Y., & Lee, B. (2019). Towards improved trust in threat intelligence sharing using blockchain and trusted computing. *Sixth International Conference on Internet of Things: Systems, Management and Security (IOTSMS).* DOI: 10.1109/IOTSMS48152.2019.8939192

Xu, F., Zhang, J., Shi, Y., Kang, K., & Yang, S. (2019). A fast low-rank matrix factorization method for dynamic magnetic resonance imaging restoration. 2019 5th International Conference on Big Data Computing and Communications (BIGCOM). DOI: 10.1109/BIGCOM.2019.00014

Xu, X. (2020). From cloud computing to cloud manufacturing. Robotics and Computer-Integrated Manufacturing. Retrieved from https://www.sciencedirect.com/science/article/pii/S0736584511000949

Yadav, S., Khare, A., & Choudhary, K. (2019). *ASK Approach: A Pre-migration Approach for Legacy Application Migration to Cloud.* 15–27. DOI: 10.1007/978-981-32-9949-8_2

Yang, K. (2005). Information retrieval on the web. Annu. Rev. Inf. Sci. Technol.

Yao, Z., Nagel, C., Kunde, F., Hudra, G., Willkomm, P., Donaubauer, A., Adolphi, T., & Kolbe, T. H. (2018b). 3DCityDB - a 3D geodatabase solution for the management, analysis, and visualization of semantic 3D city models based on CityGML. *Open Geospatial Data. Software and Standards*, 3(1), 5. Advance online publication. DOI: 10.1186/s40965-018-0046-7

Yaqoob, S., Murad, M., Talib, R., Dawood, A., Saleem, S., Arif, F., & Nadeem, A. (2019). Use of blockchain in healthcare: A systematic literature review. *International Journal of Advanced Computer Science and Applications*, 10(5). Advance online publication. DOI: 10.14569/IJACSA.2019.0100581

Young, J. (2019). Round-up of crypto exchange hacks so far in 2019: How can they be stopped.

Yu, S., Yitian, T., Zhili, Z., & Yusheng, H. (2019, October). Endpoint Protection: Measuring the Effectiveness of Remediation Technologies and Methodologies for Insider Threat. Retrieved from: https://ieeexplore.ieee.org/document/8945852

Zafar, H., Ko, M. S., & Clark, J. G. (2014). Security Risk Management in Healthcare: A Case Study. Communications of the Association for Information Systems, 34. DOI: 10.17705/1CAIS.03437

Zakaria, H., Abu Bakar, N. A., Hassan, N. H., & Yaacob, S. (2019). IoT Security Risk Management Model for Secured Practice in Healthcare Environment. Procedia Computer Science, 161, 1241-1248. DOI: 10.1016/j.procs.2019.11.238

Zavratnik, J. (2022). Analysis of web3 solution development principles. Retrieved from http://hdl.handle.net/2117/379908

Zemankova, A. (2019). Artificial intelligence in audit and accounting: Development, current trends, opportunities and threats - Literature review. *2019 International Conference on Control, Artificial Intelligence, Robotics & Optimization (ICCAIRO)*. DOI: 10.1109/ICCAIRO47923.2019.00031

Zhang, X., & Zhang, X. (2010). Information Security Risk Management Framework for the Cloud Computing Environments. 2010 *10th IEEE International Conference on Computer and Information Technology*. Retrieved from https://ieeexplore.ieee.org/abstract/document/5577860

Zhang, A., Xing, L., Zou, J., & Wu, J. C. (2022). Shifting machine learning for healthcare from development to deployment and from models to data. *Nature Biomedical Engineering*, 6(12), 1330–1345. Advance online publication. DOI: 10.1038/s41551-022-00898-y PMID: 35788685

Zhang, I. X. (2007). Economic consequences of the Sarbanes–Oxley Act of 2002. *Journal of Accounting and Economics*, 44(1-2), 74–115. DOI: 10.1016/j.jacceco.2007.02.002

Zhang, Q., & Boutaba, R. (2018). Cloud computing: State-of-the-art and research challenges. *Journal of Internet Services and Applications*, 9(1), 1–42.

Zhang, Y., Pfeuffer, K., Chong, M. K., Alexander, J., Bulling, A., & Gellersen, H. (2017). Look together: Using gaze for assisting co-located collaborative search. *Personal and Ubiquitous Computing*, 21(1), 173–186. DOI: 10.1007/s00779-016-0969-x

Zhao, Zhao, Zhao, Chen, Gao, Li, & Tan. (2019). Secure Multi-Party Computation: Theory, practice and applications. Retrieved from: https://www.sciencedirect.com/science/article/abs/pii/S0020025518308338

Zhao, J.-F., & Zhou, J.-T. (2014). Strategies and Methods for Cloud Migration. *International Journal of Automation and Computing*, 11(2), 143–152. DOI: 10.1007/s11633-014-0776-7

Zhao, Q., Wang, Y., Yang, B., Shang, K., Sun, M., Wang, H., & Xin, H. (2023). A Comprehensive Overview of Security Vulnerability Penetration Methods in Blockchain Cross-Chain Bridges. *Authorea Preprints*. DOI: 10.22541/au.169760541.13864334/v1

Zheng, Z., Xie, S., Dai, H., Chen, X., & Wang, H. (2017). An overview of blockchain technology: Architecture, consensus, and future trends. IEEE international congress on big data (BigData congress), 557-564.

Zheng, J., & Lee, D. K. (2023). *Understanding the Evolution of the Internet: Web 1.0 to Web3. 0, Web3 and Web 3. Handbook of Digital Currency: Bitcoin*. Innovation, Financial Instruments, and Big Data.

Zivkov, E., Nerandzic, B., & Kuzmanovic, B. (2015). A Correlation Between the Function of Controlling and the Process of Risk Management in the Company.

About the Contributors

Manish Gupta is Executive Vice President and Audit Director at one of the 10 largest banks in the United States, responsible for oversight of cybersecurity and technology risk management programs. He is also adjunct professor at State University of New York at Buffalo where he has been teaching graduate courses in IT auditing and IT risk management since 2012. His research has won best paper awards and has been published in MIS Quarterly, Decision Support Systems, Journal of Organizational and End User Computing, and various ACM Transactions, among others. Manish received his Ph.D. (Management/MIS) and MBA (Finance and MIS) from State University of New York at Buffalo.

Raghvendra Singh is an accomplished IT professional with five years of experience in the industry, holding a Master's degree in Management Information Systems from the University at Buffalo (SUNY). Throughout his career, Singh has developed a strong foundation in information security and audit, providing valuable contributions to various organizations. His educational background complements his practical experience, enriching his understanding of the dynamic world of information security. As a co-author of this comprehensive book on information security and audit, Singh offers readers a wealth of practical knowledge and industry insights. His unique combination of academic achievement and hands-on experience makes him an invaluable resource for those seeking to enhance their understanding of cybersecurity and auditing practices.

John Walp is an experienced information security executive and cybersecurity risk leader with broad industry and technology background. With more than 20 years of financial services and health insurance security industry experience, John is widely known as a subject matter expert in the areas of online fraud and has served in a variety of roles where his skills and knowledge provide business clients with valuable insights into various areas of information technology and cybersecurity risk management. John's areas of expertise include IS Auditing, cybersecurity, strategic information security thought leadership and technology risk management.

Raj Sharman is a Professor in the MSS Department at the University at Buffalo. His expertise is in the areas of artificial intelligence, information assurance and the use of biologically inspired computer security models, and disaster response management. Dr. Sharman has published widely in national and international journals and is the recipient of several grants. Dr. Sharman earned his PhD in computer science and a MS in industrial engineering from Louisiana State University. He served as Director of MS in the MIS program and as PhD Faculty Adviser for SUNY Buffalo's MSS department from 2005 to 2016.

* * *

Annie Bhardwaj is a recent graduate with a Master of Science in Management Information Systems and an Advanced Certificate in Cybersecurity Management from the University at Buffalo, brings a wealth of knowledge in IT auditing, information security, and risk management. With a passion for technology and a keen eye for detail, Annie has excelled in roles at Cognizant and Larsen & Toubro Infotech, where she honed her skills in IT auditing, information security, and risk management. Her knack for analyzing critical application performance and ensuring compliance with regulatory frameworks has made her a valuable asset to any team. Annie's academic projects, including research on third-party risk management and enterprise-wide IT audits using COBIT frameworks, demonstrate her commitment to innovation and excellence. With her vibrant personality and dedication to her craft, Annie is ready to make waves in the world of technology and cybersecurity.

Lokesh Bollini is a Management Information Systems graduate specializing in IS auditing, with extensive experience in risk investigation.

Mansha Chandna is an accomplished cybersecurity professional with a Master's in Management Information Systems from the University at Buffalo, SUNY (USA) and a Bachelor's in Computer Science Engineering from India. She has extensive experience in cybersecurity consulting, risk management, and compliance, having worked at Deloitte USI in various roles. Mansha is an experienced cybersecurity consultant with a passion for exploring and solving complex information security challenges. She has helped clients by assessing their existing privacy and data security policies, creating a strategic roadmap for addressing areas of enhancement, and implementing security controls that boost data security. She is experienced in providing subject matter expertise in cyber, technology and third-party risk governance and strategy for business and risk owners across industries.

Abinash Jena is a graduate with a Master's in Management Information Systems, specializing in IT Audit, IT Risk, Cybersecurity, and Cloud Security. He holds certifications in Advanced Cybersecurity Management from the University at Buffalo, CompTIA Security+, and AWS Cloud Practitioner. Abinash has experience working as a GRC (Governance, Risk & Compliance) Consultant for companies like KPMG, Transunion, and Infosys. Outside of work, his interests lie in science, the development of artificial intelligence, enjoying movies, and exploring his culinary creativity.

Rajdeep Murmu holds a master's degree in management information systems from the University at Buffalo, specializing in information security, information systems auditing, and cloud computing. He is certified in CompTIA Security+. He also has a robust six-year track record in ERP consulting, leading implementations and business transformation projects for multiple companies across diverse industries. Beyond his academic and professional pursuits, Rajdeep delights in immersing himself in the imaginative realms of science fiction novels and finds joy in cooking for his near and dear ones.

Sabyasachi Pramanik is a professional IEEE member. He obtained a PhD in Computer Science and Engineering from Sri Satya Sai University of Technology and Medical Sciences, Bhopal, India. Presently, he is an Associate Professor, Department of Computer Science and Engineering, Haldia Institute of Technology, India. He has many publications in various reputed international conferences, journals, and book chapters (Indexed by SCIE, Scopus, ESCI, etc). He is doing research in the fields of Artificial Intelligence, Data Privacy, Cybersecurity, Network Security, and Machine Learning. He also serves on the editorial boards of several international journals. He is a reviewer of journal articles from IEEE, Springer, Elsevier, Inderscience, IET and IGI Global. He has reviewed many conference papers, has been a keynote speaker, session chair, and technical program committee member at many international conferences. He has authored a book on Wireless Sensor Network. He has edited 8 books from IGI Global, CRC Press, Springer and Wiley Publications.

Prarthana Seeralan graduated from the University at Buffalo with a Master of Science in Management Information Systems (MS MIS). Her interests lie in IT auditing, risk management, and cybersecurity.

Pranith Shetty is a Senior Member with IEEE, he received his B.E. degree in Electronics and Telecommunication engineering from K.J. Somaiya college of engineering affiliated to the University of Mumbai, India, in 2010 and the M.S. degree in Information Systems with a focus in Information assurance from the University of Buffalo, New York, in 2015. From 2010 to 2014, he was a Senior Systems Engineer with Infosys, India, contributing professionally in the field of Network security, firewall administration. Since 2015, he has been involved professionally in the field of Information Security, Risk management, Data privacy, and Compliance in firms such as Morgan Stanley, Cisco, PwC, and International Paper. Pranith is a highly skilled and passionate professional with expertise in areas of Information Security, IT Risk Management, Cybersecurity and Data privacy. he has successfully designed frameworks, processes, and assessments to ensure an overall healthy risk posture across departments during his tenure at PwC and Morgan Stanley. His thought leadership and creative thinking have also been demonstrated during his current tenure at Cisco, where he leads the Risk Management program for Cloud network security offers. Pranith has earned several international recognitions in the field of Information security, Cybersecurity and Risk, and various corporate recognitions within PwC and Cisco.

Raghvendra Singh is an accomplished IT professional with five years of experience in the industry, holding a Master's degree in Management Information Systems from the University at Buffalo (SUNY). Throughout his career, Singh has developed a strong foundation in information security and audit, providing valuable contributions to various organizations. His educational background complements his practical experience, enriching his understanding of the dynamic world of information security. As a co-author of this comprehensive book on information security and audit, Singh offers readers a wealth of practical knowledge and industry insights. His unique combination of academic achievement and hands-on experience makes him an invaluable resource for those seeking to enhance their understanding of cybersecurity and auditing practices.

Index

A

B

C

R

S

T

V

www.ingramcontent.com/pod-product-compliance
Lightning Source LLC
LaVergne TN
LVHW080607300926
849162LV00005B/1070
* 9 7 9 8 3 6 9 3 4 2 1 1 4 *